DEMOGRAPHIC SUICIDE
IN THE WEST AND HALF THE WORLD

Either more births or catastrophe?

ALEJANDRO MACARRÓN LARUMBE

DEDICATION

To my father, in memoriam.

CONTENTS

Acknowledgements   Page   3

Initial remarks   Page   5

Foreword by Hans-Werner Sinn   Page   7

Foreword by Josep Piqué   Page   9

Foreword by Joaquín Leguina   Page   11

Two initial calls for attention   Page   19

Introduction   Page   22

Chapter I – A world heading towards demographic suicide   Page   27

Chapter II - The bitter consequences of low birth rates   Page   73

Chapter III – Why we have so few children   Page 155

Chapter IV – How to combat demographic suicide?   Page 221

Epilogue: Either demographic revival or demographic suicide   Page 281

Appendices. - 1.- The Kissinger report to reduce fertility in the Third   Page 289
                    World (1974)

               2.- On the accuracy of numbers and graphs in this book   Page 299

               3.- Data sources and bibliography   Page 301

ACKNOWLEDGEMENTS

I am grateful to so many people who have accompanied me on the journey to write and publish this book that, if there was anything of wisdom and merit in these pages, it would largely be due to the so-called "wisdom of the crowds." That is why too many who deserve to be acknowledged will not be individually named here. I apologize to them, and I thank them from the bottom of my heart for their help.

Among the following who are explicitly mentioned, it is worth highlighting the three generous introduction writers: the great German economist Hans-Werner Sinn, who helped me understand some key aspects of the German and European demographic decline; Joaquin Leguina, from whom I have learned so much, who has supported me so much, and with whom I have enjoyed so much during conferences and joint work; and Josep Piqué, whose ideas on the impact of demography on geopolitics led me to delve into this key aspect of the demographic decline of Europe and the West. Antonio Torres, a champion in support of motherhood and the impulse of well-intentioned endeavors, such as the RedMadre Foundation or the Avanza Project, without whose encouragement this work would not have seen the light, deserves special mention.

It is also only fair and a pleasure to thank my colleagues from the Fundación Renacimiento Demográfico - Demographic Renaissance, and specifically Vicente Boceta, Gonzalo Babé, Boris Levy, Jorge Salaverry, Rocio Monasterio, Iván Espinosa de los Monteros, Quique Ruiz, and José Luis Puerta for their invaluable support. For the edition and promotion of the book, Javier de Juan and José Luis González Quirós provided ideas and advice of essential value, and the cover image was suggested by the designer Juan Carlos González Pozuelo. I also thank Cecilia Mabilais-Estévez, who carried out, with great quality, care, swiftness and professionalism, the translation of this book into English.

Likewise, at the risk of being unfair to most of the two hundred people I thank for the ideas, information, criticism, support, advice and/or encouragement they gave me, we will explicitly mention Ana Samboal, Ángel Expósito, Ángel Pintado, Antonio Garrigues Walker, Ashifa Kassam, Carlos Bustelo, Carlos Cuesta, Carlos Herrera, Carmen Tomás, Enrique Calvet, Felicísimo Valbuena, Fernando Eguidazu, Fernando Maura, Francisco José Contreras, Gonzalo Fernández de la Mora y Varela, Götz Otto, Hans-Werner Sinn, Jaime Carvajal, Jaime Mayor Oreja, Javier Paredes, Joel Kotkin, John Müller, José Luis Rodríguez Rivera, José Luis Ruiz Bartolomé, Juan David Gómez Rubio, Juan González, Juan José Garrido, Juan Pablo Colmenarejo, Juan Velarde Fuertes, Julio Pomés, Laura Peraita, Luis María Linde, Lord Christopher Monckton, Marcos Palicio, María Menéndez Zubillaga, Mario Moratalla, Mar Montoro, Nuria Chinchilla, Pedro Alonso, Susana Burgos, Susana Criado, Victorio Valle and Vladimir Gjorcev..

Last but not least, I appreciate the ideas and support of my closest relatives.

INITIAL REMARKS

> "Most Western European states are headed towards suicide through their (poor) demographics, without even being aware of it."
> (**Michel Rocard**, Socialist French prime minister from 1988 to 1999, "Conference for families" closing, 1989)
>
>
> "There are no children in the villages to hearten the spring. Only the old ones are left contemplating their old age."
> (From a poem read in a bar in Fontibre, where the Ebro river begins, in Spain)
>
>
> "Elders should be allowed to hurry up and die, thereby reducing the state's expenditure on their treatments."
> (**Taro Aso**, Japanese Finance Minister, 2013)

In November 2011, the book, "El suicidio demográfico de España" (The demographic suicide of Spain - Ed Homo Legens) was published by the same author, and contains similar themes, as this book: where we come from and where we are, with respect to birth rates and demography, what evils are hovering over societies with few children and many elders, why birth numbers have fallen so significantly, and what can be done to increase the birth rate. For better or for worse, it was not a book written by someone with a degree in sociology or demography, but by a telecommunications engineer dedicated to strategic and financial consulting for businesses. After studying the matter in depth, the author came to the conclusion that the demographic winter, or demographic suicide, was a major problem for Spain and for many other countries, with much farther-reaching and more immediate effects than the vast majority of people believed. The author did not understand why there was hardly any mention of it in the media or why adequate public and private measures had not been taken to combat this demographic downfall, given its potentially colossal significance. The author wanted, with that essay, to share his research and thoughts on the subject, as well as provide a warning for what is currently happening and for what will happen in the future if nothing is done.

"El suicidio demográfico de España" was not a *best-seller*, but it did have a large impact among a segment of the political, intellectual, and media elites of Spain, and some significant implications outside its borders. It was even said, in an article that appeared in "Israel National News", that this book "delivered the death sentence of Europe."[1]

From 2011 to 2017, when the first version of this book was published—in subsequent versions, minor errors and typos where corrected, and some date was updated—, public awareness of the problem of aging and birth rates, both in Spain and in the rest of Europe, Russia, the United States, Canada, Japan, China, South Korea, etc., has increased considerably. The term "demographic suicide" is now mentioned more frequently in public speeches, books, articles, TV shows, etc., as can be verified with a search engine, perhaps partly due, especially in Spain, to that book. Just maybe.

Now, six years later, after countless additional hours of studying the multiple dimensions of this complicated issue and conveying the consequences of decreasing birth rates and aging societies in conferences and speeches in the media, in Spain and abroad, our goal is to more or less present the same findings in this new book, but more effectively; with more complete data; with a perspective that is not only Spanish, but also European, Western, and global; and with the different angles of the problem and their solutions analyzed in greater depth. This book contains more examples from Spain than from other countries, and more from Europe and the United States than from other parts of the world, because this research is more readily available to the author; however, these examples, in addition to their implications for Spain and Europe overall, serve mainly to illustrate situations that are more general, since this problem is much more widespread and tends to spread quickly to countries that do not suffer from it yet. Only the reader can tell if we have succeeded in this effort. In any case, we thank you very much for being interested in this colossal problem that threatens the well-being of countries and civilizations like mine, and, in the long run, their historical continuity and existence.

---

[1] "Europe is Committing Social Euthanasia" by Italian journalist Giulio Meotti http://www.israelnationalnews.com/Articles/Article.aspx/12576

FOREWORD BY HANS-WERNER SINN

Either demographic revival or demographic suicide. This is the message of this carefully reasoned book, written by Alejandro Macarrón, which is full of statistical facts and full of true and indisputable observations about declining birth rates and a distorting age pyramid in the western world. I was shocked by the imminence of the terrors he describes, because they all result from obvious mechanisms which the author lays out to the reader. The book presents the demographic facts, discusses the reasons for low birth rates, and shows the likely consequences of an eroding society that risks losing its humanitarian values. The author has convinced me that we must act to prevent the disaster and he comes up with a long list of measures for both the state and the civil society to counter the trend.

What I like is the author's soberness and objectivity. The facts he presents are shocking but he never overstates them. He puts everything into perspective, argues in a balanced view, is reasonable and comprehensible, and yet the combination of simple and indisputable truths he presents creates a mosaic that will give you sleepless nights. Alejandro Macarrón is a responsible man, a person of integrity and intelligence, who writes in a clear, lucid, and interesting style, accessible to everyone, about a problem that affects us all. We should be discussing this book with our friends to help prepare a renaissance of our societies.

HANS-WERNER SINN

Economist. Professor emeritus of Munich University and ex-president of the Ifo Institute for Economic Research.

FOREWORD BY JOSEP PIQUÉ

All the problems that afflict our societies can be approached from multiple angles. And if the method of analysis is rigorous and honest, they appear to us in all their complexity, with a great variety of edges and with the numerous and different faces of an immense and irregular polyhedron. And its interpretation requires applying the analysis and the scientific method, which can be applied not only to the conventional sciences, but also to those we have denominated the social sciences. It is often said that, in the latter case, the scientific method is more difficult to apply, since it does not originate from the mere observation of phenomena external to the observer (which, since the publication of the theory of relativity, is no longer true) but rather we face realities that vary permanently due to the very action of those who observe them. And, therefore, they introduce an inevitable subjective component in their interpretation.

Hence, the difficult scientific refutability (falsifiability in Popperian terms) of many issues related to the progress of our societies, from economics, to sociology, to politics. And that allow, in free societies (again, Popper: open societies), the expression of multiple opinions, which, on many occasions, claim to be based on data and reflections of a supposedly "scientific" character. The paroxysm of this presumption corresponds to Marx, when he contrasted "utopian" socialism with "scientific" socialism. Mere and enormously damaging "social engineering," the basis of all kinds of totalitarianism and that generate "closed" societies, in which there is no room for dissent or, of course, freedom.

And, because of this, of the real complexity of many of our challenges, and the crudeness of our realities (such as the devastating impact of the economic crisis that the West, and particularly Europe, has experienced, in recent years, or the institutional and political delegitimation of representative democracy, as a product of corruption and the perception of an insufficient response by public authorities), the easy and immediate temptation is to seek simple answers to complex problems. And there is no better way to define what we now all know as "populism." And it can only be fought with reason, civic courage, and intellectual honesty. From the defense of the deepest democratic values, which rest on the defense of humanism and ethics in behavior, with freedom of "ideas and beliefs" that, as Ortega y Gasset would say, are at the base of our modern societies, but which respond, or should respond, to the real search for the common good or, in more modern terms, for the general interest. And, as a result, we must all make the effort to identify those major, strategic, and medium- and long-term challenges that we face. And to face them with rigor and seriousness, attending to their many facets, without ideological prejudices or temporary comforts derived from the temptation to not leave the "politically correct." And this is the great theme of this book, whose author, Alejandro Macarrón, we must wholly thank for his commitment and endeavor to bring us all to the enormous and undeniable relevance of the theme. We are talking about demographics and their global impact in all directions. And, as the author himself reminds us, Augusto Comte, the founder of positivism and modern sociology, ruled that fate lies in demography. Nothing truer and more irrefutable in the long run.

It is true that, as a result of the Industrial Revolution that began in England in the second half of the eighteenth century, something that began at the time of the great Discoveries (from the sixteenth century, with Spain and Portugal as great protagonists) was consolidated: the hegemony first of Europe, and then of what we call the West, which lasted approximately two and a half centuries. And which allowed us to visualize the world from a Eurocentric perspective, at least until the end of World War I (when Europe insisted on committing suicide, once again, through a mixture of arrogance and insane ambition). But it has persisted, in its decline, until now, despite the devastating effect of World War II on Europe. And we may be facing a new suicide attempt, this time definitive.

In any case, this supremacy was possible because, in our global history, the superiority of the West from the technological and cultural point of view (nothing substantially different from other empires and civilizations of the past) was based on the "monopolistic" use of technological, and therefore productive, advances associated with the Industrial Revolution, which allowed for, in addition to military supremacy, overcoming the almost unique importance of demography. Although it should be remembered that the demographic dynamism in the West lasted a long time, until World War II, in part, due to the medical advances that allow for lower infant mortality and remarkably longer life expectancies. A temporary exception. In the end, reality is, today, indisputable. And the demographic suicide of Europe (and of that concept we call the West, which is not geographical but rather cultural in the broad sense, and which is based on the defense of representative democracy, a free market economy, and the values brought by bourgeois revolutions) is, based on the data, absolutely indisputable.

Though it is not the subject of this book, from a geo-strategic point of view, many of the things that are happening (from the weakening of Europe as a political project or the strategic expansion of powers like China, Russia, Iran, or Turkey) lead us to a geographic retreat of Western values and to a deployment of political, economic, and cultural concepts, based on the questioning of representative democracy and a return of political authoritarianism as a method of governance, as well as a "State capitalism" that, by taking advantage of market mechanisms, increases monopolist power and public interventionism, and, of course, the relativization of freedoms and basic rights around liberty, equality, and tolerance.

Because, historically, the importance of countries has been based on the combination of their demographic weight and their technological capacity. And with convergence of technologies, by definition, the most important are the most populated. And that is exactly what is happening now, as a result of the rupture of the world order that appeared at the end of World War II and disappeared with the fall of the Berlin Wall and the subsequent collapse of the Soviet Union. We are witnessing the unstoppable emergence of alternative powers, with technological and productive bases increasingly similar to those developed in the West. And with a demographic weight and dynamism that expand and sharpen these trends. And they are in the hands of powers other than the West and, often, contrary to what the West represents. All this requires many nuances and considerations of all kinds. As should be the case with topics of enormous complexity and which have multiple edges. But it is absolutely undeniable that we are facing a challenge of immeasurable magnitude. And Macarrón's book is essential for anyone who wants to approach—with rigor and seriousness, data, figures, and grounded opinions—the brutal problem of what clearly defines the title of this book: our demographic suicide. And as the subtitle also points out: if we are not able to correct the trend, we are facing an inevitable catastrophe.

There is no room for discussion on the diagnosis, because the data should not be discussed, although that happens all too often. There is room, of course, for a debate on how to apply appropriate therapy. And the book presents various treatments. May it be a spur to discuss them in depth without ideological prejudices or merely superficial approximations. Because we are risking something as serious as our sustainability as a society, in a world increasingly different and whose center of gravity is moving away from us as webecome increasingly peripheral.

We are speaking, nothing more and nothing less, of our expectations of having a future and bequeathing it to our children. The few that remain ...

JOSEP PIQUÉ

Economist, ex-minister in the Spanish Government, and businessman.

FOREWORD BY JOAQUÍN LEGUINA

Kind reader: You have in your hands an interesting and illustrated book, but also a text that can produce something chilling when considering the future. It is about demography or, as the author would say, "demographic suicide." It is, moreover, a book built with statistical rigor and without playing to the crowd.

Is the demographic evolution in Western countries a relevant social problem? Undoubtedly, it is, but it is a problem hardly detected by the citizens. Proof of this is that in opinion polls (eg the Spanish CIS) when respondents are asked: "What are the biggest problems today?" there is hardly anyone who cites demography as a problem, although there are 3% who do mention pensions as an issue.

In the Eurobarometer of 2015 (which surveys EU citizens), the first problem, which is most frequently cited, is "immigration," which 58% of respondents cite (they cite it as a problem, but not as a solution). The immigration "problem" is well ahead of terrorism (25%) and unemployment (17%).

This *demographic neglect* has, in Spain, a very particular component, namely: in our country there is hardly an academic presence of Demography as a scientific discipline, which has led to hardly any professional demographers in Spain. Only now, when great evils are announced for the pension system, have the media dealt with demographics and population aging that low fertility rates inexorably causes.

This book written by Alejandro Macarrón intends not to frighten, but to warn, and that warning is pertinent and it would suit anyone to know it. But before delving into it, I owe you, gentle reader, some background, first of all about the forecasts that have been made—and are being made—for the demographic future. I will do so now.

In the 1970s, malthusianism prevailed everywhere and international institutions made some catastrophic "demographic forecasts" to the point of writing that the growth of the population would be the end of Humanity.

In 1968, Paul Ehrlich, Professor at Stanford University published a book[2] where one can read:

"In the 1970s hundreds of millions of people will starve to death because of

---

[2] The population bomb (Sierra Club, 1968)

overpopulation [...]nothing can prevent a substantial increase in the world death rate."

It did not take much time for the UN, MIT, or Ehrlich's own forecasts to fall into the utmost ridicule, since that "terminal" demographic crisis never existed and today we face a crisis of food distribution, but not of production. In fact, more is produced than is consumed and we can even speak of an epidemic of overfeeding on the one hand and of food waste on the other. Moreover, the population needed for agricultural production has declined dramatically. Not long ago, between 30% and 40% of the employed population worked in the fields and now, with just 3%, more food is produced than is needed.

Today we speak of a very different "catastrophe," that of aging. And we must ask: how do we know for sure that this is going to be our future reality? My doubts are born of a perfectly verifiable reality, because not so long ago—specifically in 1990—the most serious Spanish demographic forecasts predicted something for 2015 that was nothing like the reality that could later be proven.

For over 30 years, Spain has had a fertility rate below the replacement level (which is usually estimated at 2.05-2.10 children per woman) without this being noticed too much in its total population, since inertia from past baby booming years and foreign immigration compensated for the deficit of births, until the arrival of the economic crisis (2008). Let's look at this in some detail.

The Spanish population, according to the Decennial Censuses, had reached a maximum growth of 344,000 annual inhabitants between 1971 and 1981; in the following decade, the increase was 190,000 people a year, and from 1991 to 1998 the growth was much lower: 60,000 people a year. But in the decade 1998-2008 this downtrend was broken and the population grew the equivalent of what it had increased in the previous thirty years, an annual average of 630,000 people, a figure never before reached in the history of Spain.

Meanwhile, the number of births dropped from 677,456 in 1976 to 365,193 in 1998. In that year, deaths totaled 360,511, resulting in a vegetative growth of less than 5,000 for a population of 39.8 million. In view of the above data, it was logical that, by the mid-1990s, specialists anticipated a population decline and a significant increase in population aging. In fact, the INE[3] projection, based on the 1991 Census, foresaw a rapid decline in population, but such projections had a very short life, since they did not foresee the immigration that occurred immediately afterwards.

---

[3] INE (Instituto Nacional de Estadística) is the national statistical institute of Spain

As of January 1, 1998, there were 637,078 foreigners in Spain, 1.6% of the population; ten years later (1/1/2008) the foreign population reached 5,268,762, 11.4% of the total. Between 1998 and 2008, the number of people living in Spain increased by 6,305,170—4,631,684 of which were foreigners. In that period there was an unprecedented expansion of the labor market. The number of employed persons increased from 13,632,900 in the first quarter of 1998 to 20,510,600 in the third quarter of 2007. The strength of the change was evident and profoundly altered our demographic, social, economic and cultural structure.

Then came the financial crisis (2008) that disrupted the whole process, starting with economic growth and continuing with the migration process, which went from being positive to becoming negative, and, as a result, the problem of depopulation and aging appeared again.

The long-term divinatory capacity of demographic forecasts is quite similar to that of card-readers, but this does not mean that there will be no demographic problems and that hypothesis sets on mortality, fertility, and future migrations are not useful. On the contrary, they are useful insofar as they show us where these hypotheses would lead, but, in 2060, will there be as many "people of retirement age" (people aged 65 and over) as the INE projections tell us today? It is not known, and it is even more uncertain, that by the year 2050 there will be 23.4 million people of working age in Spain compared to the current 30.7 million.

Demographer Juan Antonio Fernández Cordón reminded us that long-term demographic projections vary greatly depending on who performs them. For example, those carried out by the INE in 2014 and 2016 vary significantly: the number of people who are of retirement age divided by the potentially active population (16-64 years) in the 2014 projection reached 75% for 2060, while the same projection made in 2016 dropped to 66%. For its part, in 2013 Eurostat estimated that, by 2060, that same ratio would be 54% in Spain. So which is it, 75% or 54%?

On the other hand, if we want to see the phenomenon of dependent people in all its breadth, we must take into account that there are other dependents, in addition to retirees. For example, children.

According to the projection of the INE (2016), at the beginning of the 2050s there will be 15.6 million people of retirement age (today there are 8.7 million), but the number of children (under 15) will have fallen from the current 7 million to 5.2 million. Given this, in the scenario of the INE, the number of *dependents* (children + seniors) divided by the number of potentially active people would be 1.47, which is somewhat lower than what it is today.

In any case, the demographic projections lack the capacity to foresee the swings that tend to occur in migratory movements (we saw this in turn-of-a-century Spain and at the beginning of the present century). So the first thing to guess is what will happen to the millions of people who are waiting for the opportunity to enter the EU or the US. Allow me a little reflection on this.

The Mexican philosopher Hugo Hiriart reminded us:

"Walk, walk, go elsewhere. As soon as the monkey gave rise to the "clever animals who invented knowledge" (Nietzsche), they packed up and embarked on the journey. The human being, say the wise, has a single origin, born in Africa and from there moved to all parts of the globe. He populated the jungles, climbed to the cold north and crossed the ice to America."

It is not difficult to reach a conclusion: migratory processes are part of human nature and yet, these are bad times for migration. There are barriers to free movement. Restrictions and persecutions abound (migrants are arrested, confined, and deported). Border crossings have become dangerous, people die attempting to cross borders, but even this does not stop the human waves. In some places, the migrant is unfairly equated with the criminal. The natural tendency has turned into political drama. And the debate is endless. In fact, migration and its consequences are, throughout the world, one of the great social and economic issues of the political agenda of the twenty-first century.

In this regard, the philosopher Michael Dummett argues that "there is no rational argument to curb migration: borders could be opened and, with orderly and gradual transit, all who wanted to enter would be allowed, and nothing would happen (the receiving countries would benefit in the long run). Most arguments to hinder and prosecute migration are based on obscure prejudices, unfounded fears and ethnic or racial hatreds."

In any case, any politician who dares to "open the doors" is condemned to dismissal. The case of Mrs. Merkel has been paradigmatic. In addition, both the opinion polls and the "successes" that xenophobic populisms are having here (in the EU) and across the pond (the US) augur very bad times for "welcoming" foreigners. And yet, without that "welcome," or without a substantial increase in the birth rate, depopulation and aging will be unstoppable.

Several analysts and pundits deduce from this future aging—without more mediations—that "the pension system is going to be unsustainable," forgetting that in a "pay as you go" system such as Spain's, today's pensions are paid by today's employees (and by companies) and today there are more than four million people in Spain who cannot find a job—something that has nothing to do with aging—and it is precisely this lack of jobs that produces the current deficit in the pension system.

Is greater longevity, that is, the extension of life expectancy, a serious problem for future pensions? It depends. In theory, it could be enough to solve this issue by increasing the working age at the same pace as life expectancy grows so that this effect is eliminated. If that were possible, the truculent proposal that came out of the mouth of Taro Aso, the Japanese Finance Minister, would be meaningless: "Let [elderly people] hurry up and die."

We must not fool ourselves, it is the structural incapacity to create enough employment— a disease that has caused suffering in the Spanish economy for many years—that is behind most of the current deficit of Social Security in Spain (it is said that the effects of the crisis explain 70% of the current deficit).

If it were true that public pensions will not give us the means to live in the future, what we have to do, we are told, is to subscribe to a private pension plan. All demographic-catastrophic arguments seem to lead to this conclusion. But it is enough to visit a website, such as *invertia.com*, to realize that such a "solution" will actually be one for the financial entities that issue those funds (which cannot be redeemed before reaching retirement age), but not for their subscribers. In the above-mentioned web site we can read that only 3 of the 335 funds with 15 years of history had—between 2001 and 2016—a return superior to that of the stock market (5.24% for the Spanish Ibex index) and to that of the 15 year public bonds (5.27%). Worse still, the average of these 335 pension plans yielded a return of 2.03%, which did not even reach half of the two alternative returns (Ibex and public bonds).

On the other hand, any change that implies substitution (or supplementation) of the current public "pay as you go" system by a private system of "capitalization" cannot solve the demographic problems that the Spanish population will suffer.

Meanwhile, under these conditions, in Spain, "retirers," people who dedicate themselves —in private companies and in public administration entities—to force many "mature" employees to retire, thus loading tons of pensions for people who are in perfect physical and mental condition and who do not want to retire onto the back of Social Security —continue to do as they please. A bleeding example: that of the doctors of public hospitals being forced to retire. In fact, health managers in many autonomous regions in Spain have devoted themselves during the last years to forcibly pre-retire veteran doctors in order to replace them with younger ones, who are given temporary contracts. The result is that the service deteriorates, depriving the sick of the care provided by very competent people, and Social Security finances are loaded with an unnecessary cost in pensions.

All this "jubilant" zeal is based on a widespread and repeatedly refuted fallacy, according to which "to retire the old creates jobs for the young." A statement even more false than the existence of the ether or the phlogiston, as shown by the multitude of published articles, all based on empirical studies of the US and other western economies. But in any case, if we want to arrive at rational solutions, the questions that need to be asked should be other questions. For example, could a smaller working population than the present population produce as much or more than now? The answer is yes. For starters, the employment rate (percentage of employed persons over the working age population) is currently 61% in Spain and could easily reach 73% or 75%. In addition, everything leads us to think that productivity per employee under normal conditions will grow significantly.

In truth, it seems that we are headed, in the next few decades, towards the next contradiction: there is a lack of young people (because of demography), but there could end up being a surplus, if robotization soon develops all its theoretical potential. In other words, both the pension problem and the strictly demographic problem could be approached from a different perspective in the next decades, which is not just demographic: that of greater productivity, accompanied by more and more qualified work, a better distribution of work and income, and a delay in the average retirement age proportional to the rise in healthy life expectancy. But that, if achieved, would help in the economic sense in the short- and medium-term. In the long run, if fewer children are born every year than during the previous year, and the labor force continues to decline, and also decreases more rapidly than the total population, as demographic projections anticipate, things look very bad for Spain and other countries with a declining number of births.

JOAQUÍN LEGUINA

Economist, demographer, former president of the Comunidad de Madrid (autonomous region of Madrid - Spain) and writer.

TWO INITIAL CALLS FOR ATTENTION

I was born in 1960 in Asturias, a beautiful region in northern Spain that, in those days, vibrated with life. Now Asturias's liveliness is fading as more Asturians die than are born. In recent years, Asturias has been the region with the lowest fertility rate of any European country and its population is one of the oldest in Europe and throughout the world. In 1960, in Asturias, with an overall population slightly lower than today's, there were three times as many births as there were in 2015, and there were more than two births per death (about 2.5). There are now more than two deaths per birth (2.1 to 1 in 2015). In 1960, there was a greater number of little Asturians under a year old than those 80 years or older. At the beginning of 2016, you had to combine the number of all the children under 12 years old to surpass the number of octogenarian, nonagenarian, and centenarian Asturians. Asturias, the historical cradle of the Spanish and Portuguese nations[4], two nations which, in turn, became the semi-cradles of more than 25 countries in America, Africa, and Asia, is now a land where tombs and funerary urns are needed more and more each year, while the demand for cradles is decreasing. If current fertility rates are to stay the same, and if there are no migratory movements between regions or countries, Asturias will be the first Spanish and European region where, eventually, an individual will die and there will be no one around to take care of his or her remains. Alpha and Omega. Sunrise and sunset. From the cradle of Spain in its time, to the opposite. Sad paradox.

* * * * *

What did the Prime Ministers of Germany, the United Kingdom, France (President of the Republic), Italy, the Netherlands, Belgium, Sweden, Switzerland (the Federal President), Luxembourg, and the President of the European Commission have in common at the beginning of June 2017? Answer: none of them had children. And just as we were finalizing the edition of this book, it was announced that the Irish conservative party Fine Gael had chosen a childless man as successor to the Taoiseach (Irish prime minister) who had just resigned.

---

[4] The battle of Covadonga, an abrupt and forested mountainous area of singular beauty, in 722, in which the Asturians led by Don Pelayo defeated an Arab army, is considered the cradle of the present Spanish and Portuguese nations, whose overseas empires, at their sunset, resulted in some thirty new countries.

Etching of the old church of Santa María del Naranco, by Alejandro Macarrón Jaime (1928-2017), my father. Santa María del Naranco is located on the flank of Monte Naranco, about 3 km from the center of Oviedo, the capital of Asturias. It was originally built as a palace by the Asturian king Ramiro I, who reigned between 842 and 850. It is a jewel of European pre-Romanesque art. UNESCO named it a World Heritage Site in 1985.

That a few people from any human group do not have children has always occurred. It is normal and insignificant for society. But when the rulers of so many countries with so much historical and current relevance—the four European countries with the largest populations and highest GDP, five of the six founding nations of the European Economic Community, two countries of global reference such as Sweden and Switzerland, the admired "Celtic tiger," Ireland—are simultaneously lacking, we are not seeing a casual anecdote, but rather data with a high symbolic value, which reflect, at the top of their respective States, a very common social pattern. In 1937, eighty years ago, among all these European countries, which would include Spain today, if the Socialist candidate had won the 2011 legislative elections, as well as the following election, only Germany had a prime minister/Chancellor who had no children: Adolf Hitler. It was also the case of the then President of the Spanish Republic, Manuel Azaña. No one else. Now, in 2017, from the top of the social pyramid to the ordinary folks, this is what we are facing in Western Europe, and not only there.

INTRODUCTION

Imagine a country where there are so few births that, for every 100 randomly picked women who reach 45 years of age today, there are only about 60 girls and women under 30 whose mothers are one of those 100 ladies who celebrate their birthday today[5]. This means that for every 100 young adults in their 20s through 40s today, in about 30 years, there would be only 60, a century from now only around 20, and two centuries from now, only four or five. In three centuries, there would only be one young adult per every 100 that exist today. Eventually, no young adults would remain. The overall population of this infertile country, with some decades of delay, would decline at a similar pace. Moreover, this declining population would become increasingly older, because there would be a progressively smaller proportion of young people, as well as increasing longevity. With such a shockingly low number of births, this country would appear to slowly be committing suicide, as its inhabitants would be disappearing due to their voluntary infertility, which is why it is called a "demographic suicide." This phenomenon can also be called a "demographic winter" because winter is the season during which countries far from the equator experience seemingly little to no apparent life in nature.

This infertile nation would experience serious problems during several centuries leading to a population of zero. To begin, there would be a structural economic decline, due to the constant deterioration of the country's human capital——the main source of wealth for all developed nations and for the majority of developing nations——both in quality (an increasingly older population) and in quantity (fewer workers and consumers). The most well-known effect of this economic decline is the increasing difficulty of retirees to enjoy good pensions——but that is neither the only, nor most significant, effect, as we will see later on in this book.

Honoring the saying that "misfortunes never come singly," the inhabitants of

---

[5] The range when women are fertile is approximately between 15 and 44 years old. Births from mothers who are outside this age range occur in one of every 300 births in Europe, according to Eurostat data. In 2013, the mother of 0.04% of the European babies was under 15 years old and the mother of 0.27% of those babies was over 44. In the USA, percentages are very similar.

this country would suffer from the sadness and lack of affection caused by a growing solitude, by a drastic reduction in the number of close relatives (few or no children, siblings, cousins, uncles and aunts, nephews and nieces, grandchildren, etc.), in contrast to their traditional abundance. We can also predict the degeneration of the democracy of that country into a gerontocracy (government of/for the elderly), the retired being the largest electoral segment and the retired having a homogenous interest whereby the rest of society transfers money to them, via taxes, for their pensions, healthcare, and personal needs (a dependent relationship). Finally, the importance of that country in the international community would decrease, through the reduced weight of its population in the global population—something that could pose additional risks if the neighboring nations did not suffer from a similar human decline and, especially, if they decided to harbor expansionist interests.

That country has many names. One of them is Spain, a nation where each year, there are fewer births than there were at the end of the eighteenth century—although Spaniards today are 4 or 5 times more numerous than during that era—and needs fewer baby cribs than during the hard years of its civil war of 1936-1939, when the Spanish population was 45% inferior to the current one. That country is also called Germany, Italy, Portugal, Switzerland, Luxembourg, Austria, Greece, Japan, South Korea, Taiwan, Singapore, Russia, China, Poland, the Czech Republic, Hungary, Romania, Serbia, Croatia, Bosnia, Macedonia, Georgia, Thailand, Cuba, Canada, etc. With slightly softer profiles, but with the same long-term trends, if it wasn't for the continuous arrivals of foreign immigrants, the country we described earlier would also encompass the United States of America, the United Kingdom, France, Sweden, Denmark, Norway, Finland, Belgium, the Netherlands, Brazil, Chile, Australia, etc. It is a country with more and more names in a world with a growing number of people who, unlike all their direct ancestors, either do not want children or decide to have children later in their lives, when, for biological reasons, can no longer have children or end up only having one child.

There have hardly been populations as infertile as the present in the history of mankind. When those kinds of populations existed, in no case did they persist in their infertility. As in the past, infant and juvenile mortality was very high[6]. A population with a birth rate like that of the current German, Italian, Spanish or Japanese populations, would have disappeared in a matter of decades or a century,

---

[6] According to our estimates, based on historical mortality data available on the website of the National Statistical Institute of Spain (INE), at
http://www.ine.es/inebaseweb/libros.do?tntp=205002; in 1880, half of Spanish children died before they turned 12. Now, 99.5% of those born in Spain and Western Europe reach adolescence. In the great majority of the rest of the world, between 95% and 99% reach adolescence.

or would have been subjugated by other countries. Never has longevity been as high as the present, nor have there been populations with so many adults and seniors. The life expectancy of those who were born in Rome two millennia ago can be expressed with the same digits we use to express life expectancy in developed nations today—and soon, in developing nations as well—but in reverse order. In round numbers, life expectancy at birth has the same digits in Caesar's time and in our day in developed nations—and soon in the rest of the world[7]—, just in reverse order: 28 years then, 82 now. Furthermore, there is no precedent for any kind of living beings that, with greater abundance of nutrients and physical security[8] compared to their very close ancestors (three generations earlier and even less), have substantially fewer offspring.

In the absence of fully comparable historical precedents with such low fertility and so much longevity, much less with the two occurring simultaneously, we navigate into uncharted waters in this matter. For this reason, it is not possible to rely on more than a few past experiences and to analyze in detail what is currently happening in the countries and regions with the greatest aging to predict the destiny of the sterile populations, of the infertile nations of today. These are nations that should rather be called "deathions," since the word "nation" comes from "being born" (Lat. Natio from the verb nasci—to be born), and in these there tend to be fewer children born every year and a trend of more people dying than are born[9]. This lack of precedent, along with scientific, technological, and business innovations, makes it difficult to be sure what a demographic winter really means

---

[7] NB. There are a good number of mentions to sociological patterns of "developed countries" in this book. Most of them can be applied as well to the "developed" part of emerging countries, which is a growing share of the people and territory of those nations that used to be called "Third World" countries. The increasingly larger middle classes and upper-middle classes of places like México D.F., Bombay (Mumbai), Sao Paulo or Bogotá, to mention a few, display social behavior patterns in the topics of our interest (life style, consumption habits, professions, family trends, fertility, life expectancy, etc.) that are very similar to their counterparts in Europe, Northern America or Japan. Even if their countries as a whole are not "developed" yet, an increasing part of their population is very similar in nearly all aspects of interest for the subject of this book to the people of the countries of what used to be called the "First World."

[8] Current real per capita income is dozens of times higher than that of several centuries ago in Northern America, Europe and all developed nations, and much greater than historical income anywhere on Earth. The opposite has happened with homicide rates and mortality due to illness and other causes—perhaps with the exception of suicide—for the non-advanced ages. Even in the poorest continent of the world, Africa, life expectancy at birth is now close to 60 years old.

[9] For example, in the central and oldest country of Europe, Germany, deaths have outnumbered births for over forty years. In 2015, in the European Union as a whole and in thirteen of its twenty-eight countries, there were more deaths than births. In my country, Spain, there are already several provinces with more than two deaths per birth, and one of them (Zamora), reached a 3 to 1 ratio between deaths and births in 2016.

and how to fight it. In the economic productivity arena, new inventions and technologies could alleviate some of the depressive effects of the demographic decline, although it is impossible to know with certainty how much innovation could help. We should, however, project, speculate, and analyze what could happen if we continue with so few children. Removing the disappearance of some problems, such as unemployment—as each year more people would retire than young people would be entering the active workforce—and the reduction of other issues, like crime, which is much more common among young and middle-aged people than the elderly. Almost all that can be foreseen by a demographic suicide are woes, somewhat smaller or larger. By comparison, even the reduction in unemployment and crime seem to be a meager consolation. After all, there is no unemployment or crime among those who lie, forever, in cemeteries.

There's no turning back. Countries with an insufficient birth rate, like the great majority of European countries, a large part of the Far East, and a growing number of countries in other parts of the world, are inevitably aging and depopulating progressively, along with collective impoverishment and a society that languishes due to a lack of young blood. The alternative is the massive repopulation by foreigners from poorer countries and other cultures, another phenomenon not free of difficulties in management, costs, and social risks.

* * * * *

What follows is a story that will shock all people who love their country, their homeland, their city, their civilization, if it is one of those that is in serious danger of crumbling, little by little, in the coming decades due to a lack of children. This downfall suggests a panorama of impoverishment, not only economic, but also affective (in a society in which fewer and fewer people have and will have children, siblings, uncles and aunts, cousins, nephews and nieces, etc.), by the work and grace of our demographic decline. It is an attempt to narrate and describe, in terms understandable by the common readers, the sad demographic reality of countries including almost all European nations, the US and Canada, a large part of Asian countries, and in the midterm, almost the whole world. To go from the saying to the fact, from the muses to the theater, and from theory to practice, this book also points out possible solutions to the looming large problem and adaptation strategies to the tsunami of gray hair we are observing. This is a book conceived with the head, but that, because of the matter in question, cannot avoid including comments that are pure sentiments of the author, as a means of accompanying the dramatic figures that are exposed here.

Even with all the biases and errors inherent to the author's human condition, for which I apologize in advance, the facts and data this work includes are so overwhelming, so stubborn, so indisputable, that they certify, beyond any reasonable doubt that, in demographic matters, we are facing one of the largest issues, and possibly the greatest grassroots problem, that Europeans, North Americans, and natives to the countries of the Far East, and others, are facing in the 21st century. It is also worth mentioning that it is the one problem of great importance in the medium and long-term that the great majority of politicians—occupied as they are to win the next elections—intellectuals, and persons of influence, give the least importance in countries afflicted by the demographic winter. Only they know why.

As for us ordinary citizens, we can continue to passively contemplate this demographic suicide and look the other way, as we have been doing during the last few decades, or try to understand and remedy it, something that will only happen if inhabitants of the affected countries become aware of the extreme potential gravity, facilitate a new political and social impetus to birth rates, and those who are still of childbearing age actually have more children. In developed countries with a more vigorous economy, as a palliative, completing the depleted native ranks with immigrants, preferably coming from countries most like their own because of their culture and traditions, will be possible; however, facilitating the arrival of foreign workers should not be the main strategy in the face of a demographic problem, but rather, a complement to the primary commitment to increase our birth rate, due to its undesirable potential side effects.

We have few years left to get down to work and start improving our demographic prospects before it's too late. This book was written to this end: tell the problem and propose solutions. Either we recover the lost birth rate very soon or risk the wellbeing of countries affected by this decline. It is the effect the collective infertility has had in recent decades in many countries, such as mine. What has saved us a lot of effort and money in childrearing will, in the long run, be very costly, from an affective, social, economic, and political standpoint. As Americans put it, so appropriately: "there is no such thing as a free lunch," and, of course, the same applies to demographic matters.

CHAPTER 1
A WORLD HEADING TOWARDS DEMOGRAPHIC SUICIDE

Where we come from, where we are, where we are heading

"Demographics is destiny"
(**Auguste Comte**, creator of positivism and sociology)

"The demographic problem in Spain is so serious that, if it continues on the same path, Spain will disappear"
(**Juan Velarde Fuertes**, distinguished Spanish economist)

From many children, short lives and *pyramidal pyramids*, to few children, long lives and inverted pyramids

In human societies, children and well-populated families have always been bountiful. The vast majority of people did not live with great economic comfort, but their village, their city, their nation, their tribe, vibrated with life. Well, at least until about half a century ago, in Europe, North America and the Far East, more or less. Now, in the rich countries of the world, more and more gray hairs are combed, because longevity is much greater than it was years ago—a wonderful thing, provided there are enough young and middle-aged people to maintain and care for the elderly—while children, with few exceptions, become conspicuous due to their absence, because fertility is nowadays much lower.

The "population pyramid" of a country, in which the population is represented by age bands with widths proportional to the number of people in each of them, and which is called a pyramid because traditionally it has a form of a triangle with a flat base (or of a pyramid or cone if drawn in 3D) is becoming inverted in countries with few births. The population pyramid used to maintain its traditional shape due to many children, quite a few young people, somewhat fewer middle-aged people and few seniors and elderly; however, now it is a "pyramid," which, although it is still called as such, based on its morphology, no longer deserves that name. In the future, it will look more and more like an inverted pyramid. The traditional form of the population pyramid meant that countries had a great future, because there were many children and young people (the lower bands were very wide), meaning middle-aged populations could provide, without too much burden, care and support for the elderly, as the former were much more numerous than the latter.

The deformed population pyramids, such as those of present-day Germany/Japan/Spain/Italy/etc., which are typical of countries that have had several decades with few births and have a high life expectancy, mean, among other things, that those who are now of middle-age could have a tough time as retirees/seniors, because when they reach retirement age, there will not be enough youth and middle-aged people to easily support them. Thus, based on their demography, these are countries with more present than future. This can be clearly seen in the population pyramids of Spain forty years ago (1976), the year in which this book (2016) was completed, and the one predicted by the National Institute of Statistics (INE) of Spain in forty years (2056). Incidentally, and not by chance, in the pyramids of 2016 and 2056, more age bands are needed to represent the very elderly, who have reached ages that hardly anyone reached in 1976.

Population of Spain by broad age group			
Dato source: INE	1976	2016	2056(P)
Less than 20 years	35.6%	19.8%	16.1%
From 20 to 64 years	54.0%	61.4%	48.5%
65 years and over	10.4%	18.7%	35.4%
Total	100.0%	100.0%	100.0%

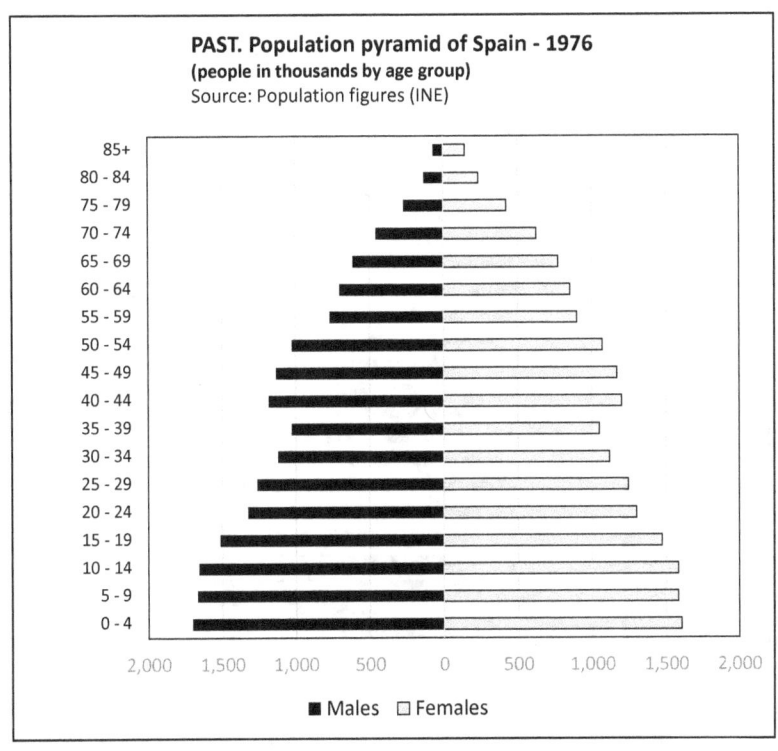

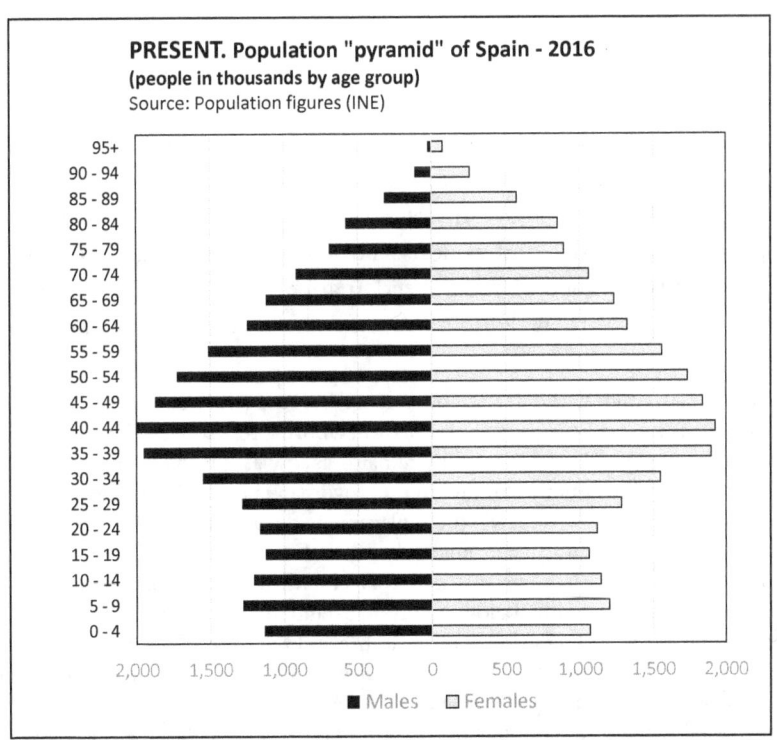

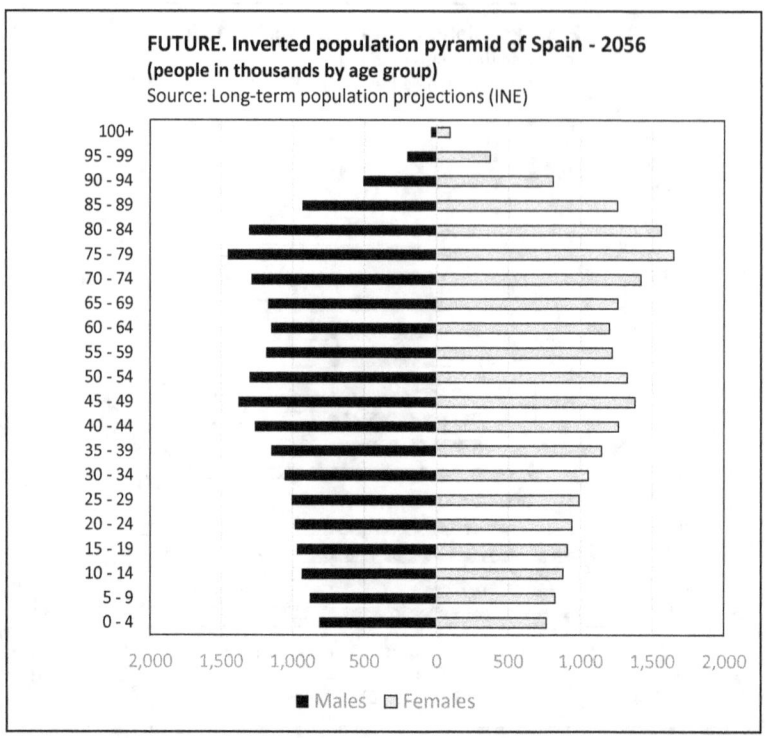

As we do not even have the number of children necessary for population replacement (an average of 2.1 children per woman[10]), each new generation of our fellow civilians is between 10% and 50% less numerous than the previous one, depending on the countries and regions. This phenomenon has most likely never occurred in history in such a generalized manner. For the first time since time immemorial, because of their demography and the average age of their population,

---

[10] 2.1, rather than 2.0, children are needed on average because a higher number of males than females are born, typically 51.6% versus 48.4% of newborns, respectively. This number is valid maintaining that infant and juvenile mortality remains as low as it is in developed countries. Otherwise, a higher average number of children per woman is needed. Traditionally, as about half of the children died before puberty, the replacement fertility rate was 4 to 5 children per woman. By 1878, in Switzerland, according to the Swiss Federal Statistical Office, 3.26 children per woman were needed to ensure population replacement, and this happened in a country where infant mortality was already below traditional standards. That is why in many still underdeveloped or developing countries, the real threshold is still higher, by a few tenths, than 2.1. Likewise, in countries where the infanticide/selective abortion of female infants continues to be practiced significantly or even massively, as is the case of the two Asian demographic giants, the required ratio of children per woman for generational replacement is greater than 2.1.

developed countries have more human past and present than projected human future. Furthermore, the bulk of developing nations follows the same path, some already quite clearly, and the rest follows only as a trend. In almost all the developing countries, fertility has plummeted in the last few decades, and there are no clear signs that it will not continue to decline. When did this begin, what consequences does it have, where are we headed?

The following graph shows the estimated evolution of the fertility rate worldwide[11] as well as by continents, from the early 1950s to the years 2010-2015. The fall from the mid-twentieth century is evident everywhere. In Africa, it started clearly around 30 – 35 years ago.

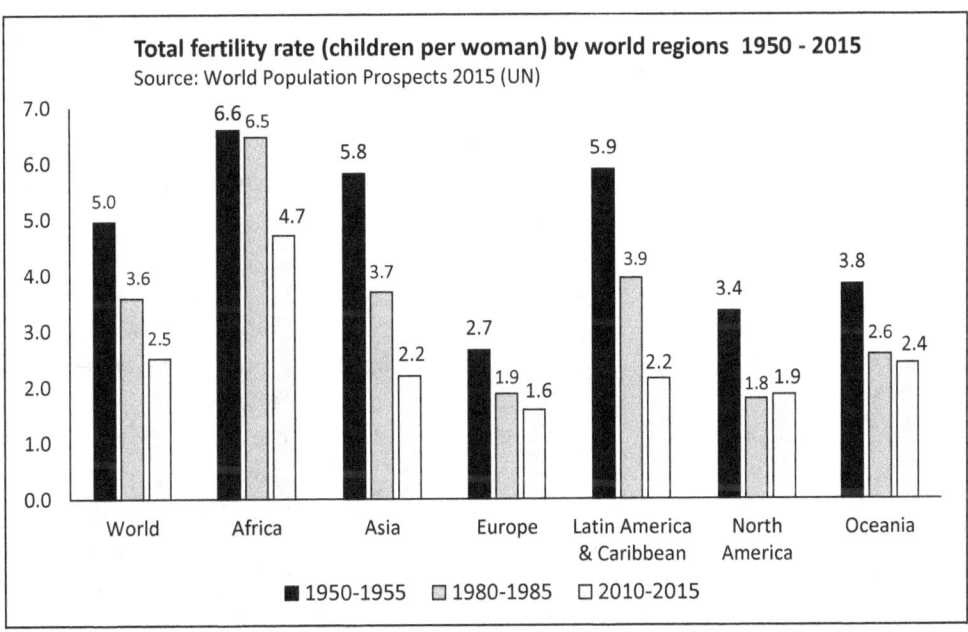

In 60 years, the worldwide birth rate has fallen by about half. As shown in the chart, in the 1950s, birth rate was much lower in Europe than the world average, and it was also lower, though to a lesser degree, in North America. Since then, the decline in fertility rates in Asia, Latin America, and the Caribbean has been breathtaking (63% - 64% fewer births since the early 1950s), to the point of

---

[11] This is called the "total fertility rate," or estimated number of children per woman. It is calculated each year by adding the ratios between the number of births of mothers of each age and the total number of women of that age. If birth rates do not change, and assuming that no woman dies before the end of her fertile years—a certainty for 99% of the women in developed countries—it is the average number of children that women would end up having by the time they concludes their fertile life.

practically reaching just the average replacement levels, and has probably already crossed that level on the way down, because the fertility in those regions of the globe, as in almost all the others, continues with an underlying downward trend. Meanwhile, in Europe, the birth rate continued a drop that, on the Old Continent, had begun half a century earlier or more (-41% since the early 1950s), to reach levels well below the replacement rate (2.1 children per woman in Europe). This decline has also been very noticeable in the last decades in North America—-a fall of 44% in 60 years, even if there has been a slight rebound in the last 30 years, mainly due to a certain recovery of the birth rate in the US, which in recent years has been falling again in the United States—, as well as in Oceania (37% decline). As can be seen in the former chart, the only continent with a remaining high birth rate in the world is the African continent, except for the North/Maghrebi regions and the southernmost region of the continent, where the current birth rate is between 2 and 3 children per woman. However, the birth rate in Africa has been falling rapidly in recent decades (-28% in the last 30 years).

Europe and the United States, pioneers in the worldwide decline of birth rates

When did the fertility rate begin to fall? As the graph above implies, the birth rate should have already fallen significantly in Europe, and in North America, as we shall see, in relation to its traditional historical levels, before 1950, since it was already much lower by that time than in the rest of the world. In fact, with some ups and downs, in some European countries, the birth rate has been slowly declining since the second half of the nineteenth century, and in some countries, perhaps since the first half. In North America, the birth rate started falling in the early 19th century. The following graphs show the evolution of the fertility rate and the number of births in several European countries. Each has followed a similar long-term pattern, starting from a historical fertility much higher than the present one, even with national differences in evolution, considering the birth rates began to decrease at different times. In some countries, partial recoveries have been experienced from the lows. Suffice to say that there is currently no European country, no rich/highly developed country, apart from Israel, whose birth rate steadily reaches 2.1 children per woman. There are some that are approaching this threshold from below, such as France, the United Kingdom, Ireland, or Sweden, although almost all of them would be significantly farther away from that number without the contribution of infants to their host countries by foreign immigrants.

In the case of Germany, Europe's central and most aging country, where, since the 70s, more people die than are born, and whose population does not diminish when there is a sufficient influx of immigrants to compensate for its vegetative negative balance—more deaths than births—the round numbers are overwhelming. During the "Belle Époque," prior to the appalling butchery we call World War I, in Germany, which was a very thriving and prosperous country, exemplary in many ways, almost two million children were born every year. Now, in the land of Beethoven, a little over a third of the number of children who were born during that "Belle Époque" are born, even with a population that is now 50% more numerous. Furthermore, of those who are born, about 30% have foreign parents. *Sic transit* Germanic fertility!

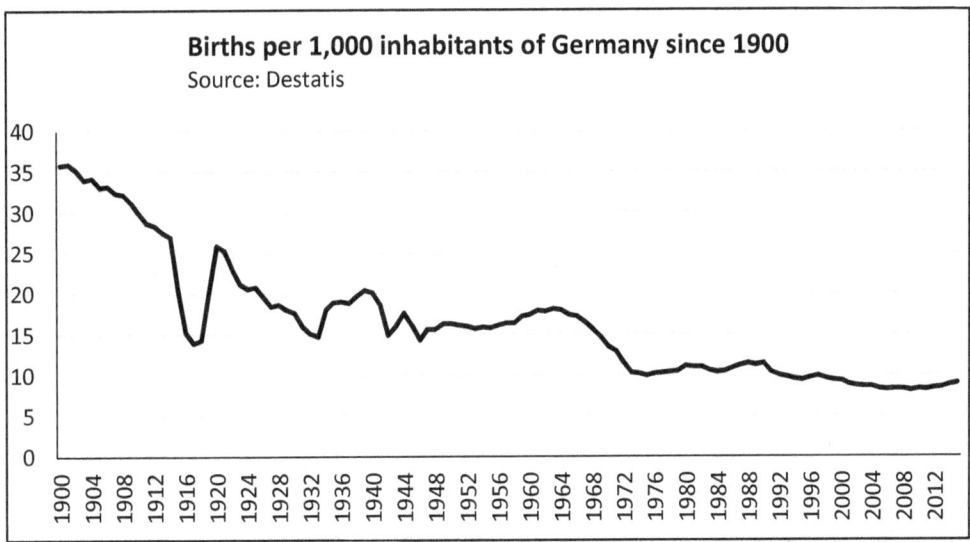

As seen in the next chart, Spain, which was significantly behind Sweden in its socio-economic development a little over a century ago, had, at the time, a fertility far superior to that of the Scandinavian country, but in decline nonetheless. During the middle decades of the twentieth century, in both countries, the trend towards a reduction in birth rates was halted. Whereas in Sweden, in the last 30 - 40 years, even with ups and downs, there has been a certain recovery in the number of births per woman, in Spain, since the late 1970s, there has been a new plunge, and since the mid-1980s, Spanish women have had a much lower fertility rate than that of the women of Sweden.

We would notice a similar trend if we were to compare the Swedish, Norwegian, or Danish fertility rates with those of the Italian, Portuguese, or Greek. The birth rate began falling earlier in northern Europe than in southern Europe, but is now higher in the north, and is still not high enough in any European country.

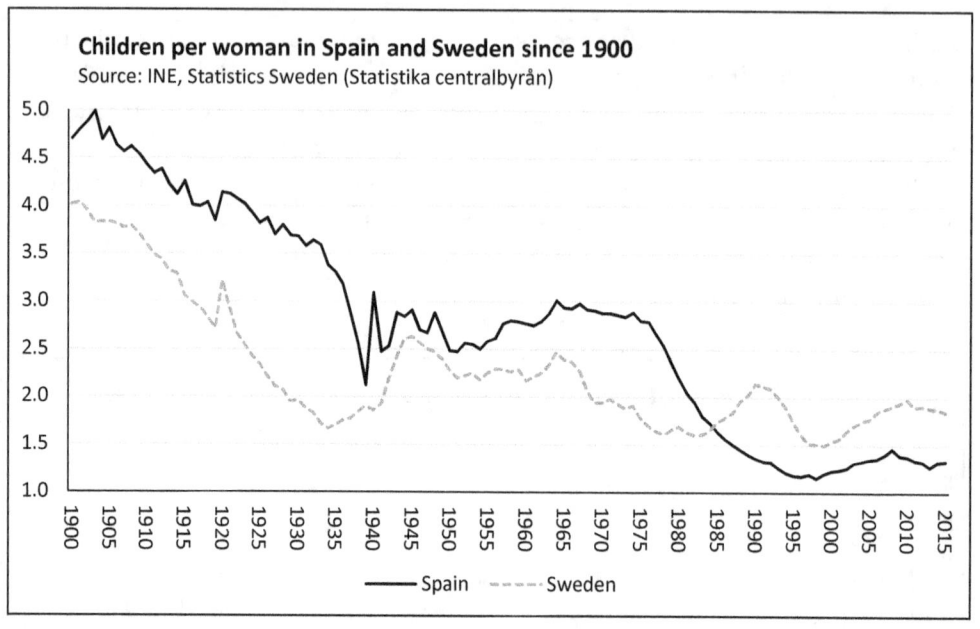

In 1901, the total fertility rate in France was already less than three children per woman, a level well below the traditional level, and among the lowest in Europe. Until the second half of the nineteenth century, in Europe and in North America— and well into the twentieth century, in the rest of the world—a human population with that level of fertility was bound to decline, because about half of the children and adolescents died before reaching adulthood, a mortality level that would make a pre-industrial society with the birth rate of France during the "Belle Époque" demographically unsustainable, in a matter of decades, prior to World War I. In the graph of France, after a continuous decline in the fertility rate in the first four decades of the twentieth century (with a sudden collapse and subsequent recovery due to World War I), there is a remarkable rebound of the birth rate, which began in 1942—curiously, when France was occupied by the Germans. The birth rate rebound then continued during the so-called post-war *baby boom*, which shows signs of exhaustion towards the mid-1960s, after which a new fall in fertility occurred, with a minor rebound beginning the mid-1990s, with a downward trend in the years preceding the writing of this book

,

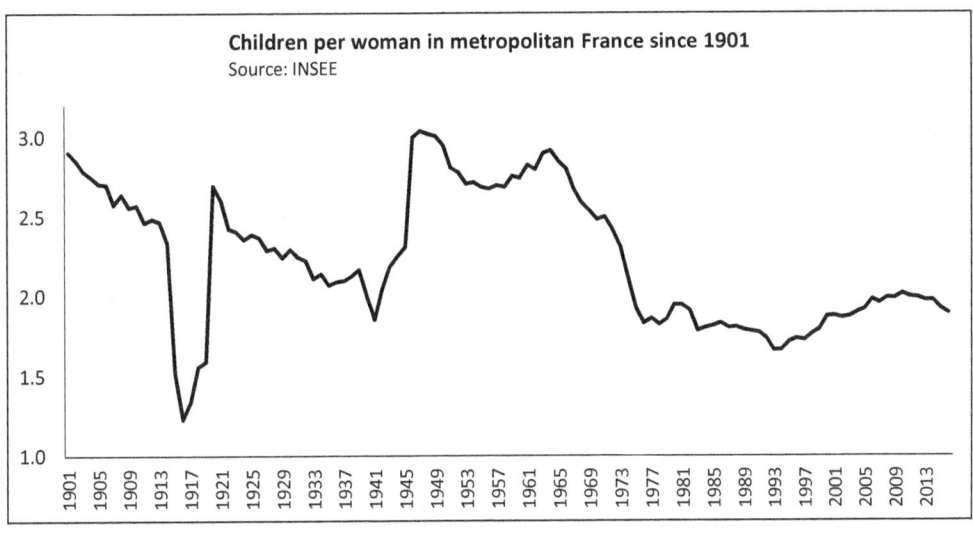

France is a country of great interest for our purpose. In addition to its international weight and influence in many areas, it has strongly been promoting high birth rates since the end of World War II, with active public policies in favor of fiscal support to the family and births. France's birth rate is less mediocre than in most other European and developed OECD countries. Nevertheless, it doesn't achieve, though it comes close to, the two children per woman (1.85 in metropolitan France in 2017, 8% less than in 2010, according to its national institute of statistics and economic studies, INSEE), and has been declining since 2011, with a drop in the number of births of 9% between 2010 and 2017. Moreover, excluding the birth rate of the immigrant population, the fertility of native French women would be around 1.70 children per woman. The additional fertility that allows the birth rate of metropolitan France to reach their global levels is attributed to, above all, the Maghreb immigrants. In 2016, the mother of 22.2% of the babies in metropolitan France was born abroad, a percentage that has risen year after year since 1999. The percentage of kids in present-day metropolitan France who are children or grandchildren of immigrants from Muslim countries (mainly, but not exclusively, from Algeria, Morocco, Tunisia, Turkey, Senegal and Comoros) and which make up the next generation of young adults in France, is at least 20%, according to our estimates, and could approach 25%, or even exceed that threshold.

In England and Wales[12], the fertility rate in the early twentieth century was far less than the historical one as well, and smaller than in less developed European countries, such as Spain. Since then, it has dropped substantially, albeit with varying ups and downs. At present, the Anglo-Welsh fertility rate, although lower than the replacement rate, is among the highest in Europe and the West, with 1.76 children per woman in 2017—it would be less than 1.70 without the extra fertility that, as in France and other European countries, is contributed by immigrants—.28.2% of those born in England + Wales in 2016 had a mother who was born abroad, a percentage that, as in France, Germany, or Scandinavia, tends to increase each year. Like France, it is striking that the birth rate began to rise starting in 1942, in the middle of World War II, in an environment of clear privations and tensions.

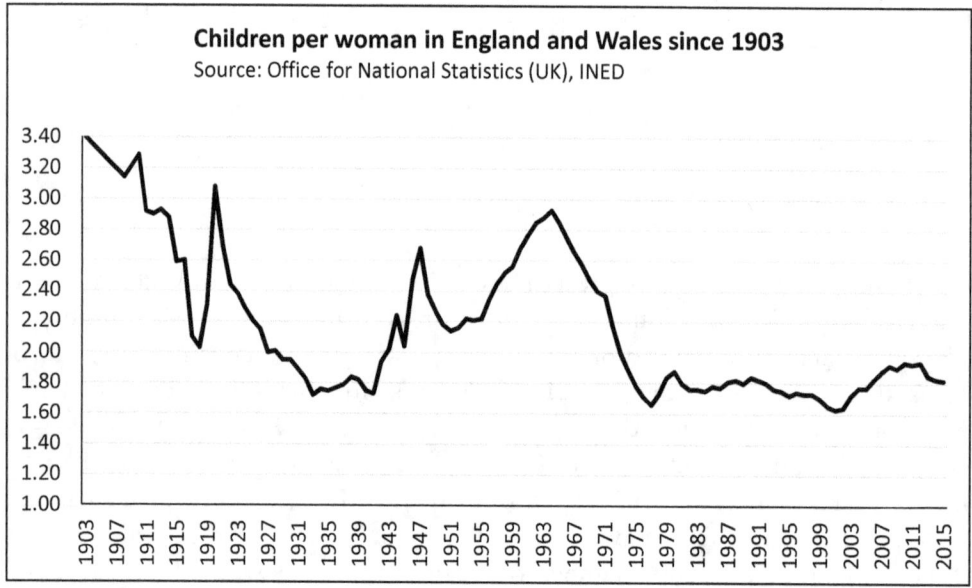

What happened in Italy, which follows the general European pattern, is also very illustrative. The typical image of Italy, like that of other Mediterranean nations, depicts a country where families were large until very recently. Actually, families have not been large for decades.

---

[12] The author has not found data for the whole of the United Kingdom dating back to the early twentieth century, and is therefore showing only England and Wales together, which on the other hand together account for 85% - 90% of births in the country since 1887, the first year for which the National Bureau of Statistics of the United Kingdom provides birth statistics. For more than 30 years, Scottish fertility has been lower than that of England. And the Northern Irish, in line with that of independent Ireland, is greater.

Since 1940, only in 1946, the year after the end of the Second World War, did fertility reach three children per woman in Italy. The post-war "baby boom," which in some countries continued until the 1970s, was particularly small and short-lived in Italy.

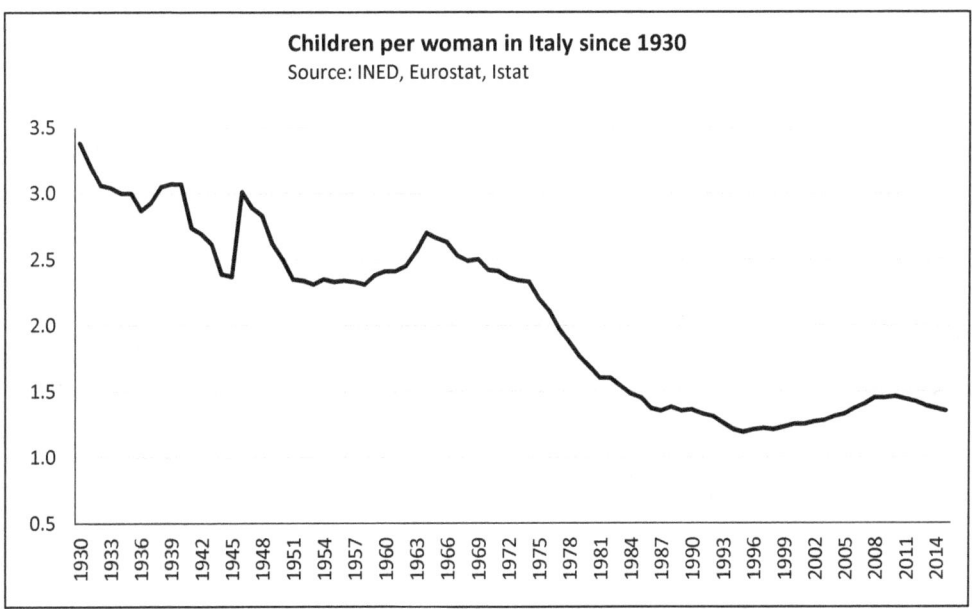

Children per woman in Italy since 1930
Source: INED, Eurostat, Istat

The United States: from the overflowing birth rate of the pioneers to a demographic winter somewhat less intense than in Europe (but still a winter)

The case of the United States is peculiar and of great interest, like almost everything related to what has been for a century now, and continues to be, the most powerful and influential nation in the world. Excluding the Native American population, the U.S. demographically stems from a population of European origin, which was initially very fertile, as well as from a large minority of people from other backgrounds, including the unfortunate Africans brought to the U.S. as slaves up until the civil war of 1861 to 1865. The U.S. data we have compiled demonstrate very significant traits for both historical purposes and the topics we deal with in this book.

The first graph displays the evolution of fertility of the white and non-white populations of the United States since 1800[13]. While the fertility of white Americans in 1800 is estimated to have been seven children per woman (7.04 in the source referenced), the rate fell by 50% throughout the nineteenth century. In this great nation, the decline of the birth rate also has a very long history. Towards the beginning of the 20th century, fertility in the United States was significantly lower than that of the pioneers of previous centuries. As for other races/ethnicities in the USA, their fertility rates were always higher than that of the whites, but the difference is now only marginal. The fertility rate of Asian-Americans, however, is even lower than that of white Americans. Nevertheless, without the contribution of White Hispanics to the global fertility of the White population in the USA, there would not be any significant difference in birth rates of "Whites" and "Non Whites", according to our estimates, based on data of the US Federal Agency CDC, [14].

The continuous drop in the fertility rate in the U.S. from 1800 until the mid-1930s indicates that the fertility rate fell <u>not only during the worst times</u> of the Great Depression but also during <u>the very prosperous</u> Roaring Twenties, as well as during other cycles of great economic expansion and social optimism. This interesting and notable factor will be discussed in more detail in further analyses throughout this book.

---

[13] Initially, the "non-white" Americans were mostly Blacks and Native Americans. We did not find their birth rates before 1850-1860, a decade from which the combined fertility of non-white Americans is estimated at 7.9 children per woman in the oldest historical data source we have used. ("The Population of the United States 1790-1920" by Michael R. Haines, published by the National Bureau of Economic Research in 1994, which, despite its title, contains demographic data until 1990). Nowadays, increasingly, other races or ethnic groups in the United States, apart from Whites with European roots, Blacks, and Native Americans, include people with personal or family origins in other countries in the Americas (mostly Hispanics but a variety of races as well), Chinese, Japanese, Korean, Filipino, Vietnamese, Hindu, Native American Pacific islanders such as from Hawaii, American Samoa, or the Marianas, etc. As for Whites, since the mid-twentieth century, they include a growing number of Hispanics (Whites), who have recently increased the global average fertility of Whites significantly.

[14] CDC, the US Center for Disease Control and Prevention, is one of the main data sources used in this book for numbers of births, fertility and other demographic statistics of the USA. It is one of the major operating components of the Department of Health and Human Services of the Federal Government of the US.

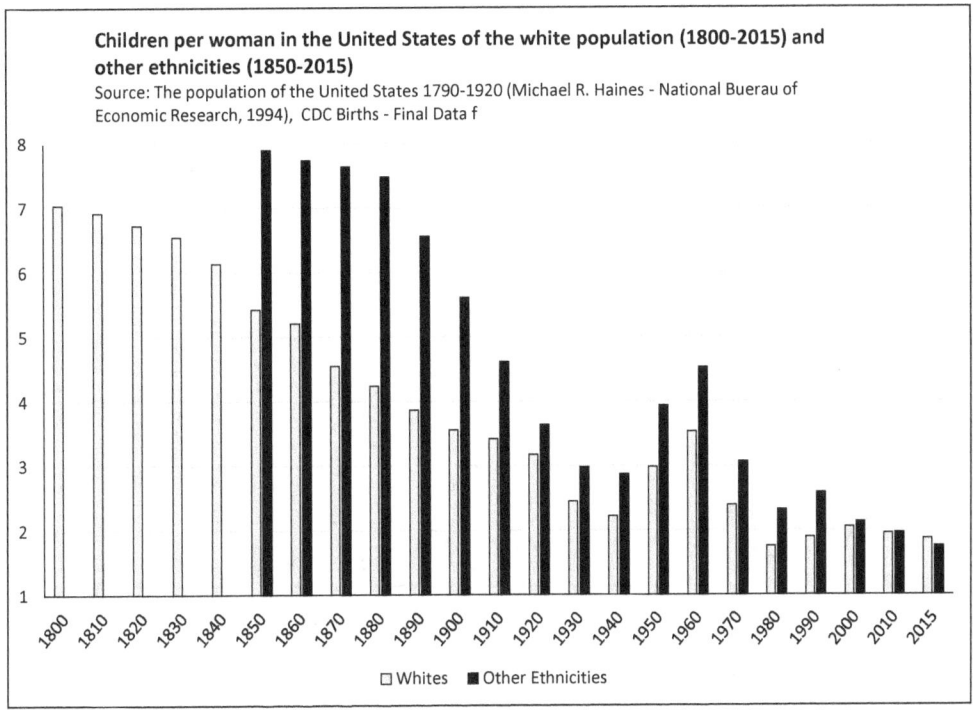

Children per woman in the United States of the white population (1800-2015) and other ethnicities (1850-2015)
Source: The population of the United States 1790-1920 (Michael R. Haines - National Buerau of Economic Research, 1994), CDC Births - Final Data f

Next graph details the evolution of the fertility rate in the U.S. during the past 100 years. While it is traditionally said that there is nothing more American than apple pie and motherhood, it is very possible that apple pie will remain the only true American symbol of the two.

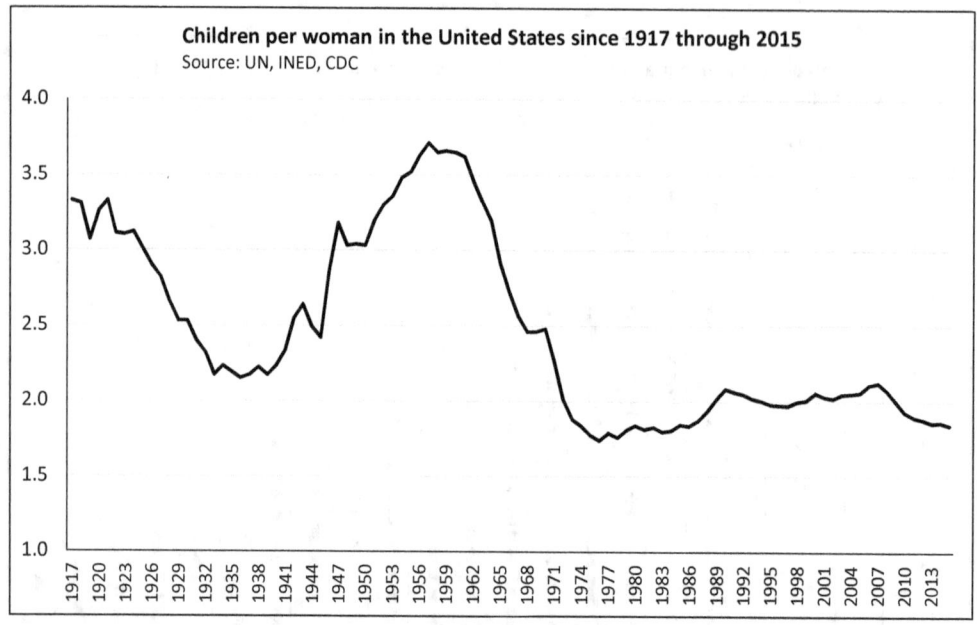

The following observations can be made from the graph:

✓ The fertility rate hit its lowest point and stabilized during the second half of the Great Depression, between 1933 and 1937/1939, for the first time after 130 years of almost continuous decline. The stabilized birth rate began after the general panic that incited the onset of the Great Depression at the end of 1929 was over, but took place during a time of economic weakness and when scarcity of material resources was the norm for a large portion of Americans. It is remarkable that a few tough years were the first to stop a falling birth rate trend that had been virtually uninterrupted for over 130 years, a century and a third during which fertility was always decreasing, despite the fact that all kinds of periods and social vicissitudes existed within that time: prosperity and poverty, optimism and pessimism, peace and war.

✓ The famous post-war American "baby boom" began around 1940, when the USA was still a non-fighting country[15]. Like France and the United Kingdom, the United States saw an increasing birth rate <u>during</u> World War II. There was a *baby boom*, as there had been in Europe, relative to the birth rates before World War II and the Great Depression (and, in the United States, almost relative to

---

[15] All babies born in the USA in 1940 and 1941, and most of those born in 1942, the first three years of the US baby boom of the XX century, had been conceived before the Japanese attack on Pearl Harbor.

the birth rates leading up to World War I), but with birth rates significantly lower than those of the nineteenth century and earlier.

✓ The post-war baby boom, which should be referred to as the "before, during and after the war" baby boom, reached its maximum of 3.71 children per woman in 1957. After the high of 1957, the birth rate fell for almost 20 continuous years, with a drop of 53% until 1976, when it reached a minimum of 1.74 children per woman.

✓ After the minimum rate of the '70s, there was a fertility rebound of 2 to 2.1 children per woman, followed by another fall every year since 2008, to an estimated 1.76 children per woman in 2017.

Delving into the elements that make up the aggregate birth rate of the United States by states and races [16], we observe significant differences in the fertility rate between states and ethnicities, as can be seen in the following tables. From the last CDC data available, we estimate that fertility in 2017 of non-Hispanic Whites was below 1.70 children per woman, and it was 1.80 or less for non-Hispanic Blacks.

Children per woman by race / ethinicity in the US - 2015	
Source: Births - Final report 2015 (CDC)	Children per woman
All races / ethnicities	**1.84**
Hispanic - Central and South America (2014)	2.81
Hispanic - All races	2.12
Hispanic - Mexicans (2014)	1.98
Whites	1.86
Non-Hispanic Blacks	1.86
Blacks	1.85
Non-Hispanic - All	1.77
Non-Hispanic Whites	1.75
Hispanic - Puerto Rican (2014)	1.68
Asians and Pacific islanders	1.64
Hispanic - Cubans (2014)	1.57
American Indians or Alaska natives	1.26

---

[16] NB for the very politically correct. On the official U.S. government documents used to collect birth and other demographic data in the United States, the words "race," "Whites," "Blacks," "Hispanics," etc. are used profusely and bluntly for purely descriptive purposes. Likewise, in the document from which we have extracted birth data in the United States from 1800 to 1990, there are no global figures for fertility, but for "Whites" and "Blacks" (which, in the document, includes actual "Blacks" as well as other non-white ethnic groups).

US states with fertility rate <u>above</u> national average Source: Births - Final report 2014 (CDC), own analysis			US states with fertility rate below national average Source: Births - Final report 2014 (CDC), own analysis		
State	Total Fertility rate (children per woman)	Difference in fertility with US average (%)	State	Total Fertility rate (children per woman)	Difference in fertility with US average (%)
Utah	2.33	25.0%	Washington	1.85	-0.8%
South Dakota	2.27	21.8%	Wisconsin	1.85	-0.9%
North Dakota	2.24	20.1%	California	1.84	-1.2%
Alaska	2.19	17.5%	Michigan	1.83	-1.6%
Nebraska	2.16	16.1%	North Carolina	1.83	-1.6%
Idaho	2.15	15.7%	Alabama	1.83	-2.0%
Texas	2.09	12.3%	Maryland	1.82	-2.4%
Kansas	2.05	10.2%	West Virginia	1.81	-2.6%
Oklahoma	2.03	8.8%	New Jersey	1.81	-2.8%
Iowa	2.02	8.4%	Virginia	1.81	-2.8%
Hawaii	2.00	7.3%	Illinois	1.81	-2.8%
Wyoming	1.99	6.9%	South Carolina	1.80	-3.3%
Arizona	1.97	5.8%	Delaware	1.79	-3.8%
Arkansas	1.97	5.8%	Colorado	1.77	-4.8%
Kentucky	1.96	5.1%	Florida	1.77	-5.0%
Louisiana	1.96	5.0%	Pennsylvania	1.76	-5.4%
Montana	1.95	4.9%	New York	1.73	-7.2%
Minnesota	1.94	4.3%	Oregon	1.72	-7.5%
Indiana	1.93	3.8%	Maine	1.66	-11.1%
New Mexico	1.91	2.4%	Connecticut	1.63	-12.2%
Mississippi	1.89	1.3%	Vermont	1.63	-12.3%
Ohio	1.88	1.0%	New Hampshire	1.58	-15.2%
Missouri	1.87	0.6%	Massachusetts	1.58	-15.4%
Nevada	1.87	0.4%	Rhode Island	1.56	-16.3%
Tennessee	1.87	0.2%	District of Columbia	1.52	-18.6%
Georgia	1.87	0.2%	Puerto Rico	1.43	-23.1%
US national average	1.86	0.0%	US national average	1.86	0.0%

These differences within the same country, whether it be in the U.S. or in any other nation, can offer interesting clues to those who seek the answers to two of the great questions this book tries to answer: why do we have so few children? and what can we do to increase the birth rate? In finding what differentiates, both culturally and in everyday life, the values between groups of people whose fertility rates are higher or lower than the average, we will surely find interesting elements to answer these two questions. For example, American states with the highest birth rates have, on average, a more religious population than those with lower fertility rates. The most fertile ethnic community, the Hispanic community, is composed mostly of immigrants who come from countries with a higher birth rate than that of the United States—which is not the case with immigrants from the Far East—, to the point that, even among them, the birth rate is higher or lower, depending on their country of origin. However, the fertility of Hispanics in the United States, and that of the inhabitants of Latin American countries, is also falling rapidly.

Likewise, there is an obvious slant in favor of the Republican Party in the states with the highest fertility rate, and the opposite in the states that typically prefer the Democratic Party presidential candidate. The following tables, based on 2014 fertility data by state provided by the CDC, show who are clearly favored in the more and less fertile states of the union. In the 2016 elections as well as those of 2012 and 2008, the fertility rate was significantly higher in the states that favored the Republican candidate in the presidential election than it was in the states that voted for the Democratic candidate[17].

Finally, a historical curiosity. In contrast with the abundance of current high-level European political leaders who have no children, this circumstance has only occurred with two of the 45 presidents that the US has had (in fact, 44, since Grover Cleveland had two non-consecutive terms and is usually counted twice on the list of American presidents): James Knox Polk, who was president from 1845 to 1849, and James Buchanan. This would total four presidents, if we also excluded the two presidents who only had non-biological children, one of whom was George Washington, whose wife was a widow from a previous marriage. The average number of children per wife of the first ten presidents in the history of the country was 5.1 and the average number of children per wife of the last ten presidents was 2.4. That is to say, this is more or less in line with what has happened to the overall fertility in their country.

---

[17] Using the number of children per woman in 2014 as reference (the 2015 figures, released after this chapter was originally written, yield very similar results), the simple birth rate average in the states won by Donald Trump in 2016 was 1.97 children per woman versus 1.75 in those won by Hillary Clinton (12% higher on average where the Republican candidate won). Using fertility data from 2012 and the presidential election results from that same year, the Republican candidate Mitt Romney won in 12 of the 15 most fertile states (all but one of which were also the most fertile in 2014), and only in 2 of the 15 least fertile. The average number of children per woman in the States won by Romney was 2.00, whereas in those won by Obama was 1.80. We have not compared prior election results and prior fertility data with the same thoroughness, but through simple visual inspection, those results seem to follow the same pattern.

The 15 US states with highest fertility in 2014, and the winning candidate / party in the last three presidential elections

Rank in fertility in the USA	State	Total Fertility Rate (children per woman)	Winner in 2016 presidential	Winner in 2012 presidential election	Winner in 2008 presidential election
1	Utah	2.33	Trump (R)	Romney (R)	McCain (R)
2	South Dakota	2.27	Trump (R)	Romney (R)	McCain (R)
3	Noth Dakota	2.24	Trump (R)	Romney (R)	McCain (R)
4	Alaska	2.19	Trump (R)	Romney (R)	McCain (R)
5	Nebraska	2.16	Trump (R)	Romney (R)	McCain (R)
6	Idaho	2.15	Trump (R)	Romney (R)	McCain (R)
7	Texas	2.09	Trump (R)	Romney (R)	McCain (R)
8	Kansas	2.05	Trump (R)	Romney (R)	McCain (R)
9	Oklahoma	2.03	Trump (R)	Romney (R)	McCain (R)
10	Iowa	2.02	Trump (R)	Obama (D)	Obama (D)
11	Hawaii	2.00	Clinton (D)	Obama (D)	Obama (D)
12	Wyoming	1.99	Trump (R)	Romney (R)	McCain (R)
13	Arizona	1.97	Trump (R)	Romney (R)	McCain (R)
14	Arkansas	1.97	Trump (R)	Romney (R)	McCain (R)
15	Kentucky	1.96	Trump (R)	Romney (R)	McCain (R)

Source: CDC ("Births: Final Data for 2014") for fertility, Wikipedia for election results

The 15 US states with lowest fertility in 2014, and the winning candidate / party in the last three presidential elections

Rank in fertility in the USA	State	Total Fertility Rate (children per woman)	Winner in 2016 presidential	Winner in 2012 presidential election	Winner in 2008 presidential election
37	Illinois	1.81	Clinton (D)	Obama (D)	Obama (D)
38	South Carolina	1.80	Trump (R)	Romney (R)	McCain (R)
39	Delaware	1.79	Clinton (D)	Obama (D)	Obama (D)
40	Colorado	1.77	Clinton (D)	Obama (D)	Obama (D)
41	Florida	1.77	Trump (R)	Obama (D)	Obama (D)
42	Pennsylvania	1.76	Trump (R)	Obama (D)	Obama (D)
43	New York	1.73	Clinton (D)	Obama (D)	Obama (D)
44	Oregon	1.72	Clinton (D)	Obama (D)	Obama (D)
45	Maine	1.66	Clinton (D)	Obama (D)	Obama (D)
46	Connecticut	1.63	Clinton (D)	Obama (D)	Obama (D)
47	Vermont	1.63	Clinton (D)	Obama (D)	Obama (D)
48	New Hampshire	1.58	Clinton (D)	Obama (D)	Obama (D)
49	Massachusetts	1.58	Clinton (D)	Obama (D)	Obama (D)
50	Rhode Island	1.56	Clinton (D)	Obama (D)	Obama (D)
51	Washington D.C	1.52	Clinton (D)	Obama (D)	Obama (D)

Source: CDC ("Births: Final Data for 2014") for fertility, Wikipedia for election results

Number of children of all US presidents

Source: Wikipedia, Wikitree, stillbirthday.com

NB. Not including extramarital offspring, stillborns or babies who died right after birth

	Name	# of children	Comments
1	George Washington	2	Biological children of his wife, a widow when she married GW
2	John Adams	5	In addition to those, one stillborn child
3	Thomas Jefferson	5	In addition to those, one stillborn child
4	James Madison	1	
5	James Monroe	3	
6	John Quincy Adamas	5	
7	Andrew Jackson	2	Adopted children. He also served as guardian of 8 children
8	Martin Van Buren	5	In addition to those, one stillborn child
9	Williiam Heny Harrison	10	
10	John Tyler	15	From two different wives (8 with the first, 7 with the second)
11	James Knox Polk	0	He served as guardian of one nephew
12	Zachary Taylor	6	
13	Millard Fillmore	2	
14	Franklin Pierce	2	He had another child who died two days after birth
15	James Buchanan	2	They were two nieces adopted by him. Only president who never married.
16	Abraham Lincoln	4	
17	Andrew Johnson	5	
18	Ulysses S. Grant	4	
19	Rutherford B. Hayes	8	
20	James A. Garfield	7	
21	Chester Allan Arthur	3	
22	Grover Cleveland	5	
23	Benjamin Harrison	2	He had another child who died shortly after birth
24	Grover Cleveland	5	
25	William McKinley	2	One of his two daughters died 21 days after birth
26	Theodore Roosevelt	6	
27	William Howard Taft	3	
28	Woodrow Wilson	3	
29	Warren G. Harding	1	It was an stepson from the first marriage of his wife
30	Calvin Coolidge	2	
31	Herbert Hoover	2	
32	Franklin D. Roosevelt	6	
33	Harry S. Truman	1	
34	Dwight D. Einsenhower	2	
35	John F. Kennedy	2	He also had one stillborn child, and one who died two days after birth. Would he have had more children if he had not been muredered so young?
36	Lindon B. Johnson	2	
37	Richard Nixon	2	
38	Gerald Ford	4	
39	Jimmy Carter	4	
40	Ronald Reagan	4	Three chidren from two different wives, plus an adopted son. He also had one daughter, Christine, who died nine hours after birth.
41	George H. W. Bush	6	
42	Bill Clinton	1	
43	George W. Bush	2	
44	Barack Obama	2	
45	Donald Trump	5	From three different wives

Average number of children per wive of the first ten presidents: 5.1

Average number of children per wive of the last ten presidents: 2.4

Rich countries, infertile countries

In all the world's most developed countries in the world minus one—almost all of them belonging to the OECD—the birth rate is less than 2.1 children per woman. The notable exception is Israel (with 3.11 children per woman in 2016 and 2017), a unique country, where a large part of the extra fertility is due to the more orthodox Jews (the "Haredim") as well as the Arab-Muslim population, ethnic groups much more fertile than the rest of the Israelis, especially the Haredim.

Japan: from being the country of the rising sun to the country of the dwindling Nippon people

Indeed, the collapse of the birth rate is by no means a uniquely European and North American phenomenon. Japan, the first Asian country to develop a modern economy, was one of the first nations in the world where the fertility rate fell steadily below the replacement level. In 1957, it entered this condition for the first time. And after years of ups and downs in fertility, since 1974, it has always had less than 2.1 children per woman. Its fertility reached a minimum of 1.26 children per woman in 2005. Since then, Japanese fertility has slightly rebounded, up to 1.44 children per woman in 2016. Between its persistently low fertility and its world record longevity, Japan is now the country with the oldest population on Earth, although Spain, with a birth rate even lower than that of the Japanese and a life expectancy almost as high, could take the crown for gray supremacy in the coming decades. Let's not forget other possible contenders in this social aging competition—a singular competition, because nobody wants to be the winner—such as Italy, Germany, Portugal, or Greece. In terms of poor demographic records, there are several, depending on the indicator and how we define the comparison period: on average, according to data from the OECD, Germany was the most infertile country in the world from 1974 to 2014, Italy from 1984 to 2014 (almost on par with Spain), and Spain from 1989 to 2014, after Hong Kong[18], which is not exactly a "country." In the middle of the second decade of the 21st century, the world's lowest fertility rate was found to be in some prosperous country in the Far East (Taiwan, Singapore, South Korea, Hong Kong, etc.), or in some Eastern European nations. If we consider the most aged and infertile regions and provinces of Europe and the world rather than whole countries, Spain has a few of them, although other European countries, such as Italy, Portugal, Greece, and Germany also "compete" significantly in these undesirable leagues.

---

[18] In this instance and in other references throughout this book to the "older," "most infertile" country or similar concepts, we have not taken into account some particular states or territories, small and sparsely populated, such as Liechtenstein, Monaco, Macao, etc., which are largely unrepresentative as a result of their small and singular populations.

Children per woman in the most developed countries by order of lowest to highest birth rate in 2014

Source: OECD, World Bank, Department of Statistics - Singapore, National Statistics - Republic of China, Wikipedia

Country	1960	1985	2014	Change 1960-2014
Taiwan	5.75	1.88	1.17	-80%
South Korea	6.00	1.66	1.21	-80%
Portugal	3.10	1.72	1.23	-60%
Singapore	5.75	1.61	1.25	-78%
Poland	2.98	2.33	1.29	-57%
Greece	2.23	1.68	1.30	-42%
Spain	2.86	1.64	1.32	-54%
Slovakia	3.07	2.25	1.35	-56%
Italy	2.41	1.45	1.37	-43%
Hungary	2.02	1.83	1.41	-30%
Japan	2.00	1.76	1.42	-29%
Austria	2.69	1.47	1.46	-46%
Croatia	2.20	1.79	1.46	-34%
Germany	2.37	1.37	1.47	-38%
Serbia	2.56	2.22	1.47	-43%
Luxembourg	2.28	1.38	1.50	-34%
Czech Republic	2.11	1.96	1.53	-28%
Switzerland	2.44	1.52	1.54	-37%
Estonia	2.12	1.98	1.54	-27%
Slovenia	2.18	1.72	1.58	-28%
Canada	3.90	1.61	1.60	-59%
Macedonia (FYR)	4.11	2.51	1.62	-61%
Lithuania	2.60	2.08	1.63	-37%
Latvia	1.94	2.09	1.65	-15%
Denmark	2.54	1.45	1.69	-33%
Finland	2.71	1.64	1.71	-37%
Netherlands	3.12	1.51	1.71	-45%
Belgium	2.54	1.51	1.72	-32%
Russia	2.56	2.05	1.75	-32%
Norway	2.91	1.68	1.76	-40%
Chile	5.11	2.66	1.79	-65%
Australia	3.45	1.92	1.80	-48%
United Kingdom	2.72	1.79	1.81	-33%
United States of America	3.65	1.84	1.86	-49%
Sweden	2.20	1.73	1.88	-15%
New Zealand	4.24	1.93	1.92	-55%
Iceland	4.27	1.93	1.93	-55%
Ireland	3.76	2.50	1.95	-48%
France	2.74	1.81	1.98	-28%
Israel	3.87	3.12	3.08	-20%

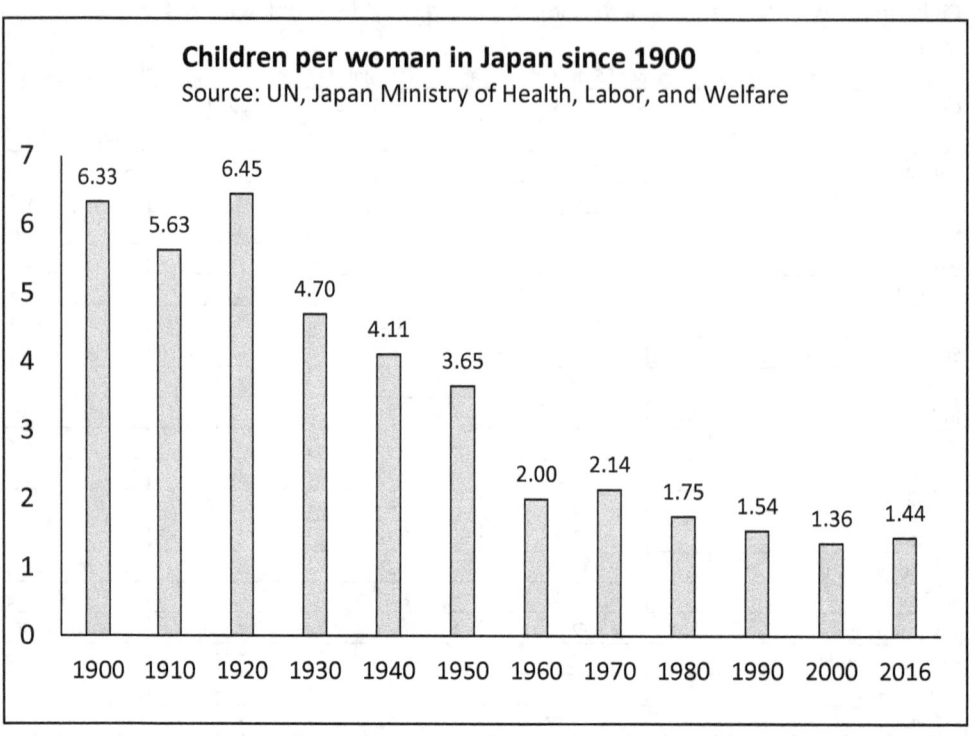

Children per woman in Japan since 1900
Source: UN, Japan Ministry of Health, Labor, and Welfare

The demographic winter that is coming, or has already arrived, to emerging countries

In large developing or already fully developed countries such as Mexico, Brazil, Iran, South Korea, and Taiwan, the birth rate has fallen similarly to Western countries and Japan, albeit in much less time. The following table, sorted by overall population, displays the fertility rates between 1950-1955 and 2010-2015 in the most populated emerging countries and those that have developed in the last decades. Overall, the fertility rate has fallen by more than 60% in 60 years and, in general, continues to fall in those countries.

Source: UN, National Statistics Republic of China - Taiwan	Children per woman in the most populated emerging, or recently developed, countries			
	1950-1955	1980-1985	2010-2015	Change 1950-2010
China	6.11	2.52	1.55	-75%
India	5.90	4.68	2.48	-58%
Indonesia	5.49	4.11	2.50	-54%
Brasil	6.15	3.80	1.82	-70%
Pakistan	6.60	6.44	3.72	-44%
Bangladesh	6.36	5.98	2.23	-65%
Russia	2.85	2.04	1.66	-42%
Mexico	6.75	4.37	2.29	-66%
Philippines	7.42	4.92	3.04	-59%
Vietnam	5.40	4.60	1.96	-64%
Egypt	6.62	5.49	3.38	-49%
Iran	6.91	6.53	1.75	-75%
Turkey	6.62	4.07	2.10	-68%
Thailand	6.14	2.95	1.53	-75%
South Africa	6.30	4.56	2.40	-62%
Myanmar	6.00	4.70	2.25	-63%
South Korea	5.05	2.23	1.26	-75%
Colombia	6.76	3.70	1.93	-71%
Argentina	3.15	3.15	2.35	-26%
Ukraine	2.81	2.00	1.49	-47%
Algeria	7.28	6.32	2.93	-60%
Poland	3.63	2.31	1.37	-62%
Irak	7.30	6.35	4.64	-36%
Morocco	6.61	5.40	2.56	-61%
Saudi Arabia	7.18	7.02	2.85	-60%
Uzbekistan	5.05	4.71	2.48	-51%
Peru	6.95	4.65	2.50	-64%
Malaysia	6.23	3.73	1.97	-68%
Venezuela	6.46	3.96	2.40	-63%
Nepal	5.96	5.62	2.32	-61%
Taiwan	7.40	2.23	1.10	-85%
Sri Lanka	5.80	3.19	2.11	-64%
Romania	3.06	2.26	1.48	-52%
Syria	7.23	6.77	3.03	-58%
Chile	5.15	2.66	1.78	-65%
Ecuador	6.75	4.45	2.59	-62%
Guatemala	7.00	6.10	3.30	-53%
Cuba	4.15	1.85	1.63	-61%
Simple average	5.91	4.27	2.28	-61%

The decline in mortality initially offset the effect of the fall in birth rates, but this is no longer the case in many countries

Not only has the birth rate in developed countries plummeted during the last century, as well as the rest of the world during the last few decades, which will be very costly if it falls below the levels required for the replacement of the population —as is already happening in half of the world, and within a few years, in three quarters or more of it—but mortality has also been drastically reduced, which is very positive, due to the increase in life expectancy/longevity. The decline in mortality rates has been particularly steep in the case of children, although it has benefited people of all ages. Not only has the typical number of years that humans live increased significantly, but also the years that we live healthily. We age more slowly. A 60-year-old was traditionally considered an old, or almost old, person. In developed countries, nowadays, and increasingly in the rest of the world, 60 is no longer considered as such. Even if we age more slowly, if a society is full of older generations and has an insufficient number of youth and other people to compensate—and almost all the developed world is going in that direction, and, in a few years or decades, much of the rest of the world as well—that society will seriously suffer, as we will see in the next section of this book when we discuss the consequences of a demographic winter / suicide. To live longer at the cost of having a difficult old age, due to a small active population, a lack of young people, society becoming impoverished, and a lack of relatives who give us affection when we are older, can be a poisoned gift.

In round numbers, life expectancy at birth has almost tripled in two centuries in developed countries, from less than 30 years to more than 80, and continues to increase. As mentioned earlier, life expectancy at birth in Western Europe, and soon in the rest of the world, has the same digits as that from the time of the Romans until the beginning or middle of the nineteenth century, but in reverse order. In Roman times, or in Spain 150 years ago, it was around 28 years. Now, it's 82 years. In almost all developing countries, it is now comfortably above 70 and on its way to the 80s. The poorer countries on Earth, most which are in sub-Saharan Africa, have life expectancies ranging from at least 50 to 60 years. It is estimated that at least half of the children born today in developed countries will live more than 100 years. The number of centenarians is growing everywhere at a dizzying pace. For example, in Spain, in only 14 years, from January 2002 to January 2016, according to data from the INE, the population 100 years old and older increased four-fold and the number of people living to 105 or older increased thirteen-fold.

Historically, life expectancy began to increase first in European countries that were modernized and developed in the 19th century, as well as in the United States, Canada, and Australia. Countries that developed later in Europe, such as those in the south, once they left underdevelopment, quickly approached the former in their longevity, as the following graph shows for the cases of Sweden and Spain, for example. If we included in it the so-called "emerging" nations (which, combined, used to be considered the "Third World"), we would see how life expectancy has converged in these nations within the last few decades even more rapidly than what had happened between Southern and Northern Europe.

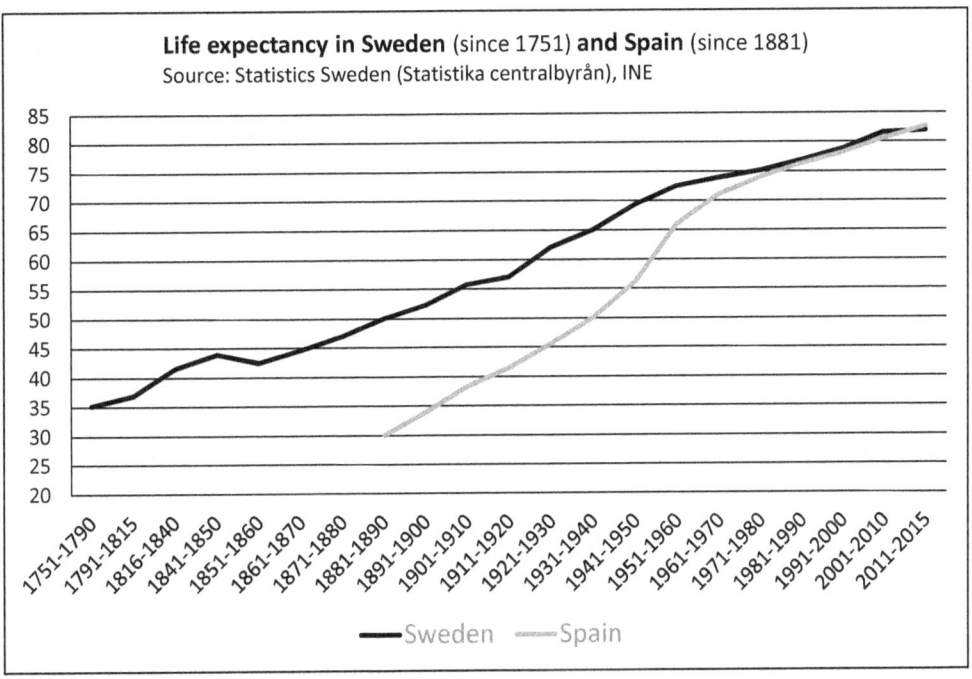

As a curious fact, although the United States is the country that, by far, has contributed the most to the development of humanity in virtually every field since the beginning of the 20th century, and its per capita income is among the highest in the world, life expectancy in the Yankee colossus is several years lower than in Western Europe or Japan. As an even more curious fact, in the US, among the three largest ethnic groups (or "races," in the words of the American authorities in all official documents, whites, blacks and Hispanics), the Hispanic, not white, population has by far the longest life expectancy, with black Americans/African-Americans having the shortest longevity. Both the shorter life expectancy of the United States compared with other wealthy countries in the world, as well as these interethnic differences, makes us pause to consider.

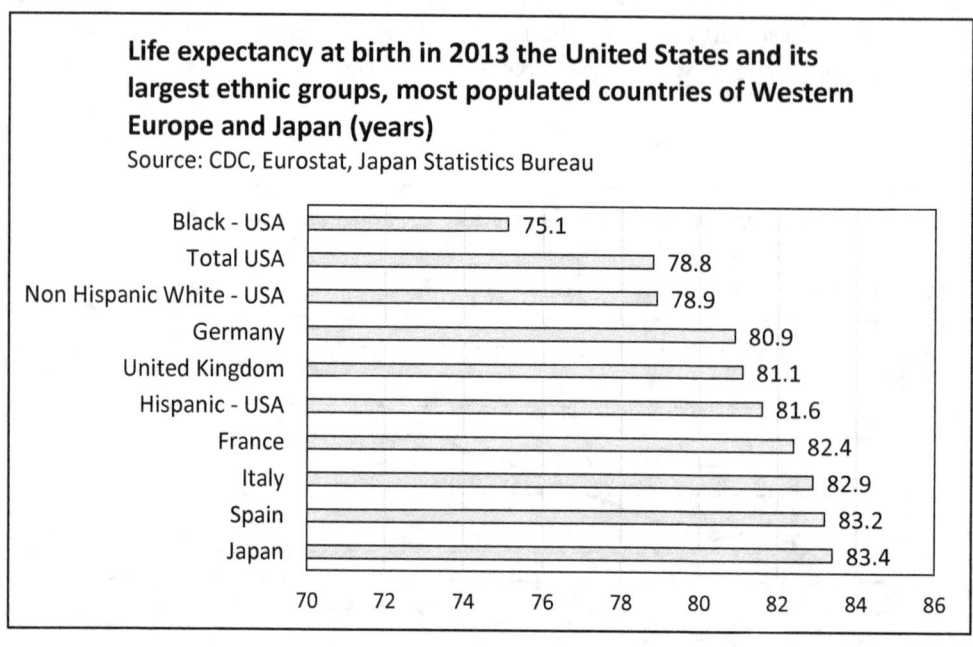

Life expectancy at birth in 2013 the United States and its largest ethnic groups, most populated countries of Western Europe and Japan (years)
Source: CDC, Eurostat, Japan Statistics Bureau

Group	Years
Black - USA	75.1
Total USA	78.8
Non Hispanic White - USA	78.9
Germany	80.9
United Kingdom	81.1
Hispanic - USA	81.6
France	82.4
Italy	82.9
Spain	83.2
Japan	83.4

Beyond the rich countries, the widespread growth of life expectancy around the world, particularly in the least developed nations, since the mid-twentieth century is cause for celebration. Without over-exaggerating, we believe this is one of the greatest achievements of mankind ever. Although this book contains bitter messages, warnings, and gloomy projections, while discussing these issues, it is pertinent to not forget to appreciate what the figures in the following chart mean, as they imply joy for billions of human beings who are not as likely to become seriously ill or die before they reach old age, for parents who will not prematurely lose their children and vice versa, for the siblings who will rarely see their siblings die young, for the friends who no longer suffer for the same reason as much as they used to. On a global scale, in round numbers and on average, humans who were born in the past decade will live at least 25 years longer than those born during the generation of their grandparents and will maintain better health for many more years. A real achievement, for which we owe gratitude to those who have played a leading role in the hygienic, technical, scientific, economic, and political advances that have made a higher quality of life possible.

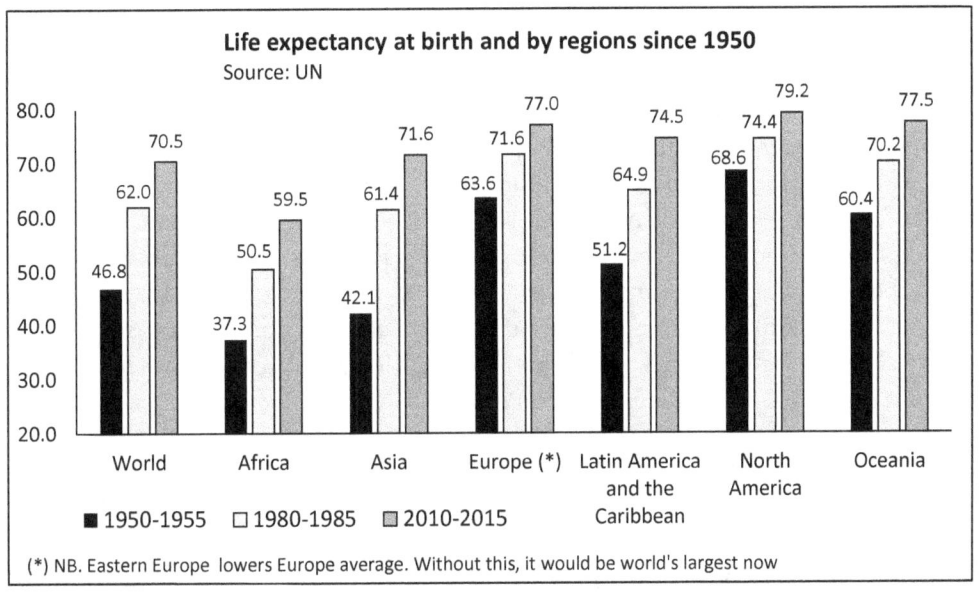

This wonderful extension of life expectancy in quantity of years, and in quality of life at all ages, and more strikingly at the most advanced age, has been possible thanks to great advances of civilization—vaccines, antibiotics, and other medicines; better health care means, techniques, and habits; greater abundance and variety of foods and nutrients; greater housing sanitation, including potable and chlorinated water, and sewerage; a drastic improvement in safety and hygiene conditions in the workplace; in recent decades, a major reduction in environmental pollution—which have reached increasing layers of the population, and, in many cases, almost all the members of a population. It goes without saying that in developing countries, which still only partially enjoy all these benefits, diarrhea and pneumonia in the first years of life continue to be the causes of a large number of deaths, and especially among the least developed of these countries[19].

The decline in childbirth and postpartum mortality in women, in homicides, wars, and work-related accidents—whose victims have generally been mostly male—as well as the recent reduction in fatal road accidents, have contributed to the increase in longevity, which continues to grow at a rate of two to three years per

---

[19] In line with what is still happening in very poor countries, as an example, in Spain, a century ago, in the five-year period 1911-1915, according to data from INE, 7% to 8% of children died before reaching the age of two due to diarrhea and gastroenteritis alone. Now, practically none.

decade in rich countries, at a faster rate in developing countries, and at a much higher rate in those that are "in the process of becoming" developing countries. Paradoxically, along with this increase in longevity and an improvement in global health, which goes hand in hand with economic development and an impressive decline in poverty—in actuality, not relatively—and illiteracy in the world, we are also witnessing the "pathologies of abundance": more and more people are obese, diabetic, and have dyslipidemia (excess cholesterol or triglycerides in the blood, among others); the growth in drug use shows no sign of stopping; nicotinic habits have become weapons of mass destruction; and the excess—in more than a few cases—of prescription drug consumption also takes its toll. These phenomena (more obesity, diabetes and related pathologies, drugs, tobacco), however, do not prevent the global growth in life expectancy.

In particular, the fall in infant mortality worldwide, and specifically in the less wealthy areas of the world, is especially beautiful and comforting. In the early 1950s, more than one in five human babies did not reach the age of five. Now, that statistic is less than one in twenty. In Africa, where three of every ten young people would die before reaching five years of life in the past, the number of individuals who do not reach five years old is now less than one in ten. While infant mortality rate there and in many countries and places in other continents is still too high, the improvement is spectacular, and the trend elicits hope. Overall, the mortality rate per 1,000 live births before the age of five has fallen by 77% worldwide between 1950-1955 and 2010-2015, according to UN estimates, and continues to fall. In Western Europe, Japan, and the world's most developed and healthiest countries, only 0.2% to 0.5% of children born today will die before reaching their fifth birthday, and as that percentage continues to decline, the whole of humanity is quickly approaching it as well. By stark contrast, in 1950-1955, over 21% of the children worldwide left us before blowing the candles on the cake of their fifth birthday. What a delightful change!

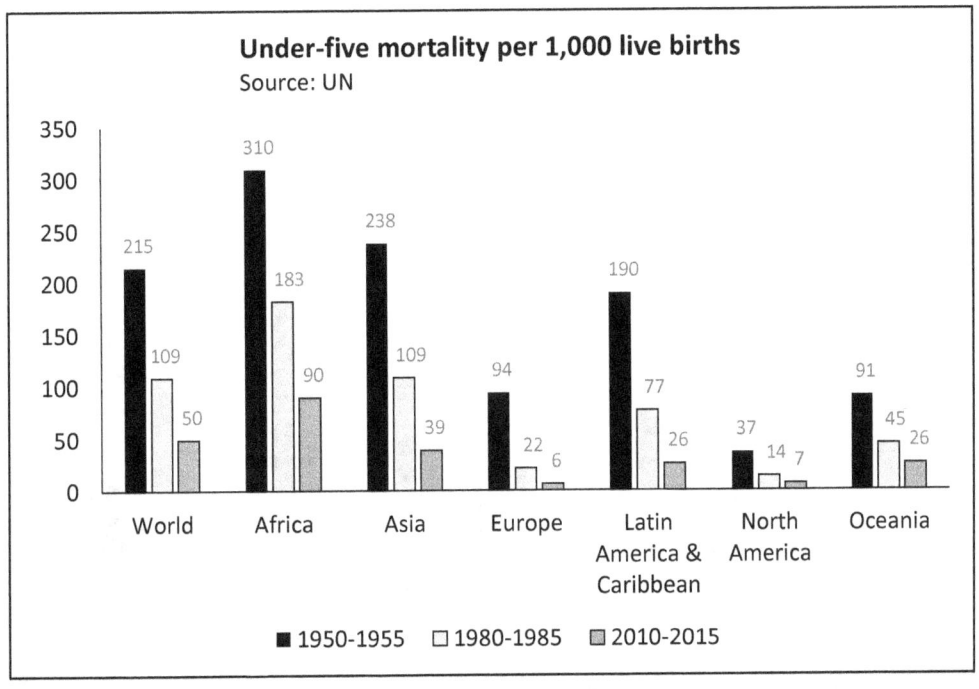

As mortality rates, historically and in general, began to fall before birth rates, and the difference between the two ratios began widening in the eighteenth century, during the Enlightenment period, and even further in the nineteenth century, a considerable population increase resulted. It is estimated that humanity was multiplied by just over 1.5 in the eighteenth century, and by almost 1.7 in the nineteenth century[20]. This trend accelerated exponentially in the twentieth century, so much so that the world population in the year 2000 was about 3.7 times that of 1900. Although the growth of the size of humanity in the sixteenth and seventeenth centuries (when it was multiplied by 1.12 and 1.14, respectively) pales in comparison to the past three centuries, in the first two full centuries of the Modern Age, the world population also increased at a rate significantly higher than the average of all previous centuries since the Neolithic era[21].

---

[20] There is no unanimity among the sources consulted about the world population prior to the twentieth century (and even in the twentieth century, there are reasonable doubts, especially about those time periods farther away from the present time), so that these numbers are only estimates, given the difficulties in retrospectively estimating the worldwide population. We assume, however, that the trend is correct: world population growth took a big jump in the eighteenth century, an even greater jump in the nineteenth century, and soared in the twentieth century, reaching rates that might never be equaled again in the future.

[21] According to population estimates for around 5000 BC, in the midst of the Neolithic period (about 5 million humans in total), the average population growth per century since then, up to the year 1500, should have been close to 7%.

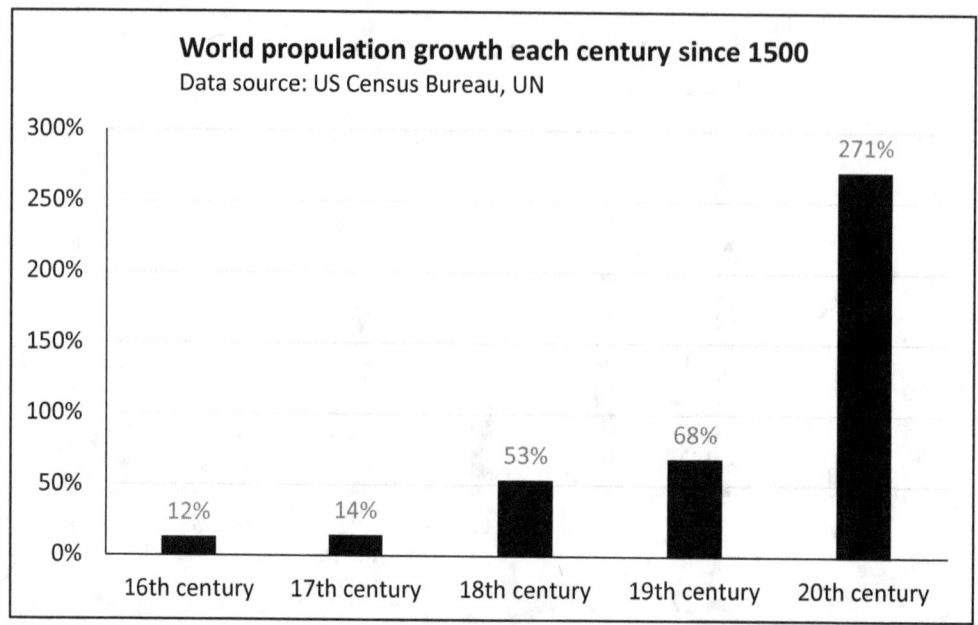

World propulation growth each century since 1500
Data source: US Census Bureau, UN

Data Source: US Census Bureau, UN	1500	1600	1700	1800	1900	2000
World population estimates (millions)	500	562	640	980	1,650	6,127

NB: 1500, 1900 and 2000 world population quoted are UN estimates in its most recent revisions
1600 and 1700 figures are the average of the low and high estimates in several sources quoted by the
US Census Bureau in https://www.census.gov/population/international/data/worldpop/table_history.php

Given these figures, we must be aware that if humanity continues to grow indefinitely, as it did in the twentieth century, by the year 2400, in less than four centuries, there will be one trillion (1,000,000,000,000) human beings, something that, besides being unimaginable, would most likely be unsustainable in strictly physical terms, due to the proportion of all terrestrial biomass that humanity would represent. Humans currently represent about one part per 5,000 of all the existing biomass (from which we eat and with which we live). If there were a trillion souls on Earth, we featherless bipeds would be a part per 35 or so. Before the end of the twenty-seventh century, if humanity continued to increase in the current millennium as it is increasing in the twentieth century, human earthlings would take up ALL terrestrial biomass (!!!). So, at some point, humanity will need to stop growing in quantity. What is questionable is whether that should be now. What is even more questionable is whether we should switch from the traditionally uninterrupted population growth to an accelerated decline, accompanied by a strong social aging, in only a few decades. And it is simply unacceptable, at least for the author of this book, that the inhabitants of the nations on the path to demographic suicide should have to resign ourselves to it, simply to compensate for the population growth—until recently "runaway," and in some places, seemingly still—of other nations.

Sweden, one of the most developed and civilized countries in the world, offers particularly interesting data on how large population growth occurred as mortality fell. Sweden is one of the earliest places on the globe to leave underdevelopment and poverty behind, and its birth and death statistics date back to the mid-eighteenth century. The following two graphs show how birth rates have been falling in Sweden for about 150 years while mortality has been declining for over 200 years, perhaps even 250[22]. The excess of births over deaths Sweden generated until the birth rate reached very low levels, resulting in many more Swedes on the face of the Earth, was one of the reasons many Swedes emigrated to the US in the final decades of the 19th century and the early decades of the 20th century.

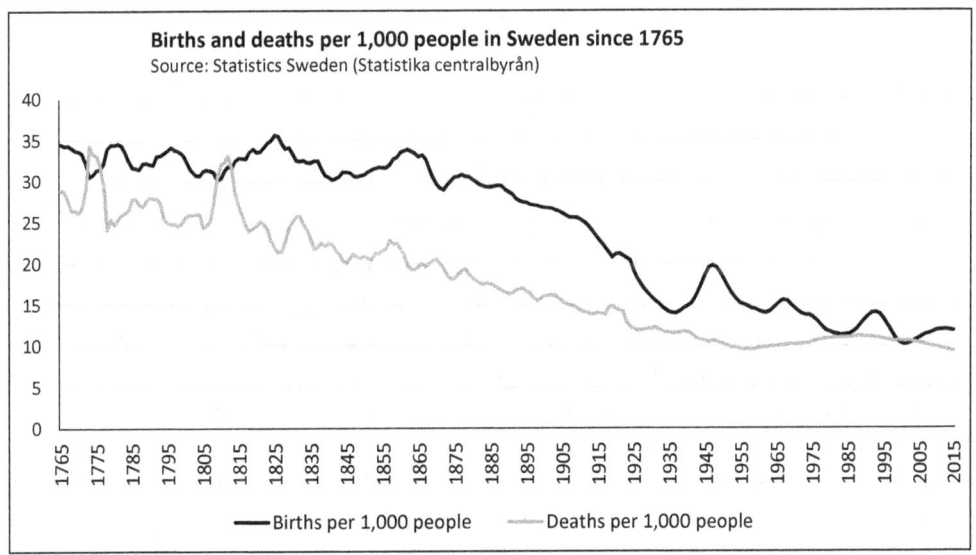

_____

[22] The graph has been drawn to represent each year using the average numbers for that year combined with the previous four, in order to soften the ups and downs that occurred each year, especially those steepened with respect to mortality (for example, in a year with wars, epidemics, or bad harvests). This allows for greater insight into the underlying trends.

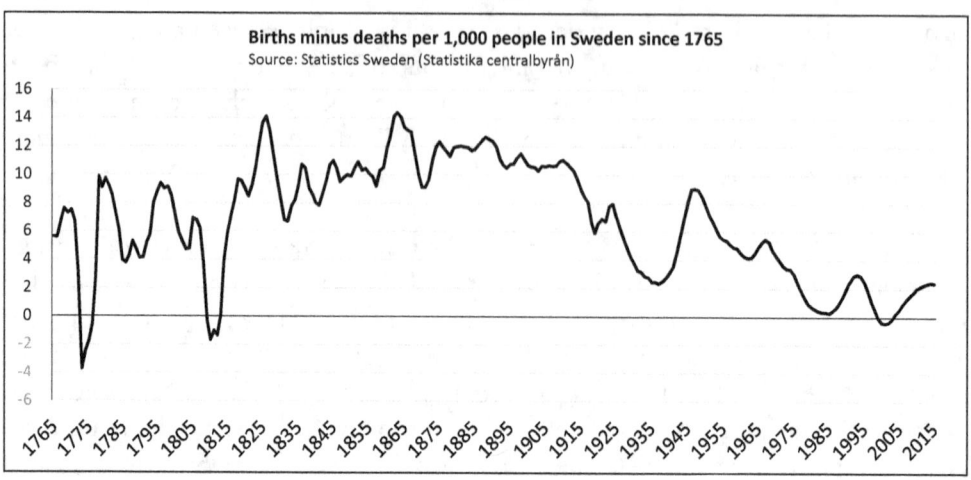

Births minus deaths per 1,000 people in Sweden since 1765
Source: Statistics Sweden (Statistika centralbyrån)

Thus, we have moved from a pre-modern world, in which, since the dawn of time, many children were born but few lived long lives, to another time in which the birth and death rates are, simultaneously, much lower than what history is accustomed to. This process, going from a pattern of high fertility and high mortality to another in which both are low, is known as the "demographic transition." In this transition, globally, there has been a large population growth in the last two centuries, especially in the last one, because, in general, death rates initially fell earlier/more than birth rates. At present, the world population continues to grow, but at rates that tend to be increasingly milder and are mostly due to a fall in mortality rates, because the number of babies born each year is barely growing, if at all, and in a few years will begin to decrease, if it isn't already. Approximately half of humanity currently lives in societies with a fertility rate below the replacement rate (almost all of Europe and Russia, Northern America, Brazil, and some Latin American countries, Australia, China and the Far East, Iran, etc.). Given the trends, this will probably impact 75% or more of humanity in a decade or two at most. India is about to join this category of countries—among other reasons, because the replacement threshold is 0.1 to 0.2 higher than 2.1 children per woman, due to the higher infant and juvenile mortality that persists, as well as the infanticide/selective abortion of female babies still practiced with tragic frequency, the latter occurring even more commonly in China[23]—if not already there in 2017.

---

[23] According to information from the 2010 Chinese Census, population data from the UN, and the typical proportion of female to male infants (between 105 and 107 boys per 100 girls at birth), in China, approximately one in every ten little girls will go missing. In the 2010 census there were 100 female infants for every 118 males in China. This scarcity of girls may be due to four reasons: selective abortion of females (which would also imply that these were late abortions if the sex was known through an ultrasound, since the sex of the fetus generally cannot be determined with this technique until the fourth or fifth month of pregnancy), the murder of babies for the mere fact of having been born female, girls whose existence has been

India, alone, represents almost 1/5 of the world population. The same is true for Mexico, where fertility is at the edge of the replacement threshold, as well as other Asian and South American countries with sizeable populations, or South Africa.

Therefore, the growth of human population in the coming decades will consist of, above all, middle-aged, older, and elderly people. If the birth rate continues to decline—and there are no strong signs that this will not be the case, except for small rebounds registered in some European countries and elsewhere, mainly in places where the fertility rate has been low for decades, and in others where the decline in the birth rate was especially steep in the last quarter of a century—by the middle of this century, the world population could reach a maximum, and from there, begin to decline.

In any of the predictable scenarios, whether that be a fertility rate even lower than the current one, or remaining the same as now, all societies tend to be older, or much older, something only preventable with a birth rate much higher than the current one, which seems unlikely, except in areas of the world where it is already so low that, if their governments and their societies take the issue seriously, those societies could experience rebounds. Another factor is that, if longevity increases in the coming decades as some visionaries predict[24], population reductions could become softer or may not even happen at all. However, the children and youth population, at the very least, with birth rates below the replacement level, will inevitably experience widespread declines, as is already the case in many countries, and will continue to affect many more.

---

hidden from the authorities (something that would have been caused by the one-child policy that, in 2015, China announced it would no longer be following), and girls given in adoption to foreigners (this fourth cause would only explain a very small part of this tragedy, according to the available data on trans-border adoptions). Most likely, it is a mix of all four factors. In total, through these means, the first two being true feminicides, and the third one being only a virtual feminicide, in China, between early 2010 and late 2014, between 4 and 5 million girls conceived or born in those years would have been eliminated, either physically, or for the purpose of officially counting them. This would between 9% and 10% of the total. If the main factor were the concealment of females for the purposes of the census, this will probably be a population that will surface in future censuses. Unfortunately, the most plausible factors are the first two causes: the elimination of fetuses or babies in mass only because of their female condition. There are similar occurrences in India, but with a little less than half the frequency (according to our estimates, in the pyramid of the Indian population in 2015 there were around 2.5 million little girls missing, or 4% of the total). In the case of India, there is no such one-child policy.

[24] There are those who even announce that we will see soon "the death of death," if the biological process of aging can be halted. If they indeed prove to be right, they will deserve the positive epithet of "visionaries." If not, they will deserve to be depicted, in hindsight, as "charlatans".

Countries and regions of the globe either in serious demographic decline or only a few years away

The demographic decline, characterized by the downward trend in the native population counts—and, without enough immigration, in total population—and an intense social aging, has already begun in the countries that have spent the most amount of years on the path to demographic suicide due to their low birth rates, such as much of Europe, North America, and Japan. Among these countries, those that have attracted a significant mass of foreign immigrants have been able to soften or counteract the decline in their global national figures, with the pros and cons the influx of immigrants has brought to their economy and social cohesion. This excludes Japan, a country that predominately believes that certain risks linked to immigration, such as increased public insecurity, does not compensate for the potential benefits.

Eastern Europe, the worst demographic health on the planet

Regarding population loss, the region on the planet with the worst birth-to-death ratio is Eastern Europe. For many years, in most Eastern European countries, more people die than are born, as the birth rate in these countries is low or very low, and life expectancy is several years shorter than it is in Western Europe. To make matters worse in terms of their demographic health, Eastern Europeans can migrate relatively easily to Western Europe—countries that have a per capita income 2 to 4 times higher in current money—where they integrate very well and gain access to better jobs, or to Russia, in the case of the former Soviet Republics. As a result, several countries in Eastern Europe have suffered considerable losses of population, some of them experiencing serious bleedings, as can be seen in the following data:

✓ In Russia, between 1991 and 2011, a total of about 13 million more people died than were born. The Eurasian giant compensated about half of this loss with the influx of immigrants from former Soviet republics, mainly ethnic Russians, who in more than a few cases had become second-class citizens in the smaller countries (compared to Russia), which emerged after the dismemberment of the Soviet Union. Since 2011-2013, because of measures taken by the Russian government to stimulate the birth rate and the immigration of ethnic Russians, the Russian population hemorrhage seems to have been halted, although it is still too early to know whether this is a sustained trend.

✓ In Ukraine, in that same period from 1991 to 2011, things were proportionally even worse. There were 5.7 million more deaths than births, a loss of 11% of the population, to which should be added during those 20 years a net emigration of more than 700,000 people.

✓ Bulgaria, Hungary, Estonia, Latvia, Lithuania, Romania, Serbia, Croatia, and Moldavia, among others, have also experienced far more deaths than births in recent years, with population losses between 4% and 10% during 1995-2014, due to the imbalance between deaths and births. Their birth deficit has been accompanied by declines in population due to emigration, which in some of these countries has reached almost exodus proportions. For instance, approximately 10% of the population of Romania emigrated to Italy (6%) or Spain (4%) between 1999 and 2011. Since those who leave are also younger, on average, than those who remain, this emigration causes an additional aging of the country[25].

✓ The Czech Republic, Slovakia, Poland, and some countries of the former Yugoslavia, such as Slovenia or Macedonia, show not so negative, or slightly positive, balances between births and deaths, although in cases such as Poland, which has experienced a considerable emigration to the West, the net result is a population loss.

The good news in this small disaster is that several Eastern European countries have finally been reacting decisively to their serious demographic issues for years. Their governments are strongly encouraging more births, taking measures of various kinds, such as providing economic incentives and pro-family and pro-birth advertising campaigns, among other initiatives. Among these now "pro-birth" eastern European countries, apart from Russia, as far as this author knows, Hungary stands out—the second OECD country that dedicated the most of its GDP in 2011 to fertility, after Denmark, and may be the first in 2016—as well as Poland and Macedonia.

Western Europe, very low birth rate, very high aging

In Western Europe, the demographic health of Germany, Italy, Portugal, Greece, and Spain is extremely precarious and is expected to worsen. In addition to all these countries being very old, for years, there have been more deaths than births in the first four, a phenomenon that occurred in Spain in 2015 and 2016, and

---

[25] A similar phenomenon is occurring many thousands of kilometers away, in Puerto Rico, where the ease of emigrating to the US, and the low birth rate, are causing a serious demographic hemorrhage in the Puerto Rican population.

is expected to occur again in coming years, and that had already been happening with the Spanish Native population for years. That is one of the reasons— combined with the desire to wash once and for all / continue to wash, the cliché of Germany as a "hard/inhuman" country, an image it inherited from the mega-murderous psychopath Hitler— that led Chancellor Angela Merkel, in 2015, to open the doors of her country to over one million refugees from Syria and from other areas of conflict, a decision which disrupted the German society, mainly for fear of Jihadist terrorism and public insecurity (fed by the Islamist attacks suffered in Europe since the horrendous attack on Charlie Hebdo, or episodes such as the massive sexual assault on New Year's Eve 2015 in Cologne). In Germany, the working-age population declines from year to year, so this country will either need to "import" labor from the outside or gradually languish. Since 1972, more people have been dying in Germany than are born. Between 1995 and 2015, both included, Germany recorded 2.85 million more deaths than births, a negative balance which in Italy was of nearly 800,000 people.

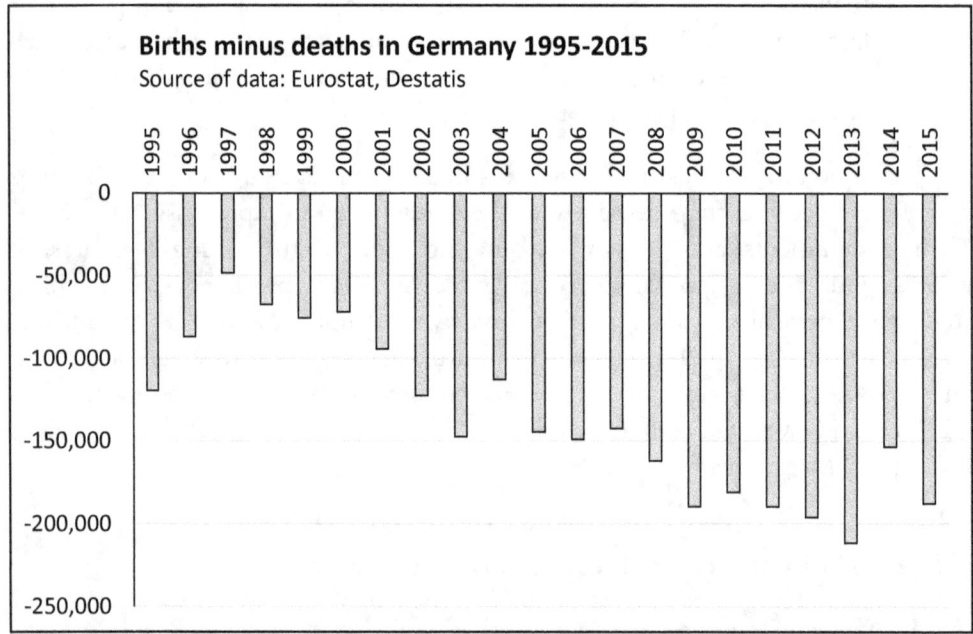

To its credit, to combat the effects of the demographic winter—as long as such winter is not too intense—Germany can count on its economic-industrial strength, in addition to its traditional seriousness and rigor, which has allowed the Germans, so far, to better weather their first decades of an intense demographic winter. This economic robustness and geographic location facilitate the arrival of immigration from Eastern and Southern Europe. The German outlook for medium and long-term economic growth is weak, however, precisely due to its demographic decline. Likewise, the German authorities have acknowledged that the lack of births is one of its most fundamental problems and have been offering substantial birth incentives/economic compensation for years. These incentives have so far achieved a success ranging from insignificant to moderate—there seems to have been some rebound in birth rates since 2012, although it is still too early to assess whether this is sustainable or not— among other things because, as we will see later in this book, money is important when it comes to having children, but the available data unequivocally show that money is nowhere near being the most important factor. Anyway, these incentives could be a good start for Germany to both display its aforementioned seriousness and address the root of the matter, of people not wanting to have enough children, and for Germany to not limit itself to only economic aid to fertility, as is usual in Europe. Hopefully.

Italy is almost as aged as Germany, and although it has spent fewer years with a negative balance between births and deaths, the magnitude of the red numbers in its income statement on life and death is growing exponentially, and already shows a percentage similar to that of Germany's with respect to population. Italy is the European country—and perhaps in the world, although we have not been able to verify this with data—in which, in 2014, women were, on average, the oldest when having their first child (30.7 years), followed very closely by Spain (0.1 years less). Since immigrant mothers are younger, on average, than both native Italian women and in most of Europe, the average age of primipara natives—women giving birth for the first time—is already over 31 years old in both countries. Unfortunately for both Italy and for the bulk of other countries seriously affected by a demographic winter, Italy is not an economic and technological powerhouse like Germany[26], except for its prosperous and industrious northern third. Portugal and Greece merit the same comments as Italy—for years there have been more deaths than births, although for fewer years than in Germany—but they have even less economic capacity to use against their demographic crumbling, and especially after the devastating Great Recession that started in 2007-2008.

---

[26] Japan has a technological and industrial strength comparable to that of Germany, but it is financially much weaker, as it was not able to recover from its huge financial real estate bubble, which broke out in the early 1990's. Japan continually postponed the cleansing of its deteriorated banking system to avoid the mass bankruptcies and the immediate impoverishment that this would have caused to its citizens. Because the Japanese State has been the least austere in the developed world ever since, with continued enormous public deficits, to which a growing cost of pensions and healthcare for the Japanese retirees—the most numerous in the world with respect to the population of the country—has been progressively contributing more and more. As a result, by the end of 2015, Japan had by far the largest ratio of public debt in relation to its GDP: 238%.

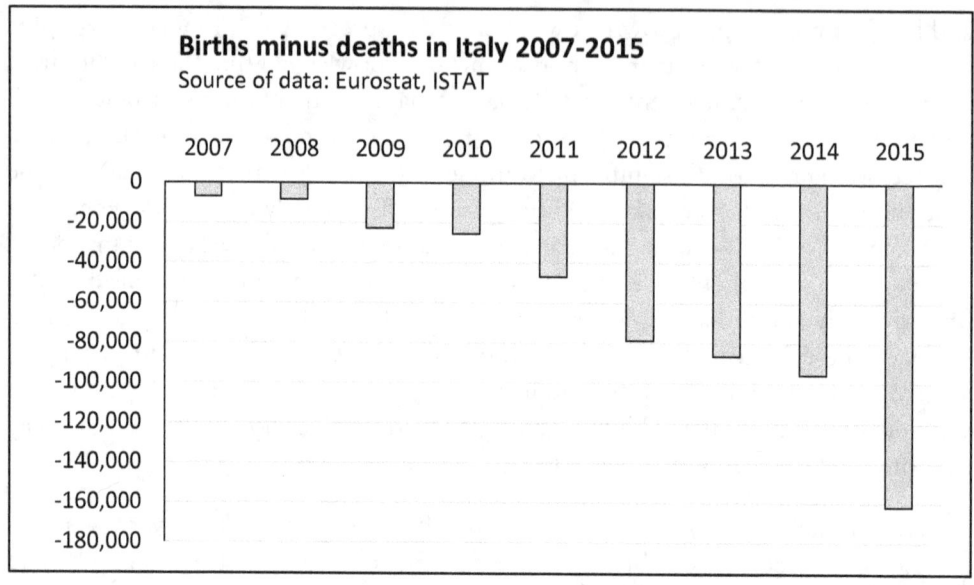

Births minus deaths in Italy 2007-2015
Source of data: Eurostat, ISTAT

Spain, despite its very poor demographic prospects due to the very low birth rate it has had for decades—whose aging effect on society is aggravated by the happy fact that Spanish life expectancy is especially high, as is the case of Italy— is not yet the least demographically healthy country in Western Europe. This is due to the flood of immigration it experienced from around the mid-1990s to 2008-2009 and because the drop in the birth rate below the replacement level began somewhat later than in the other European nations, due to the unique political regime it had until 1975-1976, which was morally conservative and openly promoted high birth rates. By contrast, Spain's birth rate has been declining particularly rapidly since 1977 and since Spain's life expectancy is the highest in Europe, the country is aging at a torrid pace and some of its regions and provinces are the most infertile and oldest of Europe[27]. Although Spain globally began to have more deaths than births

---

[27] The three most infertile European regions in the five-year period 2010-2014 (out of a total of 276 regions among all European countries, according to the official division from Eurostat) were, in this order, Asturias (the birthplace of the author of this book), the Canary Islands, and Galicia, all three in Spain. There were two more among the top ten with the lowest birth rates: Castile and Leon and Cantabria. The fourth least fertile region in Europe was the Portuguese Madeira —second in 2015 in the European "regional infertility contest"—and the fifth was the Italian Sardinia. Among the six European regions with the highest percentage of population aged 80 or older at the beginning of 2014, headed by Liguria in Italia, were Asturias (second), Castile and Leon (fourth) and Galicia (sixth). The third was Limousin in France, and the fifth, Umbria in Italy. The seventh and eighth were also Italian: Molise and Marche. The ninth, the

in 2015, this had been going on for years among the native Spaniards. Spain also does not have the economic and technological strength of Germany to soften the rigors of the demographic winter in its first decades—in the long run, no one has the strength, if the population decline and the runaway aging of that population persist, not even Germany—but it enjoys very favorable conditions in terms of climate, geography, culture, and lifestyle, as well as having magnificent infrastructures and health services[28], to attract a foreign population that can integrate reasonably well or very well: retired Europeans who come to live in Spain as a "European Florida" and spend their pensions there; many Western Europeans of working age would be happy to go and work in Spain if they had the opportunity; Eastern Europeans who integrate very well culturally (for example, Romanians); Latin Americans who speak the same language and who have a similar culture, etc. Anyway, whatever its specific strengths to cope with the first eaves of harmful effects of its intense demographic winter, Spain, as any other very infertile country, should ideally recover a healthy birth rate as soon as possible, or else.........

Greek Peloponnese, and the tenth, Tuscany, whose wonderful Florence was the cradle of the Renaissance. The three provinces or equivalent (smaller than "region") of any European country with the highest percentage of population aged 65 or over, and at least 100,000 inhabitants, were the Spanish Orense, Zamora and Lugo, in that order.

[28] Between 2012 and 2015 —the last years available when writing this book on Eurostat— Spain had the longest life expectancy in Europe, and this has to do with, among other things, the quality of its health services and various aspects of its lifestyle and food. It is one of the most visited countries in the world (for its climate, scenic beauty, historical-cultural heritage, gastronomy, tourist infrastructure, amusements), and is probably the most desired place to live in Europe. There is a reason Spain receives more foreign exchange (Erasmus) students than any other European country, and is the country where most British reside outside the UK. Its homicide rate in recent years per 100,000 inhabitants is among the lowest in Europe. It also has especially low rates of other horrendous crimes such as rapes and suicides.

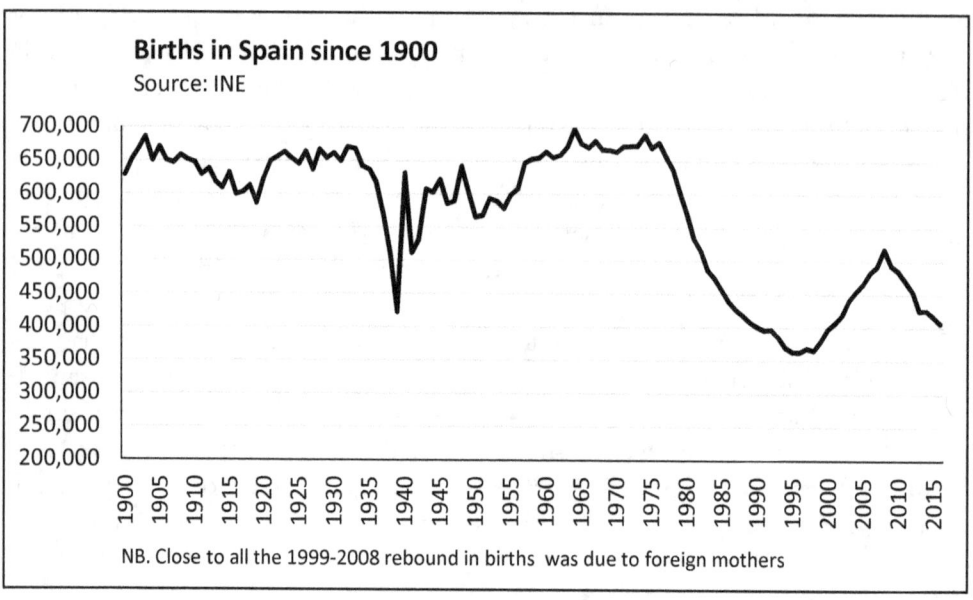

Births in Spain since 1900
Source: INE

NB. Close to all the 1999-2008 rebound in births was due to foreign mothers

Switzerland and Austria are two very aged countries with low birth rates. They counterbalance in their nominal demographic numbers with immigrants and their children, their already pronounced native demographic decline. Furthermore, as in the German case, their economic strength, especially for the Swiss, allows them to work around the first damages created by the demographic winter. Switzerland is an extreme case in the contribution of immigrants to the birth rate, as no fewer than three out of eight babies born there have a foreign mother—whose average fertility is far higher than Swiss women's—not even counting the children of immigrant women with dual nationality.

As shown in the following graphs, Swiss fertility began to fall, at least 140 years ago, if not earlier. The fall of the Swiss birth rate goes back a long time. Between 1922 and 1941, both years included, births were below the replacement threshold, which at that time was higher than 2.1 children per woman, since the mortality at that time was much higher than the current one, at any age, and especially during the infant years. And in Switzerland, as in the United States, the United Kingdom, or Canada, the so-called "post-war baby boom," comparatively mild in Switzerland, actually began before World War II, after the birth rate hit rock bottom in 1937, after 60 years of virtually uninterrupted decline, and began rebounding in 1938. All of this makes you think, especially since Switzerland has been one of the most prosperous and admired countries in the world for over a century, and is internationally considered a model for civic responsibility, where everything is in order. But not everything is in order with regards to fertility, as the current rate does not ensure sustainability in the future of the Swiss population!

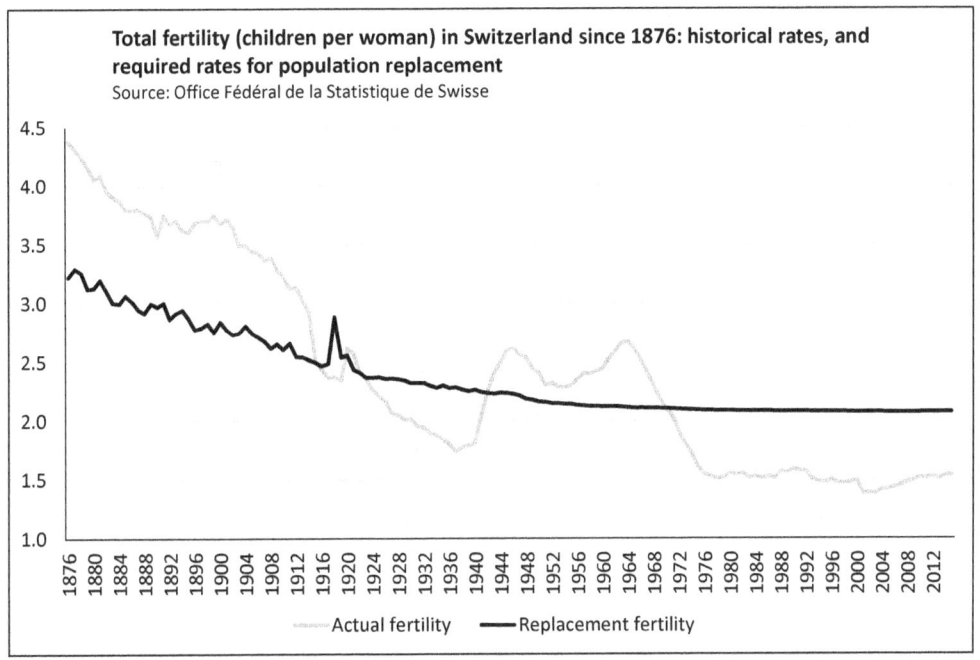

Total fertility (children per woman) in Switzerland since 1876: historical rates, and required rates for population replacement
Source: Office Fédéral de la Statistique de Swisse

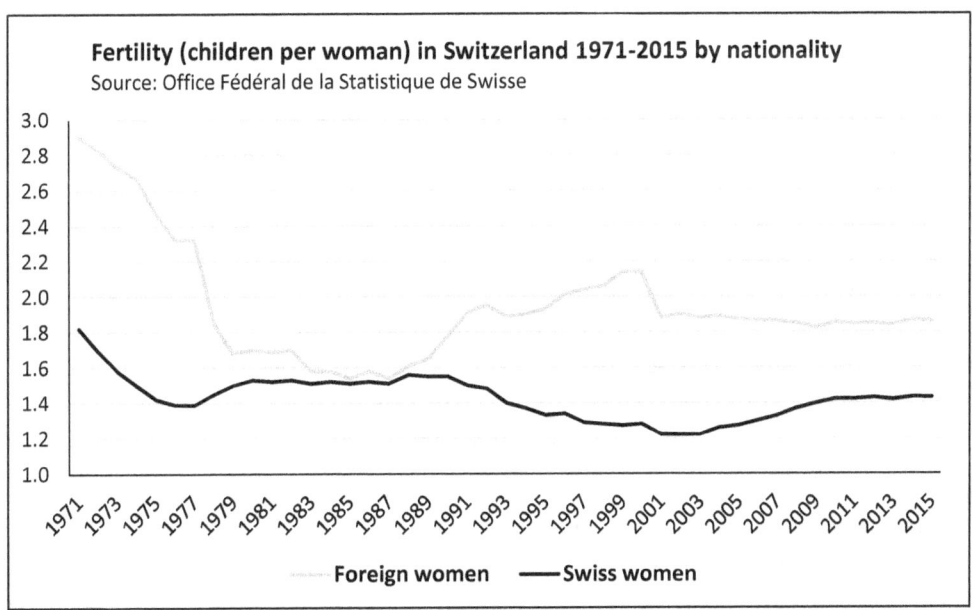

Fertility (children per woman) in Switzerland 1971-2015 by nationality
Source: Office Fédéral de la Statistique de Swisse

The Far East, beating the infertility records

In the East, Japan, where, for years, more diapers have been sold for the incontinence of the elderly than for babies, is the local (and worldwide) reference on aging and low birth rates. While the Japanese fertility is no longer the lowest in the area, it has been the longest-running fertility rate at low levels. Between that, and the fact that the Japanese are the longest-living humans, Japan is the oldest country in the world, closely followed by Germany and Italy, which curiously were its allies during World War II. In the Land of the Rising Sun, there are fewer and fewer rising Nippons, and the number of births has been lower than the number of deaths since 2007, with a divergence that grows each year, as can be seen in the following graph. Japan's birth deficit will last indefinitely, unless birth rates rise sharply, because births tend to decline, with fewer women of childbearing age every year, while deaths tend to increase as more and more people become older. Since it is a country that is very closed to foreign immigration, immigration does not seem to be a feasible way to achieve a rejuvenation of the population or additional births.

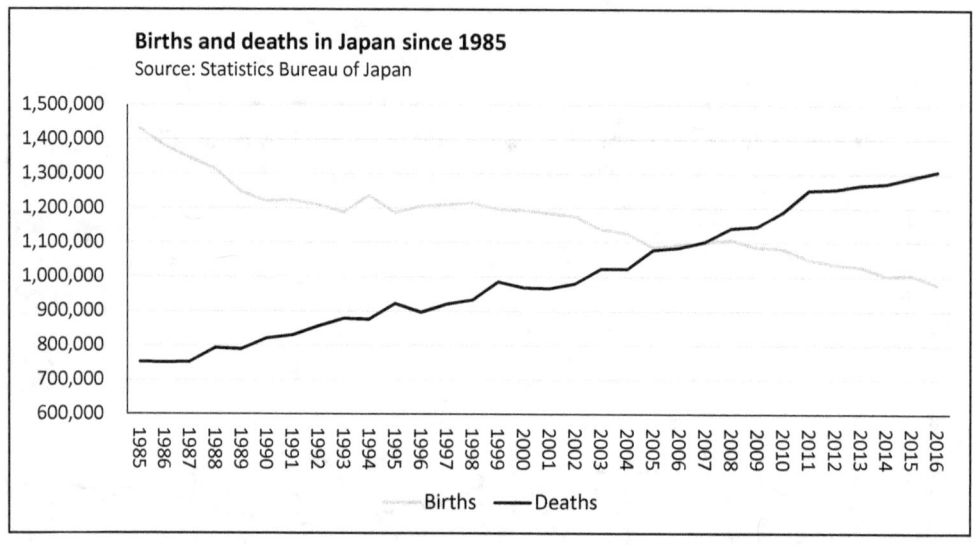

Finally, in this review of the primary countries that already present very poor demographic prospects, in the Far East there are nations like the Chinese giant, South Korea, Taiwan, Singapore, or Thailand, with low or very low birth rates. As the drop of the birth rate below the replacement level occurred in those countries more recently than in Japan or Europe, and it dropped from very high fertility rates, by inertia, they still have relatively young populations and many women of childbearing age, factors which have so far prevented their death rates from overtaking their birth rates, which will occur, if they continue at the same pace, within a few years. The same evolution—a decline in fertility rates in a few decades to levels below the replacement rate—has occurred in a country as special and relevant as Iran, although at 1.7 to 1.8 children per woman, its current level of fertility does not reach the extreme lows of 1.0 to 1.3 of the Asian "Tigers" of the Far East. In the latter countries, the fall in birth rates has been so abrupt, and life expectancy has grown so rapidly, in parallel with its accelerated socio-economic progress, that aging is occurring at very fast rates, even if it has not yet reached the worst levels of Europe or Japan by way of inertia of their traditional demographic profile, since up until not so long ago, they enjoyed a very high fertility rate.

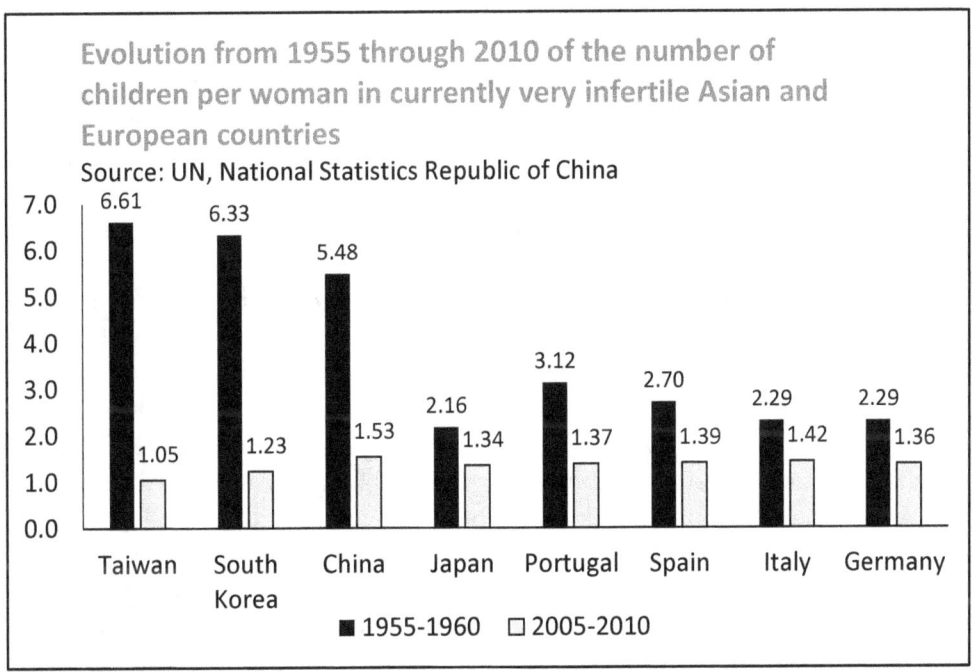

China, for example, already has a median age—the age that divides the population into two halves—which is barely below that of the United States, and higher than those of fully developed countries like Ireland, despite being less developed, as there are still large areas of the Asian giant with insufficient, or very insufficient, levels of development. For this reason, China is said to run the risk of "becoming old before becoming rich," as part of the human-economic resources needed to achieve such high economic growth as it has experienced were obtained at the cost of people having far fewer children, that is, investing much less than traditionally in their human-demographic future. Neither the official Chinese economic statistics nor those of other countries reflect the contribution of "traditional" women who have (many) children and who do not work outside the home and seemingly do not contribute to the GDP. Nor is the work and cost of raising the next generations explicitly seen in those statistics. Yet, without children now, there is no future GDP.

Other emerging countries whose prosperity levels are lower than that of the current Chinese run a similar risk of aging long before they sufficiently develop, with even greater force than China, and are already aging at a strong pace, as the birth rate is dropping while, fortunately, life expectancy is increasing—for instance, Brazil, Cuba, and other Hispanic countries, Morocco, or some former Soviet republics.

Some other developed countries with an insufficient birth rate have also aged significantly, but not to the extent of countries in Southern, Central, and Eastern Europe, or the infertile countries of the Far East: France, Ireland, the Scandinavian countries, the United Kingdom, the United States, Australia, New Zealand. However, for most of these nations, this is due, in large, to the contribution of births by immigrants. Furthermore, fertility has had a downward trend in almost all these countries prior to writing this book. For example, in Sweden and Norway, two countries that are often mentioned as examples, because their birth rates have somewhat recovered from their lows, and their fertility rate is not far from 2.1 children per woman as in other parts of Europe, the children born to immigrant mothers represented about 28% of the total number of babies born in 2015—similar to what is occurring in the UK and Belgium. Ireland is the European country with the highest native birth rate (France barely edges it out in total birth rate, but would not be able to do so without the contribution from its abundant Muslim immigration) and the lowest degree of aging, and yet, in recent years, it has not even reached 2 children per woman. In 2017, the birth rate in Ireland was 1.8 children per woman, with no less than 25% of babies born to mothers born abroad, after falling every year since 2009.

* * * *

Ultimately, although the demographic health of humanity as a whole still appears to be in good shape, when looking at global numbers, it is rapidly deteriorating and the trends are negative. Delving from the global to the specific parts, the demographic health is already worrisome for half the globe, due to the fall of the birth rates experienced, and in the worst half of that half, which includes the country where this book was written, Spain, it is very troubling, almost dreadful. In the half of the world where this health is still good, it is on the path towards becoming deficient within the next few decades, as the average number of children per woman continues to fall. So far, some of the effects of falling births have been compensated by a simultaneous increase in life expectancy, although the downside of an increased longevity is the high degree of aging that certain human populations have already reached—a phenomenon that is spreading to all populations, as birth rates continue to be low and/or continue to fall. In the countries that are worse off in terms of birth rate and aging (especially Japan and those in Europe), and even more so in those regions within these countries that have the worst demographic health, the present situation is between pre-dramatic and dramatic, already immersed in a slow but inexorable spiral of demographic death—demographic suicide—and in the midst of a very worrying process of social aging.

% population aged 65 years and over							
Year	World	Europe	Germany	Spain	Italy	Northern America	Japan
1950	5%	8%	10%	7%	8%	8%	5%
2015	8%	18%	21%	19%	22%	15%	26%
2050(P)	16%	28%	32%	36%	35%	23%	36%

% population under 20							
Year	World	Europe	Germany	Spain	Italy	Northern America	Japan
1950	44%	35%	31%	36%	35%	34%	46%
2015	34%	21%	18%	19%	18%	25%	18%
2050(P)	28%	20%	17%	17%	18%	23%	17%

Number of people aged 20-64 for every person aged 65 years and over							
Year	World	Europe	Germany	Spain	Italy	Northern America	Japan
1950	10,0	7,2	6,2	7,8	7,0	7,0	10,0
2015	7,0	3,5	2,9	3,3	2,6	4,0	2,1
2050(P)	3,5	1,9	1,6	1,3	1,4	2,4	1,3

Data source: World Population Prospects. The 2015 Revision. Medium variant projections scenario

What are the implications of all this? How do we recover a healthy birth rate? We are in a sociodemographic dynamic that has never before occurred in the entire human history, since birth rates have never been so low and life expectancy so high. Therefore, one can only speculate and analyze on both of these issues, without being able to sufficiently contrast the conclusions drawn from these ponderings with all the empirical/historical data that would be desirable. What the logic indicates, and what is beginning to happen in the countries and regions where the demographic suicide is at a more advanced level, is that this process—besides leading in the long run, if there is nothing to stop it, to the extinction of the population affected by it—has serious consequences in four fields of great importance that we will analyze in depth in the next section of this book: economic (material impoverishment); affective and of a bad old age (affective impoverishment, increasing risk of non-voluntary "euthanasia" and/or mistreatment of invalid elderly people that are expensive to take care of); political (denaturalization of democracy, leading to gerontocracy), and geopolitical (loss of international weight and reduced defensive capacity against external threats with a decreasing population). If massive foreign immigration is the only intent to avert the evils of a demographic winter/suicide, the international/ historical experience indicates that this is an eventful pathway not devoid of dangers, and that, in the long run, it is also not a complete solution to the local demographic problems derived from a low birth rate, because immigrants also age, collect pensions, and receive other social services.

CHAPTER 2
THE BITTER CONSEQUENCES OF LOW BIRTH RATES

"What future does a country of old people have?"
(**Juan Velarde Fuertes,** distinguished Spanish economist)

As we have discussed in other parts of this book, what is said, and especially in this section, about what a structural insufficiency of births would imply, is mainly an exercise of looking into the future, conjecture or speculation—carried out, assuredly, with logical and factual rigor—as there are no historical precedents to validate that our projections and hypotheses reflect what would really happen if such poor fertility levels were to continue. There has never been such a low birth rate (three to four times lower than the rate that prevailed for centuries on end), nor such a high life expectancy (between two and a half and three times the one for centuries on end), in the currently developed countries. It is logical to fear, as we will analyze in detail, that the demographic winter triggers very negative consequences in the following key areas for human welfare: economic, affective-family, quality of democracy, and geopolitical.

Towards a decrepit and shrinking society, with a tendency towards extinction

"A nation does not have the right to commit suicide, because it does not only commit suicide "for itself' but 'for others' as well."
(**Miguel de Unamuno**, Spanish writer and philosopher)

Before we go into the specific economic, affective, political, and other consequences, we will speak of three inevitable social trends for a society in the process of a demographic suicide, which are undesirable from a human or anthropological standpoint, and for anyone who loves their homeland. Here we are no longer dealing with hypotheses or conjectures, but with mathematical certainties, in the case the birth rate does not increase. Specifically, we talk about the following trends:

✓ A trend in losing population and the disappearance of a society that has a structurally insufficient birth rate.

✓ A decreasing number of children, young people, and young adults.

✓ As a consequence of the two previous factors, an increase in the average age of the population and a tendency towards social aging, due to the increasing ratios between the number of senior and elderly people and the rest of the population.

Even with just these three trends, the demographic suicide in which so many countries are immersed in should already alarm us, and combatting it would need to become one of our greatest national/regional/local priorities.

For indicative purposes, to compare and understand how the population of young adults would evolve—for example, the number of people aged 18-40 years— in countries with very low fertility rates using two scenarios, one with the current very low infant and youth mortality, and the other with historical mortality, the following graph gives us an illustrative idea, with approximate numbers. The graph shows the size of the youth population every 31 years, starting from a base of 1,000 in 2016, in a country where fertility would indefinitely be 1.34 children per woman—the simple average between 1990 and 2015 of the combined fertility rates of Germany, Italy, Spain, and Japan—with two assumptions: with the current mortality rates—which implies that 2.1 children per woman suffice for generational replacement—and with the typical historical mortality in any country up until about 150 to 200 years ago, with which we have estimated that at least 4.5 children per woman were needed to ensure the generational replacement. Additionally, it has been assumed that a new generation is formed every 31 years [29], and that historically, it occurred approximately every 25 years, because in the past, people had children at ages significantly lower than today's parents do. As shown in the table, with the current fertility and mortality rates, countries such as Japan, Germany, Italy, or Spain have very poor demographic prospects, and not only in the long-term: every 30 years or so they will lose about 35% of their young population, and a few decades later, of their total population. If present fertility were combined with historical mortality, in a few generations, their populations would have vaporized into thin air.

---

[29] The average age at motherhood in Germany in 2014 was 30.9 years, in Italy, 31.5 years, and in Spain, 31.8.

NB. Very often, in public media, two different concepts are confounded: mean age of women at childbirth / motherhood, and mean age of women at birth of first child. The former is the average age of mothers when their children were born, including them all. The latter is the average age of women having one child for the first time, and it is necessarily lower than the former, since many first-time mothers end up having more than one child from later deliveries.

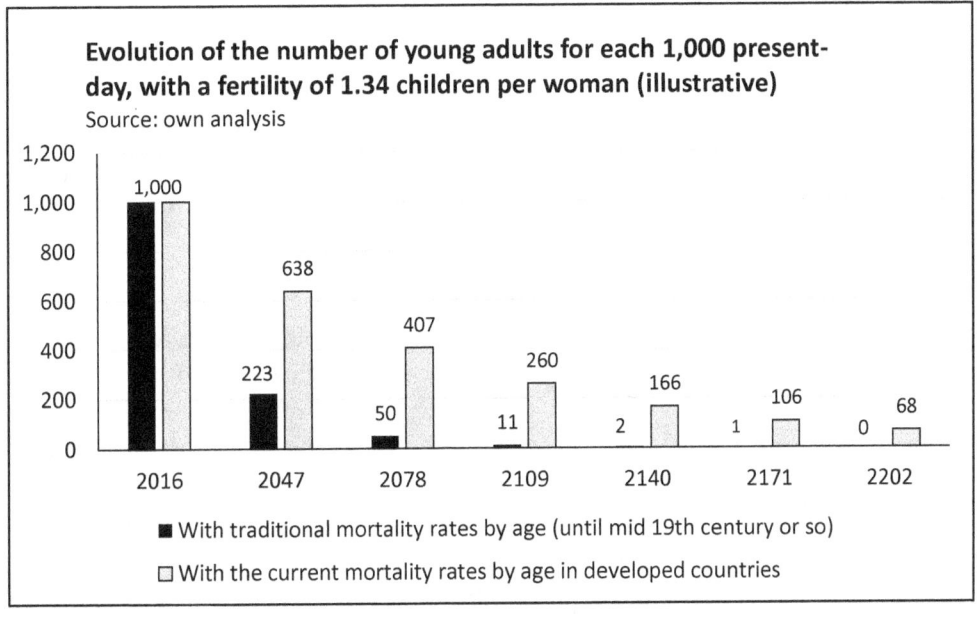

Evolution of the number of young adults for each 1,000 present-day, with a fertility of 1.34 children per woman (illustrative)
Source: own analysis

■ With traditional mortality rates by age (until mid 19th century or so)
☐ With the current mortality rates by age in developed countries

Earlier, we were saying that we are sailing on demographically uncharted seas. In addition to having no birth and life expectancy precedents reflecting what is happening in our time, we also do not know to what extent the new developments in productive technology and business organization and the sciences and techniques in healthcare, will help us compensate for the negative effects of the demographic winter in the production of wealth. We also do not know how well we will be able to adapt to it in other areas, especially now, as long as the demographic winter is not excessively "wintry" and while it is in its initial stages. We certainly do not know at what pace life expectancy will continue to increase or whether that pace will slow down or accelerate in relation to the current one, nor do we know what will become of life expectancy with good health[30]. It seems difficult to refute a priori

---

[30] Life expectancy, at birth or at a given age (for example, at 65 years old), is calculated very accurately each year, based on the observed mortality of people of different ages. Life expectancy with a good health status/quality of life is less easy to calculate accurately, since a narrow and homogeneous definition of "quality of life" or "health status" is required. Eurostat provides statistics by country for years of healthy life expectancy (Healthy Life Years), but the numbers it displays show a somewhat erratic progression and much more disparity year-over-year than those of the plain life expectancy (which change very little year-on-year, and generally in a positive way), which gives an idea that they must not be easy to calculate in a homogeneous way. Notwithstanding this variability, some clear conclusions are drawn from the Eurostat figures: life expectancy with good health is (only) between 65% and 85% of the expected total number of years of life; the expected years of healthy life for men and women are similar, and since women live 4 to 6 years more on average than men, they spend more years of their life in poor health; part of a growth in life expectancy is living more years without good health. Thus, in European societies, and undoubtedly in the rest of the world, there is a growing percentage of

the idea that the consequences of a persistent demographic winter would be between bad and catastrophic. It also seems clear that for the countries that have been most demographically unhealthy for decades, such as Japan or those in much of Europe, it would be well-suited to have a fertility rate around three children per woman for an extended period of time (e.g., half a century) to recover from their previous decades of great infertility. However, realistically, if birth rates just stabilized at around or slightly higher than 2.1 children per woman, the demographic outlook of these countries would greatly improve.

On the other hand, if global birth rates were to continue at a rate higher than 2.5 children per woman, there would eventually be, in an amount of time difficult to estimate (probably, between one and several centuries), a quantity of human population on Earth which would cause more than a few difficulties, especially in those poorer countries where GDP does not grow much faster than population, the basis of historical fears of overpopulation of Malthus ("An Essay on the Principle of Population"), Aldous Huxley (among other works, in "Brave New World Revisited"), Paul Ehrlich ("The Population Bomb"), or an initially secret US government report, known as the 1974 "Kissinger Report"[31] (due to its importance, we dedicate an annex to this book to it), etc. In summary, what many economists and sociologists thought during the past 50 years is that countries with low/very low per capita income would not get out of poverty if their populations grew at high rates—not much lower than their GDP growth rate—because per capita income would increase very slowly[32], and to make matters worse, a large portion of the wealth produced would need to be devoted to raising a huge mass of children and young people. On the other hand, as we saw in the previous chapter, if humanity continues to increase indefinitely in number, unless we invent ways of

---

senior and elderly people with deteriorating health, mostly women, whose care, logically, consumes a growing volume of resources.

[31] The so-called "Kissinger Report" was a secret memorandum of the United States government in December 1974 (http://pdf.usaid.gov/pdf_docs/Pcaab500.pdf), later declassified (1980) and made available to the public (1989), on the implications, for national security and of US interests abroad, of the explosive population growth that then occurred in the world and what had to be done to try to slow it down. See annex of this book dedicated to it.

[32] This was the case of post-colonial India, in general terms, until it liberalized and modernized its economy. In the 50 years following independence, the combined population of Pakistan, India and Bangladesh (the former British India) increased almost threefold, implying an average population growth rate of 2.2% in that half century. This means that, of the annual GDP growth, 2.2 percentage points did not go towards increasing per capita income, because they were absorbed by the increase of "capita." Worse was the case of the Muslim states of the former British Raj of India, Pakistan, and Bangladesh (called East Pakistan until its secession in 1971): the number of its inhabitants was multiplied by 3.6 from 1950 to 2000, with an average annual growth of 2.6% for its population.

continually generating new net biomass in great quantities—which seems to be difficult or impossible—or that massive emigration to other planets or celestial bodies be within reach of humans—something equally unlikely today—, at some point this would be the unavoidable factor that would prevent the human species from continuing to increase in quantity.

As for the aging of the population, it can be measured in various ways, such as the mean age of the people or their median age, the percentage of people over 65 years old, the percentage of the population over 80, the quotient between the number of those over 65 and those under 15 or 20, etc. By any of these measures, we are progressing towards societies with levels of aging without historical parallel, and, that are, additionally, growing. For example, in Spain there are already provinces where the global average age is nearly or above 50 years old (particularly, the provinces of Orense, Zamora, and Lugo), some even reaching a mean of 52 years, in the case of women of Spanish nationality. If, globally, for the first time in history, it is expected (by the UN) that before 2020 there will be more humans over 64 than under 5, there are already four Spaniards over 64 for each under 5. According to projections from the Spanish INE, by the beginning of 2040, less than 25 years after the publication of this book, for each Spaniard under 5 years there will be eight 65 years old or older. Other countries impacted by a low birth rate problem and aging display similar figures, a little up or down. One of the most representative indicators of aging, the percentage of the population aged 65 or over, continues to grow worldwide, with Japan, with 26% in 2015, the country that leads the world ranking. A Spanish province already exists where people over 64 exceed 30% of the total, which, on January 1st, 2016, reached 33% of the residents born in Spain, excluding immigrants.

Social aging, in countries with low/very low birth rates, is mainly due to the lack of children and young people. For example, the average age of the Spaniards, my compatriots, has gone from 33 to 43 years between 1976 and 2016, with an average of 1.5 children per woman in that span. By contrast, between 1930 and 1976, with an average fertility of 2.9 children per Spanish woman, life expectancy grew in Spain by 24 years, but the mean age of the Spanish population increased by just 4.7 years. According to my approximate calculations, based on estimating what would have happened had the birth rate maintained the same level as in 1976 level in Spain and had the death rate dropped as it has since then, 75% of that 10-year increase would be due to the drop in fertility and only the remaining 25% would be caused by increased longevity[33]. This last increase of 2.5 years on average, on the

---

[33] In this scenario (constant fertility rate of 2.8 children per woman from 1976 to 2016 and a decline in mortality in that interval equal to that actually experienced), Spain would have no fewer than 15 million additional inhabitants, all children, young people, and adults under the age of 40 in 2016; its population would be similar to that of France, the United Kingdom, or Italy;

other hand, would have had no effect on real social aging, since in the last 40 years, not only has life expectancy increased, but the expected years of survival in good health as well, as we age and physically deteriorate at lower rates than traditionally. An average person 60, 70, 80, or 90 years old is now "younger" and healthier than their counterpart 40 years ago, let alone 100 years ago. This means that so far VIRTUALLY THE ENTIRE aging problem suffered by societies afflicted by the demographic winter like Spain is due to the low birth rate, and it has virtually nothing to do with the increase in life expectancy, since a part of the increase in the average age does not result in any harm to society, because health and average physical force for the same age also continue to improve.

Negative economic consequences of the demographic winter

"A crisis acts on the economy like dynamite, explosively. (Bad) demographics acts like the termites, undermining its fundamentals in a slow but inexorable way" **Alfred Sauvy** (French economist, demographer and sociologist)[34]

"Where there is no flour, everything is sadness" (Poverty breeds discontent) (Spanish proverb)

The economic consequences of the demographic winter seem clearly impoverishing for the generation of wealth/GDP, and for the value of accumulated wealth (financial assets, houses, and other properties); the more intense the demographic winter is, the stronger the consequences will be. This impoverishment can be, more or less, appreciable in absolute value (mild, moderate, very serious), depending on how intense the demographic decline in each society is, how technologies and productivity continue to improve—in particular, among other, through robotic technologies—or the degree of openness of world markets to trade, among other factors. This impoverishment will fall somewhere between large

---

the average age of its population would be 7 to 8 years lower, and the percentage of those over 64 years would be significantly lower than the current one.

34 It is not a literal quote, word for word, but it sticks to its actual content. I borrowed it from my friend Joaquín Leguina, one of the distinguished pupils of Mr. Sauvy, and writer of a foreword of this book..

and immense, in any case, compared to the prosperity that could be enjoyed without its impact. That is, no matter what, it will entail a huge opportunity cost. The reasons for this are easy to understand.

Deterioration of human capital in quantity and quality

The main economic resource for wealth creation has always been the human being. That is why the term "human capital" is increasingly used. The human capital of a society, with the demographic winter, deteriorates in quantity (as there are fewer people) and quality (as the people that remain become older and older). Without human beings, no wealth is created and there is no economic supply. Without them, there is no economic demand for consumer goods and investments either, in the absence of which the possible supply of those would be equally useless, since the economy takes two to tango—supply *and* demand—and one, alone, cannot dance.

From another angle, for all economic agents individually, the key to their particular economic health is to earn more than they spend overall, including their production and maintenance costs. What is left after consumption—what is saved—should not be devalued, and if possible, should increase in value through successful investments. To be able to earn money, customers who consume—who buy—are needed. With a population declining in total number, and with the ones left being less likely to consume, because of their increased average age, the revenue of the majority/great majority of companies, their employees and their shareholders, *ceteris paribus*, tends to decrease, to deteriorate. If companies' revenues decrease, the consumption of goods and services of the companies themselves will also be impacted, as will public revenues from taxes, social contributions and taxes (and with it also the State's consumption and investment capacity), which would occur at the same time the State, to make things worse, has to spend more and more on retirement pensions, healthcare for the elderly, and assisted living and long-term care for those who cannot take care of themselves. A depressive-impoverishing spiral, in short.

On the other hand, in all modern economies, a not insignificant part of the economic activity, the jobs and the personal incomes that these jobs bring to the corresponding employees, the taxes generated and the business profits, come from the investment in new infrastructure, additional productive capacity and new business ventures that are created when growing demand is expected. Now, why build more houses, if there are fewer and fewer people alive? What is the purpose of building new roads, if there will be fewer cars on the existing ones? Apart from new nursing homes, hospitals, and funeral homes, or what foreign tourism might require, assuming the latter is growing, demand for new infrastructure will be minimal in the coming years and decades in countries experiencing a demographic decline. These reduced investments lead to the reduction or disappearance of jobs, taxes, and corporate profits traditionally generated by these investments in societies with demographic vitality. In other words, these societies will have a (much) lower GDP and total wealth.

As for production itself, a scarce labor force tends to become more expensive, to the detriment of the competitiveness and viability of companies, a phenomenon which would not exist if salaries increased because employees were becoming more productive, but a real disadvantage when the reason for salary increase is that potential employees are depleting. The employees' happiness with their salary increases is likely to be short-lived—if they even notice it—because of the correlative increase in taxes needed for taking care of the elder of their country, which will also impact companies and because the number of viable businesses that need workers will also decrease. On the other hand, not only would we deal with a scarce labor force, but also with an increasingly older one, something questionably good for productivity and competitiveness[35], with minor exceptions where more experience compensates for less vitality and future prospects, as in certain predominantly intellectual positions and professions.

Likewise, with a lower demand for goods and services in general, there is a loss of economies of scale in their production and supply, one of the keys to lowering the cost of so many products and services—at equal quality—in modern economies. This is something that equally impacts the productivity of companies—although a minority of them, especially medium and large industrial ones, can find new demand in exporting more production—and individuals, the State, and the companies themselves, in their capacity as consumers/buyers of products and services. For example, in public or private education, the cost of educating a student, when there are 30 students per classroom, is much lower than educating only 15 or 20, because there are fewer children and young people in a certain space. With the demographic winter, there tends to be fewer and fewer students per class, which results in a higher unit cost per seat, and an impoverishment of the social learning function students experience with their peers. Of course, theoretically, in order to compensate for a shrinking number of students, the number of teachers

---

[35] For example, an interesting article in the Spanish digital publication "El Confidencial," on the negative effects of aging on public administration employees in Spain, published in mid-2016, was titled "Demographic crisis in the public administration. Civil servants grow old: less eager, more cynical, and with many ailments." http://www.elconfidencial.com/sociedad/2016-07-10/funcionarios-edad-media-bajas-asistencia_1213918/#!pu6MGKXkoxwehD0

could be reduced, classrooms/schools could be closed—and in the long term, this would be inevitable—these measures are not only painful, from a human point of view, but complicated to carry out, especially in schools that economically depend on the public sector, because of the adverse reaction of educators and other affected civil servants, as well as voters in the locality in which closing an entire school, due to a lack of students, is being considered.

On the other hand, in an aging and declining society, it is expected that there will be less innovation and entrepreneurship, two major keys to economic progress (but not the only ones), because innovations will be less accepted, and the majority of innovations are created by young or relatively young people—whose numbers tend to decrease in societies with low birth rates—for two main reasons:

1. The young person (or relatively young) still believes he or she can change/take on the world. When youths innovate/start a business, they take no prisoners. Most innovations and ventures fail. As in almost everything, however, quality comes from quantity. The more attempts there are, the more innovative successes that will result (in technologies, techniques, products, companies, etc.)

2. For a young individual, embarking on a venture or innovation is much less risky than for a mature/older/elderly individual. The youth typically has few or no family burdens, and, above all, time is on their side to recover from failures.

As the demographic winter continues, accumulated wealth—people's savings, their houses, family wealth—tends to lose value. The value of property significantly depends on how much the potential buyers believe it could be worth in the future. If the economy is expected to grow and demand is expected to rise, the value of assets tends to rise. On the other hand, if expectations are the opposite, if it is predicted that there will be more supply than demand, valuations tend to go down. For example, real estate—one of the great sources of accumulated wealth in modern societies—tends to decrease in value in areas in which there are more and more empty houses, and it is foreseeable there will be even more in the future. A similar trend occurs with local business stocks, whose future prospects are bleak when demography declines. The decrease in the value of many assets hurts not only the wealth of their owners, but their investment possibilities as well, since, to be able and willing to invest, one must first possess wealth. The money that is invested in whatever fashion typically comes from the sale of other properties and/or from loans one obtains, by, among other things, placing other property(ies) as collateral. In a world where the value of assets and properties is declining, so will investment and consumption, as owners of these assets feel poorer.

Less economic growth—if not structural recession—with a declining and aging population

Population growth has been one of the traditional engines of demand and economic growth in countries that developed. Although this is not the only relevant/favorable factor for economic growth (other factors such as business and trade freedom, technological innovation, an adequate, and stable legal/institutional framework, an independent and professional justice, improvements in business management systems and financing, a good educational level for the population, a reasonable social cohesion, etc. also play a role), *ceteris paribus*, the more people producing and consuming, the more economic growth there will be in a country. By contrast, if a population declines and ages continuously, it is very difficult to avoid small growth (or even a structural recession), which is exactly what native demography leads us to predict for Europe and Japan in the coming decades.

In simple terms, approximately, the Gross Domestic Product (GDP) generated annually in any country is the product of two things: how many people work, multiplied by the average productivity per worker. Obviously, if fewer people work, it is harder for the economy to grow, although productivity, which depends on factors such as the use of technology, the training of workers and work techniques, tends to increase because those factors, and others, improve. As an example, real GDP in the United States grew, approximately, six-fold between 1955 and 2015. According to data we have gathered from JP Morgan, the average productivity per worker in 2015 was 2.5 times that of 1955, and the American labor force was 2.4 times that of the mid-1950s. According to these figures, if the US population/labor force had not grown in the last 60 years, the country's current GDP would be 58% lower than it is today and the 2016 US economy would be less than half the size of the European Union's or China's

As for the first factor of GDP—the size of the labor force—since modern capitalism began to emerge in the late Middle Ages in Europe, there has always been a double demographic driver of economic growth. Demand and value of those assets whose prices largely depend on expectations (business stocks, houses, etc.) that:

✓ The total population grew more or less continuously.

✓ Many people migrated from the countryside to the cities. In doing so, they went on to work in the modern economy, became literate, and thus became GDP producers and consumers to a much greater extent than in the countryside. The total population with "modern productivity" was therefore increasing.

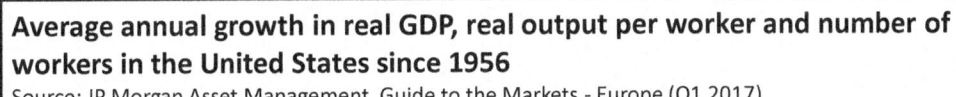

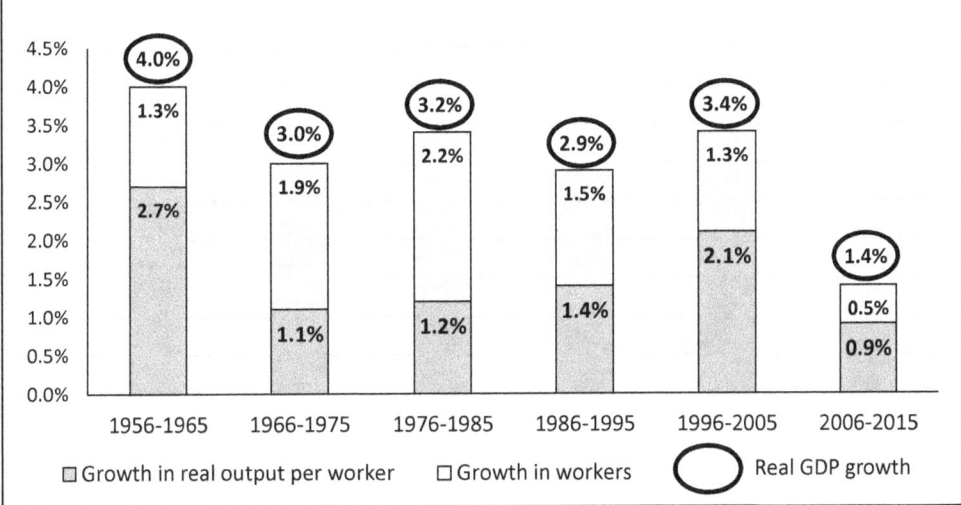

This growing demand, coupled with the increase in population, and in the population with "modern productivity," in addition to driving up consumption, drove the creation of capital based on expectations for centuries (to give two examples of this kind of intangible capital: i) the difference between the stock market value of companies and their net book value or ii) the difference between the market price of houses and their cost in materials and construction[36]). In turn, these expectations improved overall prosperity and served as a guaranty / collateral for loans that were used for new investments or consumption. To sum it up: there was a virtuous cycle of a self-fueled expanding economy, with population growth as one of its major engines or drivers. With an aging population and an eventual contraction of it, in the coming decades, this is no longer going to be the case, and we are actually exposing ourselves to live through exactly the opposite: a declining, structurally depressed economic demand and a generalized depreciation in assets and local properties, which will have depressing effects on the economy.

---

[36] The value of the land on which houses are built depends almost exclusively on the expectation that, in the future, that land will be used for buildings that will be sold at a good price or that the already-existing buildings on that land will sell well. If you do not plan to build anything on a particular ground due to a lack of demand, or if the land is not going to be used for other productive purposes, it tends to be worth very little. By contrast, the best square meters of urban land, in places with the highest demand for houses in the large cities, are highly valuable.

During the last 30-50 years, when the growth of the native Western European population began to slow down and there were no longer illiterates among us, the next demographic drivers were the massive incorporation of women into the workforce and foreign immigrants.

Number of employed women per 100 employed men in the most fertile, post-university ages, by country in Europe (annual average of 2015)		
Source of data: Eurostat	**Total population aged 25 - 39**	**Country nationals aged 25 - 39 (*)**
Portugal	97.9	98.8
Lithuania	94.8	94.7
Norway	94.2	96.3
Sweden	92.9	95.4
Cyprus	92.7	95.9
Austria	91.9	95.4
Belgium	91.3	94.3
Netherlands	90.0	91.7
Spain	89.7	92.6
Denmark	89.6	93.1
Iceland	89.4	89.7
Latvia	89.4	91.1
Switzerland	89.1	93.2
Slovenia	89.0	90.7
Germany	88.8	92.4
Ireland	88.7	92.1
Luxembourg	88.7	94.0
Bulgaria	88.4	88.4
Croatia	87.9	87.9
France	87.5	90.1
Finland	86.5	87.9
Eurozone	86.4	89.3
European Union - 28	85.3	87.3
Poland	84.4	84.5
United Kingdom	84.1	85.8
Estonia	81.1	81.0
Romania	80.7	80.7
Greece	79.3	81.0
Malta	78.8	79.2
Hungary	76.9	76.8
FYR of Macedonia	76.0	76.4
Italy	75.2	78.6
(*) NB. Includes immigrants with dual citizenship		

The first of these last two demographic drivers of economic growth is virtually exhausted—at least in Europe—because in this day and age, the vast majority of young and middle-aged European women already work, as displayed in the table: there is almost no difference between the rate of female and male labor activity, although the latter is always slightly higher. For the main characteristics of the socio- economic model of the developed countries to be sustainable in general, it is imperative to ensure that female labor outside the home be compatible with a fertility rate not lower than the replacement rate, 2.1 children per woman on average, which has not been the case for decades. If, in order to produce more GDP we must incur (a large) shortage of children, there will be bread for today and hunger for tomorrow, equivalent to *eating* the future, in addition to the terrible affective and vital impoverishment that not having children would mean for women (and men).

As for immigration, the massive and growing arrival of foreign workers in Europe and the United States does not seem viable/prudent either in the foreseeable future, due to the rise of populism, the fear of jihadism, the increased unease related to immigration in Western societies, and the fortunate fact that many of the countries that traditionally "issue" immigrants are finally developing, among other reasons. This is not to say that immigration, in doses that can be assimilated without trauma, and with the appropriate professional and cultural profile, will not, in the future, continue to be one of the resources developed countries use to address their labor and population rejuvenation needs, but immigration as a sufficient demographic resource in low-fertility countries is a complicated issue, for the above reasons, which are discussed in more detail below.

The negative effect of a demographic decline on productivity

The argument developed above applies to the impact of demographic changes on GDP, based on the number of workers and consumers. Demographic change is however, in our view, also having a negative impact on productivity growth. Many influential people—for example, the economists Nouriel Roubini and Larry Summers, or Francisco González, the president of BBVA bank, among many others—have wondered in public arenas why productivity has not been growing in the West for years as had been expected, despite great technological innovations within the last few decades. The potential productivity of individuals and companies depends, among other factors, on technology, work practices, training, and workforce motivation. Real productivity, in addition to the above, depends very much on aspects closely linked to demography—for example, demand levels. As a significant part of business costs is fixed, and companies seldom operate at full capacity, businesses often enjoy economies of scale with increasing sales volumes. When sales rise, *ceteris paribus*, the productivity per worker, per office or factory square foot / meter, per dollar of capital invested in machines, etc., also rises.[37]

As we mentioned before, it takes two to tango—supply and demand—in the economy. If one of them is lame, even if the other one is not, they will not dance well together. Although potential productivity tends to increase steadily due to technological advances, if demand growth slows down or even decreases, because the number of consumers also decreases, and if consumers grow older and have fewer needs, except for things like medicines and healthcare, it is to be expected that productivity growth, notwithstanding the technological revolution, will not be that of the glorious 1950s, 60s, or 70s. One of reasons is the decline in the rate of increase, if not an outright decrease, of traditional economies of scale resulting from an ever-increasing native demography, which is especially important in the services sector. In addition, and this would have a negative impact on supply, it is doubtful, if not impossible, that the aging of the labor force does not affect productivity, except in certain intellectual tasks.[38]

---

[37] Let's illustrate this with a simple example. When an economic crisis arrives and the clientele of a neighborhood pizzeria is reduced, in the absence of layoffs—not always possible or viable, as well as humanly undesirable—real productivity per employee of the pizzeria also decreases. Let's imagine that before the crisis, the pizzeria in our neighborhood, with three employees, sold 160,000 dollars a year in pizzas and complements (drinks, desserts, etc.) and had total external costs (raw material, rent, electricity, etc.) without including personnel, of 40,000 dollars. Thus, the average productivity per employee was 160,000 dollars of revenue minus 40,000 euros of external costs, divided among three workers, equal to 40,000 dollars of net production / added value each on average. Then comes the crisis, and as a consequence, sales fall by 20% (typically, as demand falls, prices must be lowered in an effort to lose less clientele and/or gain new customers, both factors contributing together, with a multiplying effect, to lower total sales), and costs can be reduced by about 15% (some costs are often essentially variable with the sales volume, such as, in this example, raw materials or home delivery, but others are fixed, such as renting the premises, the net result being that, in general, external costs usually fall less than revenue in times of crisis). Average productivity per employee now becomes (128,000 - 34,000)/3 = 31,333 dollars of added value per worker. Employees know how to make pizzas just as well as before, or even better, because they are increasingly experienced and because difficult sales have probably pushed them to innovate to improve quality and processes—but their economic productivity is 21.7% lower. Getting back to our topic, the advanced demographic winter implies a continuous reduction in demand, equivalent to a structural recession. This alone, apart from other economic ills, tends to lower productivity by generating diseconomies of scale.

[38] Workers' productivity grows rapidly in the first years of their working life. During those years, they first learn to work, then each time they are doing the job better, aspire to promotions which give them an extra motivation; after a few years they begin to supervise/direct other people, etc. Later on, as people master the trade and settle into a "comfort zone," their productivity tends to grow less or stagnate, unless they are ambitious/very capable/highly motivated people and continue to strive and to be promoted/rewarded, or that new

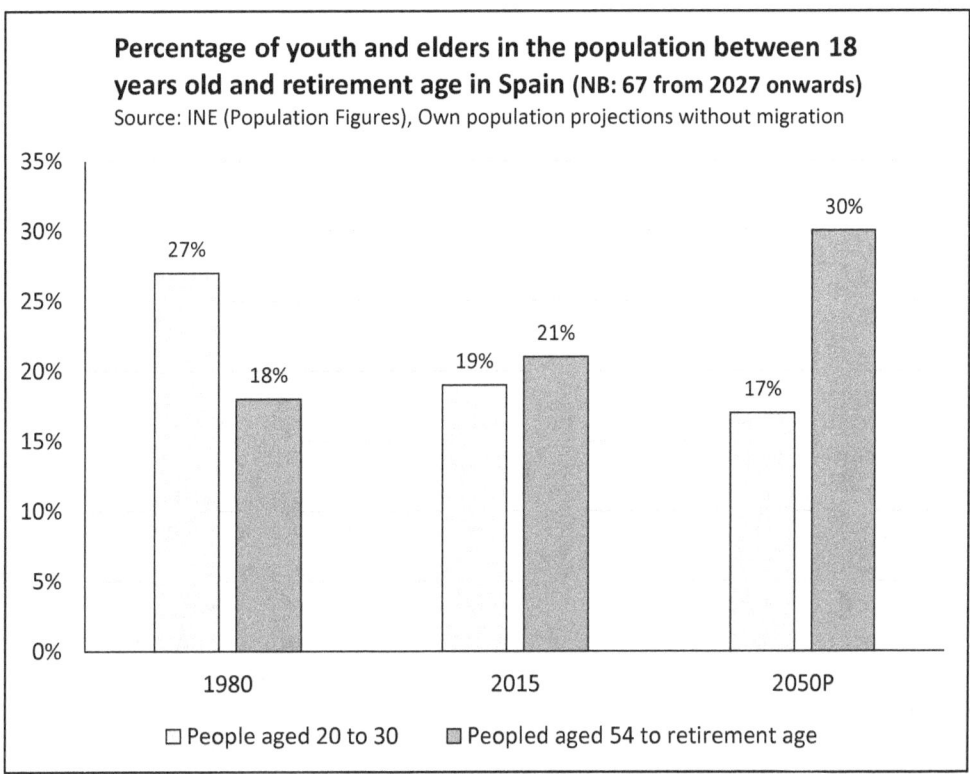

Percentage of youth and elders in the population between 18 years old and retirement age in Spain (NB: 67 from 2027 onwards)
Source: INE (Population Figures), Own population projections without migration

□ People aged 20 to 30   ▣ Peopled aged 54 to retirement age

Likewise, the growing weight of low-skilled foreign immigrants in the European and North American workforce—workers who have alleviated the decline in the number of native young adults due to the lower birth rate in the West—could have some impact on average productivity. This possible impact, in turn, could be temporary or long-term.

---

technologies are introduced that have a great positive impact on their work. As people reach maturity (in their forties, and even more so in their fifties), and many stagnate in their professional career, their productivity does not grow, and can even decline, with the exception of a smaller and smaller minority who continue to rise and grow professionally. In the 10 to 15 years prior to retirement, this is even more noticeable, as the increased experience, in a large number of personal cases, does not compensate for the lower motivation and the lower physical vigor and poorer health. In addition, at more advanced ages, there is a larger percentage of people already incapacitated, totally or partially, due to accidents and diseases suffered over the years. To make matters worse, as older people generally earn more or much more than young workers, the relationship between what many of the seniors produce and what they earn tends to be less attractive to companies than that same equation for young and middle-aged employees. For this reason, companies carrying out staff reductions try, preferably, that oldest workers—who are going to be more and more numerous—be the ones who leave the company.

Headwind in the economy of countries suffering from demographic decline

Thus the economy of the more developed countries, traditionally driven by a demographic tailwind, now flies with a demographic headwind. The same phenomenon will soon happen to the newest arrivals in the group of countries affected by the demographic suicide (China, Taiwan, South Korea, etc.). Starting to remedy this structural defect as soon as possible, by acknowledging the problem and with a higher birth rate, is essential so that the evolution of Western GDP will not land between mediocre and very poor in the coming decades (like Japan, or worse).

A major additional risk resulting from these demographic headwinds affecting the economy is the gap between expectations for robust GDP growth—usual expectations until recently in the West and in Japan, except for periods of recession—and a more mediocre reality, causing governments to feel pressured by the public opinion and the elites to force an economic growth that does not occur naturally, through larger public deficits and artificially low interest rates, with the goal of boosting demand. This results in increasingly indebted States, financial and asset bubbles (real estate, stock market), two situations which always end badly[39]. According to some economists, such as the Italian Ettore Gotti Tedeschi, who once headed the Vatican Bank, this has been the major cause of the Great Recession that began in 2007-2008: the demographic decline in the West had already been damaging its structural growth capacity for 10 years to 20 years, which led the Central Banks of the US and Europe to inject money into the economy at very low rates in the early years of the twenty-first century. This very cheap money provoked the large bubbles in real estate and other assets to burst in 2007-2008, which led to the great economic and financial crisis that ensued, from which we had not yet fully recovered in 2016, when we wrote these lines. Had we recovered sooner, neither the FED in the US nor the European Central Bank would have kept the money (interest rates) at such ridiculously low levels.

A final thought on this point: the traditional demographic push on demand and the economy is a bit like good health: as long as we have it, we do not pay attention to it. Adam Smith, Marx, Keynes, von Mises, Hayek, Friedman, and all the right-wing, left-wing, or moderate economists, analyzed an economy with a more or less constant underlying demographic driver that provided new labor nonstop, that

---

[39] This idea is developed very credibly in the article "Mind the (Expectations) Gap: Demographic Trends and GDP, of Rob Arnott and Denis Chaves," which can be read at http://www.mauldineconomics.com/images/uploads/pdf/2013_08_07_OTB.pdf, introduced by John Mauldin, best-selling author on financial investments.

requested more products, more services, more houses, more transportation vehicles, etc., and that encouraged businesspeople to invest to meet this new demand. Since it was a constant element, it did not logically appear among their great concerns or objects of intellectual muse. Probably for this reason, the demographic factor has not been given the relevance it deserves in economics until now. This will change in the twenty-first century—it is already beginning to change: economists and economic opinion-makers are talking about it more and more in pubic—because the growing demographic languor of many countries will strengthen the importance of this variable in economic analyses and theories, business planning and public policies. In fact, there is a growing number of economists, businesspeople, and politicians who speak of the demographic brake on growth in the West and more than a few of them even use the term "demographic suicide"[40].

Let us see below in detail various negative impacts on the economy of a demographic decline, a population reduction and the aging of the remaining population.

With fewer young people comes less entrepreneurship and innovation

With customary exceptions, the typical entrepreneur who truly creates new companies, taking risks and innovating, usually begins to do so at a young age. In order to take the plunge for the first time and take risks, it helps to have the vitality, the boldness, and even the folly of the youth. It would suit anyone well to have many years ahead to recover from a possible failure in a business venture. All this together offers prospects of having much to gain (money, glory: "I will do things that no one has ever done," "I will do things better than others, because I have the talent") and little to lose ("if it doesn't go well, I will recover, as I am young"). Of course, whoever does well when starting a business young will normally continue to do so in their middle age and older. It is better, however, to be entrepreneurial

---

[40] Since we published the book "El suicidio demográfico de España" ("The Demographic Suicide of Spain") in 2011, we have found that the negative impact of demography on the Western economy is a subject gaining more and more weight in international but also Spanish economic analyses. We do not believe that this is substantially due to our book, beyond the grain of sand that it has contributed in this area, especially in Spain, but that, as the demographic deterioration of the West, and of Spain in particular, progresses at an exponential rate, the awareness that this is an element to take more into account is growing in parallel as might be expected. In particular, the term "demographic suicide" is much more commonly used now than it was before 2011.

before the years begin to weigh us down.

As I as writing these lines, in August 2016, the seven richest people in the world, all self-made (who did not inherit their fortune), were, in order of personal wealth, according to the magazine "Forbes":

1. Bill Gates, who founded Microsoft when he was 20.

2. Amancio Ortega (Zara), who founded his first company, Confecciones GOA (a bathrobe maker), when he was 27.

3. Warren Buffett, who founded his first (and successful) company, Buffett Associates Ltd, when he was 26.

4. Jeff Bezos, who founded Amazon at 30.

5. Carlos Slim, who founded his first company at 25.

6. Mark Zuckerberg, who founded Facebook at 20.

7. Larry Ellison, who founded Oracle at 33.

On average, these seven billionaires, whose business ventures have had huge social impacts and have yielded major innovations, began their entrepreneurial careers at 27 years old. The legendary John Davison Rockefeller launched his first venture at age 18 and amassed such personal wealth that he is considered the richest man of all times in constant money. The unique technological innovator and great businessman Steve Jobs (the genius of the Macintosh, iPod, iPhone, iPad, Pixar, and many other disruptive products and companies) founded Apple at 21 years of age. The great inventor and entrepreneur Thomas Alva Edison, to whom we owe feats such as electric light (the incandescent filament lamp), the recording and reproduction of sounds (the phonograph), or the founding of the only company that continues to be part of the "blue chips" from the Dow Jones Industrial Average since its inception in 1896—General Electric—likewise patented his first invention at the age of 21. The Lumière brothers patented the cinematograph when one was 30 and the other 32 and with it presented their first film shortly thereafter at a session in Paris. The five founders of the German software giant SAP were between 28 and 37 when they started it up. The Italian Luciano Benetton launched his first tailoring and clothing business at the age of 20 and launched the company that bears his name at 30. The Scottish James Watt patented his steam engine, which was not the first of his great inventions in that field, at age 33. The also Scottish Alexander Graham Bell, who created his first invention when he was only 12 years old, patented his telephone at 29 in the USA. The Spanish Juan de la Cierva Codorniú, inventor of the gyroplane, the ancestor of the helicopter, founded his first company and built his first airplane in 1912 when he was only 16 years old. He built the first gyroplane in Madrid at the age of 25. Swedish engineer Ingvar Kamprad founded IKEA, the inexpensive furniture giant, at 17. Danish Arnold Peter Møller founded the freight container giant Maersk at the age of 27.

Logically, then, in societies with fewer young people, *ceteris paribus*, there will be fewer entrepreneurs and less technological-business innovation, especially the disruptive kind—the kind that truly transforms people's lives and companies' processes. As there are more and more seniors and elderly individuals, the aversion to taking risks, innovating, and adopting possible innovations will generally increase. These factors, among others, will lead to lower increases in productivity and wealth for the majority of people. They will also lead to fewer income-improvement opportunities for those at the bottom of the social ladder.

The smaller the youth population, the less general demand for goods and services

In a population with a decreasing number of young people, the demand for many types of goods and services tends to weaken. Young and middle-aged people tend to consume more of almost everything except healthcare products and services. When the number of births begins to fall in a country, the effects of the nascent demographic winter are first noticed, after a few years, in the reduced number of children and young people. Among other things, the demand for education falls, a sector of activity that directly or indirectly employs more than a small percentage of the working population of any modern country. In addition, of course, this affects the demand for other goods and services children and youth require. Let us examine the next three examples from Spain, transferable *mutatis mutandis*—with a somewhat greater or lower intensity, but following the same direction—to many more countries afflicted with a persistent low birth rate for some time.

The Spanish figures showing the decrease in the population of infants or school age children are shocking. Between 1980 and 2030, in only 50 years, Spain would lose 50% of its population under 15 years old and 60% if we only focus on the children of Spanish mothers.

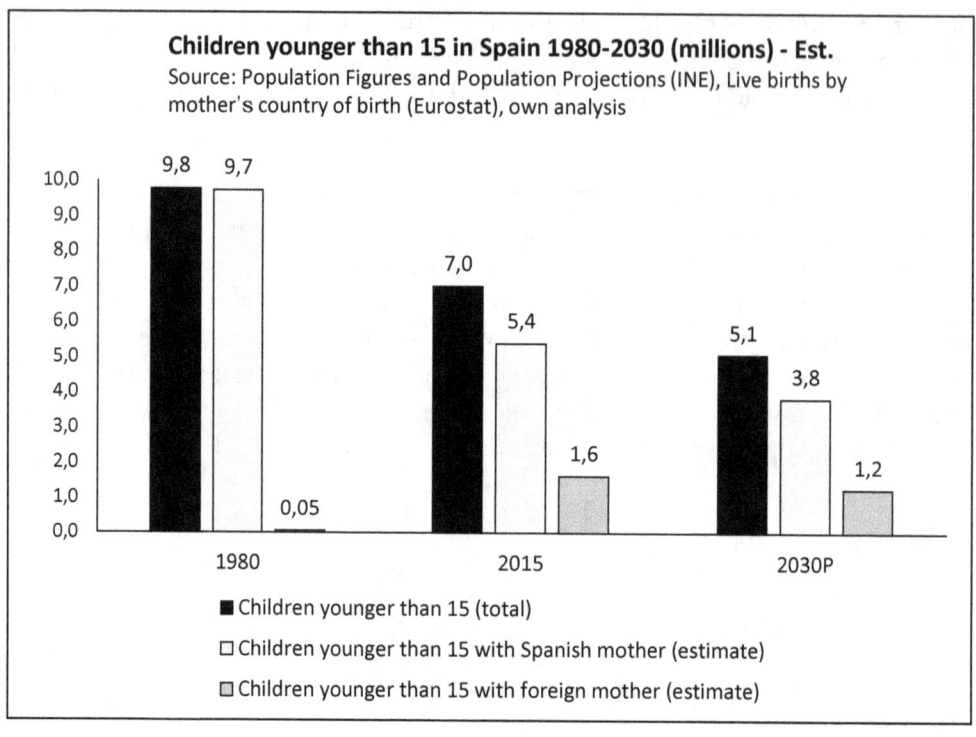

Children younger than 15 in Spain 1980-2030 (millions) - Est.
Source: Population Figures and Population Projections (INE), Live births by mother's country of birth (Eurostat), own analysis

- Children younger than 15 (total)
- Children younger than 15 with Spanish mother (estimate)
- Children younger than 15 with foreign mother (estimate)

Change 1980-2015-2030 in population younger than 15 in Spain			
Source: INE, Eurostat, own analysis	Change 1980-2015	Change 2015-2030	Change 1980-2030
Children younger than 15 (total)	-28%	-28%	-48%
Children younger than 15 with Spanish mother (estimate)	-45%	-29%	-61%
Children younger than 15 with foreign mother (estimate)	3210%	-23%	2441%

Following the drastic reduction in the number of children caused by the demographic winter, the same depletion happens with university-aged youth or prior to entering the workforce. Thereupon, the same happens with the young work force—people, for example, between 25 and 39 years old—one of the engines of the economy, since these are people who are starting to work, learning to perform their trade, performing it better every time, moving up the ranks and earning more money, consuming, renting houses to live and/or buying their first home whenever they can afford it. In the Eurozone countries, despite the arrival of foreign immigration, largely young or middle-aged, between early 2000 and early 2015, there was a 13% decrease in the population aged 25 to 39, with levels greater than or equal to the Eurozone average in Germany (-22%), the Netherlands (-19%), Italy (-17%), Denmark (-15%), Spain (-14%), and Austria (-13%).

While I was writing these lines (July 2016), I came across the most recent unemployment figures and resident population for Spain, from the INE, for a slightly wider age range. My country, between the second quarter of 2008 and the second quarter of 2016, lost 20% of its population from 20 to 39 years old (-2.8 million people in that age band), which was mainly due to the present effects of the fall in the birth rate from 1977 to 1999 in Spain, and only in a very secondary part, to the net emigration, a consequence of the Great Recession. In only eight years, the number of young adults from 20 to 39 years dropped by 20%! In those same eight years, Spain gained 1.1 million people over 64 years and now has 15% more people in that age group than during the second quarter of 2008. There are now far fewer youth and many more older and elderly people in just eight years: a pure and simple demographic decline.

Continuing with Spain, approximately half of the real estate transactions are carried out by people who buy their first home and who are the drivers of a market of enormous importance for the economy as a whole. The average age of these buyers is around 35 years old. Now, the total number of people in the typical first-time buyers age-range (from 30 to 39 years) will suffer a major collapse until 2030 in Spain. Barring net immigration flows with the rest of world in this age group, and based on current population figures—people in that age group are already born—Spain will lose 45% of its people in this age group between 2010 and 2030. This means that, except for coastal areas that benefit from a demand by foreigners—especially Europeans—who like to spend their vacations in Spain, or who reside there during retirement, and in large cities like Madrid, Barcelona, Valencia, Malaga, etc., that should continue to attract national and foreign populations, the value of real estate in the rest of the country faces a huge depreciation due to lack of buyers and an increase in the number of empty houses as more people die. It will hardly make sense to build new houses in the vast majority of the Spanish territory experiencing a serious demographic decline, except in some small select areas and some second homes. Consequently, the direct and indirect jobs that the construction activity has traditionally generated in Spain, as in other countries when they developed and grew in population, will also disappear. This means a lower accumulated real estate wealth (existing homes) and a lower new real estate wealth (since new constructions would hardly be required).

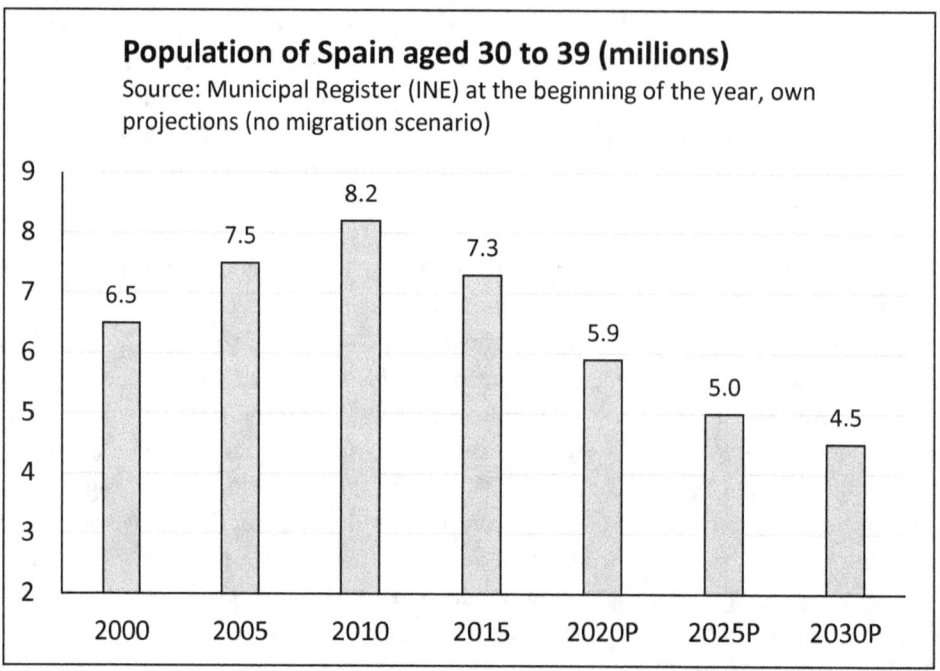

Population of Spain aged 30 to 39 (millions)
Source: Municipal Register (INE) at the beginning of the year, own projections (no migration scenario)

With an inverted age pyramid, older people are less employable

Traditionally, the older people are and the longer they have been working in companies and organizations, the more money they earn, for the same position. Employers used to pay (and still pay, in many cases) significantly more in exchange for a lot of experience, as it was a valuable and scarce resource, when there were higher numbers of middle-aged individuals with limited experience and the more inexperienced youth abounded even more. As the age pyramid is reversed, what is abundant in the workforce is the amount of people with the most experience and what is lacking is a large population of young people. In this situation, companies are increasingly deincentivized to pay higher wages to older workers, despite their greater experience. Mature workers undoubtedly know more than young people. On the other hand, they have less physical vigor and less motivation if their professional career has been stagnant for years, as tends to happen with a large number of people from a certain age, among other reasons, as they reach a certain point in their professional life known as their personal level of incompetence, according to the famous "Peter principle," a level past which, normally, no further promotions are received. This is why companies that are in the process of restructuring, whenever they can, prefer to lay off older workers, who for the same position (for example, secretary, salesperson, waiter, concierge, etc.) can cost between 1.5 and 3 times what their peers with 20 or 30 years of less experience cost, but who do not perform two or three times more than the younger employees, and are sometimes even less productive than the young workers who already have some experience, because of the latter's superior motivation and vigor. Companies act in accordance with who they believe that provides them with a higher benefit and who does not, because of the relationship between personal performance and salary. This is one of the reasons why unemployment and inactivity rates among people who are a few years away from retirement are higher than among their middle-aged peers in developed countries. Without enough young people among which to dilute their higher wages, most of the older people, in times when they are abundant, are less attractive as employees. This would require significant changes in the work models and the compensation of senior workers, as well as in their mentalities and expectations and of those of the business managers in relation to them, leading to new balances between the interests of older workers and those of companies, as well as those of society in general, as senior unemployment no longer suits it. If this is not achieved, among the evils of social aging, the unemployment of people 5 to 15 years away from their normal retirement age will not be one of its minor issues—which is already occurring significantly.

Increased burden on the taxpayer and the economy of social benefits for retirees, in an aging society with few young people

"The old pact between generations is no longer valid. The generation that will retire in the next few years had very few children and it is no longer reasonable for our generation to finance their pensions and medical care as it has until now."
(**Hendrik Wuest**, Young Christian-Democrat German politician, in 2003)

"Social Security medical expenses for the elderly have to be cut ... Let the old people use crutches, as before, instead of requesting hip prostheses."
(**Philipp Missfelder**, leader of the Christian-democrat German youths, in 2003[41])

---

[41] This German politician, born in 1979, when criticized for "showing a lack of solidarity," retorted that his duty was to defend the people of his generation. It is therefore expected that when this gentleman retires at an old age, if he continues in politics and continues to defend "those of his age," he will argue the opposite and will label the young people of that time as

It is clear that, with fewer working people per retiree, traditional public pensions (based on the fact that pensioners receive what active workers are contributing/paying in taxes, under a "pay as you go" system[42]), public healthcare services and the costs of caring for dependents, who need long-term care because they can no longer take care of themselves either totally or partially, will be an increasingly heavy burden on the economy. In the economies of the developed countries, these three sources of expenditure related to the elderly already consume between 15% and 25% of the wealth produced, of GDP, in large part by means of public expenditures, but not limited to these. In addition, these spending sources are increasing, as the ranks of the more senior citizens are increasing and their combined voting power also increases.

Modern Social Security was established in the United States in 1935, under the presidency of Franklin Delano Roosevelt. There were then fifty-two workers per retiree in the Yankee giant, who also lived on average only a few years more after retiring. Of course, with some 50 active workers for each pensioner, if a small fraction of the salary—for example, 2% —is deducted from each worker in the form of taxes or social contributions for retirement purposes, very good retirement pensions can be paid out. Without reaching such extremes, when in 1908, the Spanish Minister of the Interior, Juan de la Cierva Peñafiel, father of Juan de la Cierva Codorniú, inventor of the gyroplane, and grandfather of my friend Juan de la Cierva Hoces, himself a genial inventor[43], founded the National Welfare Institute

---

unsupportive, even though they will say things similar to what he was saying when he was young.

[42] The alternative to the pay as you go pension system is the individual system of "private savings with capitalization," and is being introduced in more and more countries, including some so little suspected of being addicted to "unbridled capitalism" such as Sweden, as a complement or substitute to the pay as you go system, due to its clear advantages over the latter. It consists in keeping the mandatory retirement contributions, or at least a significant fraction of these contributions, in some kind of piggy bank or in some account in the workers' names (notional accounts), which can then be invested in various types of financial assets, such as stocks, bonds, bank deposits, etc. This system has several advantages: what is saved belongs to the worker and is outside of the hands of politicians; effective savings rates increase; and if the worker dies at any time, the money in that account belongs to his or her heirs. In addition, if the money is invested well, the capital saved can be multiplied, thanks to the "magic" of stock market returns (historically, 5% -10% per annum on average, once inflation has been subtracted and including corporate dividends) and compound interest, which, according to Einstein, is "the most powerful force in the universe," since the money that can be capitalized multiplies in an almost incredible way at a significant compound interest over a large number of years.

[43] See the article titled "Perfecting the Future. Oscar-winner Juan de la Cierva invents it all, from the photo-finish to smart bombs to interactive TV".
https://www.bizjournals.com/southflorida/stories/1997/03/17/story6.html

("Instituto Nacional de Previsión" or INP), a precursor to modern Spanish Social Security, there were about ten people of working age per person of retirement age in Spain.

In the United States and in almost all of Europe, for every retiree there are now between 1.5 and 3 active workers—a significant proportion of whom are part-time workers— with a downward trend towards having less than two in the future, something that is already happening in more than a few countries and certain regions that have significantly aged. Correspondingly, the cost of retirement pensions is already a very substantial burden on the economy and on taxpayers. Because of demography, the scenario we are headed towards is one where public retirement pensions are increasingly smaller in relation to the typical worker's salary, and at the same time, cause an increasing burden on the economy as a whole. The following graph shows the number of people employed in 2013 in Western Europe per pensioner, accrued either through their own work when they were younger or through widowhood, that we have calculated using data from Eurostat on employment, retirement, and widowhood pensions. In Eastern Europe, the proportions are similar (data also from 2013): 2.1 active worker per retired pensioner or widowed in Slovakia; 1.9 in the Czech Republic, Estonia and Poland; 1.7 in Hungary, Romania, Latvia, and Croatia; 1.6 in Lithuania and 1.5 in Slovenia.

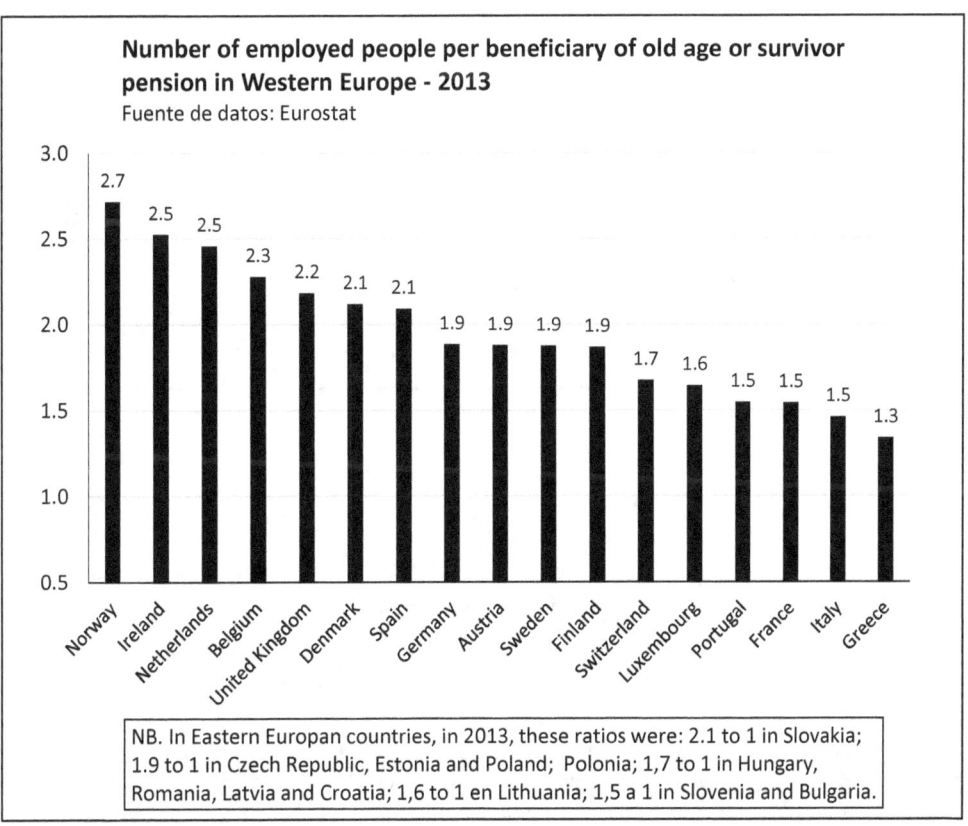

Number of employed people per beneficiary of old age or survivor pension in Western Europe - 2013
Fuente de datos: Eurostat

NB. In Eastern Europan countries, in 2013, these ratios were: 2.1 to 1 in Slovakia; 1.9 to 1 in Czech Republic, Estonia and Poland; Polonia; 1,7 to 1 in Hungary, Romania, Latvia and Croatia; 1,6 to 1 en Lithuania; 1,5 a 1 in Slovenia and Bulgaria.

The following graph shows the evolution of the number of people of theoretical active age (16 to 64 years old) in Europe, the United States, Japan, China, and India in 1975 – 2015 - 2055, who support retirement pensions, health, and long-term care for each person of theoretical retirement age (65 years and over). The decline in this ratio observed over time, which, when it was still high, allowed for the good care of the elderly without them being a heavy burden on the economy, is enormous, and is especially fast in Asia, because the drops in birth rates and the increases in life expectancy over the last 30-50 years have been more intense on that continent than in the West, as economies developed later and birth rates have been falling faster.

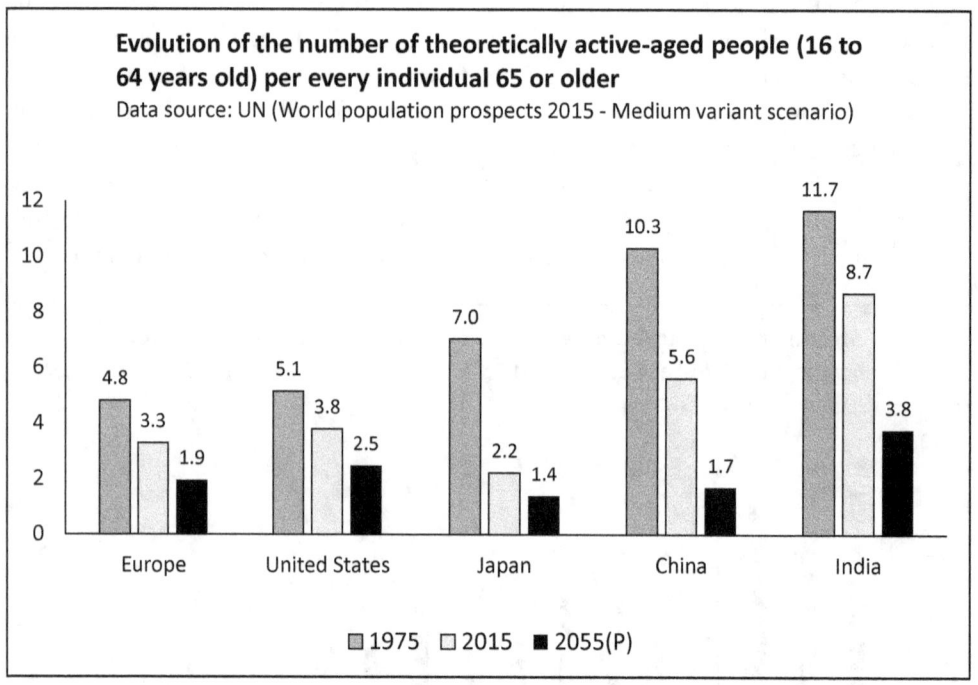

Evolution of the number of theoretically active-aged people (16 to 64 years old) per every individual 65 or older

Data source: UN (World population prospects 2015 - Medium variant scenario)

■ 1975 □ 2015 ■ 2055(P)

To make matters worse, there are several factors that reduce (therefore, worsen) the ratio of active people to retirees/pensioners with respect to people who, based on their age, could produce wealth and taxes in support of retirees. Not all people of a theoretical "working age" actively participate in the productive economy. They also do not all contribute to the GDP that is officially measured[44],

---

[44] Work in the home—cleaning, cooking, administration, and orderliness, etc., and the effort in raising children, typically and traditionally performed by females—although men in developed countries, in this day and age—carry out a minor but not insignificant part of this job, are

nor do they generate Social Security contributions or taxes, as a result. The number of "inactive" people of working age (students; the unemployed; women who take care of their children and homes and do not work outside the home; the disabled), is greater than the number of people of retirement age who do not receive a pension. Although the theoretical working age is 16-64 years, the average effective age of entry into the labor market is well beyond 16 years in developed countries, because the vast majority of people continue to study beyond that age, something that did not happen 50 to 100 years ago (in fact, in the past, many people started working before 16 years old). The average actual retirement age in many countries is less than 65 years. The result is that, from the age of 16 to the day 65 candles are blown on the birthday cake, in Western Europe, people only work about 70% of these 49 theoretical years—or 588 months—between those two birthdays. Specifically, in 2014, the expected number of years of effective working life, according to Eurostat, was 35.3 years per person, or 72% of those 49 "official" years, with a minimum for all of Europe being in Italy, at 63%. To make matters even worse, those percentages and those of the previous graphs do not include the fact that more than a few people who work do so part-time.

On the other hand, from the present decade onwards, and especially from the next decade, in the more developed countries there will be an additional worsening in public retirement funds, health for seniors and assisted living expenses, because of the massive retirement of the baby-boomers, while the life expectancy of retirees continues to lengthen. In addition, the massive incorporation of women into the workforce from the 1960s to 1980s-90s, as well as foreign immigrants who have arrived since then, which allowed the real ratios between active workers and pensioners to improve during the last decades, will lead to additional increases in public spending for the elderly when these new waves of workers massively begin to retire ("new" with respect to native males, traditionally the vast majority of the labor force).

Medical expenses per person shoot up starting at 50 to 60 years old. Although I do not have exact data to verify, I was told that a Spanish Health Minister used to say that, on average, the Spanish generate an expense in medical care and medicine, during their last two years of life, equal to or exceeding that of all their previous years put together. It is assumed that things will be very similar in the case of citizens of other developed countries. This is largely due to cancer, a disease that is

---

activities that result in quality of life and, in the short or long-term, in economic value. Official GDP statistics, however, do not include the economic value generated by such activities when they are produced without resorting to persons outside the family, although there would be enough data to be able to estimate them, at least in average/standard terms. For example, there are data on what households pay to contract domestic staff for cleaning, cooking, babysitting (with references such as the cost of daycare places, or what caregivers/nannies charge), etc.

not only cruel and very hard to cope with, but is also very costly to treat, and is responsible for the death of just over one in four Europeans, according to Eurostat mortality data. A similar amount must be added to these numbers, to account for people who suffer from cancer throughout their life.

In Spain, according to data published by the newspaper "El Mundo"—I don't have such precise numbers for other countries, although they should be similar—half of the pharmaceutical expenses in 2011 were generated by people aged 75 and older, who represented 9% of the Spanish population that year. Another 30% was originated by people aged 65 to 74, who, in 2011, accounted for just over 8% of the country's population. 80% of pharmaceutical expenses were due to people 65 years of age or older, who represent 17% of the population, and 50% was generated by only 9% of people! As those over 65 will double in percentage of the Spanish population within the next 40 years—and practically all that growth will be due to those over 74—according to forecasts by the UN, Eurostat, and the Spanish INE, Spain, like any other country suffering from a demographic winter, will need to either succeed in substantially reducing healthcare costs per patient / person, or it will need to allocate increasing and very substantial portions of its GDP to healthcare spending, or do both things at the same time.

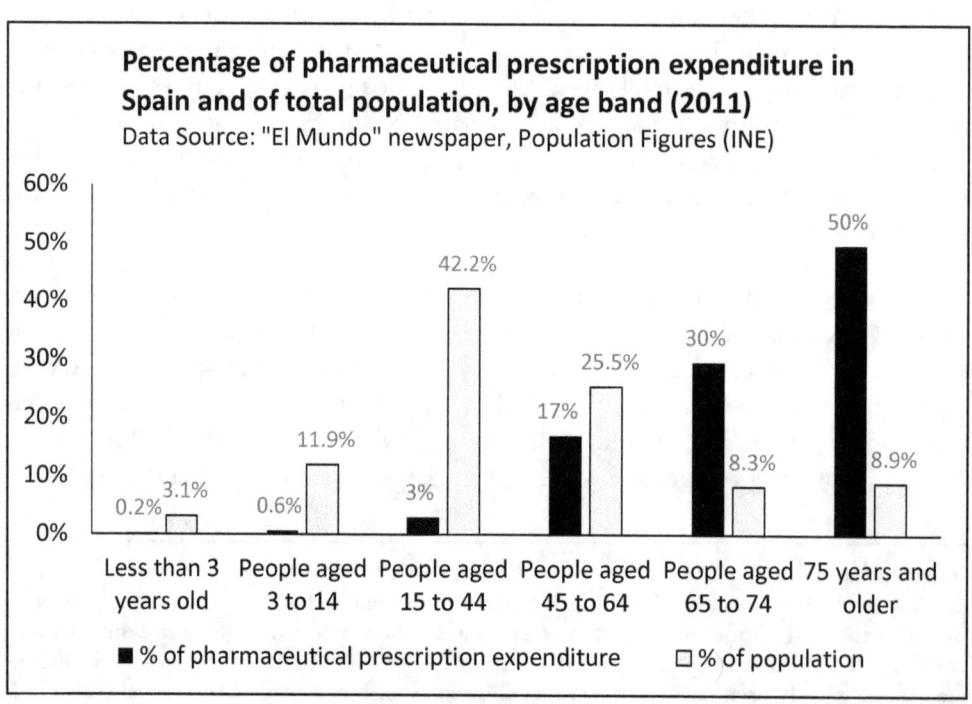

In line with their increased aging, countries tend to allocate a growing percentage of the wealth they produce to healthcare spending. On average, the OECD countries spent 9% of their GDP on healthcare needs in 2015, reaching almost 17% in the US that year and 10% in Western Europe. In the 25 years from 1990 to 2015, the share of healthcare spending in relation to GDP has grown substantially, around 50% in developed OECD countries, from an average of about 6% of GDP to 9%, particularly in some countries, as shown in the following graph for the period 1990-2015 in the OECD countries—tremendous loss of wealth and a growing burden for the taxpayer and the productive economy!

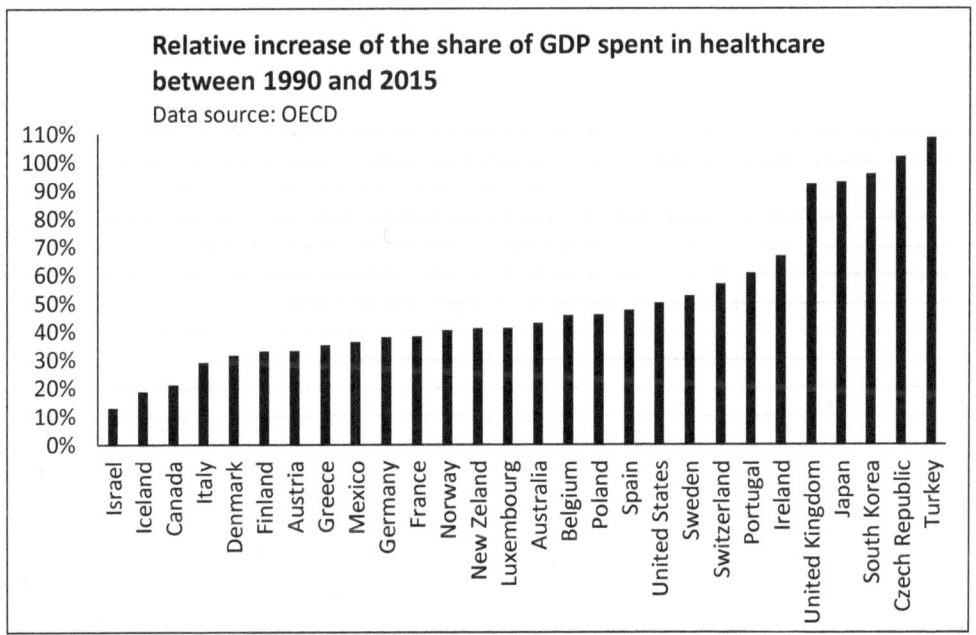

Beyond the cost of medical care for the elderly, the number of dependent people, who are unable to take care of themselves in whole or in part, whether due to physical impairment or mental deterioration, is also growing exponentially in aging countries that are in the process of becoming even older in the future. This will result in either neglecting these people or incurring a tremendous expense for their long-term care, or both.

In particular, the number of people with nervous/brain-damaging illnesses, including Alzheimer's and Parkinson's, has been increasing tremendously in the last decades, as shown in the graph below, which displays the evolution between 1992 and 2012 of the leading causes of death in Spain. What happened in other developed and aging nations is very similar.

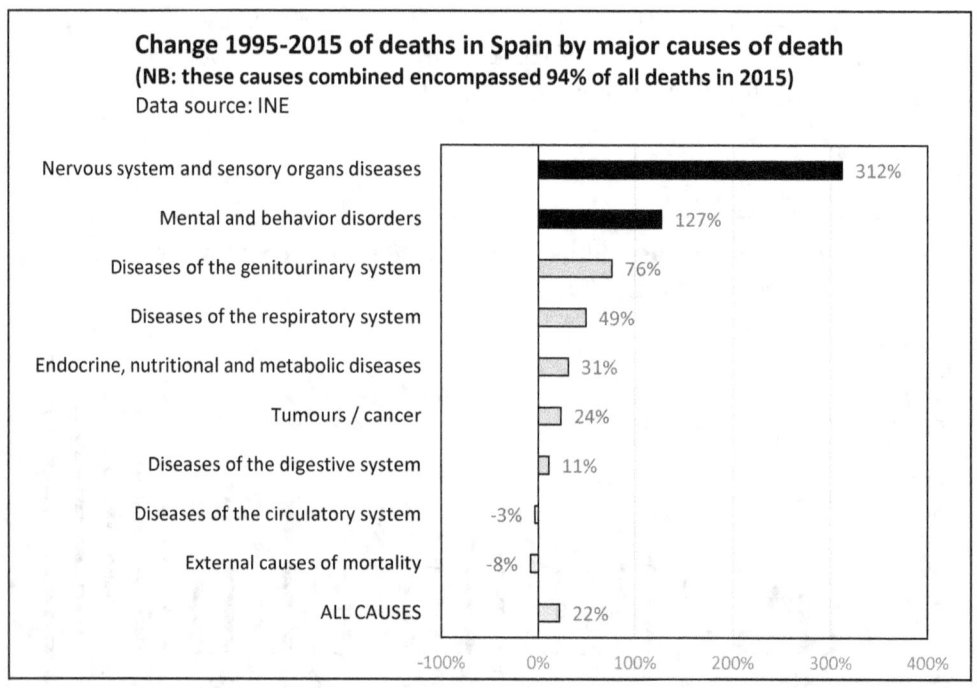

Change 1995-2015 of deaths in Spain by major causes of death
(NB: these causes combined encompassed 94% of all deaths in 2015)
Data source: INE

Nervous system and sensory organs diseases	312%
Mental and behavior disorders	127%
Diseases of the genitourinary system	76%
Diseases of the respiratory system	49%
Endocrine, nutritional and metabolic diseases	31%
Tumours / cancer	24%
Diseases of the digestive system	11%
Diseases of the circulatory system	-3%
External causes of mortality	-8%
ALL CAUSES	22%

In the United States, the number of deaths due to Alzheimer's disease—in about 70% of cases, women—has grown by about 90% between 1999 and 2013 and the number of deaths from Parkinson's disease, more than 70%. Treating people afflicted with these types of disease, especially when they are in the more advanced stages of it, is very expensive. According to the Alzheimer's Association of the United States, in the country of Uncle Sam, about 5 million people suffer from this terrible ailment. It is projected that, if there are no medical advances to prevent it, there will be 15 million cases of Alzheimer's in 2050. One-third of Americans over 85, and one in nine aged 65 or older, currently suffer from Alzheimer's disease in the United States. According to the association, caring for Alzheimer's patients and other dementia costs US taxpayers a total of $236 billion a year, 1.5% of the country's GDP, equivalent to more than $32,000 a year per Alzheimer's patient, between medical expenses and long-term care.

In order to address these challenges, governments and public administrations of various countries are trying to contain the increase in public spending on pensions, healthcare, and dependent care that result from this demographic evolution, trying to make private pension systems, private healthcare, health and public care services copayments, instead of the State, responsible for a growing part of the cost. They also seek to make the public system more sustainable through a slower deterioration in the ratio between retirees and active people. To this end, in addition to helping the economy create more jobs, and preferably high value-added jobs (which generate the most tax revenue for governments), they are delaying the retirement age, and in some cases, are making it easier for retirees to work—and as a result, pay more taxes—which is very logical, because we now reach 60/70/80 years in much better average health than we did 50 or 100 years ago, and in this day and age there is a much higher percentage of workers who do not perform manual/physically hard work, instead participating in information and service management activities that can be performed even when one no longer has the physical stamina of a 20-50 year-old.

In the United States and Italy, the theoretical retirement age is already 66 years, one more than the traditional 65, and in Norway is set at 67 years, as in the case of Israeli men. In other European countries, such as Germany, Denmark, Spain, France, Ireland, Holland, or Poland, the retirement age is gradually increasing, or will in a few years until it reaches 67 in the next decade, and 68 in Ireland. In the countries where the age is still under 65, the trend is to raise it to 65. In the United Kingdom, it is expected to reach 68 years before 2046. It is also expected that the retirement age will rise above 65 in emerging countries such as Mexico or Morocco, and that it will approach 65 in other countries where retirement occurs at a younger age. Furthermore, in many countries, women have or have had a lower retirement age than men, something that does not make sense considering their longer life expectancy. The trend is now for the retirement age for both sexes to become equal through increases in the retirement age for women. One of the ideas being tossed around, for implementation in a decade or two, in countries like Denmark, which I heard during a lecture in Madrid in 2015 from a Danish expert on the subject, would be for people to retire when their remaining life expectancy is 15 years. Such a measure, as is occurring nowadays, given that the theoretical retirement age is the same for all—with the exception of professions that seriously impact health, such as mining—would favor those who want to retire and are in better-than-average health or have a better genetic background with respect to aging effects. This is already the case between men and women. As men's life expectancy is lower, at an equal retirement age, on average, female pensioners receive their retirement pension for 4 to 6 more years.

In spite of the above, although the delay in the legal and effective retirement age seems unavoidable, because of the negative impact on a State's financial health that increased expense in retirement pensions would cause, if these actions were not taken and because we are in increasingly better health at any age, particularly between 65 and 75, this measure is not without drawbacks, since:

1. There are some jobs in which the years "do not weigh" much and sometimes even carry weight in a good way, such as intellectual occupations, true. But there are many others where physical deterioration and loss of vigor make a strong dent in people, even in this day and age, and with an improved quality of life, especially those occupations intense in physical wear/stress/physical and mental speed/physical skills, etc.

2. Much of the workforce, in the last years of their working life, is looking forward to retirement. Employers wish that many of their senior employees would retire, as they are people who earn (a lot) more than younger workers in similar positions, but the motivation of most employees tends to stagnate or drop from 50 years-old on or so, unless they continue to climb the ladder, are given challenging responsibilities, or are people with a greater personal motivation and/or have well-established incentives, linked to their productivity.

Drop in value of assets and properties: wealth in stocks and real estate could fall 50% to 75% due to the demographic winter

Most of the market value of "re-sellable" assets and properties, such as stocks or real estate, derives from their future price expectations (from 50% to 80% of their value in general)[45]. Where there are fewer people and fewer potential buyers

---

[45] The difference between the market value of a company and its net book value (its assets or total equity, less its debts and contingencies), also called intangible capital or goodwill, is the present value of all the expected profits that the company will earn in the future. The better the expectations, the greater the goodwill. For example, Apple, the company with the highest stock market value in the world, at the closing of the market on August 10, 2016, when we were writing these lines, was worth 581.9 billion dollars, but its net equity was less than 25% of that amount, "only" 126.4 billion dollars. This means that investors estimated its "future" aggregate value to be 581,950 - 126,400 million = 455,550 million dollars. If Apple's business stopped generating profits, its market value would approach its net book value, which would result in a drop in value of more than 75%. Moreover, if it had recurring losses, it would end up with a value less than its net equity, because expectations would be that Apple would have less and less equity, not more. Something similar can be said about real estate. The value of houses and buildings in general is the sum of the value of the land on which they are built and of the construction itself. While the latter can be assessed with some objectivity using the cost of the materials and the cost of the construction itself, the value of the land depends almost exclusively

for these assets, regardless of their own evolution or quality, they will tend to become less valuable, since when there is a lot of demand for an asset or property, its selling price to a new owner is greater than when demand is scarce. In particular, by the end of August 2016, at least two-thirds[46] of the aggregate value of the 500 largest publicly traded US companies, whose aggregate performance forms the Standard & Poor's stock index, was derived from their expectations of future profits. Without these expectations, some $12 billion of wealth in the hands of all kinds of people and economic agents, from the US and around the world, would evaporate: large fortunes, small and medium investors, pension funds and others, companies, non-profit organizations, governments, etc.

A similar phenomenon happens with the value of houses and properties. If many houses become empty in a neighborhood whose population is decreasing, and the facades of buildings are covered with "for sale" signs, the prices of those homes will be worth less and less, and a growing fraction of them won't be sold except through tremendous price reductions. In principle, this is good for those who need a home, as properties become more affordable—although if the building/neighborhood in which they want to buy their property is becoming emptier, living in that neighborhood or building is not a very desirable prospect, as was already mentioned—but for the economy, as a whole, it has an effect similar to that of the declining stock market values in destroying the wealth of families and businesses: very negative. Moreover, whoever buys a cheap home because of these depressed values will also, in the long run, become a victim of the same circumstance, as their property will tend to depreciate. It would then seem wise not to buy properties, but to rent them instead, in order to avoid this risk—decisions which would further reduce the possibility of selling these properties at a good price, as the number of potential buyers would be even lower: there would be few buyers due to the decline in population and even fewer due to the remaining people interested in renting, rather than buying, these properties. Along these lines, the report titled "Ageing and asset prices" by Elöd Takáts of the BIS (Bank for International Settlements, headquartered in Basel, Switzerland) published in August 2010 forecasted enormously negative impacts due to demographic declines on the

---

on the expectations that in the future it will cost, more or less, depending on the expected demand for it. What are the houses and the land worth in a village that is being abandoned? They tend to be worthless. When the village was inhabited, they were worth much more. Gold coins in the desert are not worth anything either.

[46] We say "at least," because it is actually more than two-thirds, since accounting or "book" value of many companies in the US and other countries also includes intangible and goodwill items—for example, through the acquisition of other companies acquired at a premium over their net book value—which may or may not materialize. For example, research and development expenses for new products and services that have been "activated" are included in the accounting assets of the company, as if they were a cash amount deposited in a bank.

average real value of real estate, in aging countries with a declining population. This report, for instance, projected, in constant money, a 75% drop in the average value of housing and other real estate between 2010 and 2050 in Germany and Spain, through a *ceteris paribus* analysis and accounting only for the effect of the demographic winter. In Portugal, the expected drop was over 80% and in Italy, just over 70%[47]. Other countries, with a demographic profile somewhat less mediocre, would not fare as badly. In Belgium, France, and Finland, according to that study, houses would "only" fall by between 40% and just under 50% by 2050.

Is this drop in the price of assets and property caused by a declining demography good or bad? Although few things are entirely black or white, in our opinion, and using the metaphor of colors, we would be faced with a phenomenon which would be dark gray, with a tendency to increasingly approach black. In general, in structurally downward price markets (experiencing deflation), although in the short-term buyers tend to gain, in the long run, the adage which says that "Where there is no flour, everything is sadness" (Poverty breeds discontent) is fulfilled. The exception to this rule are those markets in which sellers and producers can offset falling sales prices with increases in the volume of sales transactions and/or reductions in production costs for those goods or services[48].

Apart from the obvious damage to millions of people through the reduction in value of their assets in societies where a majority of adults—or a very large majority—has some property(ies) of not insignificant value (their house; shares of

---

[47] Of course, as the author of the report pointed out, demography is not the only relevant factor explaining the evolution of real estate prices, but it is one of the fundamental factors, as it is one of the main drivers of demand (more/fewer people, more/fewer demand), and even of supply. For example, when a society ages, if the house itself is the main asset owned by retired people, as it is in Spain, and they want to sell it to convert it in cash they can use to live better in the final stage of their lives, house prices could tend to fall additionally, as there would be fewer buyers (fewer young people and people in general) and more sellers (retirees). A similar comment can be made about the stock market: shares may suffer in the future from structural depreciation due to the need for many retirees to sell them.

[48] An example of structural and at the same time virtuous price deflation is that of the telephone service, which has become cheaper and cheaper for about a century, a phenomenon that has allowed the whole population to access it in economically viable terms for both users and telecommunications operators. The key has been that, thanks to the increase in call volumes and the drop in the cost of providing these calls, telephone operators have been able to offset the drop in sales prices. This is more likely to happen in goods and services with a high technological component than in more "classic" industries, such as housing and a host of "traditional" goods and services, where it is more difficult to incorporate revolutionary technological elements or systems that multiply the productivity of those who generate or provide these goods and services, unlike what happened, for example, in the automobile industry with the help of robots, in agriculture with the introduction of mechanized machinery, or in information management services with the use of computers and automated databases.

companies in the stock market or shares in mutual funds; businesses; in more than a few cases, second homes, art collections, etc.), that destruction of capital also has depressive effects for the economy as a whole. When everything is going well, as owners of financial wealth or real estate count on these assets, they spend and invest more than if they did not have those assets and they can go into debt using their assets as a guarantee to buy houses, start companies, consume, etc. These actions move the economy and create jobs, through a phenomenon that economists call the "wealth effect." If expectations of economic growth and future profits fade or disappear, this wealth based on expectations is reduced or disappears. This happens temporarily when the economy enters a recession or crisis. With the demographic winter, the real threat is that this begins to occur structurally.

Geopolitical risks from the demographic suicide

At the international level, a country or geographic region with a demographic evolution worse than its neighbors and/or those with which it openly or partially competes loses strength—either for the purpose of peaceful negotiations or for the purposes of war—and loses its relative position with respect to these other countries, all other factors being equal.

Sic transit European glory

Europe, as a whole, is a textbook case. Although still a very rich area of the planet, since the mid-twentieth century, its economic and political global weight has been decreasing in parallel with the decrease in the number of human beings living in Europe, as a percentage of global population, as can be seen on the following graph.

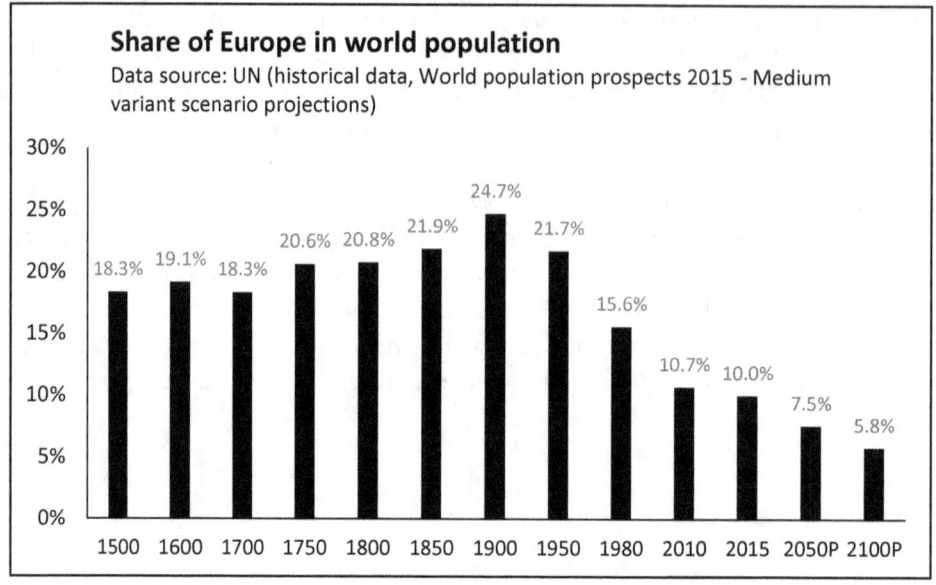

In the fifteenth to the seventeenth centuries, there were four major poles in the world, considered developed in those days, excluding significant but less important states like Japan: the Chinese Empire, the Turkish Empire, the Mughal Empire in India (all three Asiatic empires, especially the first and third), and Europe. Europe was not a unified country—it has never been a single country, although the European Union, and especially the Eurozone, bears some characteristics of a country—but, taken together, consisted of a large number of nations and states with a high degree of similarity in religious and moral values, institutional organizations, ethnic composition, and with important commercial, human, and information flows among them. Europe had, in the fifteenth century, a noticeably lower population than the other three great developed empires/human poles put together. Moreover, each of the major Western European countries that developed large overseas colonial empires (Spain/Castile, the United Kingdom/England, France, Portugal, the Netherlands, Belgium, the future Germany, etc.) had a much lower population, taken individually, than any of the other three great empires. Russia, in turn, managed to dominate the entire northern part of Asia and a large fraction of its central lands. Between the fifteenth and mid-nineteenth centuries, the total European population was about three times smaller than that of Asia. Despite this demographic inferiority and its lack of political unity—quite the opposite, the intra-European belligerent quarrels were commonplace—since the end of the fifteenth century and especially since the sixteenth century, Europeans dominated the world and transformed it forever through their colonial expansion in America, Africa, Asia, and Oceania. In economic terms, the fact that they could achieve so much with so few people can be explained because their economic productivity and military effectiveness were far superior to the rest of the world, thanks to their scientific-technological advances and developments—as well as in all branches of knowledge and thinking—in the manner they carried out productive and commercial activities, and in the political-legal-institutional arena. These advances and developments far outweighed the numerical inferiority of Europe in relation to the great Asian empires and, specifically, of each of the European countries. At the height of its power, in the so-called "Belle Époque," towards the beginning of the 20th century, the weight of the European population in the world also reached its peak.

Since the mid-twentieth century, and especially since the final decades of that century, the political and economic weight of Europe in the world has fallen progressively, through the combination of two major factors, not including, since the last third of the nineteenth century, the outstanding development at all levels and the weight in the world of the North-American "great son" of Europe, the US:

✓ The average productivity of the once called "Third World" countries, now called "emerging" countries, tends to approach that of the developed countries by gradually incorporating new technological advances and modern production processes and because their populations are massively becoming literate. With the convergence in productivity, the number of people who live in each country, in relation to the population of its potential rivals, has, once again, the importance it used to have in the medieval and ancient world[49]. Comte's maxim that "demography is destiny," partially suspended for some time when Europe—and then the US and Japan—took a great leap forward in economic productivity and military efficiency, while the rest of the world had not yet followed, is once again quantitatively true.

✓ The human weight of Europe in the world keeps falling, and even more so when we look at future adults, that is, the children and youth. If, from 1950 to 2015, Europe has lost half its weight in the whole of humanity, when we look at the future humanity, that is, children, young people, and young adults, we see an even greater reduction of the weight of Europe: Europeans under 30 were in 2015 a third of what they were in 1950 in relation to world totals.

---

[49] This idea was developed after reading this basic statement in the great book "Cambio de era" (change of era) by Josep Piqué, who was a minister in Spanish governments several times, business manager and entrepreneur, and the writer of a foreword for this book: in this day and age, through the generalization of the use of technologies and production techniques, the workers' productivity of the various nations of the world tends to converge, following centuries where it was greatly superior in Europe and the United States, and allowed the western countries to dominate/lead the world, even though their population was a minority as a fraction of the whole of humanity. Given a similar productivity per person, the number of inhabitants of each country once again has a great, and in many cases, decisive, weight in international relations.

Because of its undesirable world leadership in the demographic winter, Europe tends to become irrelevant in the world. Let us see some additional examples that illustrate this statement.

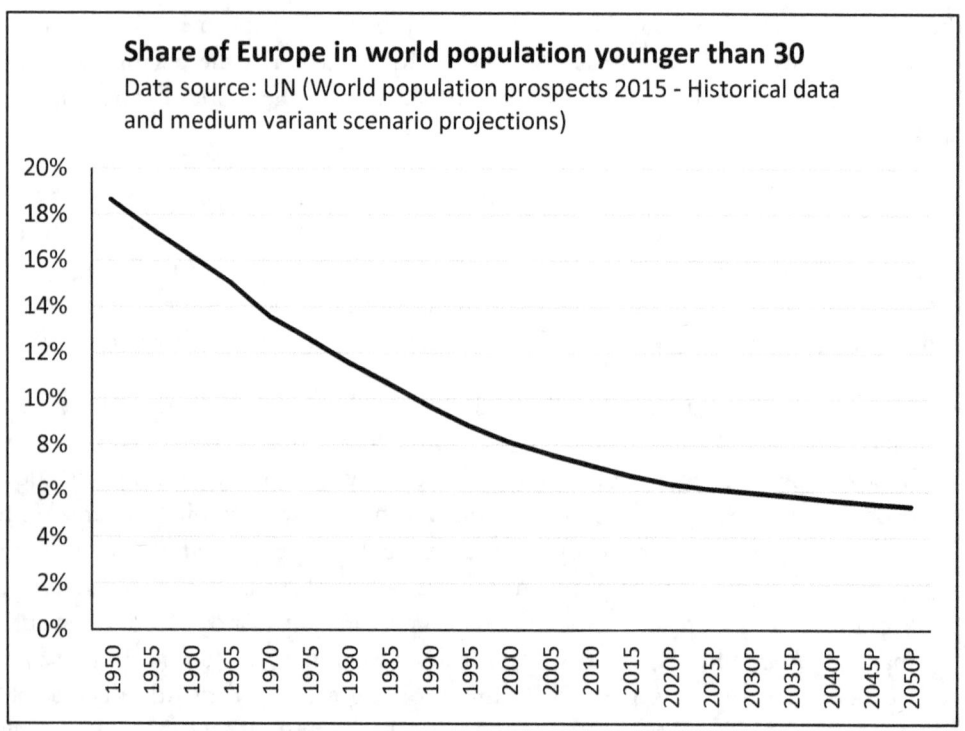

Share of Europe in world population younger than 30
Data source: UN (World population prospects 2015 - Historical data and medium variant scenario projections)

The last Franco-German wars and demography

"There are twenty million Germans too many!"
Georges Clemenceau, French President, after World War I

Due to its much greater fertility between the second half of the nineteenth century and the Second World War, Germany had a demographic strength far superior to that of its French neighbor, whom it defeated in the Franco-Prussian war of 1870-1871, would have defeated in 1914 -1918 if not for Anglo-American support, and outright defeated in 1939-1940, despite British support. The following graph shows how the population of both countries evolved between 1867—a few years before the Franco-Prussian war, when both countries had comparable population—and 1939. It is worth noting, for example, that between 1900 and 1914, the French population grew by one million, while Germany's grew by 12 million.

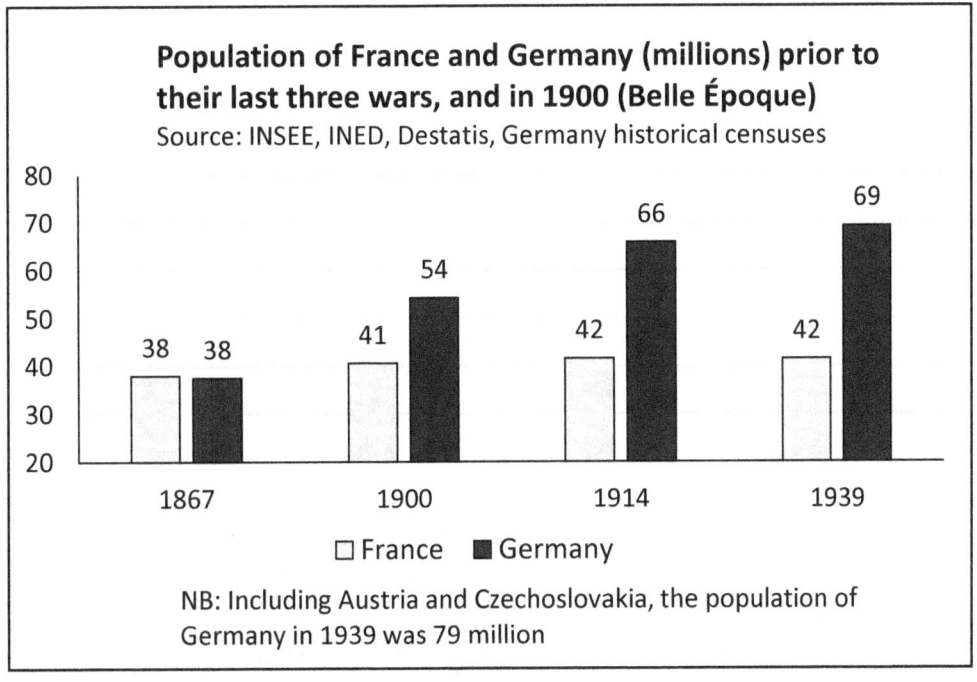

Population of France and Germany (millions) prior to their last three wars, and in 1900 (Belle Époque)

Source: INSEE, INED, Destatis, Germany historical censuses

☐ France ■ Germany

NB: Including Austria and Czechoslovakia, the population of Germany in 1939 was 79 million

In the 21st century, the tables turn: France will surpass Germany in population in two to three decades (and so will the United Kingdom)

If, since the late nineteenth century, Germany has had a higher number of inhabitants than France, with the gap growing for many decades, the current population numbers, birth rates, and aging in both countries are turning things around. If these trends do not change, according to Eurostat projections, in a few decades—between 2040 and 2045, assuming both countries will have similar migratory flows—Germany will have a smaller population than France, given the higher Gallic birth rate and the milder degree of aging of its population. With this "sorpasso" (overtaking), Germany will lose its status as the most populous country among those that currently form the European Union, something that would happen before 2020 if Turkey were to become a member of the European Union. According to these projections, the United Kingdom will also outnumber Germany, only a few years after France will, before 2050. Several years before, by 2033, according to our estimates, also based on projections by Eurostat, France and the United Kingdom will each have more inhabitants under the age of 65 than Germany: children, young people, and working-age people combined.

The German demographic decline, if the fertility rates of the main European countries do not change, or if Germany does not receive many more foreign immigrants—with the consequent integration challenges a massive immigration would imply—would be unstoppable, both in absolute numbers as well as in relation to the other large countries of Europe, a phenomenon which would be reflected in their relative power in Europe, to the detriment of Germany.

Among the large European countries, Italy—which for many years had a population similar to that of France and the United Kingdom and therefore a similar representation in key European institutions such as the European Parliament—, due to its persistently low birth rate, will also suffer a relentless population decline, and correspondingly, a decline of its political-economic weight in Europe. The fifth country by population of the European Union (Spain), as well as the sixth (Poland), will experience declines in population in the 21st century, and consequently of political weight in Europe, in line with those of Germany and Italy.

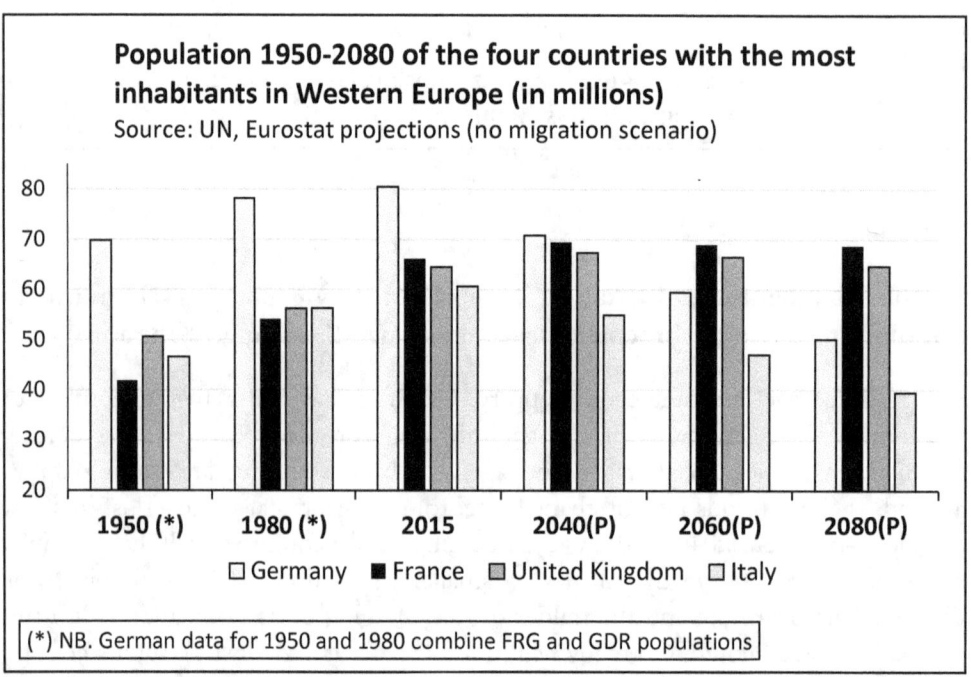

Population 1950-2080 of the four countries with the most inhabitants in Western Europe (in millions)
Source: UN, Eurostat projections (no migration scenario)

□ Germany ■ France ▨ United Kingdom □ Italy

(*) NB. German data for 1950 and 1980 combine FRG and GDR populations

Within countries, some regions/provinces lose political and economic weight relative to others, because of their demography

Without as much drama as between countries, something similar is occurring within them: areas and regions with greater demographic dynamism (due to higher birth rates and to greater domestic and foreign immigration) gradually gain internal weight compared to those with less dynamism. For example, in the United States, the change in the demographically based electoral weight of the major States, between 1960, when John Kennedy was elected President, and 2016, when Donald Trump was elected, has been tremendous. The relative weight of California and New York has been reversed during that interval, in favor of the former. New York has gone from being the most populous state and having the most votes, to sharing third place with Florida, one of the biggest winners in political weight because of its demography. In 1960, eighteen US states were more populous than Florida. In 2016, only California and Texas had a larger population. In 1960, Texas was the sixth state in number of electoral votes. In 2016, it was the second. The decline of other large Eastern states, or of the Northern and Midwest industrial center, such as Pennsylvania, Illinois, Ohio, and Michigan, has also been notable in the past 56 years. At the other end of the spectrum, Nevada's electoral representation has doubled since 1960. Arizona has seen its share multiplied by 2.75. The home of the unparalleled Grand Canyon of Colorado is the state that has seen the largest increase in its share of electoral weight since 1960, after Florida, whose electoral representation has been multiplied by 2.9 since then.

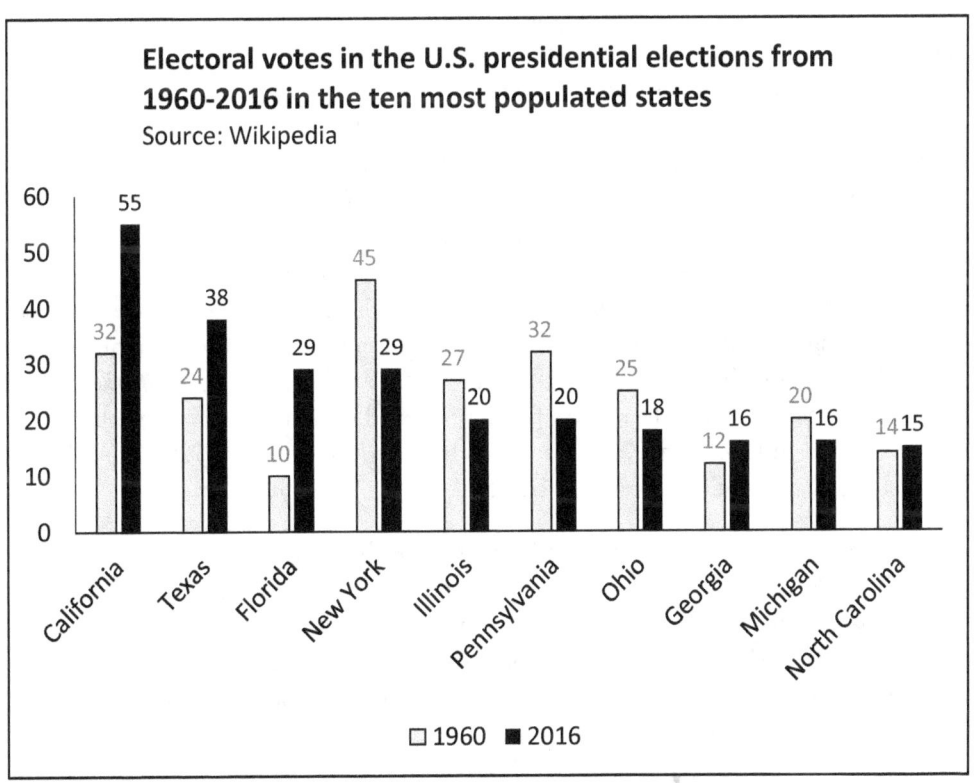

In Spain, Madrid, the provinces of the Mediterranean coast—with the exception of those of Catalonia, overall stable in this respect—and of the South, the Balearic Islands and the Canary Islands, have gained political-demographic weight for about 40 years relative to the rest of the country, whose demographic and national political weight is in constant decline. In Germany, the more prosperous and demographically healthier states in the south, such as Bavaria or Baden-Württemberg, are gaining weight in their nation. More than half of all the population growth of Germany since 1960 (West + East) is due to those two *länder*.

Spain, Morocco, Ceuta and Melilla

Spain will continually lose strength against its southern neighbor, Morocco, in the next 20 to 30 years, due to demography, *ceteris paribus*. In 1950, Spain had more than three times the population of Morocco, a country then divided into a French protectorate and a Spanish protectorate. By 2015, the Spanish population was only one third higher than that of Morocco and was already smaller among those under 30. Morocco has been claiming Ceuta and Melilla, two Spanish cities, as its own for more than 500 years, when there was no Moroccan state. In the last 40 years, due to the strong Moroccan population immigration that both cities have had and the higher birth rate of these immigrants, the Maghrebi population of Ceuta and Melilla has gone from being a clear minority to being about half of the total population and a large majority among the new generations. In other words, in the future, the immense majority of the population of Ceuta and Melilla will be of Maghreb-Muslim roots, and with it, the annexationist claims of Morocco on these two cities could be easier than ever. The historic precedent of Kosovo is very clear. Historically, Kosovo was the cradle of the Serbian nation, but in the second half of the twentieth century, Albanian-Kosovars—Muslims in Kosovo—reached an overwhelming majority based on a continued immigration and greater birth rates than ethnic Serbs. Finally, when Albanian-Kosovars reached about 90% of the population, they managed to secede from Serbia. The international community did not accept the independence of Kosovo at first. In the end, *realpolitik* prevails and "de facto" situations like this usually end up becoming "de jure."

On the other hand, even if there were no changes in the sovereignty of a particular territory, it is evident that, for example, for a person from Melilla of European-Christian roots, living in his or her city would not be the same if there was a 70%-80% Maghrebi-Muslim population compared with traditional Melilla, a city with a mostly Hispano-Christian cultural and ethnic background, along with a significant population of Hebrew roots.

From the US-Soviet bipolar world to the great (demographic) weakness of Russia and the Chinese hegemony in the making, not to mention India

The most globally significant case of geopolitical weakness due to demography is probably Russia, which has led its authorities to take birth rate matters very seriously in recent years. The largest country on Earth, which has very long borders to protect, among whose neighbors is the Chinese giant—with whom it maintains territorial disputes on certain borders—is becoming empty and counts less and less in relation not only with the US, but with its Chinese neighbor especially. The "Russian bear" can no longer offset, through its former economic-technological superiority in Asia, its inferiority in population with respect to China. Between 1991 and 2011, thirteen million fewer people were born than died in Russia. By size, Russia could fit Germany forty-eight times, but has less than twice as many people and a lower GDP than that of Germany. While Russia is almost twice as big as China or the US, in 2015, there was only one Russian for every 9.6 Chinese or every 2.2 Americans. In 1960, the year I was born, in the midst of the Cold War, the geopolitical power of the Soviet Union, near its peak—although it had another name and a different internal political regime, from a geopolitical standpoint, it was essentially the old Russia—fewer people lived in the United States than in Great Russia (the current Russian republic as such, and the rest of the Soviet republics). For its part, in 1960, China had three times the population of the Soviet Union, and almost 3.5 times that of the United States, but it was a country so behind[50] that, despite its immense human mass, did not pose a real threat to its Russian neighbor—although on occasion there were sparks of war between the two countries, as in the Sino-Soviet border conflict on the Ussuri River in 1969—let alone to the United States. Things are now very different, as the combination of a demographic weakness—a loss by the country with its capital in Moscow of half of its actual population through the dissolution of the Soviet Union, as well as further population losses since then because of its relatively low birth rate and relatively high mortality rate—, and the slower economic growth in the last decades of Russia relative to the US, and above all, vis-a-vis China, is radically disturbing the world's balance of power and emphasizing Russia's weakness against China.

---

[50] In the late 1980s, in a visit of top-level Chinese rulers to Spain, both sides were stunned to exchange economic data and find that China's total electric power generation capacity, with more than 1 billion inhabitants at the time, was half that of Spain, which had a little less than 39 million inhabitants and a significant level of development, but did not reach the levels of the United States or the richest countries of Western Europe. The post-Maoist China had about 50 times less Kwh per capita than a country like Spain, which was developed but is still somewhat behind in wealth per person from the G-7 countries and the Scandinavian or Benelux countries! Since then, in barely 30 years, much water has flowed under the bridge.

Dato source: OECD, UN (World Population Prospects 2015)	Population in 1960 (millions)	Population in 2015 (millions)	GDP in 2014 - trillions USD PPP (Purchasing Power Parity)	GDP per capita 2014-2015 (thousands USD PPP) (2)	Apparent per capita productivity of active age population (3) in thousands USD PPP (2)
Russia	120	143	3.4	23.7	33.9
Soviet Union (1)	214	292	N/A	N/A	N/A
United States	186	322	17.3	53.8	81.1
China	644	1,376	18.0	13.1	17.9

(1) In 2015, this number combines the Russian population and the people living in other former Soviet Union republics
(2) Per capita figures for GDP and productivity are an estimate, since GDP numbers are from 2014, and population is from 2015
(3) This is not actual productivity per worker, since it has been calculated inclusding all working age people, employed or not (students, housewives, sub-65 retirees...). It also includes working people aged over 65. In any case, this ratio helps to quantify the economic output that each country actually obtains in average per person tehoretically aged-suited to work.

Because of demography, the US is facing challenges in the medium and long term against China, with the growth in Chinese productivity, as the country continues to develop. Since 2014, China has been producing more total GDP, in purchasing power parity, than the US, and the gap continues to increase. Since the seeming productivity of the Chinese working age population is still only one-fifth that of the United States, or slightly more (calculated using the purchasing power parity GDP from 2014, and with UN population data for 2015), and is closing in on that of the Yankee giant, if nothing substantial changes, in one or two decades, the United States will become second-best in terms of economic size with respect to China. If the productivity of China's working-age population reaches only 65% that of the Yankees—the current level of Spain, a rich, but not the richest, country, in relation to the US—which it will most likely reach in not too many years, the Chinese GDP will then be three times the GDP of Uncle Sam's country. The only good news for the Americans on this issue is that China is forecasted to experience a much worse demographic evolution than the United States (by population loss and aging), but given the huge differences in population size between the two countries, and the slow movement of demography, the United States will only mitigate a minor part of its growing economic inferiority to China in the long-term as a result.

Russia's current demographic-economic imbalance vis-a-vis China, however—with which it shares more than 3,600 km of border—and the even greater imbalance it will face as the productivities of both countries level more, makes the US imbalance with China pale by comparison, and can have far worse consequences for Moscow in its disputes with Beijing, because of its stratospheric order of magnitude and its geographical proximity. By 2014-2015, China already had a GDP that was more than five times that of Russia, with an apparent productivity of its working population only half that of Russia. The Chinese working age population is ten times the Russian's. With just the Chinese and Russian productivity being the same, the Russian economy would be one-tenth that of the Chinese.

In the next decades, as China achieves a military power in line with the size of its economy, the US world hegemony of the last 70 years and the security of Russia will face more and more challenges. Based on demographic projections on its economic production, China will have a clearly dominant position in the world between 2020 and 2040-2050, when India is forecasted to take over as the world's leading economic power, due to the demographic suicide in China, whose negative effects on its economy will become quite noticeable around 2020-2025 and will be very intense starting around 2035-2040. According to the UN, India will be the most populous country on Earth starting in 2022, ahead of China. It is already the most populated among people under 60, and by far, among those under 40. In 2009, the last year for which we had complete data on the Indian economy, its productivity per active person was about half of China's. If India were able to approach the Chinese level of development, it would become the world's leading economic power in the second half of the twenty-first century. Regardless, India seems very likely to surpass the United States in GDP between 2030 and 2050. Its active age population is already almost four times that of the US, and by the middle of the century it will be almost five times, according to UN population projections. Once again, demography seems to be one of the keys to destiny in the 21st century!

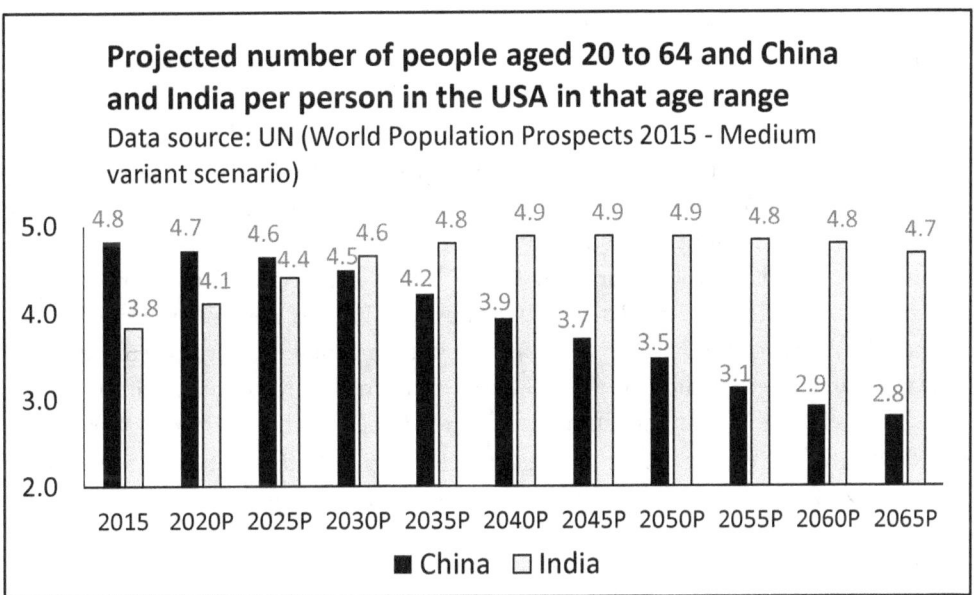

Israel, a country that is unique, as well, in fertility and demography

Israel is a unique country in many ways. In the matters of interest in this book, it is the only Western/fully developed nation with a birth rate clearly above the replacement level, at just over three children per woman (3.08 in 2014, according to the Israel Central Bureau of Statistics). Therefore, its population is much younger, on average, than that of any other Western country. The median age of the Israeli population was 30 years in 2015, according to the UN. By comparison, in the European Union, median age was 42 years in 2015, and it was 38 in the US.

Although the fertility rates of non-ultra-Orthodox Jewish Israelis is enviable by contemporary Western standards, Israel manages to surpass, on average, the 3 children per woman thanks to ultra-orthodox Jews (Haredim), whose birth rate is so high they are currently doubling in number approximately every 15 years, a rate that will lead to a ten-fold increase every 50 years. In 2009, for example, Haredim were estimated to have 6.2 to 6.5 children per woman[51], compared to 2.4 for non-Haredi Jews. Similarly, Arabs living in Israel, who account for about 20% of the population, have a higher birth rate than non-Haredi Jewish Israelis, although their birth rate is experiencing a significant downward trend. In 2014, non-Haredi Jewish Israelis still represented 65% of the Israeli population, a declining percentage, due to greater fertility of the Haredi Israelis and, to a lesser extent, the (still) higher birth rates of Israeli Arabs compared to those of unorthodox Jewish Israelis.

Thanks to this high fertility, as well as the immigrant, and predominantly Jewish, population that continues to move to Israel, the country manages to maintain a demographic balance with its potentially hostile Arab neighbors. Fortunately, Israel's relations with some of their neighbors, such as Egypt and Jordan, have been mostly peaceful and cooperative for several decades. Since the Six-Day War (1967), the combined population of Egypt, Jordan, Lebanon, Syria, and the Palestinian territories has been about 16 times that of Israel's. The disproportion is considerable, but it does not increase in relative terms, something directionally good for the security of Israel. That's the good "demography" news for the Hebrew state, as it relates to its security. The bad news would be that the Haredi Jews, who traditionally refuse to perform military service, represent a growing percentage of the population—and an even faster growing fraction of the Jewish Israelis—and that the number of Arab Israelis, who are exempt from the mandatory military service, is also growing more rapidly than the number of unorthodox Jews in Israel. As a result, currently only about 50% of Israeli babies are children of non-Haredi Jews, a fact which could have implications for Israel's security in the future. It also isn't ideal for the current and future security of Israel that the populations of its Arab neighbors and that of the Palestinian territories are significantly younger than the Israeli population, with the following median age in 2015, according to the UN, being: 19.3 years in Palestinian territories; 20.8 in Syria;

---

[51] It was 6.2 according to the Myers-JDC-Brookdale Institute, a non-profit organization created by the Israeli government and the American Jewish Joint Distribution Committee, while the Israel Central Bureau of Statistics estimate was 6.5 children per Haredi woman in 2009.

22.5 in Jordan; 24.7 in Egypt; 28.5 in Lebanon. Finally, it is worth mentioning some impressive demographic numbers from Egypt, that should keep Israel up at night: the Egyptian population, more than eleven times the Israeli population in 2015, grows at such a rate that the country of the pharaohs adds "one new Israel," in population, every 4 or 5 years (9 million additional Egyptians from 2010 to 2015, compared to a Israeli population in 2015 of just over 8 million people). On the other hand, 98% of the more than 90 million Egyptians live in only about 35,000 square kilometers, along the fertile banks of the Nile, a strip of land with a very high population density.

As for the Gaza Strip, it is not surprising that it is a human powder keg if we combine the structural dispute it has with Israel with its demographic evolution: a very young population, which increases in size at a rate that indicates doubling itself every 25 years—because of its high birth rate of 4.2 children per woman in 2014, with a huge population density, which logically, if nothing changes, will also double every 25 years, a rate that will supposedly multiply by sixteen in a century.

Risks arising from the growing presence of immigrant populations in Western countries that are in the process of demographic suicide

"One day, millions of men will leave the Southern Hemisphere to go to the Northern Hemisphere. And they will not go there as friends. Because they will go there to conquer it. And they will conquer it with their sons. The wombs of our women will give us victory."

(**Houari Boumedienne**, President of Algeria, in 1974, at the United Nations)

"I wish French society would not even try to integrate the Moroccans. They will never integrate. [...] Integration is possible between Europeans, because the cultural fabric is the same. [...] But here we are talking about another continent, another religion. [...] They will be bad Frenchmen. They will never be 100% French."

(**Hassan II**, King of Morocco, in 1993, during a conversation with the journalist Anne Sinclair, broadcast on the French TV channel TF1)

One of the obvious ways to combat demographic decline—the favorite of most politicians in the West, though not in Japan—is to resort to foreign immigration.

When the arrival of foreign labor helps a country grow its economy and/or address certain specific needs, such as dependent care (babies, the elderly, others), and there are people from other countries ready to emigrate to that country to carry out these tasks, it generally creates a clear basis for a "win-win" situation in economic terms, both for the foreign immigrants and for the country. In addition, as foreign immigrants are usually younger on average than the natives of the host country, they generally have a rejuvenating effect on the resident population. If this arrival and settling of foreigners is well managed and legal, and if they assimilate well—which typically requires, among other things, that the number of immigrants who come each year more or less matches the needs of the host country, that the majority of them have a professional qualification and cultural values that facilitate their integration, and that their main attraction to the host country is not its free public services as a Welfare state, but rather the desire to work there—then all are happy. This is true despite the personal uprooting that their expatriation generates in many immigrants and the sadness that it brings to their relatives and very close friends in their country of origin. Let us not forget that to encourage immigration to the developed country du jour, among other things, is also to foster personal uprooting.

Things are generally less idyllic in this matter. If the main reason for immigration is the decline of the native population due to the demographic winter in the host country, what immigration leads to is a population substitution and a continuous increase in the number of those who have foreign roots that are different than the traditional roots of the majority. History teaches us time and time again that populations of different ethnic-cultural characteristics cohabiting in the same territory can collide. In particular, this can happen when there is a mixture of religious sensitivities that produces conflicts. An extreme case is that of the former Yugoslavia in the 1990s, especially in Bosnia-Hercegovina, Croatia and Kosovo, with bloody wars and criminal massacres where Orthodox Serbians, Catholic Croats, and Muslim Bosnian and Kosovars all alternated between being victims and perpetrators. As I write this book, there is great concern in Western Europe and the United States for the integration of its abundant immigrant Muslim population, especially in the wake of the jihadist attacks of 2015, 2016 and 2017 in countries such as France, Belgium, Germany, UK, the United States, Sweden, Spain…. We do not know if these will remain as relatively low intensity conflicts and isolated terrorist incidents or become something much worse. In Germany, specifically, this concern grew enormously due to the flood of Muslim war refugees and the rosary of incidents, such as rapes and sexual abuses, related to this massive immigration. Incidentally, the decision made in 2015 by the government, headed by Angela Merkel, to welcome many refugees was very controversial because of its evident risks to the internal fabric of Germany, its non-negligible economic cost, and the shockwaves it created in other countries within the European Union—probably contributing, inter alia, to the success of Brexit in the 2016 British referendum. The decision was made for a mixture reasons: humanitarian, wanting to improve the international image of Germany[52], and demographic considerations ("We need foreign manpower to counter the effects of our demographic winter").

In economic terms, in modern welfare states, the consumption/receiving of free public benefits, for the same age group, is much higher among immigrants than among the natives of the host country and the tax revenue generated by foreigners is significantly less. This is logical, since immigrants are, on average, less skilled than the citizens of the developed country, work in jobs that are, on average, lower paying, and, in almost all countries, are unemployed and underemployed in greater proportion than the natives. Another factor contributing to unemployment or underemployment among immigrants is the fact that, for a significant number of immigrants coming from countries with a much lower per capita income, the free benefits they receive without working, or better yet, that are compatible with underemployment in the shadow economy, provide a standard of living far superior to the one they left behind in their homeland, an alternative the natives of the developed country do not consider. Between their greater natural difficulties in the labor market due to language and cultural barriers, and the greater attractiveness that subsidies for those who do not work have on immigrants, their unemployment rates can far exceed that of the nationals, as we saw in Spain, following the "Great Recession" that began in 2007-2008, when unemployment reached very high levels among Spaniards and stratospheric levels among immigrants (nearly 40% at its peak in 2013, reaching 50% and over in some ethnic communities), after the prolonged previous economic boom caused by the real estate bubble. The table in next page shows, for example, the unemployment and shadow employment rates for the largest foreign communities in Spain. If we exclude the Chinese, who have a lower unemployment rate than the Spaniards, the figures for other nationalities are chilling.

---

[52] Because of the devilish Hitler regime, and, previously, of German militarism, decisive in triggering World War I, Germany has been negatively dragged with an international image of a potentially harsh/ruthless country, which is a very harmful antagonist to the virtues that are typically attributed to Germans: laborious; serious; educated; very technically capable and inventive; excellent in manufacturing; having made great scientific, philosophical, and literary contributions to humanity, etc. Therefore, in 2015, when the German government decided to welcome many hundreds of thousands of refugees, mainly Muslim, more than one German leader probably thought that this action could finally end the "Black Legend" that loomed over Germany, certainly an unjust reputation after the defeat of 1945.

Social Security (SS) affiliation, unemployment and undeclared work among nationalities with the greatest presence in Spain in September 2015 Data source: Affiliation by nationality to Seguridad Social by 09/2015 (Spanish Social Security), Employment Statistics (INE - EPA Q3-2015), Municipal Register of Population by 01/2015 (INE)		
Nationality	**% SS affiliated people in population aged between 16 and 64**	**Combined rate of unemployment plus undeclared work (est.)**
Morocco	35%	50%
Foreign, non EU	43%	40%
Pakistan	46%	35%
Foreign, European Union (1)	47%	34%
Latin American countries with more people in Spain (2)	49%	32%
Ukraine	50%	30%
Total Spain (Spaniards and foreigners)	56%	21%
Spain (3)	58%	19%
China	65%	9%
Rest of countries	39%	45%
(1) Around half are Romanians or Bulgarians. The other half are Western Europeans		
(2) Argentina + Bolivia + Colombia + Ecuador + Peru + Paraguay,		
(3) Native Spanish + immigrants with dual citizenship		

Across Western Europe, the unemployment rate of foreign immigrants is higher or much higher than that of those who are natives, as shown in the following chart, using data from the OECD. The graph shows, for example, that in eight European countries, headed by Norway, Sweden, and Belgium, unemployment among those who are foreign-born is at least twice as much as among native-born. In other words, immigrants are more likely to be recipients of unemployment and welfare subsidies—not a small cost for public coffers. We lack country data detailing whether second generation immigrants have a higher or lower unemployment rate than citizens of non-immigrant roots, although there are probably important differences among ethnic communities as well.

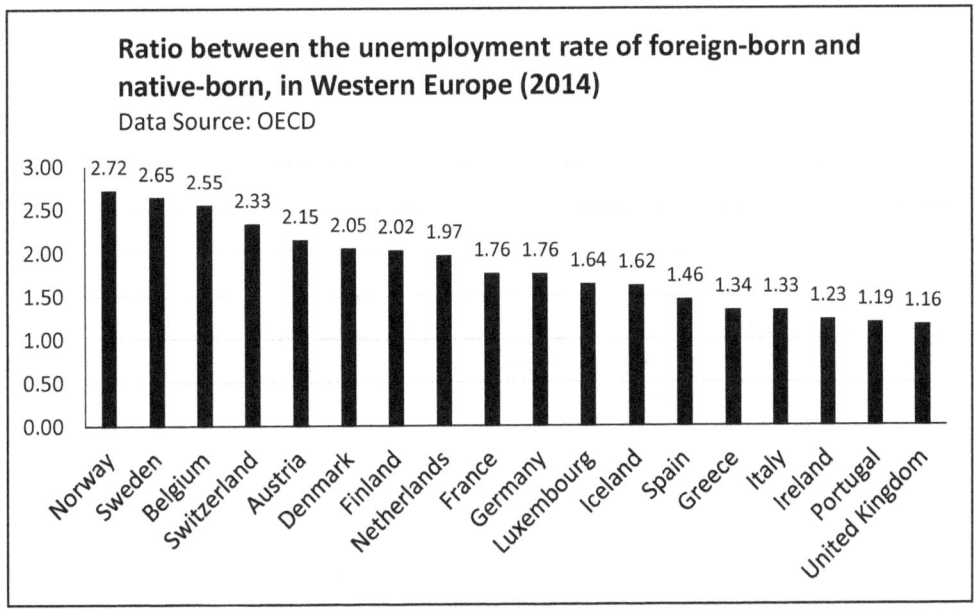

In addition to the direct cost of unemployment benefits and other benefits given to people of foreign origin who do not generate much in tax revenues to the States, the existence of this additional mass of unemployed people contributes to depressing wages for the lower and lower-middle classes of the population. It also causes more competition for vacant jobs, one of the great sources of resentment felt by the lower-middle class against immigration throughout the West. Politicians opposed to mass immigration have grasped and exploited this discontentment in the last few years. Karl Marx said that it was in the interest of capitalism to have what he called "a reserve army of labor," so that wages would be kept low. In this day and age, an excess of immigration, beyond what a country can easily assimilate, would, de facto, play that role in the lower-middle segments of the labor market, by increasing the supply of labor without subsequently increasing demand—hence a great source of support for the National Front party of Le Pen in France is from many working-class districts that formerly voted for the Communist Party.

Furthermore, the arrival of immigrants from countries with relatively high crime and homicide rates, at least in relation to those of host countries, generally leads to increased criminality in the host countries. The following figure shows the ratio of foreign inmates to native inmates, calculated for those over 15 years of age in both groups. As can be seen for all countries, apart from Ireland (whose immigration is mostly European and largely skilled), there is a much greater probability of being a convict if one is a foreigner—supposedly deserving to be incarcerated—than if one is a native. Curiously, the country where the ratio is by far the lowest, not counting Ireland, is the UK, where concern about immigration is high (61% of the British people considered it the top problem in Europe in the Eurobarometer survey conducted at the end of 2015) and dissatisfaction with "excessive" immigration was one of the main complaints of the Brexit supporters in the referendum on whether or not to leave the European Union.

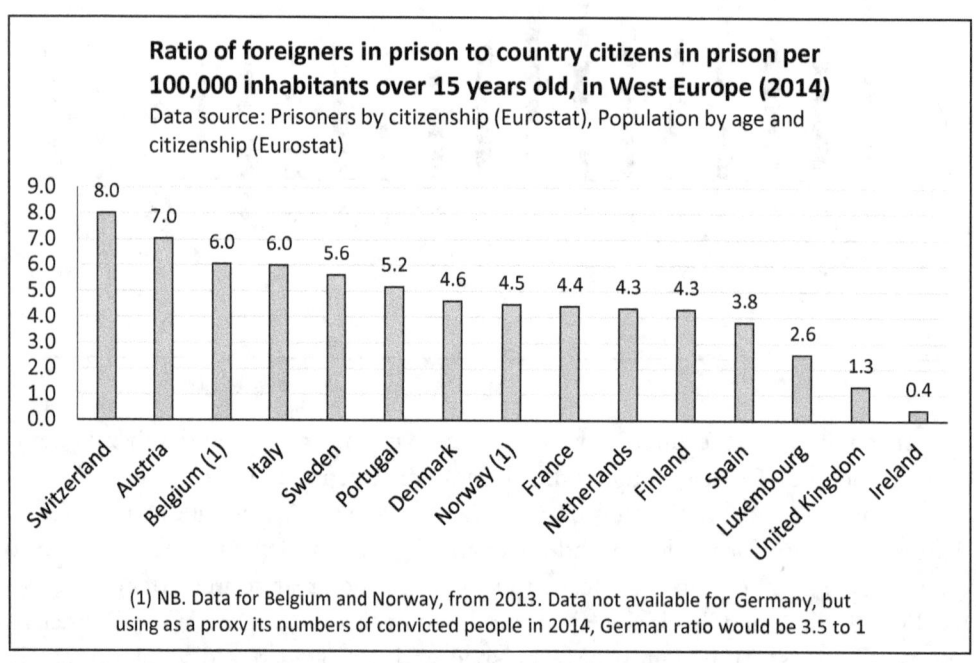

Ratio of foreigners in prison to country citizens in prison per 100,000 inhabitants over 15 years old, in West Europe (2014)
Data source: Prisoners by citizenship (Eurostat), Population by age and citizenship (Eurostat)

(1) NB. Data for Belgium and Norway, from 2013. Data not available for Germany, but using as a proxy its numbers of convicted people in 2014, German ratio would be 3.5 to 1

In Spain, in particular, the immigrant population, since the mid-1990s, although it has generally integrated fairly well, has resulted in additional crimes and crimes previously unknown in the country, such as "express kidnapping." Similarly, almost all perpetrators of the largest terrorist massacre perpetrated in the history of Spain and Western Europe, the March 11, 2004 bombing of several crowded trains, in which 191 people were viciously murdered and 1,856 were injured, some seriously, were immigrants from the Maghreb region, as were also the terrorists of the deadly attacks in Barcelona in August 2017, nearly all from Morocco or sons of Moroccans. The official prison terms sentence records in Spain in 2014 by continent of birth provided by the Spanish INE, combined with the size of the respective immigrant populations, show condemnation rates per 100,000 inhabitants—at comparable ages and for the same sex—that are between 4 and 20 times higher for Spanish residents born outside of Spain than for Spanish citizens. The exception is Asians, with conviction rates as low as the Spanish. To be fair, the vast majority of immigrants do not commit crimes, whether in Spain or in any other country, but their overall crime rates almost always widely surpass those of the natives in developed countries. This factor, logically, generates fear and resentment among native citizens.

For the United Kingdom we have attached a chart with very meaningful data about prisoners by religion, a topic quite related to immigration and delinquency (the great majority of the British people with a religion other than Christian or Jewish are first or second generation immigrants), which we have calculated from a document written by the British House of Commons[53]. Among other things, this report contains, on page 15, the percentage of prisoners by religious affiliation and the percentage of people of each religion among the 15-year-olds residing in the United Kingdom, as of March 2016. Using these data, we have created the following graph and table.

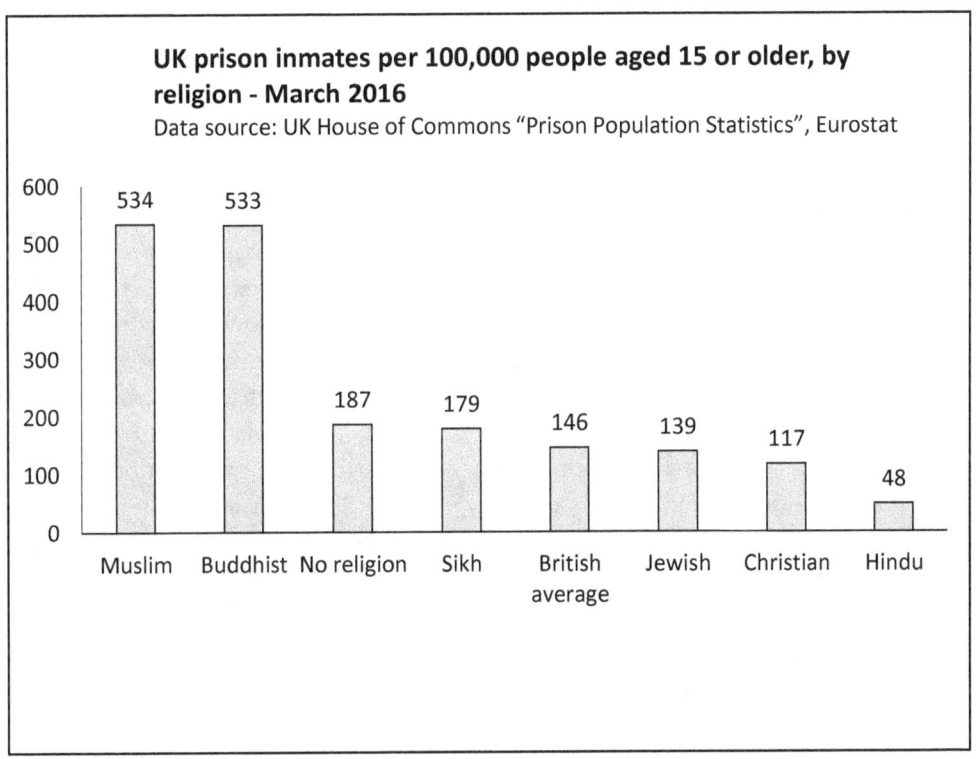

---

[53] **See** (http://researchbriefings.files.parliament.uk/documents/SN04334/SN04334.pdf).

British prison population by religious group - March 2016				
Source: "People in prison" (UK House of Commons	Number of inmates	% of prison population	% of general population aged 15 or older	Number of times their inmate rate per 100,000 with respect to the other religious groups combined
Christian	41,940	49.1%	61.3%	0.6
Muslim	12,506	14.6%	4.0%	4.1
Hindu	421	0.5%	1.5%	0.3
Sikh	732	0.9%	0.7%	1.2
Buddhist	1,558	1.8%	0.5%	3.7
Jewish	406	0.5%	0.5%	1.0
No religion	26,349	30.8%	24.1%	1.4
Other	1,437	1.7%	0.5%	3.4
Not recorded	92	0.1%	7.0%	N/A
Total	85,441	100%	100%	1.0

As a result of these factors (job competition with the local workforce, high unemployment, and associated crime—whether of the common type or the Islamist terrorist type), immigration is one of the issues that most worries, agitates, and tears Western societies. In the United States, a tough stance against illegal immigration was key to Donald Trump's election to the Presidency. In France, for similar reasons, the National Front of the Le Pens has gained enormous strength. The same is true in Germany with AfD, in the Netherlands with the Party for Freedom (PVV), led by Geert Wilders, or the FPO in Austria. In the latest Eurobarometer survey available when writing these lines, in the year 2015, immigration was the issue that most concerned the citizens of 27 of the 28 countries of the European Union. In the only country on the list (Portugal) where it was not the first issue, it was the second. No less than 58% of Europeans said they were concerned about immigration. The second most important problem for Europeans, a subject closely related to immigration, specifically Muslim immigration, was terrorism.

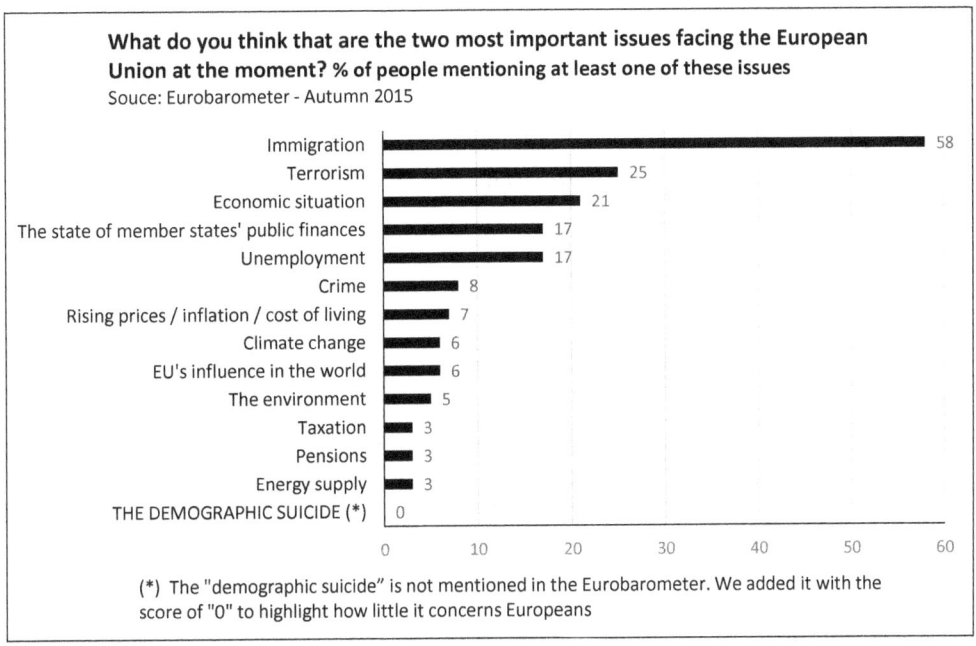

What do you think that are the two most important issues facing the European Union at the moment? % of people mentioning at least one of these issues
Souce: Eurobarometer - Autumn 2015

(*) The "demographic suicide" is not mentioned in the Eurobarometer. We added it with the score of "0" to highlight how little it concerns Europeans

Affective impoverishment and the risk of a poor end to life

> "Man shall not live by bread alone."
> **(Jesus Christ)**
>
> "We are moving from a society in which a grandparent used to care for four grandchildren, to another in which a single grandchild is supervised by four grandparents."
> **(Tomás Burgos**, Spanish Secretary of State for Social Security)

Beyond the negative material impact the demographic decline causes, or its debilitating effect on a country's international position, a low birth rate leads to enormous emotional impoverishments. What a pity to see in Europe, and the other places where demographic suicide is happening, a growing number of villages, neighborhoods—and soon entire cities, many of them with a splendid past—that are becoming human deserts, mostly with old people remaining in them. A few decades ago, one could see their streets teeming with human life, with many kids and young people hanging around in them, along with a number of middle-aged adults and some elderly people. Those streets are now much emptier, decaying, sad. They are much less noisy, certainly, but the same is true for deserts or cemeteries.

Smaller and smaller families

More and more people without children/siblings, or with one at most, without grandchildren, uncles and aunts, cousins, etc., are an inevitable consequence of the demographic suicide. In its "single child" version, in particular, everyone would be raised without siblings, and in future generations, other "lateral" relatives, such as uncles and aunts, cousins and nephews and nieces, would also not exist. The table below shows the number of close relatives by type, if everyone had the same number of children (assuming a rate of almost 0 mortality until women's fertile age is over, which is more or less true in developed countries). In the past, families were very large. Currently, they are much smaller.

Average number of close relatives per person, if everybody had the same number of children (fractional numbers for illustration purposes only)							
Children per person	1	1.3	1.7	2	3	4	5
Siblings	0	0.3	0.7	1	2	3	4
First cousins	0	0.8	2.4	4	12	24	40
Aunts plus uncles	0	0.6	1.4	2	4	6	8
Nieces plus nephews	0	0.4	1.2	2	6	12	20
Grandchildren	1	1.7	2.9	4	9	16	25

The first column represents the "communist Chinese" scenario of the last decades, with its forced single child policy, whose end was announced in 2015, in view of the future demographic catastrophe it was generating and of the undesirable fact that everybody was raised without siblings. With regards to this second point, the expression "Little Emperor Syndrome" was coined in China, referring to so many only children, who in many cases were spoiled by their parents, grandparents, and uncles and aunts. To have a small minority of only children in any society is inevitable, but for not having siblings to be the most common case is very undesirable, because the temptation to pamper an only child too much is difficult to resist and because the only child grows up without a littermate(s) from whom to learn, with whom to also sometimes argue and train in the art of competing and negotiating—two essential skills in human life—within the controlled environment of the family, whom to love fraternally, and on whom to count for support as siblings when one gets older…

The second column reflects the estimated average scenario[54] of the developed

---

[54] In reality, these averages are broken down into families that disappear downstream due to lack of children or grandchildren, and some more numerous, since in a society with X children per woman, those who have children always have somewhat more than X on average, as the average is reduced because of those who have no children at all. This table nevertheless serves to

countries with a very low birth rate (1.4 children per woman or less) such as Germany, Italy, Spain, or Japan. The third column, 1.7 children per woman/man, reflects the case of the Western countries with a slightly higher, but still insufficient, birth rate. Finally, the columns on the right reflect the traditional families, full of siblings, cousins, uncles and aunts, nephews and nieces, grandchildren, etc…full of family life, in short.

With the fall of birth rates, families tend to be like those in the left-hand columns, and the reduction in family size is noticeable in almost all family sagas, especially those stemming from a couple who had many children a generation or two ago. A journalist from Madrid, about 60 years old, who interviewed me in 2011 when I published "El suicidio demográfico de España" told me: "My father had ten children, myself included, and we gave him thirty grandchildren between all of us. I have three children, who have given me only a single grandchild." From thirty grandchildren to the father, to only one to the son! What a pity! More modestly, without reaching such dramatic proportions, my story goes along the same lines as does almost every family's, with few exceptions. I have twenty-two cousins. My children have six. My parents and their siblings, born between the mid-1920s and the mid-1930s, had, on average, almost four children each. The next generation, born between the mid-1950s and 1970s (my twenty-two cousins, my siblings and myself) have had, on average, less than half as many children as our parents.

From the point of view of the quality of the upbringing of the new generations, children in larger families are exposed to a much greater variety of relationships between siblings and relatives than those of smaller families. Brotherhood is a great school of love and cooperation, not exempt from certain doses of competition and rivalry, the two basic modes of human interaction. In large families, not only does each brother benefit from having many dittos for these purposes, but that very same diversity is valuable in and of itself, since, in every type of human relationship, each different group has its own dynamics and its members live specific experiences and learn unique lessons from these experiences. An only child lacks relationships with siblings. In families with two children, each child interacts, apart from his parents, with a single sibling. In families with three children, diversity begins to appear in the fraternal groups that are formed. Each of the three siblings participates in three types of groups, each with its own dynamics: a group of three together, as well as a group of two with each of his or her two siblings separately. In families of four and more, diversity grows exponentially, with the consequent educational and affective benefit for each sibling, as shown in the following chart and table.

---

illustrate what it would mean, on average, to have these numbers of children, for the purpose of calculating the number of close relatives.

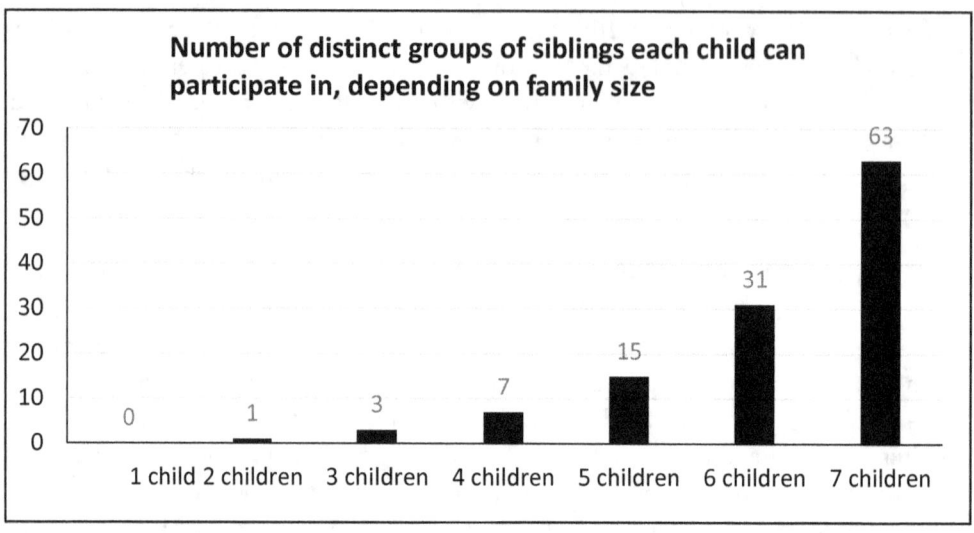

Number of distinct groups of siblings each child can participate in, depending on family size							
Number of children	Groups of 2	Groups of 3	Groups of 4	Groups of 5	Groups of 6	Groups of 7	Total groups
1 child	0	0	0	0	0	0	0
2 children	1	0	0	0	0	0	1
3 children	2	1	0	0	0	0	3
4 children	3	3	1	0	0	0	7
5 children	4	6	4	1	0	0	15
6 children	5	10	10	5	1	0	31
7 children	6	15	20	15	6	1	63

Sadly, that wonderful and fruitful abundance of siblings—and other close relatives—that always characterized family life is now only enjoyed by a small minority. In Spain, for example, only 10% of the families in this day and age have three children and less than 2% have four or more children. Therefore, the vast majority of children—more than 80%—are raised without siblings or with only one. In other countries with a similarly low birth rate, such as Germany, Italy, Portugal, Austria, Switzerland, Japan, South Korea, etc., things are very similar. Even in European countries where the birth rate is closer to the replacement level, a large majority of people are raised without siblings or with just one. If a revolution like the French Revolution were to happen again, one would hope that "Liberté" and "Égalité" would remain as two of their claims / slogans, but would "Fraternité" also remain in societies with such a high percentage of people who grow up without even a little brother or sister? Overall, in Western Europe, using data from the 2011 Census, roughly 85% of children under the age of 25 lived either without siblings (43%) or with only one (42%). Only 12% lived with two other siblings, and 3% with three or more, as seen in the following graph[55].

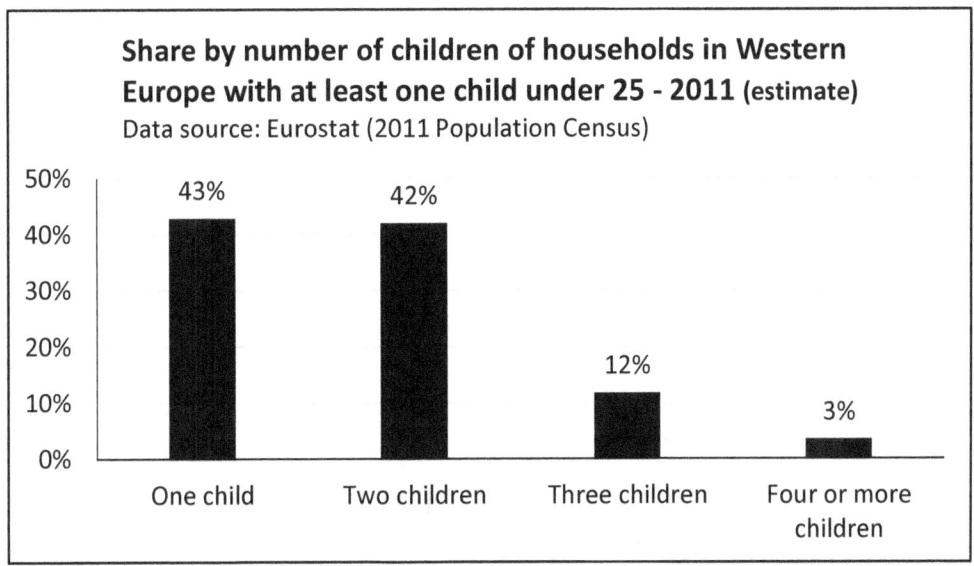

To make things worse in terms of the emotional impoverishment that the demographic suicide process leads to, there is an increasing percentage of children growing up without one of their parents—typically their father—and parents, usually the father, who do not live permanently with their children. The main reason—aside from the misfortune of suffering the premature death of one of the parents—is the abundance of divorces and breakups, which, as detailed in the next section of this book, leads, in turn, to a decrease in the birth rate. The secondary reason, impacting a small but growing minority of cases, are the modern

---

[55] The percentages of the graph have been calculated with the aggregate data on the number of persons per household in which at least one child under the age of 25 lives and subtracting the parents, for Austria, Belgium, Denmark, France, Holland, Ireland, Iceland, Italy, Norway, the United Kingdom, Sweden, and Switzerland. It does not take into account that in some households, families have not yet had all the children they will eventually have, and that in other families, some siblings have already left the home, factors that would tend to overestimate the number of households with few children. On the other hand, and acting as a counterweight in these estimations, all members of the household who are not parents are hereto counted as "siblings" although some homes also contain grandparents, other relatives, domestic personnel, etc., together with the parents and children. All in all, even if these are not exact percentages reflecting how many only children there are and how many households with siblings there are, the graph does correctly illustrate the direction things are taking. Along these lines, Eurostat birth statistics based on birth order show a slightly higher proportion of only children and children with more than three siblings and a somewhat lower percentage for children with a single sibling. Eventually these statistics will surely result in similar numbers of siblings.

possibilities/techniques—and the laws that protect them—of having children outside the "traditional" method and system (a couple made of a man and a woman in a committed relationship, almost always married yesteryear, who copulate to have children with the intention of raising them together). As for single-parent households caused by the death of one of the progenitors, that have always existed, there should now be fewer than before, since, although we have children later than in the past, mortality rates at any age are very much lower than before. Globally, there is a continued growth in single-parent households, and in the number of parents (especially the father) living without their children, which is mainly due to the separation of the parents, as well as some formed outright by a single-parent.

The long shadow of a lonely old age

The number of people who will spend their old age alone is growing in the modern world. Between low marriage rates, divorces, and the few children and siblings we have, who, in a very open world, can easily go to live in another part of the country—especially in a nation as extensive and with as much internal mobility as the United States—or to another country, and how long we live in this day and age, the scenario of a long solitary old age, especially for women, is more and more probable. This was not the case in the past, since there were many children and it was very normal for one of them to accommodate their widowed parent in their home. In some cultures, it was traditionally a (or the) male child upon whose shoulders this duty fell. Likewise, people had more siblings and nephews and nieces. If one reached an advanced age, there were also many grandchildren—and grandnephews and grandnieces—one of the few pleasures of old age. There were also few legal or de facto marital breakups. Now we seldom get married, often divorce, have few children, young individuals have few siblings, middle-aged people do not make much effort to take their old father/mother into their home, and we die at very old ages. As for grandchildren, with birth rate trends of the last 25 years in countries like Spain, between 25% and 30% of people born since 1970 end up not having even one child. If the percentage of people without children does not drop, in a generation, between 40% and 50% of people will not even have a single grandchild. Not one! The result: more and more people live a lonely old age and lack family affection—this does not sound very positive. Even if elderly parents no longer live as often in their children's home, the children do somewhat take care of their elderly parents. Of course, if there are no children, or at most one or two, who most likely do not live nearby, the chances of receiving direct affection and direct physical care from the children are now a fraction of what they were in the past.

Thus solitude and the lack of affection in old age is another bad consequence, actually one of the worst, of the demographic winter, and of its traveling companion—cause and effect—the disintegration of the family. Spending the last 15 to 25 years of life, in physical and often mental decline, with the bitterness of solitude and lacking affection, can be very hard. In fact, as I read in a study, in developed countries, the priority for the elderly, after health, is not money, but love (affection) among the classic trio of the great vital necessities (health, money, and love).

A desire of more than a few: that old people die (there are many, they are costly to maintain, it is a burden to take care of them)

In the very striking Japanese film "The Ballad of Narayama," elderly people of a village, when their physical deterioration becomes quite significant, voluntarily go to Mount Narayama to end their days, in order to release the others from the burden they cause. The village is poor and cannot feed/care for adults who have become "useless" due to their age. Heartbreaking story. Well, in a society with more and more elderly people, who are economically expensive (pensions, healthcare, assisted living for those who cannot take care of themselves) and difficult to care for, when their deterioration is advanced —like those who have advanced Alzheimer's or other similar ailment—the temptation to get rid of them, either "by force" or through the cellophane wrapping of "euthanasia"[56], also called "death with dignity," as if it were not decent to die without resorting to assisted suicide, or not being liquidated in an unsolicited manner when in an allegedly terminal situation, under the guise of sparing suffering to the "suppressed," is a growing temptation. Along these lines, the quotation from the Japanese finance minister that we reproduce in the beginning of this book, went around the world when he said it. It is of an extreme crudeness and gravity, because it was not simply uttered by some demagogue in an underdeveloped country, nor from one of those psychopathic doctors or nurses who, from time to time, make national or international headlines under the appellation of Dr. Death, because they kill elderly people who are in their care for non-life-threatening or not necessarily life-threatening ailments, performing "euthanasia" without their consent, which should really be called "Cacothanasia" (ugly death), because it truly is murder. No, this lapidary phrase came from the lips of one of the key ministers of the government of Japan, a country of the highest international importance, with a high level of development and civility, whose economy is the third largest in the world by its GDP.

Another situation that occurs frequently is the question of what to do with

---

[56] Euthanasia literally means "good death," although these two concepts, death and good, don't rhyme well, at least for those who love life.

cancer patients in pre-terminal stage, as there are more and more people affected in the developed world, as well as in aging countries with fewer resources, impacting them even more from an economic standpoint. Increasingly, in certain cancer types, there are medicines for patients with metastases that slow the disease in a not insignificant number of cases, and, in some cases, even cure it completely, but without achieving the former in a majority of cases, and in much fewer cases the latter. The problem is that these treatments are very expensive (tens of thousands of dollars or euros as an order of magnitude). Is it ethical/fair/adequate/possible to spend 50,000 dollars / euros of public money in prolonging, perhaps for only two months, the life of the patient? For people who can spend that money out-of-pocket without much effort, or with direct relatives who can afford these costs for them, it is possible for them to make that decision. For a large number of people, however, these are amounts of money that are not within their means or that they would even prefer to leave to their children after they die. As the percentage of people with cancer continues to increase, as the probability of contracting this disease increases at an older or advanced age, and there are more and more people in these age brackets in aging societies, this dilemma becomes increasingly larger. It will most likely result in loss of life, or a few months of life, for more and more people.

From an economic-humane point of view, the pressure towards euthanasia, whether viewed as something ideal or at the most macabre we refer to as "cacothanasia," seems inevitable in countries with an advanced demographic winter. It could be countered (or not), by the electoral power of retirees—which is discussed a few pages further, especially in legal matters, and in a theoretical manner. If it were to be counteracted, as would be ethically desirable, public and private spending on the elderly would increase even more, unless science surprises us with truly effective advances in the cure for diseases like cancer. There are signs and hopes for a cure for it, but not certainties. At the individual level, however, in specific residences for the elderly, in some on-shift hospitals, with less scrupulous caregivers, the potential risk seems, in any case, difficult to avert altogether.

Elderly people sedated or tied up so they do not disturb

Without resorting to murder, the risk of mistreatment of the elderly who require a lot of long-term care is also there, for example, in keeping them bound or sedated (almost) all day, so they are not a disturbance. A few years ago, I read in the Spanish newspaper "El Mundo" a story (dated March 28, 2012) with the disturbing title "Drugged to not disturb. A quarter of a million elderly and mentally ill indiscriminately sedated to require less staff in Germany." The article quoted a report from the Center for Political Studies at the University of Bremen, which said that of the 1.1 million patients with dementia in Germany—a chilling figure which will not stop growing, there and everywhere else, as societies are getting older and senile dementias of all kinds, such as Alzheimer's, are on the rise—some 240,000 were given psychotropic drugs normally prescribed for psychosis or schizophrenia, in order to save money and require less personnel for their care, by keeping those patients sedated.

In a similar vein, barely a month after the previous article, I read a report in the Spanish newspaper "El País" titled "One in five elderly people living in assisted-living residences spends the day immobilized"[57]. The article refers to a study conducted by the Catalan autonomous government, in which this practice had been denounced in Catalonia. The news began as follows: "One in five elderly people living in assisted-living residences remains immobilized or tied up most of the time, a figure that doubles among those who suffer some form of dementia. This practice, which seeks to avoid falls and other risks arising from the agitation and cognitive problems of residents, further deteriorates their condition and, in addition, could be avoided in many cases with the adoption of simple measures such as physical stimulation—walking, exercise, etc.—the use of ergonomic seats, more frequent changes of posture, and a more precise care for the residents' health to discover what causes their agitation or aggressiveness." In other words, measures that require either more time from the people who take care of these elderly patients or more investments. That is to say, more money and/or more inconvenience for caregivers. Scandalized by this news, I mentioned it to a friend of mine who is a nun and who had a management position in the Madrid Episcopate and had much knowledge on these issues. She was not surprised and told me "it is the same in the residences for the elderly in Madrid."

The Spanish news and opinion website "El Confidencial" published an article along the same lines on 09/22/2010: "Spain overuses straps in residences: 100,000 elderly sleep while tied up."[58]

I ignore whether or not things have improved since the publication of news like this in Germany and Spain, and I lack data on what happens in other countries. What is certain is that the number of elderly people and people with Alzheimer's and other senile dementias is increasing exponentially worldwide and that the temptation to perform these kinds of abuses towards the elderly, whether partially or sporadically, is increasingly present as the population is aging: for States and

---

[57] http://ccaa.elpais.com/ccaa/2012/04/29/catalunya/1335723378_543613.html)

[58] http://www.elconfidencial.com/alma-corazon-vida/2010-09-22/espana-abusa-de-las-sujeciones-en-residencias-100-000-ancianos-duermen-atados_240065/

administrators of nursing homes, whether public or private, to save costs; for the caregivers, to alleviate, with these types of horrible practices, the burden that they often feel when taking care of defenseless elderly, especially if suffer from dementia.

Degeneration of democracy into gerontocracy, potentially self-destructive

Retirees will become the increasingly powerful homogeneous electoral segment in any democracy, to the point of being highly likely to dominate it in terms of their particular interests. They have already reached that point to a large extent in developed countries, but will have more and more power. In the public sphere, these interests translate permanently, above all, into higher spending by the State and public administrations on pensions, health care, assisted living, and other services for the elderly. In other words, increasing amounts of money are taken away from those who create wealth and are transferred to the elderly. It is logical. When you are young, you have your whole life ahead of you and can afford to be an idealist and try to "change the world." When you are older, with customary exceptions, it is normal to be disenchanted with the possibility of "changing the world" and idealisms. At an older age, one does not have much life ahead as to indulge in experiments that could compromise their well-being and needs to ensure it. For this reason, it is logical that in material matters, an average/typical pensioner be much less idealistic, for example, than a university student, who has not yet faced the difficulties of procuring and securing their own means of subsistence. These difficulties are not insurmountable, but do require an effort, sometimes significant, to overcome. Since the human capacity to think that "I deserve it" is very high, it is normal for politicians who seek the vote of retirees, in other words, practically all of them, to tell them just that: "you deserve the best pension/healthcare/long-term care," although giving them all these benefits results in a great burden for those who work and for the economy in general, as we saw earlier.

In our opinion, this poses a serious risk to the ideal that in democracy, the majority of voters think mainly about the common good, or, at the very least, that elections result in governments that reasonably harmonize competing social interests and do not satisfy above all the interests of homogeneous pressure groups, as numerous as their members may be. From a general prosperity standpoint, this gerontocracy (the government or predominance of the elderly) may lead to, if not necessarily "kill the goose that lays the golden eggs," though it is not impossible to get dangerously close to that situation, a very strong burden on the economy.

Let's look at two examples of the political weight of the older electorate in the last few years.

No Brexit without demographic winter?

In the June 2016 referendum on the departure of the United Kingdom from the European Union, which divided the country in almost two equal halves—the option to leave, the "Brexit," won with almost 52%—with a significance and final scope that are still unknown as I write these lines, the "no" to the EU would not have won if the voters 65 or older had not largely opted for this option. The numbers are resounding. Voters aged 65 and over were about 24 percent of the census, but they voted in a substantially larger proportion than the rest of the voters, as they cast almost 30 percent of all votes, according to exit polls 60% of them chose Brexit, versus 47% of those under 65, 44% of those under 55, 39% of those under 35, 33% of those under 35, and 27% of those under 25, age segments that, in addition, participated less the younger they were, as can be seen in the next page graph. The vote of the retired, many of whom were frightened by the pro-Brexit politicians, who were telling them that the health care they receive and need so much was in jeopardy if continuing in the EU—one of the main claims of the "out" vote—tipped the scale.

Only 15 or 20 years ago, or perhaps less, with significantly larger percentages of younger voters and smaller percentages of mature voters, if the British had held a similar referendum, and people had participated and voted the same for each age group, the result would have been favorable to the "Bremain," the permanence in the EU. Going back further in time, when the population was even younger, the margin would have been even wider. Another interesting reflection that was published in the post-referendum analysis is that those who had decided the outcome of the referendum, the majority of those over 65, would live with the consequences of their vote for far fewer years, due to their advanced age—16 years on average—than the younger voters—some 69 years on average—who were mostly opposed to Brexit, something that was perceived as an unfair paradox.

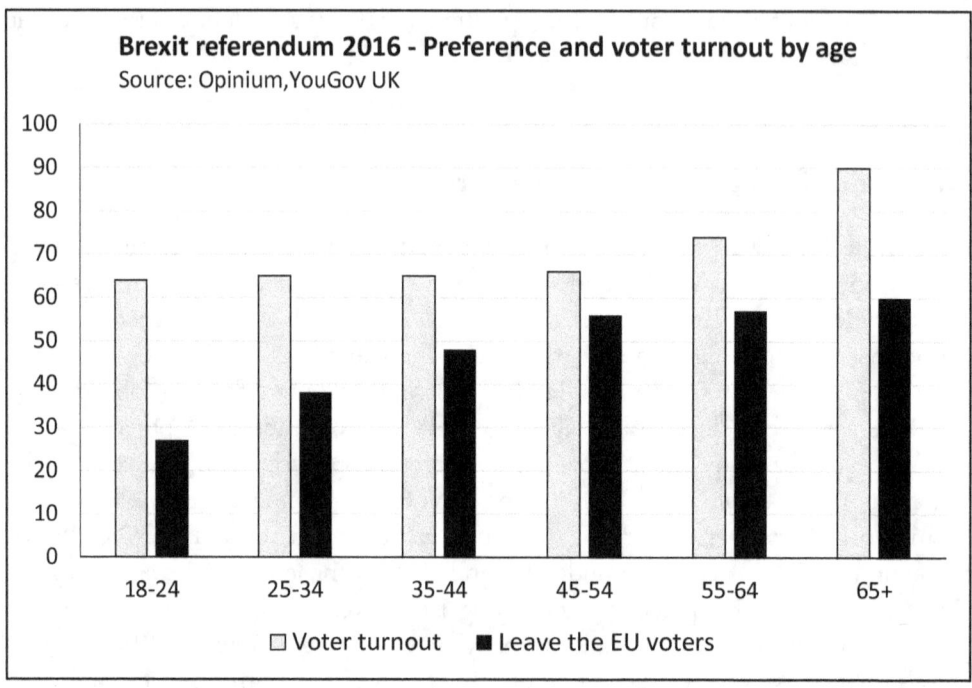

A Spain on the brink of bankruptcy, among other reasons, due to the electoral power of its pensioners

General elections took place in Spain in 1993. In the second and last electoral debate among the different contenders, the then-prime minister ("presidente del gobierno"), the Socialist Felipe González, suggested that the policies proposed by his rival, the conservative Jose Maria Aznar, would pose a risk to retirement pensions. It was said then that insinuation was decisive for González to win the debate, and then, the elections. Since then, a dominant gene was established in the DNA of Spanish politicians that says loud and clear: "Retirees are sacred. Without them, it is impossible to win elections." In subsequent years, with the retirees becoming an increasing percentage of voters, it was so observed. In particular, this "dominant gene" manifested its power in the harsh years of the Great Recession.

From 2008 to 2013-2014, Spain experienced a terrible economic crisis, deeper and more destabilizing than the rest of the great Western economies. In the Eurozone, only Greece and Portugal were worse off. The Spanish unemployment rate reached unheard-of levels in a modern economy, peaking at nearly 27%[59]. The general government deficit—all public administrations together—soared since 2008, peaking in 2009 at the stratospheric level of 11% of the GDP. Since 2009, efforts to reduce it to reasonable levels have resulted in huge sacrifices for many beneficiaries of public spending, as well as for taxpayers, but results have been very slow to arrive. In fact, in 2016, when the Spanish economy grew at a very healthy 3.3% growth rate, the total fiscal deficit still represented 4.5% of GDP, a level above the 3% set as the acceptable maximum for the medium and long term financial stability of countries in the Eurozone. As a result of these continuous budget deficits, between 2007 and 2016, the total Spanish public debt increased by more than 700 billion euros, or more than 60 percentage points of GDP, and continued to grow in the first half of 2017.

Why has Spain been unable to reduce its public deficit more quickly and, as a result, has been forced to go into debt so much? In a not insignificant part because, while the Spanish economy was declining or stagnating, one of the major public budget entries did not stop growing: spending on pensions, in their vast majority

---

[59] Such high levels of unemployment were due to several reasons. But probably the most important of all was that the pre-crisis economic boom was driven above all by the construction of a huge number of houses over a period of several years, when, each year, between two and three times the number of houses commonly needed in Spain in previous decades—200,000 to 350,000 new homes per year—were built. When new homes were no longer needed/sold, as there was no demand for them and prices had reached their highest levels, almost all the people who worked in the construction of houses lost their job, as well as many workers in sectors offering products and services related to the construction and the equipment of furniture and household appliances and services. Since a large part of the labor force employed in the Spanish economic boom from 1995 to 2007 were newly arrived immigrants, but only a small minority— between 6% and 8% in net numbers, according to our calculations, based on official population figures by INE—left the country because of the crisis, despite many more being unemployed, the result was monumental unemployment rates, something as socially undesirable as costly for the State in the form of subsidies and other free benefits. The rise of unemployment in Spain between 2007 and its peak of 2013 was approximately equivalent to the immigration arrived before the crisis. Although it is a rude and populist simplification to say that "unemployment is the fault of the immigrants: if they left Spain, there would be no unemployment," certainly an infusion of 5.7 million foreign immigrants such as those who arrived in Spain between 1995— when the country had 39.6 million inhabitants—and 2010, if not reversed because a large number return to their country of origin when economic crises such as the Great Recession arrive, contributes very much to increasing the levels of unemployment. Why did only a small minority of unemployed immigrants return to their country with the crisis? Because even without employment, they live better in Spain than in their country of origin, because of the subsidies and free benefits they receive, such as healthcare and education, as well as the great citizen security there is in Spain compared to that of more than a few countries, especially the most insecure in Latin America. The morale is once again one that we have tried to present in various parts of this book: well-managed immigration is very beneficial for the host countries. Poorly managed—as in this case—and with high unemployment rates, its overall benefit to the recipient country is much more questionable, if not, in aggregate terms, negative.

retirement and survivor's pensions.

Between 2007 and 2013-2014, four million people lost their jobs in Spain, the total compensation of the vast majority of workers was frozen or reduced, and hundreds of thousands of employers went through a lot of difficulties, many of them ending up ruined. Taxpayers suffered large tax increases in almost all tax categories, possibly in all of them. Pensions however were not only untouchable but even gained purchasing power during the crisis. While Spanish GDP declined between 2007 and 2014 by 2.1% in current money (and more in constant money, in purchasing power), pension spending grew by 43%, as can be seen in the following table, with retirement pension spending increasing by probably 50% or more[60]. Average pensions gained purchasing power during this deep economic crisis...less so for public pension beneficiaries. Pensioners were the population segment Spanish politicians spoiled and privileged during the crisis, to the point of even canceling out the spirit of the reforms made to contain its long-term growth[61]. Why? Nominally/officially, because the mechanisms regulated by law for the annual revaluation of pensions are applied automatically. In actuality, because the voting power of retirees is enormous, and has led to an application, not only "automatic" (due to the continuous increase in the number of pensioners, as the population ages), but also "generous" of those laws in a country on the brink of default and needing to be bailed out by its more solvent European partners during the worst years of the crisis. In 2015, 24% of Spanish voters were of the theoretical retirement age (65 or older), but that percentage rises to 25%-26% if we take into account the average real age of retirement in Spain in 2014 (under 65 years old), or

---

[60] The official data of the Spanish Social Security do not allow an apple-to-apple comparison between 2007 and 2014 by type of pension, because in 2007 they did not distinguish between the contributory and the non-contributory parts (contributive meaning the portion linked to what the taxpayer paid in taxes while he or she was working). Prorating the non-contributory part in the 2014 data using the proportions of 2007 would result in an increase in spending on retirement pensions between 2007 and 2014 of around 50%, a period when the economy contracted, on the brink of default in repaying sovereign debt, and borrowing up to their eyeballs during that period!

[61] For example, the last pension reform of 2014, designed to limit future growth, created ceilings to its annual revaluation to offset inflation, but stipulated that in the worst case each individual pension would increase annually by at least 0.25%. The first time this reform was implemented was at the end of 2014, when that 0.25% increase was applied for 2015. Since inflation had been below zero (deflation) in 2014, with a negative 1% Consumer Price Index (CPI), in fact, if pensions had been reduced by 1% in current money, they would not have lost purchasing power, and the State would have achieved very valuable savings in its efforts to reduce the public deficit and to contain future pension expenditures. Of course, there was no political courage to do so. The result was that, with a Spain suffocated in public deficit and public debt, with 25% unemployment, pensions still gained 1.25% in real purchasing power in the 2014-2015 revision. The reason: the pensioner vote is a mighty knight! Gerontocracy!

about 30% if we measure the number of voters who actually go to the polls, since older folks vote more than the rest of the census, as was seen in the case of the Brexit referendum (British voters 65 or older represented 24% of the total population but casted around 30% of the votes, because of their much greater electoral participation). It is a segment of voters too powerful to not cultivate.

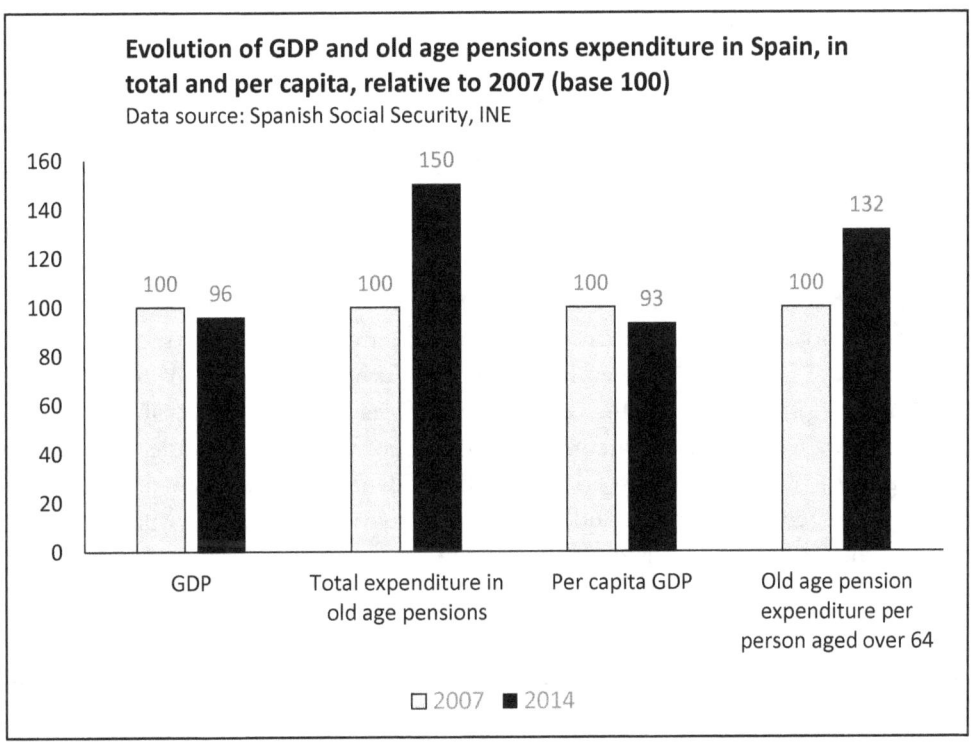

If public spending on pensions in Spain had increased during the crisis at the same pace of the economy—in other words, no increase or rather a slight decrease, as was the case of Spanish GDP in current money—something which would have been possible if the number of retirees had not increased (approximately +14% between 2007 and 2014), and if the crisis had forced them to suffer from the same income adjustments as experienced by any other sector of the Spanish economy and any other population group (something politically impossible because of the great electoral power of retirees), Spain's economic-financial health would have improved much earlier, and would now be less precarious. In fact, if pension expenditures had varied at the pace of the economy since 2007, Spain would have been able to reduce its public deficit to the 3% of GDP considered acceptable several years before this book was published—we do not know, as we write these lines, in what year this financial stability level will be achieved— and the public debt of Spain in 2016 would be about 200 billion (200 thousand millions) euros lower, both because of less accumulated pension spending since 2008 and less interest expense on the public debt as per the author's calculations, and the risk premium on the Kingdom of Spain with respect to the interest paid on the German public debt would have been considerably lower for several years, which would have resulted in an accumulated interest saving of tens of billions of euros for the public sector as well as Spanish companies (since this risk premium also affects, in one form or another, private financing). These improvements have not been possible, even partially or moderately, due to this gerontocracy which, despite being only in the initial stages of its demographic winter, the Spanish democracy has already largely become. One crucial remark: this is not the "fault" of retirees. They simply are many, they worry about what is natural for them to worry about, and politicians who seek their vote know this.

We are therefore headed towards democracies dominated by the "silver/gray" vote, towards gerontocracies, which could very well be self-destructive, because they might crush or "semi-crush" the productive society, which, in the future, will probably be subjected to an even higher tax pressure than the current one, in order to be able to pay all the benefits required by retirees. This, in turn, will damage the economy as a whole and encourage the migration of young and middle-aged people to countries with a milder taxation...These dynamics are sometimes almost inevitable, given the human condition and the rules of the political game, but its final result, sooner or later, is bad for everyone.

Antithesis *ma non troppo*. The other side of the coin: pros of the demographic winter

Since no one-sided coins exist, and this book intends to give a balanced view on the multi-faceted subject at stake, the demographic winter would also have some beneficial collateral effects, typically derived from the reduction in suffering. This is similar to how death results in the suppression of the problems and dangers that lurk during our earthly existence, the reason for the existence of suicides, and that there are many. When one dies, one gets rid of all the evils of this world! An increased life expectancy and aging also provide certain analogous benefits with regards to the typical problems of the youth and the working age. When you finish your studies and start working, you no longer suffer from the stress of exams, and when you are retired, you no longer have the stresses of losing your job or trying to find a good job, or to achieve this or that promotion. For those of us who love life, blessed is the young age when we were nervous about exams. Blessed is the work/professional stress at ages younger than those who are retired. Blessed are the problems that come with living, because having to face them means that one is alive...

Less unemployment from a decreasing active population

Along these lines of relief produced by aging or death, the reduction of the workforce population due to the demographic decline would lead to the disappearance or a drastic reduction in unemployment, unless immigrants, foreign or national, massively reach the country or area in question. For the same reason, the shortage of labor would make it easier for wages to rise, which is, in principle, good for workers but bad for businesses, as previously discussed, since these wage increases would not be linked to higher labor productivity, but to staff scarcity, which would hurt the competitiveness of companies and would hinder the viability of the least profitable ones. The demographic winter also augurs a corresponding rise in taxes to cover State spending on pensions, healthcare, and on those who depend on others for care, which would reduce in part or in whole that possible additional gross wages potential. Likewise, the labor shortage would most likely be mitigated with more foreign immigration, which, in addition to the other social advantages and disadvantages that it entails, would prevent or make it difficult for wages to rise due to a shortage of (native) labor.

Savings in the education and upbringing of children and young people

The countries and societies' expenditure in education and child-rearing—in fact, a very profitable "investment" for society in the long run, and not an "expense" consumed when made, even if it implies an immediate disbursement of money and dedicating economic resources—tends to decrease with the demographic winter, as the number of members of the new generations decreases. However, it is likely that these savings in educational expenditures will only occur in part and/or with some delay with respect to the decrease in the number of children and young people, because closing education centers and classrooms, and suppressing teacher positions, as student numbers are dwindling, can be painful and difficult to carry out, especially in the case of public education, due to the political cost this would mean for the local representatives who would try to implement it.

Housing prices crash: better for buyers/renters...if they want them

With the demographic winter, a slow but inexorable collapse of the prices of the real estate properties (land and houses) can be expected, as more and more of them are empty through the death of their residents, without being replaced by others. Although this results in a loss of wealth for the owners of these real estate properties, as well as, in aggregate terms, collectively for society, at the same time, it will mean cheaper access to homes for new people, whether to own or to rent. Of course, living in a semi-empty, or almost empty, town, neighborhood, or building, with hardly any other neighbors, does not seem to be a very pleasant prospect. Therefore, in the dynamics of depopulation we are heading towards in so many places and in many already noticeable cases, it is foreseeable that people will prefer to concentrate on regions/provinces/cities/neighborhoods/buildings that are more pleasant to live in, i.e., those that continue to be more populated. In those, for that reason, the decline in real estate prices would become less noticeable—and in some places, such as the best downtown areas of each major city, little or not at all—while other neighborhoods or buildings would become empty. In the latter, real estate would end up being worthless or almost worthless, although that would not benefit residents (buyers or tenants), because they would not want to live in them.

Less crime in an aging society

Population aging would also lead to less crime and social conflict, since these are both much more typical of young people than of seniors and the elderly. The propensity to commit crime, to judge by the convict statistics in Spain—and presuming that the data is similar for other countries—decreases drastically with age, as shown in the chart.

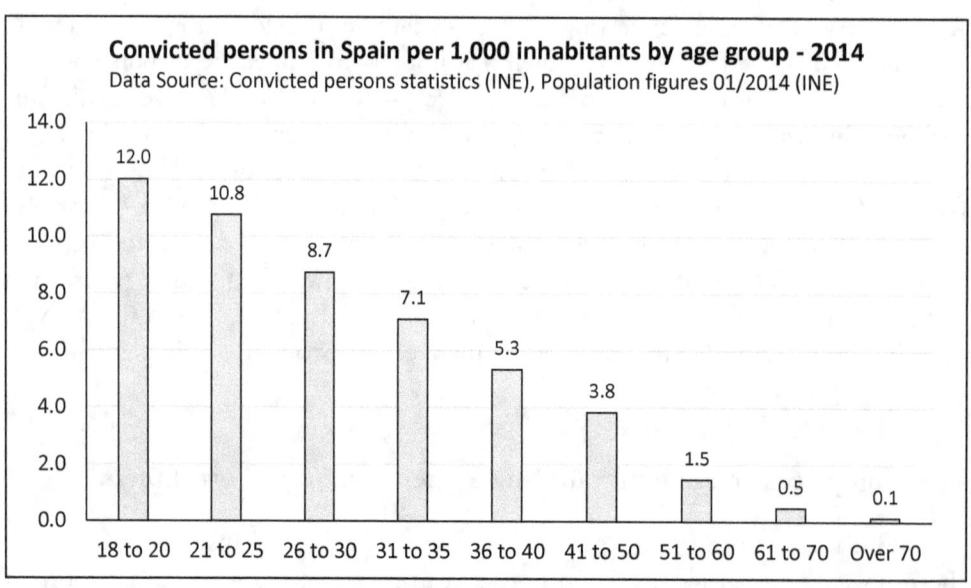

Convicted persons in Spain per 1,000 inhabitants by age group - 2014
Data Source: Convicted persons statistics (INE), Population figures 01/2014 (INE)

Fewer revolutions and social-political upheavals in aging societies

> "Anyone who is not a revolutionary at 20 years of age has no heart. Anyone who is still a revolutionary at 40 has no head."
> (Adage[62])

Idealism, the naivety of believing that the world can be changed at once (for the better), the desire for adventure, ignorance and vitality are ingredients that have made many young people, throughout history, hit force, if not cannon fodder, in belligerent or revolutionary enterprises (pro-freedom/democracy, pro-independence in real or imaginary colonies, anarchist, communist, Nazi-fascist, indigenous rights, Islamists, etc.), often with the use of terrorism and violence, at the service of charismatic leaders and with the desire to "change the world." Much older societies, by contrast, do not seem the best ground for such social upheavals. The inclination to embark on idealistic-revolutionary adventures, on the street, storming Winter Palaces, putting bombs, etc., declines with age. Of course, the fact that there are many young people in a society does not necessarily imply that there will be strong social upheavals, but it does facilitate them. The fact that young people are scarce certainly does make these upheavals more difficult, when it does not directly prevent them. The dry grass does not inflame without a spark, but the wet grass does not even inflame with a spark.

The Nazis triumphed in a Germany with many young people

In the late 1920s and early 1930s, when rising Nazism subjugated a large part of the German population[63], Germany was a country where teens and very young

---

[62] This phrase, or a similar one, is originally attributed to Winston Churchill. It was apparently reused in a modified form by the Social-Democrat German Chancellor Willy Brandt as "a man who is not a Communist when he is young, has no heart; who is a Communist when he is old, has no head." In Spain, there is a more cynical variant of the same idea attributed to the Count of Romanones, a key center-leaned politician in the first third of the twentieth century, who it is said was once approached by a young man from a good family, an admirer of his, who asked him for advice on how to achieve a successful political career like Romanones. "Are you from the left or the right, young man?" The Count asked. "From the right, Monsieur le Comte, from the right," replied the young man, to which the Count replied: "Move to the left, you'll have time to be on the right."

[63] To be fair to the German people of that time, who many condemn en bloc for the rise of Nazism, the best election results obtained by the Nazis in free elections was 37.3% of the votes cast (July 1932). In other words, five out of eight German voters (62.7%) preferred other political options, not the National Socialist party, in the best result ever obtained by the "Brownshirts." In fact, in the next free election, in November 1932, the Nazis dropped to 33.1% of the votes. Later, in March 1933, they won 43.9% of the votes with Hitler already in power. Of course, with Herr Adolf running the country, these were no longer free and fair

adults abounded due to the overflowing German birth rate until 1914, in stark contrast to the infertile, aging, and peaceful present-day Germany. This large mass of German youth played a major role in the rise of Nazism, as a force of shock and intimidation in the struggle for power.

Islamic revolutions, "Arab springs," and jihadism in countries brimming with youth

In today's boom of Islamist extremism and jihadism, the countries where the movement has been the strongest (the main Arab nations, in addition to Iran, Afghanistan, and Pakistan), bustle with young people. The average age of the 19 terrorists identified as the perpetrators of the hijack of the four planes crashed on September 11, 2001 was 24 years. In Saudi Arabia, the birthplace of 15 of these 19 terrorists, the median age of the population at that time was 22 years old, less than half that of, for example, the aging modern-day Germany. These Saudi terrorists were born when the birth rate in their country was slightly higher than seven children per woman, and population growth was explosive, as infant mortality had already dropped significantly from its traditional levels, but birth rates had not.

The following chart shows the (very low) median age of the populations of the main Arab countries and other Muslim countries where there have been revolts and strong social upheavals in the last decades, at the beginning of the political-social outbreak that was denominated "Arab Spring" (2010-2011). The "Arab Spring" movement, which began with the immolation in Tunisia of a 26-year-old, Mohamed Bouazizi, and that later spread to other Arab nations, ended in a reasonable manner in only Tunisia—though at the significant price of more than 200 human lives— whose society, although very young by developed country standards, is the oldest of all Arab societies. In the other countries where he took a strong turn, this peculiar "Spring" led mainly to tragedies, notably in Syria, Libya, and Yemen. The net result of this movement in Egypt was significant bloodshed and little democratization.

---

elections, among other things, because the Nazis themselves had burned down the German parliament, the "Reichstag," a few days before, and had blamed the Communists. This event and its emotional exploitation by the Nazis shocked Germany. Despite this event, as well direct or indirect coercion, and the voting manipulations that took place, the National Socialists did not even come close to winning half of the votes in the March 1933 elections.

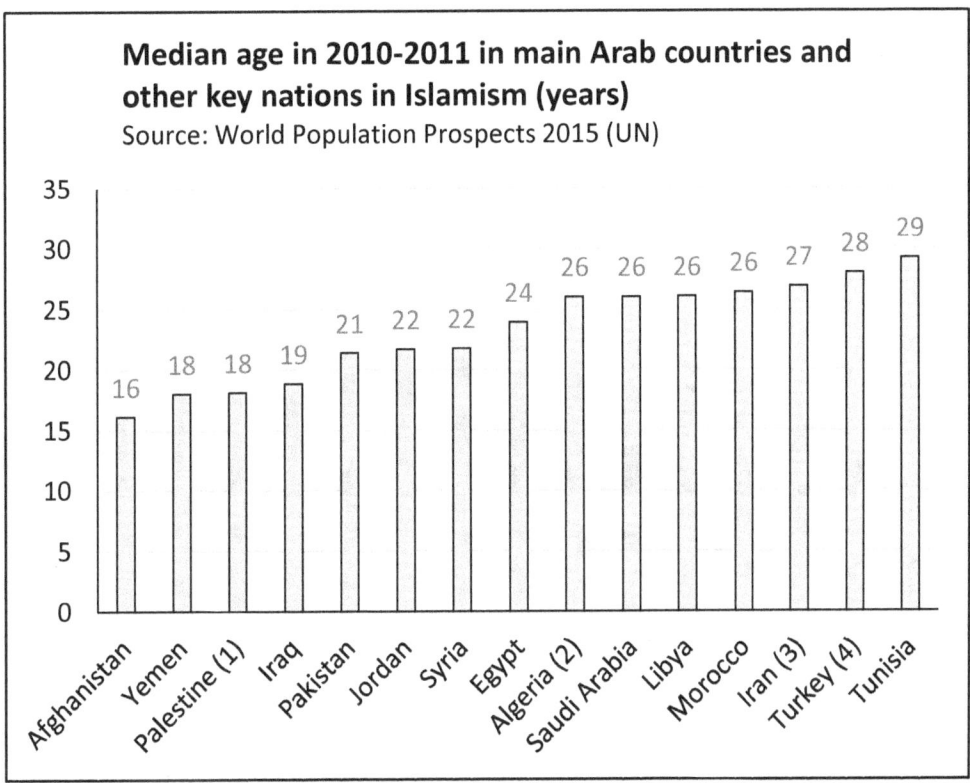

Median age in 2010-2011 in main Arab countries and other key nations in Islamism (years)
Source: World Population Prospects 2015 (UN)

Comments
(1) The UN calls it "State of Palestine"
(2) 18 years at the outbreak of the civil war with the Islamic Salvation Front in 1991
(3) 18 years when the 1979 Islamic Revolution took place
(4) 25 years when the Islamist Erdogan came to power in 2003

Because of these sociodemographic reasons, *ceteris paribus*, we believe that, as these countries become older, Islamist extremism, as well as jihadist terrorism overall, should recede. In general, the Arab and Islamic countries herein referenced are aging rapidly, due to the declines experienced in their birth rates and the increases experienced in the life expectancy of their populations, as evidenced by the considerable increase in their median age between 2000 and 2015, according to UN data, with the exception of some of the countries that were at war or other conflict in 2015-2016 (and not all, partly because some of these conflicts began after 2010), as shown in the following graph.

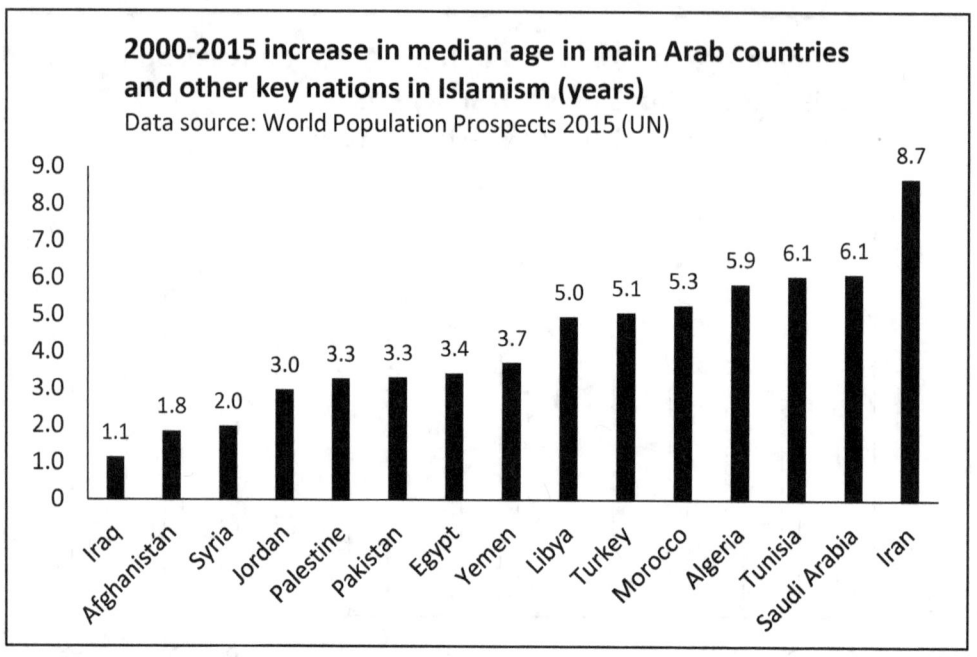

From a young Spain prone to civil war, to the aged and peaceful Spain in this day and age

"Blood that does not overflow,
youth that does not dare,
it is neither blood, nor youth,
it does not shine, nor does it blossom."

Verses of "Llamo a la juventud" (I Call to the Youth) by the communist poet **Miguel Hernández**, written in 1937, during the last Spanish Civil War

As I am writing these lines (July 18-19, 2016), it has been exactly 80 years since Spain began its greatest tragedy of the last 200, or more, years: the cruel civil war of 1936 to 1939. That fratricidal conflict occurred largely because of the exacerbated political passions of the time, and because the sociological foundations of those who fought (the left allied to the Catalan and Basque separatists, against the right) did not resign themselves to the triumph of the other side, to the point of being ready to fight to death, something very few Spaniards would do today for their ideals. Before the war itself, during the Second Republic, from 1931 to 1936, more than 2,000 people died from political violence, more than half of those in the socialist-communist insurrection of October 1934 in Asturias. In Spain at that time, for every person aged 15 to 34 (the youth and the young adults), there was roughly one person 35 years or older[64]. The median age was about 24-25 years. In 2016, with the inversion of the population pyramid, for every Spaniard between the ages of 15 and 34, there were three compatriots over 34 years old: three times the ratio 80 years ago. The median age of the native Spanish population at the beginning of 2016 was about 43 years old, 42 if we include immigrants in the calculation. In 1936 it was about 25 years old. Bloody social conflict and political violence in Spain today are minimal, and the prospects of a possible civil war, despite the potential risk of secession in Catalonia, seem fortunately almost nil, if not completely nonexistent. Of course, the current peaceful scenario is far from being due to only the societal shift towards aging. But it is logical to think that the current abundance of middle-aged and older people in relation to young people is one of the main reasons as to why there are no major risks of bloody civil wars or revolutions in Spain, or anything similar, after the long, turbulent century from 1830 to 1940, a period during which Spain was embroiled in four national, as well as some regional, civil wars, and experienced its fair share of coups d'état, suffered various revolutions and revolts, and saw innumerable individual episodes of politico-social violence.

The Basque case: a society that grew older than usual because of terrorism, which in turn languished largely because of social aging?

Something similar can be said about the demographic evolution of the Spanish Basque Country and the separatist and anti-capitalist terrorist organization ETA, which emerged in a Basque society that in the 1960s and 1970s boiled with births and youth. This terrorist movement gradually faded starting at the turn of the century. Apart from police assaults and political and social developments, which were separate issues in and of themselves, the gradual drop, through the years, in the recruiting of young men to their ranks who were willing to take personal risks by committing the barbarities of the ETA separatists was also probably a factor. The actions of ETA, in turn, may have been a factor in the drop in the number in young Basques in total, and in the much faster aging of the Basque Country than in any other part of Spain. The tremendous collapse of the demographic health of the Spanish Basque Country, which reached a birth rate lower than in any country in the world in the mid-1990s (0.91 children per woman in 1994 and 1995, 68% less than in 1976, a level only surpassed by another Spanish region, Asturias, with 0.84

---

[64] These were the exact proportions in the 1930 population census data, which did not change significantly, if at all, in the six years between 1930 and the beginning of the civil war in 1936. The current population figures, by age, are from the Municipal Register as of January 1st, 2016 (INE).

children per woman at the time, and 0.81 in 1998) must have played a significant role in the extinguishing of ETA. Furthermore, mainly due to its tense political climate, the Basque Country suffered from a strong population emigration to other parts of Spain between 1976 and 2014, with a net exit of people of Spanish nationality—native Basques as well as people with family roots in other parts of Spain—during that period, equivalent to 8% of the Basque population in 1976. Also, to some extent, due to the same political climate and its socioeconomic ramifications, the Spanish Basque Country probably received far fewer foreign immigrants than other regions of Spain between the mid-1990s and the beginning of the Great Recession (somewhat less than half the immigration of Madrid or Catalonia in proportion to their respective populations, and about 35% less than the Spanish average), despite being the area of Spain with the highest per capita income, along with Madrid and Navarre.

Inversion of the population pyramid in the Basque region and the rest of Spain from 1976 to 2016					
Data source: Population Figures at 01/1976 and 01/2016 (INE)		1976 - Total population	2016 - Total population	2016 - People born in Spain	Relative change 1976 - 2016 of people born in Spain
Basque country (Spanish side)	Population aged 15 to 24	318,671	186,349	159,829	-50%
	Population older than 59	244,167	605,437	592,443	144%
	Persons aged 15 to 24 per person over 59	1.31	0.31	0.27	-79%
	Population aged 15 to 24 as a % of total	15.8%	8.6%	8.0%	-50%
	Population older than 59 as a % of total	12.1%	28.0%	29.5%	144%
Rest of Spain	Population aged 15 to 24	5,285,657	4,656,607	3,781,050	-28%
	Population older than 59	5,044,957	10,664,460	9,946,200	98%
	Persons aged 15 to 24 per person over 59	1.05	0.44	0.38	-64%
	Population aged 15 to 24 as a % of total	15.6%	10.5%	9.8%	-37%
	Population older than 59 as a % of total	14.9%	24.1%	25.8%	74%
NB: In 1976, only 0.5% of people in Spain were foreigners. In 2016, foreign-born people were 12.7% in Spain and 7.3% in the Basque region. For estimating the 1976-2016 relative change, we have assumed that 99.5% of Basques and Spaniards in 1976 were people born in Spain					

As a consequence of the above, the number of Basques most likely to join a terrorist group based on their age—adolescents nearing adult age, and very young adults, that is to say, people mainly between 15 and 24—has fallen by 50% between when ETA was on the rise and at its peak, in the mid-1970s and 1980s, and the present day. On the other hand, the segment of the Basque population that is already mature, very old, or elderly, has more than doubled since then. The inversion of the population pyramid (from many young people and rather few very old people to the opposite) has been considerably more pronounced in the Basque Country than in the rest of Spain. Basque society was younger than the Spanish average when ETA was growing and expanding. Now, 40 years later, compared to the rest of Spain, Basque society has a smaller youth population, and a much larger older population, as can be seen in the table above.

Likewise, as a result of the brutal fall of the Basque birth rate, the strong net emigration to other parts of Spain, and a lesser foreign immigration (younger, on average, than the rest of the population) between early 1975 and 2015, the increase in the median age of the Basques has been tremendous, higher than that of any other region of Spain, as can be seen in the following table. In fact, no European country, except one that was plagued by a terrible war (Bosnia Hercegovina)—and not even there if we only count the Basque population born in Spain, in other words, not counting foreign immigrants—saw such a growth in the median age of its population as the Basque Country between 1975 and 2015. Worldwide, only South Korea, Singapore, and Thailand, countries whose birth rate crashes have been vertiginous, have surpassed the median age increase of the Spanish Basque Country in the last four decades.

Median age of the Basque population, Spain as a whole, and of several countries and continents (in years), in early 1975 and 2015				
Data Source: UN (World population prospects 2015), INE	1975	2015	Change 1975-2015	Change % 1975-2015
Basque country	28	45	17	61%
Spain	29	42	13	45%
Japan	30	47	17	57%
Germany	35	46	11	31%
Italy	33	46	13	39%
France	32	41	9	28%
Canada	27	41	13 (*)	48%
South Korea	20	41	21	105%
Singapore	22	40	18	82%
United Kingdom	34	40	6	18%
Russia	31	39	8	26%
United States	29	38	9	31%
Thailand	19	38	19	105%
China	20	37	17	85%
Brasil	19	31	12	63%
Israel	24	30	6	25%
Asia	20	30	10	50%
Mexico	17	27	10	59%
India	20	27	7	35%
Africa	18	20	2	11%
World	22	30	8	36%
(*) 13 actual years, although rounding of 1975 and 2015 medians would appear to give a difference of 14.				

In our opinion, it is no coincidence that the demographic health of the Spanish Basque Country followed a parallel with the rise and decline of the separatist-communist terrorism of ETA, which conditioned Basque politics, economy, and society from 1974-1976 to the beginning of the second decade of the twenty-first century. With all the negatives its demographic collapse has brought and will continue to bring to this fascinating land, in the end, its demographic decline seems to have played a significant role in its pacification. Every cloud has a silver lining, although globally, as in this case, it is not worth it.

A very aged nation = a nation defenseless against tyrannies?

"Youth always pushes
youth always prevails,
and Spain's salvation
depends on its youth."

Verses of "I call the youth," from the communist poet **Miguel Hernández**, written in 1937 during the last Spanish civil war

Notwithstanding the above, this positive element of fewer social conflicts and less violence in societies experiencing a demographic winter would, in turn, also entail a potentially colossal theoretical risk in national and international politics. If the aging of societies contributes a great deal to these societies being substantially less violent/belligerent, and if, in the future, they should face serious external or internal threats (a threatening neighboring country, widespread terrorism, mob rule, heinous tyranny, etc.) that could not be successfully fought without legitimate liberation struggles/rebellions, this same lack of youth and abundance of senescence could potentially condemn such societies to impotence, and therefore to succumb to such threats and not be able to free themselves from them. Such a scenario could be, indefinitely, an ugly "end of History," or at the very least a dreary "parenthesis in History," much less happy than the one predicted by Francis Fukuyama's when communism fell, when he proclaimed the thesis that liberal democracy had triumphed as the only viable political system forever. Orwell ("1984" and "Animal Farm") and Hayek (on "The Road to Serfdom"), among many others, imagined a world subjected to tyrannies of a greater or lesser harshness. If they get it right in the end, may God have mercy of the tyrannized societies that are very old!

In cemeteries, there is no violence, no unemployment, no problems for their eternal inhabitants

As we see, then, this demographic winter coin also has two faces. In our opinion, the "good" face is far from making up for the "bad." For those who prefer a demographic winter/suicide to good demographic health, with many children and youth, for their country/homeland/city, as there would be less unemployment and crime/violence, it is worth remembering that in cemeteries none of these exist—instead, there is absolute peace. Moreover, if humanity were to disappear, gone would be diseases, economic crises, wars, public deficits, public debt, environmental pollution, racism, sexism and all harmful "isms," bad taste, etc. All the bad of mankind would end! (in exchange, everything good would also go, including our own lives).

CHAPTER 3
WHY WE HAVE SO FEW CHILDREN

> "Man's best friend (in the animal kingdom) is not the dog, but the scapegoat"
> **(Carlos Rodríguez Braun**, Spanish-Argentinean economist)
>
> "The worst enemy of the intelligence analyst is his/her own ideology"
> (Warning of the **American CIA** to their intelligence analysts)

What is causing the decreased birth rates in so many European countries, Asian countries, and much of the world? What prevents Europe and so many other places from having more children?

Like many other major man-made disasters, the demographic winter we are suffering from seems to have multiple roots. Problems of a large caliber, like this one, are not usually the product of a single cause, although among the various concurrent factors, there are always some that weigh more than others. There is no unanimity among those who have studied this phenomenon about the roots of the contemporary low birth rate, either because this issue is relatively recent and has not yet been studied in depth, because of its complexity, because of ideological prejudices or partisan interests or interests of some factions, or because it is uncomfortable to admit that an insufficient birth rate highlights a huge structural failure in the social model of developed and developing countries. Or, perhaps, due to a combination of the above reasons. Besides listing these factors, we will try to analyze them in the light of the available data, to try to separate what is true and logical from what is a fallacy or a myth.

Why we should be having more children, and not fewer, than before (food for thought!)

Before we discuss why we have so few children, we will begin by arguing why the opposite should happen, since, curiously, there are substantial reasons that should lead us to have <u>more, rather than fewer, children than before</u>. As we have far fewer children than in the past, despite these reasons, the inevitable conclusion is that the modern society elements acting against higher birth rates (values, cultural, customs, legal, etc.) must be very powerful and must be very deeply rooted in the current social model / lifestyle. Thus, these factors can difficultly be countered with only some isolated measures, one patch or another, and appeal for us to have more children. However, it will always be better to take some measures than to do nothing at all. But aspirin is not enough to treat cancer with any chance of success. We need much more for major diseases like this. And first of all, we must know that the disease is cancer and not a temporary indisposition.

The main reason we should have more, and not fewer, children than ever before, is the drastic drop to a near-zero level in maternal mortality in developed countries. In the past, one in every 15 to 25 women died during her last pregnancy, delivery or postpartum. As an anecdote (or an example), both the mother and the wife of the great German physicist Rudolf Clausius, one of the parents of Thermodynamics, died because of their last childbirth. As a rough order of magnitude, in the currently developed countries, until about 150 years ago, or even less, the mother died during, or as a result of, one out of every hundred deliveries. Even today this is the case in very poor countries, including some in Africa. In particular, in Somalia, in 2010, women died in one of one hundred live births (source: CIA). As the birth rate in Somalia is estimated to have been 6.87 children per woman during 2010 (source: World Bank), if we put these two figures together, assuming there are no changes in the future, we fear that one in every fifteen Somali women will die as a result of her last pregnancy or childbirth. One in fifteen!

Do we voluntarily undertake any action in the developed countries that carries a 1% probability of death? Even professional soldiers (volunteers) in Western countries do not face such high death risks when they fight in modern wars. In one of the deadliest wars for them, the war in Iraq from 2003 to 2011, the risk of death in combat for American GIs was significantly lower than the traditional risk women faced in childbirth worldwide, a risk our grandmothers, great-grandmothers, and all their ancestors confronted with great love for their families when giving birth (THANK YOU, HEROES! Without your courage and desire to bring children into the world, none of us would exist). There was, on average, no more than one American soldier killed in Iraq for every two hundred deployed there.

Despite such tremendous danger linked to childbirth in other times, and childbirth being traditionally much more painful before epidural anesthesia started being used, there were many more children than now. In the European Union in 2012, for every 100,000 births, less than five women died—a rate that was less than half of the EU average in countries such as Italy or Spain, where, incidentally, the average number of children per woman is one-fourth or one-fifth of the traditional rate and the birth rate is lower than the already meager European average. Even today, in countries like the US, the average risk of women dying in childbirth or during the postnatal period is six times that of Spanish or Italian women[65]. Despite this higher risk, North American women have 30% to 40% more children, on average, than Italian or Spanish women.

Data for 2011	Maternal mortality (*) per 100,000 live births	Total fertility rate (children per woman)
United States	17.8	1.89
United Kingdom	6.6	1.91
France	6.3	2.01
EU-28 average	5.4	1.58
Germany	4.8	1.36
Spain	3.0	1.34
Italy	2.6	1.44
(*) During to pregnancy, childbirth or puerperium		
Data sources: Eurostat, US Census Bureau, Scientific American - CDC		
https://www.scientificamerican.com/article/has-maternal-mortality-really-doubled-in-the-u-s/		

Secondly, if many now do not want children for whom they could not provide sufficient comfort and good studies[66], we should remember that perhaps half of the babies born before a little over a century ago in Europe were exposed, if not condemned, to economic/material precariousness in childhood and youth. If they reached adulthood, many of them illiterate, they were bound to perform miserable occupations if they were male (laborer, pawn, porter, miner, etc.) or become servants if they were women. By contrast, now, in more and more countries, and indeed throughout Europe, the State guarantees the entire population of children and young people access to education, food, clothing, housing, and quality medical care through free public services or services financed with private wealth. Virtually any child born in developed countries today, with enough effort, has the potential to attend higher education and thrive as an adult, regardless of his or her starting social status. Yet, we have far fewer children than before. Ironically, Marx could no

---

[65] Data from the Center for Disease Control and Prevention, CDC, for the United States, /www.scientificamerican.com/article/has-maternal-mortality-really-doubled-in-the-us/ and Eurostat

[66] "What some should understand is that the best gift you can give your child is not to pay him a master's degree at Harvard, but to give him a little brother," said Javier Echevarría Munguira, the presenter of a public event in Madrid at which the author participated as a speaker, discussing the demographic winter.

longer call the low-middle class Europeans "proletarians" because the contemporaries in that social layer—or any other stratum—have no progeny (proles in Latin). Yet, even though the fate that once awaited many children was not exactly a path of roses, people still had many little ones.

Thirdly and closely linked to the above, the vast majority of human beings in this day and age, in developed and emerging countries, have a real level of income and material prosperity unmatched in the past. I remember hearing Miguel Boyer, the vice-president of the first Spanish socialist government and Minister of Economy from 1982 to 1985 at a conference in Madrid in either 2009 or 2010 comment that economists estimate that the real per capita income of Spaniards had been multiplied by 40 between 1500 and 2007. It first multiplied by 5 until 1950 and then by 8 since 1950. In other developed or developing countries, multipliers of real personal income compared to what existed a few centuries ago may be somewhat higher or lower than the Spaniards', but their values are, in all cases, very substantial. Therefore, although many people say that today "raising children is very expensive," by whatever objective measure we might use, almost everybody today is much more prosperous than populations were a hundred or more years ago.

In addition, and even if it goes in the opposite direction of something that will be discussed below, in the past, fathering and raising children brought terrible suffering to a majority of parents, from seeing one or more of their offspring die. Let's illustrate this with an impressive example, already mentioned in these pages: only a century ago, in the five-year period from 1911 to 1915, according to tables of historical data of the INE, each year, on average, 44,349 children under the age of two died of diarrhea and gastroenteritis. It was the most prominent cause of death, accounting for 10% of all deaths. In 2013, according to official statistics, only one child died in Spain of the same cause. Raising children now, of course, is not a bed of roses, free of thorns and complications, but the supreme pain from when a little one of yours does not make it, often after great physical sufferings, is something that very few parents suffer from nowadays. Formerly, while the majority suffered from this tragedy, they still did not shy away from the adventure of being parents. Nowadays, many of our fellow countrymen avoid this adventure entirely and another large quantity only experiences it once.

Finally, today there are wonderful innovations facilitating pregnancy and childbirth that were not available until relatively recently. We now enjoy modern systems for gynecologists to monitor pregnancies—what a great invention the ultrasound was—and to treat pregnancy-related problems, for the benefit of both the pregnant mother and the unborn baby. The epidural, as well as various types of painkillers that can be administered during baby delivery or throughout the pregnancy, provide a huge relief of delivery pains for the mother. Furthermore, treatments against infertility and techniques of assisted reproduction, once unthinkable due to their lack of effectiveness, are available now. Without in vitro fertilization, it is estimated that 1% to 8% fewer babies would be born in the West (the latter figure corresponds to Denmark[67]). It must be said that, if these fertility treatments generate the misleading expectation that the age at which children can be born can be extended indefinitely, the net effect on the number of births would be lower than that mentioned, since many women today, believing indeed that modern techniques of assisted reproduction allow them to postpone motherhood for more and more years, end up putting it off until it's too late, even with such modern techniques[68].

Nevertheless, despite such powerful reasons and today's ease of having more children than before, exactly the opposite occurs, and by a wide margin. This underlines the depth of the causes and the magnitude of the material and mental impediments that, currently, act against having children. Let us review them.

Reasons for the current low fertility rate: truths, half-truths, myths, fallacies, urban legends....

Excerpt from the article "Fertility: fewer children, older moms" from Statistics Canada[69]

---

[67] According to ESHRE, the European Society of Human Reproduction and Embryology, in the following countries, at least 3% of babies were conceived in vitro around 2014: Belgium, Czech Republic, Denmark, Estonia, Iceland, Norway, Slovenia and Sweden. In the US, however, that figure is under 1% (https://www.eshre.eu/guidelines-and-legal/art-fact-sheet.aspx)

[68] Towards the end of 2013, one of the most outstanding Spanish gynecologists specialized in assisted reproduction commented to the author of this book that, for the professionals in the field, it was more and more frequent to have to communicate sad and unpleasant news to patients: that even with the most modern therapies, it was impossible to overcome their infertility problem, because of the deterioration of their reproductive system due to their age. On the other hand, for the not-so-young women who consult other specialists in an attempt to overcome their age-induced infertility, the last technically viable option offered is generally not easy to accept, for obvious reasons: that the fertilized ovum to be implanted be not their own but, rather, from a young donor.

[69] http://www.statcan.gc.ca/pub/11-630-x/11-630-x2014002-eng.htm

"Let's see, your great-grandfather was 1 of 7 children. Your grandmother was 1 of 4 children and you are 1 of 3 kids. You are thinking of having 1 or 2 kids, or, if you happen to be a statistician, that's currently an average of 1.61 children per woman.

Over the past 150 years, Canada has changed from a high-fertility society where women had many children during their lives to a low-fertility society where women are having fewer children overall and at increasingly older ages. Until the early 20th Century, when people were still living primarily in rural settings, it was advantageous for couples to have large families. Children were expected to share daily chores, both in the home and on the farm. This added directly to the family's productivity and prosperity.

The economic benefits of a large family, combined with the influence of religious teachings and a lack of reliable contraception methods, resulted in an estimated total fertility rate of 6.56 children per woman in 1851. For a woman of this era, childbearing would have continued throughout her reproductive years for the duration of her married life, as it was more difficult to control the timing and number of births.

Although fertility remained relatively high during the following decades, it began falling in the late 1800s and early 1900s. By the turn of the century, women were having close to five children, on average This fertility decline was associated with many factors, including a transition to greater urbanization, a growing dependency on wages earned outside the home and the rising cost of childrearing.

Then came the Great Depression, followed soon after by World War II. With the inherent uncertainties and upheavals of the times, fertility levels fell further during the late 1920s and throughout the 1930s. By 1937, the total fertility rate had fallen to 2.64 children per woman, on average. From 1946 to 1965, thanks to a strong post-war economy, the reunification of families following the war and high marriage rates, Canada's baby boom was born. [70]. The boom peaked in 1959 when the total fertility rate reached 3.94 children per woman.

By the end of the 1960s, that all changed. The influence of religion on daily life was in decline, contraception was now more effective and readily available than ever and the participation of women in higher education and in the paid labor force was

---

[70] It actually was not like that. As we saw in the first chapter of this book, and much like the United States, the United Kingdom or Switzerland, the Canadian baby boom began before World War II. Specifically, the Canadian birth rate (in number of births and in fertility rate) reached a low in 1937 and began to pick up in 1938. On the other hand, the 1920s, during which the birth rate continuously fell in Canada (as in the US), are known as the Merry Twenties because they were years of great economic expansion and optimism. Yet, in the 1920s, Canadian fertility experienced a very clear decline.

on the rise. Fertility levels fell rapidly.

Changes to divorce legislation in 1968, and again in 1986, allowed for easier access to divorce and a subsequent increase in the number of divorces, likely affecting both the number and timing of births for couples."

Let us begin by enumerating the main causes of infertility that those who speak on this subject mention. There are quite a few:

- ✓ Decline in infant and juvenile mortality.
- ✓ Less need for children in an urban society than in a rural one.
- ✓ Less need for children as "staff of the old age" nowadays, as the welfare state provides pensions, healthcare, and long-term care for to the elderly.
- ✓ Incorporation of women into the workforce outside the home (and the opposite is also mentioned by some: insufficient female labor participation).
- ✓ Difficulties in reconciling work and maternity.
- ✓ Higher educational level of women, whose achievements would delay motherhood as well as open other horizons and interests in life.
- ✓ Lack of physical comfort to raise children in urban households, smaller than the rural homes of yesteryears.
- ✓ Delay in age of having a first child [71].
- ✓ Abundance of contraceptive instruments and mechanisms (pre and post-coital pill, preservatives, abortion, IUD, vasectomy, tubal ligation, better knowledge of infertile days in the menstrual cycle, etc.).
- ✓ High rates of family break-up and weaker marital ties.
- ✓ Less religiosity and patriotism than before.
- ✓ High emancipation age from moving out of the parental household and forming one's own.
- ✓ Lower paternal authority against the State in relation to children.
- ✓ Survival of macho patterns in society.
- ✓ Feminist trends against motherhood and the father figure.
- ✓ Ecological trends against human impact on the planet.
- ✓ Increased homosexuality and dissemination of gender ideology.
- ✓ Parents who do not push their children to have (many) children.
- ✓ Inconvenience of having children with current lifestyles, because of the freedom, time for fun, and money that raising children takes away from parents.

---

[71] For instance, on average, in 1977, Spanish women had their first child at 25. Currently that number is 31. In the nineteenth century and before, most likely, that age was several years younger than 25.

✓ Increasing cost of raising a child until he/she is emancipated.
✓ Much greater fiscal pressure than before.
✓ Insufficient wages to have and raise children, high unemployment rates, and job insecurity.
✓ High housing costs.
✓ Lack of aid from the State.
✓ Etc.

Without trying to be exhaustive, so that this book does not consist of 1,000 or more pages, let's examine below whether these potential causes of the low prevailing fertility are essentially justified or not.

Fewer children now, because children and adolescents rarely die

The first of all these mentioned causes—the lower infant and juvenile mortality—seems quite logical. Formerly, over half of children died before reaching adulthood, and almost all those died before reaching adolescence. The table below shows the probability of surviving after a certain age in Spain in 1880 and in 2013. If a mother had a child who died very young, then another who also died shortly, later had two more who survived into adulthood, and finally decided not to have any more children, in total, she would have given birth four times to end up having only two children. Likewise, thinking that some of their children would most likely die young, more than one couple would have "one more, just in case." Nowadays, when a woman has two children, it is highly unlikely that both of them will not survive beyond their youth. Today, only 1% of children born in France, Spain, Italy, Switzerland, Sweden or Japan, for example, will not reach the age of 40. That same 1% figure can be applied, minus a year or two with respect to the age of 40, in any other developed country, and will end up being true, in no time, in developing nations as well.

Probability of not surviving in Spain beyond certain ages, around 1880 and in 2013 (both sexes)			
	Average 1878-1882		2013
Age	Deaths by 1,000 people	Probability of not surviving beyond this age	Probability of not surviving beyond this age
0	256	25.6%	0.27%
1	149	36.7%	0.29%
2	93	42.6%	0.30%
3	42	45.0%	0.31%
4	27	46.5%	0.32%
5	20	47.5%	0.33%
6	13	48.2%	0.34%
7	10	48.7%	0.35%
8	8	49.2%	0.36%
9	7	49.5%	0.37%
10	6	49.8%	0.37%
11	6	50.1%	0.38%
12	5	50.4%	0.39%
13	5	50.6%	0.40%
14	5	50.9%	0.41%
15	6	51.2%	0.42%
20	9	53.0%	0.51%
25	10	55.3%	0.64%
30	10	57.5%	0.79%
35	11	59.7%	0.98%
40	13	62.1%	1.29%
50	19	67.6%	2.85%
60	39	75.6%	6.91%
Data Source: Mortality tables for 1878-1882 and 2013 (INE)			

This very high survival rate implies that today, even though we bring about far fewer children than before, we should end up having the same number of adult children as we did back then and our society should have the same demographic vigor. According to our estimates, with the data in the table below, we now need approximately 60% fewer children than when life expectancy started to increase, as almost 60% of the population died before the age of 35, whereas now, in the countries with the highest life expectancy, that figure is less than 1%. Thanks to this, we can save the effort, suffering, and cost of about 60% of the pregnancies, childbirths, and child rearing, formerly destined to have a painful premature end. Nowadays, for this reason, 2.1 children per woman is the average that guarantees the generational replacement. Towards 1880, with the data in the table below, in

Spain—with a life expectancy at birth of slightly below 29 years—it took about five children per woman, more or less, to replace the population. This figure was similar in countries with a similar level of development, before and after 1880. A significant natural increase in population implied that the average number of children per woman had to have been higher than five, and even higher in women who did not die as a result of pregnancy or childbirth—a frequent thing in those times and previously, as already mentioned—or from other causes, before having been able to give birth to all the children they would have had without their premature death.

The current problem is that in Europe and in countries with a low birth rate, we do not have 60% fewer children than before—we have between 70% and 80% less children. We have taken advantage of this margin, and have even *exceeded* the margin, to have fewer children than in the past, provided by a radical decline in infant and juvenile mortality. To illustrate this concept, it would be as if, collectively, we were someone who used to have a salary of 10,000 dollars a year and spent 9,000, received a raise resulting in a 20,000 salary, started spending more and more, and ended up with a structural expense level of 25,000.

After examining the first major cause among the many that are put forward to explain the low birth rate, and that probably accounts for a large part of the historical fall in the number of children per woman, we will analyze the rests. Some seem quite logical, others, not so much, and the rest will turn out to be pure myths or fallacies in light of the available data and common sense. Although some of these logical causes for a low birth rate are inherent to the modern world, as we will see, we remind the reader that, thanks to the lower mortality, we should have plenty of room in matters of fertility to cope with these other causes, provided we do not fall below the population replacement threshold (2.1 children per woman)—a level we are well below in many countries. On the other hand, whether they are logical or not, if we do not sufficiently counteract the effect of some of these real causes of a low birth rate, we are faced with a demographic decline/suicide. Therefore, resigning ourselves to the fact that there is no way to increase birth rate because some of these causes are supposedly "untouchable" does not seem like a good idea, especially when the drop in the number of births below replacement thresholds occurred only a few decades ago. Not much has been done in many countries to combat the low birth rate, and, only recently, and still insufficiently, has there been a general awareness that it is a serious problem for these countries.

Fewer children as we live in cities and not the countryside

It seems widely accepted that, in the rural environment where a vast majority of the population traditionally lived, children were wanted in part because, from their adolescence, and in a few cases even before the beginning of their adolescence, they were a valuable source of labor. Therefore, as they could be raised using moderate resources, to have children was a profitable investment in over a few years, from a purely economic point of view. Certainly, we no longer live in this type of society, and therefore, if this hypothesis were correct—as it seems to be, to a good extent—this reason would also be one of the real causes as to why we have fewer children than before. Although this correlation does not necessarily imply a cause-and-effect relationship, we observe that, for at least 150 years, in Europe, in general, the greater percentage of urban population there is, the lower the global fertility. Even today, in developing countries, birth rates are much higher in rural areas than in large cities. For example, according to data from INEGI (National Institute of Statistics and Geography of Mexico), in the capital Mexico City, in 2000, the birth rate was 1.9 children per woman versus 3.6 in the most backward and rural state of Chiapas. In 2013, there continued to be a considerable difference between the two Mexican states, although much smaller than thirteen years earlier: 1.8 children per woman in Mexico City and 2.5 in Chiapas. In Russia, between 1974 and 2014, fertility in rural areas averaged 46% higher (0.69 additional children per woman) than in urban areas.

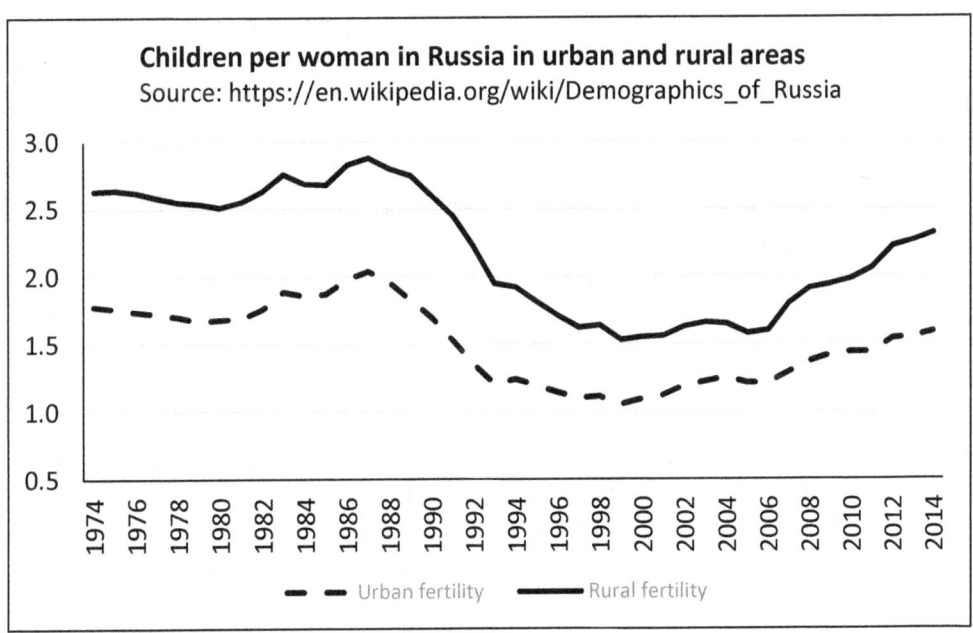

Fewer children because we live in cities and in less spacious homes than in the past

Along the same lines, there are also those who argue that, in order to raise (many) children, the discomfort of living in smaller houses in cities, compared with the larger homes of the past in rural areas (the houses themselves, plus the adjacent space available for the little ones to run around freely), is one of the factors that leads people to have fewer children than before. It does not seem unreasonable that this has a negative effect on fertility, especially for those who want to have a lot of offspring. Since the vast majority of modern homes in developed countries have at least two bedrooms, the lack of rooms is not an insurmountable obstacle to having at least two children. Of course, those who really want to have quite a few children, but do not have a big house, can resort to bunk beds to extend the bedroom space, the sort which abounded, for example, in the house of a family very close to and loved by the author, with seven children born in the 60's, when, in Spain, the average birth rate was about three children per woman. In that house, the three sisters slept in a triple decker bunk bed in a room while the four brothers slept in two regular bunk beds in another room.

What happened with the fertility of the heads of the Spanish Royal family, or the British Royal family, will prove very illustrative of this phenomenon. Royal families certainly do not have a problem with space in their homes to raise offspring, in addition to having abundant domestic service to discharge the parents, and indeed the mother, from all the aspects of raising children they do not want or cannot handle. Nor do they have financial problems in raising children. The mother is also not dismissed or harmed in her professional career for being pregnant or any other of the typical obstacles that are claimed as reasons for barely having children. Well, the great-grandfather of the present king of Spain, King Alfonso XIII, had seven legitimate children. His grandfather Don Juan, Count of Barcelona, who did not come to reign due to the complicated vicissitudes of the Spanish monarchy in the 20th century, had four children. His father, King Juan Carlos I, had three children. Finally the current king, Philip VI, has two daughters. If this trend continues, the heir of the future queen Leonor will be a single child, who in turn will not have any descendants (!!!).

Prior to this, in the nineteenth century, Queen Isabella II of Spain had twelve children—five of them stillborn or dead immediately after being born—and King Alfonso XII had "only" three children, but he died very young (when he has 28). If he had lived longer, it seems likely that he would have had some more children.

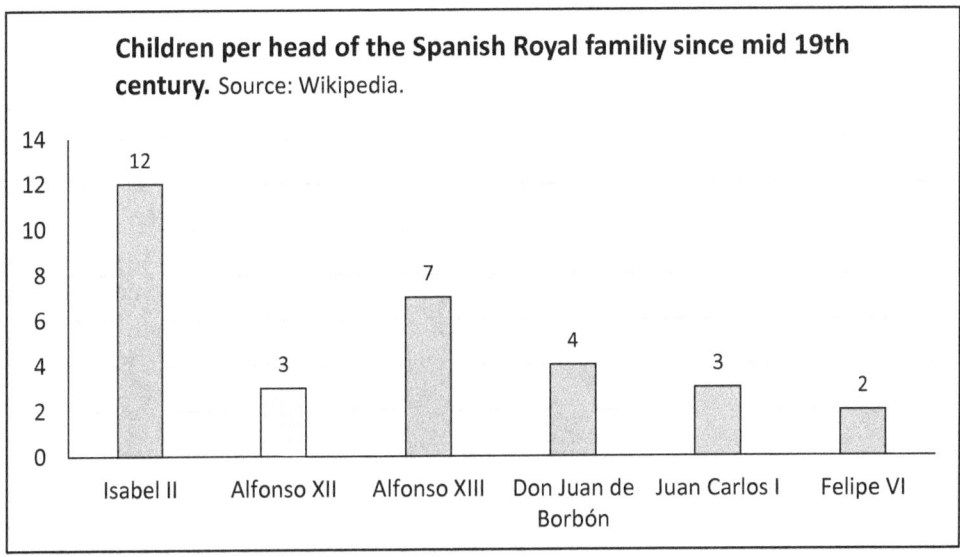

Children per head of the Spanish Royal familiy since mid 19th century. Source: Wikipedia.

Going North, in the British case, the pattern is very similar, from the nine children of the Queen of the golden age of Britain, Victoria, to the two children of Prince Charles. His son, Prince William, has two children. He might still have more, but it is unlikely that they would be many more. Kate Middleton, his wife, when she delivered her third child, was 36 years old, an age at which female fertility tends to drop very rapidly, and women seldom have many additional children after it, if they already have some.

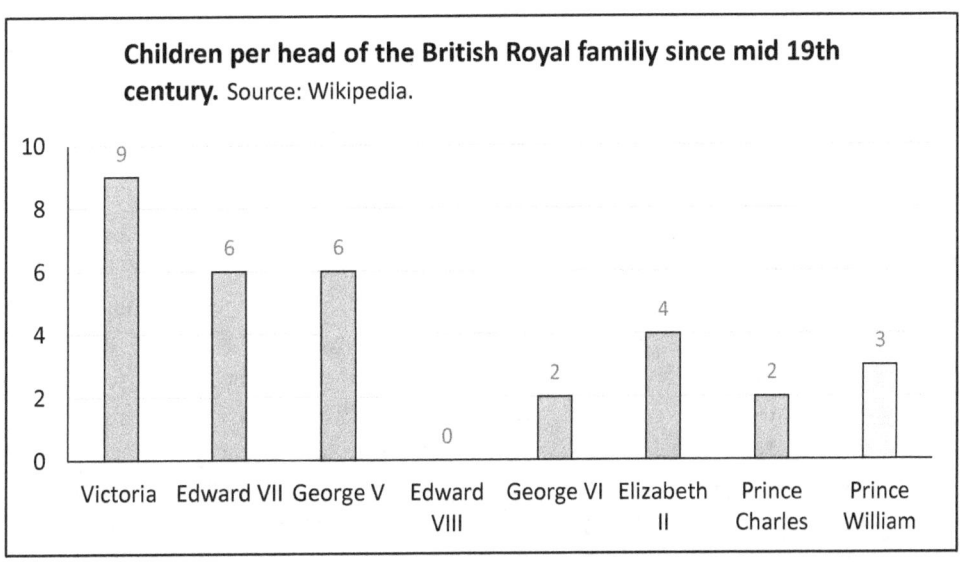

Children per head of the British Royal familiy since mid 19th century. Source: Wikipedia.

Going South, the sultan of Morocco, Mohamed VI, has two children. His father, Hassan II, had five. His grandfather Mohamed V had seven (from three wives, five with one of them, and one with each of the other two). Going East, the former emperor of Japan, Hiro Hito, had seven children. The current emperor, Akihito, has three. His heir, prince Naruhito, has two. Hence, fertility trends in these four royal families are very similar, despite their significant cultural diversity: European-Catholic, European-Protestant, African-Muslim, Asian-Shintoist. The morale of this royal example, if it were not a mere coincidence, is that the vast majority of people follow the general trends of society in their time, whether commoners or royal stock, rich, poor, or middle class. Another lesson in matters of children is that, most likely, almost all those who want to have children, can have several. When children are not desired, although all material conditions are favorable, people do not have them.

Fewer children because the State promises to take care of us in our old age and we no longer need them as we used to in the autumn years

For parents, children were considered to be their "old age insurance" in yesteryears. Parents told their children: "You will be the staff of my old age." In modern societies, however—with a State that gives us a retirement pension that oscillates between modest and significant, provides us with free medical care and, eventually, gives us or finances long-term care if we cannot function on our own and must depend on others—children are no longer necessary for our old age. It is convenient to have them for their affection and the little or much long-term care they provide us, but they are no longer perceived as indispensable for these needs, as in the past.

The author heard the prestigious German economist Hans-Werner Sinn, director of the Munich IFO economic think tank, and who kindly wrote a foreword for this book, comment, during a lecture in Madrid in 2015 at the headquarters of the BBVA bank, that modern retirement pensions were created by Bismarck in Germany in the 19th century to alleviate the hardships of the old age for those who had not had children. With the generalization of public retirement pension systems and other benefits that are necessary for the elderly, the State would have made a significant contribution to making it less necessary for people to have children. The "Kissinger Report" already mentioned against fertility in the least developed countries, to which we dedicate an Annex to this book, precisely includes, among the measures intended for people to have fewer children, the introduction in Third World countries of social security systems that give economic protection to the elderly. As a result of that lower birth rate, the State itself will have increasing difficulties—it already has some, in societies as old as those of the West or Japan—

to fulfill its promise of giving us good retirement pensions, free or nearly free medical care, and long-term care services for those who need them, because of the abundance of elderly people in a society in which people of active age tend to diminish. It would be a textbook case of the so-called law of unintended consequences: you act with good intentions in pursuit of something desirable, and in the long run, unexpected problems—equal or greater than the ones you attempted to address—are created.

Fewer children due to women's new roles in the workforce and their higher education level

Regarding the incorporation of women into the workforce outside the home, and the fact that the achievement of a higher educational level for women would delay the age of motherhood and open other horizons and interests in life beyond being a traditional mother / housewife, it seems logical that both these factors have a negative impact, structurally, on the number of children born. There would be a different number of children when the personal priority of women in their prime is to have children and raise them compared to when this is secondary to the development of their professional activity. The "Kissinger report" also proposed, as two key measures to cause birth rates to decline in the Third World, to encourage female education and for women to perform paid jobs.

It is true that, in the modern world, a large proportion of women (and couples) do not plan to have children until they achieve a stable and satisfactory employment horizon, for reasons of economic well-being as well as to give "the best" to their children, reasons that would lead many women to postpone motherhood, and a few of them, thereby, to delay it so much that when they finally want to, they can no longer conceive. Along this idea, there are some countries, such as Sweden, where a high rate of female employment is accompanied by one of the highest birth rates in Europe, though is still insufficient and going down. This correlation, however, does not occur equally in other countries with birth rates elevated by Western standards, such as France, Ireland, or the USA. Conversely, there are countries with very high female labor rates, such as Switzerland, Austria, or Germany, where the birth rate is extremely low. It is also important to separately analyze the fertility of native and immigrant women in the various countries, since the latter, with some exceptions like the Chinese, generally have higher jobless rates and higher birth rates than native women. When the contribution in number of births of foreign-born women to the host country is high, and their average fertility is much higher than that of native women (as is the case in most of Western Europe), the conclusions reached on the relationship in those countries between birth rates and female employment rates may be significantly distorted because of this impact.

On the other hand, it is evident that the maternity of an employed woman causes an appreciable direct cost for companies—unless this is compensated by the State—due to maternity leave, as well as the absences from work, by either parent, to care for their children (mainly related to medical care and school obligations), for something that directly benefits the parents and society, and, only in the much longer term and if they survive, the companies: the children of their employees. Likewise, for the parents' co-workers, their child-care related work absences often involve extra workload, especially in companies without the critical mass to easily replace employees absent for these reasons, e.g., a restaurant with three waiters, where one of them must suddenly step out because the school has called saying his/her child has a fever and must be taken to the doctor as soon as possible. Therefore, unless companies are compensated and/or their managers and employees are very pro-maternity and aware how essential it is for society for more children to be born, it is logical that companies tend to frown when their female employees get pregnant or when employees are absent because they are caring for their children. It is also logical that co-workers do not rejoice much when working with those who often take time off work because of their children, especially if it inconveniences them in carrying out their own mission or if they have to assume additional volumes of work.

It is one thing for these difficulties and costs of motherhood to be a reality, and therefore denying them would be counterproductive, and another thing for it to be considered negative for women to fully equate men in education levels—actually, today, in almost all of Europe, combined, women exceed men in education—that those who so desire work outside the home, and that working women have children. Therefore, if we really want to effectively solve this difficulty, given the fact that children are a benefit to their parents and a necessity for society, and often are the opposite in material matters for companies and colleagues, it is necessary to discharge the companies from the economic damages that the parenthood of their employees entails. Otherwise, we should expect to have lower birth rates and/or fewer working mothers and/or pay working mothers less (probably a little of each), as well as men less responsible for the upbringing of their children when it may affect their professional performance. Compensating co-workers for the absence of mothers and fathers from work seems more difficult, as several companies probably do it themselves upon seeing their additional effort, at the expense of fewer salary increases and promotions for the fathers and mothers who miss work often to care for their children. In any case, co-workers will always be more willing to take on a part of that extra workload if they are pro-birth themselves (because they have children themselves, and understand such situations first-hand, or because they are aware that children are desirable in a society) than if they do not give importance to this matter.

What is much more debatable as far as its beneficial effect—and especially in countries with a serious birth deficit—is that the State, the intellectuals, and the media promote the idea that what is essential for a woman to have a full life is to develop a successful career, while motherhood, implicitly or explicitly, is presented as superfluous. For society, the maternity (and paternity) of a small part of its members is only superfluous if other members of society compensate for the infertility of that group by having enough children, as it used to be, when there were, for example, many more celibate religious people (priests, monks, nuns) than now, in addition to quite a few infertile people for health reasons, and many women who did not have children because they never married in times when almost all babies were born in wedlock. Thus, nothing bad happened if a few people did not have children, since those who were parents had many. Nowadays, this is not the case in country after country, where, despite having a deficit of births, ranging from significant to enormous, in the dichotomy between female labor outside the home and fertility, the only thing that is prioritized, promoted, and extoled in the laws and the media is the former, despite its negative effect on the latter, instead of researching how it would be possible to reconcile the two in a reasonable way.

In our opinion, if there is any place where society could use the tremendous benefit of the almost nonexistent child and youth mortality, with the implication that far fewer children are required than before, it is precisely where women and men enjoy the same access to higher education and career opportunities, something that in the past would have rendered human populations unsustainable in the medium term, because of the lack of children and young people—as long as this does not end up resulting in a birth rate as insufficient as that of Germany, Spain, Italy and many other countries already mentioned. Of course, female work outside the home makes it difficult, in a structural way, to have as many children as was common in the past, because of the complexity of attending to both external work and a large progeny, apart from some "super-mothers" (and "super-fathers")—really the exception—who have as many children as women did before but who also work outside the home as women do now. However, since a pattern of two children per woman (and in some cases, three or more) is enough to guarantee the demographic health of modern societies, this number of average descendants and having a satisfactory professional career do not necessarily seem incompatible.

We do not have children due to the difficulties of reconciling work life/professional career and maternity

Closely linked to the above, nearly the same, but said in other words, in modern societies, very much committed to the creation—and later consumption—of economic wealth, the large number of hours that non-retired adults spend per day outside the home, between commuting to the work place and the working day itself, interferes with family life and makes it inconvenient to have and raise (many) children. Who takes care of them on a daily basis? Formerly, except for the better-off and wealthy households, who could use paid nannies / domestic services for these chores, and even in the majority of them, it was mainly the mothers. And today? In part, children are cared for in schools and nurseries. Even so, parents, and more often the mother than the father, still have to balance family and work, especially when children are under the age of two. Young adults who have not yet had children hear those who have children complain about this, and logically, it doesn't help them to decide to have children of their own. A part of those who have already had one or two children, because of these difficulties lived in their own flesh, give up having more, which is why, in general, women who do not work outside the home have more children. Furthermore, the percentage of women working part-time soars with the number of children they have, as shown in the table below.

Percentage of women aged 25-49 with part-time employment in 2014 in the EU-28, the five most populated western European countries, and two European countries less populated but with relatively high fertility					
Data source: Eurostat	Childless	One child	Two children	Three children	Increase in the part-time employed rate from 0 to 3 children
European Union	20.0	31.3	39.2	45.1	25.1
Germany	25.3	59.4	74.6	77.8	52.5
France	19.3	24.7	34.2	42.9	23.6
United Kingdom	16.3	44.5	58.2	62.0	45.7
Italy	27.8	35.7	42.1	45.1	17.3
Spain	21.5	29.7	29.9	30.7	9.2
Ireland	16.2	32.7	37.2	47.3	31.1
Sweden	24.5	32.8	37.1	40.7	16.2

Yes, the difficulty of reconciling work and family life is one of the things that most complicates having and raising children. Of course, companies, in general, prefer to have female employees who do not have to leave work because of pregnancy, childbirth, or child care, which has a negative impact on many women's desire to have children in this day and age. It would not be logical if this were not the case, unless the companies were sufficiently compensated (for example, with very significant reductions in Social Security contributions for companies that employ women with young children).

However, this doesn't seem to be the main factor as to why so many people in developed countries do not have children, or, at most, have one, as some evidence indicates:

✓ In Germany, Austria, or Switzerland, countries with fairly reasonable work hours—and very low levels of unemployment—the birth rate is almost as low as in others, such as Spain, where many argue that the difficulties mothers have in reconciling family life and work are the main reasons we hardly have children. It is also striking that, although the birth rates of Germany, Italy, or Spain are similarly low (with a rebound in Germany since 2012, which we hope will strengthen and increase), the table shows that part-time employment rates are very different in these three countries.

✓ Part-time work is more common in the Netherlands than in any other developed nation. It is so frequent among women—75% of Dutch females aged 25 to 54 have a part-time job—that their average number of effectively work hours per week was around 25 – 26 hours in 2015. However, fertility rate in the Netherlands is not impressive (1.66 children per woman in 2015, 1.65 in 2016).

✓ The birth rate for women who do not work outside the home, because they have chosen to be more "traditional" women ("Stay-at-home-moms"), is greater than the rate for women who work, but it is not "explosive." For example, in Spain, the birth rate, according to our rough estimates obtained by crossing birth data by age and occupation of mothers and women in general, among ladies between 25 and 44 years old, is about 1.8 children per woman, compared to about 1.2 for those who work. 1.8 is 50% higher, which is a lot, but only 0.6 more children per woman in absolute terms, which is not that much. Moreover, it is, of course, much less than the historical Spanish birth rate of 4 to 6 children per woman.

✓ Female public servants, in addition to having a stable job and an employer (the State) who advocates against discrimination of sex, generally have reasonable working hours, but do not appear to have an abnormally higher fertility rate than the overall average, based on partial indicators available to the author of the book[72], and the information the author has been able to

---

[72] In OECD countries, women, despite representing only 43% of the total workforce, occupied 58% of public positions in 2013, a percentage that tends to be higher among the younger staff. In Spain, where women are also the majority, and growing, in public service, in some regions of the country, public servants constitute a very high percentage of the female workforce. In spite of this, in these regions, the overall birth rate is very low. This is the situation, for example, in Extremadura, where 36% of the women working in that region in 2015 did so in the public

gather informally from leaders of diverse public administrations in the past. Nevertheless, in honor of the truth and the factual rigor with which we have tried to produce this work from end to end, this is a point where the author lacks sufficient data to issue a judgment with the same assurance as many others in this book. For this reason, the author urges anyone who can provide real and unbiased data about it, or who can publish these data, to do so, since this hypothesis (that the female public servants do not have a much higher fertility rate than the rest of the women) might only be true in part. And it's very important to validate it, as it is a key group when it comes to understanding whether discrimination against working mothers by businesses, and the difficulty in reconciling a working life and maternity, are or are not key elements when deciding to have more or fewer children.

✓ In the United States, there is little legal protection against firing pregnant women or women with young children, and yet fertility rates in the North American giant far exceed the European average, and even more in relation to countries with special legal protection but with very low fertility rates, like Spain.

✓ A very high percentage of European women have a part-time job, but despite this, in Europe, people have the few children that they have. In countries like Spain, there is labor legislation especially favorable for mothers to have reduced working hours. A Spanish working mother, if she wishes, can request—and must be granted by her company—a reduction of her workday between one and five hours a day, with a proportional reduction of her gross salary[73]. The woman who receives this workday reduction is given a reinforced protection against termination equivalent to the one given in case of pregnancy or the maternity leave, until the youngest of her children is twelve years old.[74]. Despite such favorable

---

sector, a percentage probably even higher among Extremaduran women of Spanish nationality and of childbearing age. Despite this, the birth rate for Spanish women residing in that region was 1.26 children per woman in 2015. The correlation by regions between the fertility of Spanish women and the percentage of women working in the public sector in 2015 was -10%. In other words, there is no correlation (the relationship is even slightly negative, although by so little that no conclusions can be drawn).

[73] This wage reduction, except in the case of very low salaries, exempt from taxes, is smaller in terms of net salary, as progressive taxation in this case acts in favor of the employee, through a reduction in the average personal income tax rate due to the salary reduction.

[74] Until the government of José Luis Rodríguez Zapatero (socialist), that age limit for the youngest child was three years old. Zapatero increased it to eight. Under Mariano Rajoy (center right) as president of the Spanish government, it was raised to twelve.

conditions to keep their job and have a customized work schedule, the birth rate for women in Spain, and especially those working outside the home, is still very low.

✓ Finally, as an anecdote, probably representative, let us recall what was said earlier about the decreasing fertility in the last 150 years of the heads of the British and Spanish royal family and their royal consorts, without balancing problems between maternity and work, lack of economic resources or any other material obstacle to have children.

Ultimately, everything that facilitates a better balance between work and family life should be a positive factor to promote more births, in addition to being able to raise children better and enjoy them more. But the data and the previous rationale indicate this cannot be the main key of a low birth rate. On the other hand, it has been known for centuries that you can't square the circle. Female work outside the home is not utterly incompatible with maternity and satisfactory child rearing, yet their simultaneity presents undeniable difficulties. The denial of these difficulties, or the attempt to solve them by putting the burden on businesses, is likely to lead only to failure in the very important fact that women who wish to can have a satisfactory professional life and be mother at the same time, or that society have the children it needs for its future viability.

Delay in the age at which we have children

The delay in the age at the first child—and subsequently the others, if any—is one of the fundamental reasons why we now have so few children. Several centuries ago, especially among less civilized peoples, women used to have their first child before the age of 20, often around 15 or 16. Currently, in the European Union, the mother of more than 99% of newborns is 18 or older. In Spain, in 1976, with a birth rate of 2.8 children per woman, 32.9% of the babies born that year had a mother under 25 years old and 10.8% were over 35 years of age. In 2014, with a birth rate of 1.3 children per woman, only 9.3% of the newborns had a mother under 20 years of age, while the mother of 28.7% of the babies was over 35. Nowadays, if we consider the data sets representing the average age women first become mothers together with the birth rate in the fifty provinces of Spain, using data from 2014, there was a negative 70% correlation between the average age of access to maternity and the number of children per woman[75].

Having children and forming a family is not a vital goal for the young people of this day and age, as it once was. The high percentage of young people who attend university, especially women, who now represent a large majority of the university population in almost all European countries, facilitates postponing access to maternity. The sad thing is that when they finally want to have children, it is too late for many women, and "they are over the hill" / their biological clock for maternity has passed, or for having as many children as they would want, because they delayed maternity excessively, as they first sought—men and women alike—to consolidate their professional prospects and to put their material life on track (a good job and, if possible, a house of their own), while trying to find, often unsuccessfully, the ideal partner. The result, in the end, is that, nowadays, a lot of people wish they had had more children (or at least one more child), but they cannot, or no longer have the stamina to do so, because they had their first child at an increasingly older age.

The difficulty in getting pregnant, the female infertility rate, is very low until 30 years of age, increasing slowly from 20 to 30, but then growing faster from 30 to 35, much faster from 35 to 40, becoming very high between 40 and 45, and is maximal from 45 on. Ergo, because of the delay of motherhood, many babies that were wanted are lost, because they were not conceived. Or, since the first child born in a family arrives with a delay of several months or years after the first attempt to conceive, due to insurmountable difficulties in the following attempts, they end up without a little brother or sister.

Male infertility, which increases at a slower rate with age than female infertility, also plays a significant role, among other reasons, because, on average fathers are several years older than mothers in almost all families. As a matter of fact, fertility specialists consider that when a woman fails to become pregnant, in about one-third of the cases, it's due to her male partner's infertility, in another third of the cases, it's due to the woman's own infertility, and in the last third, either both are infertile, or it is not possible to determine who is. Therefore, although the theoretical age range within which males can fertilize a woman is wider than the age range women are able to become pregnant, in practice, the male contributes approximately the same, on average, as a woman, in couples' infertility. One of the reasons for this is that the father is generally several years older than the mother

---

[75] The correlation between two sets of data does not imply causality, but does indicate that there could be causality. The fact that in this case we are studying it is -70% indicates that there could be a high degree of negative interrelation between delayed access to maternity and infertility (the older women are when they become mothers, the fewer children they have).

(for example, according to our estimates, in Spain, the father is almost three years older on average).

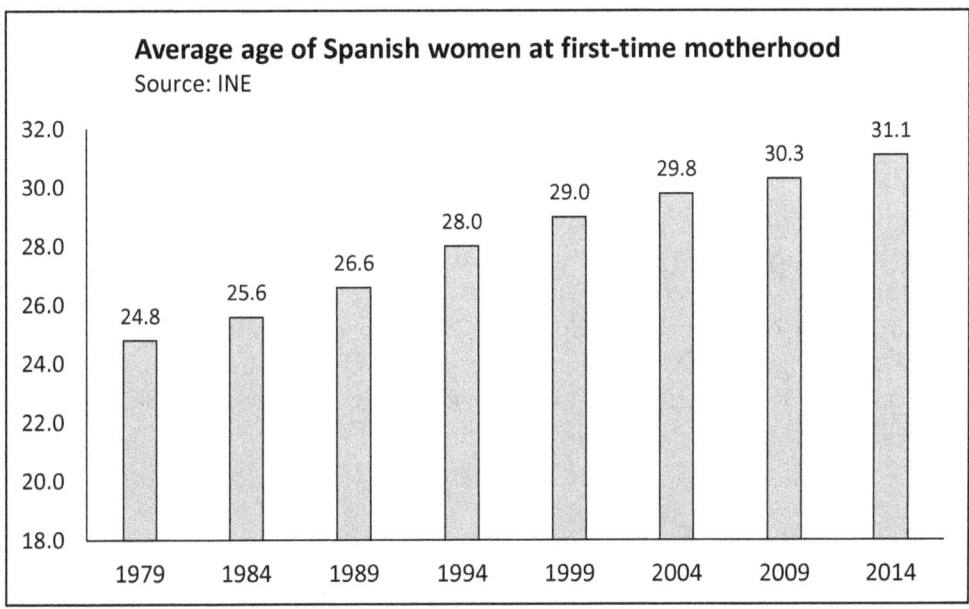

With the increase in the age of motherhood, birth rates are adversely affected not only because of the increasing difficulty for older women to become pregnant, but also because, if the long wait to expect a "Happy Event" is finally over, it is much more likely that the promise will not be fulfilled if the expectant woman is older. There is a larger number of miscarriages in women whose biological clock marks an hour / age too late to have uncomplicated pregnancies, a proportion much higher than among young women. A 40-year-old woman who becomes pregnant is three to five times more likely to suffer this terrible misfortune than a 25-to-30-year-old woman. In Spain, the average maternity age in 1976 (mean age of women who gave birth that year) was 28 years old and the average age at which women had their first child was 25. In 2015, the average maternity age was about 33 years old and Spanish women had their first child, on average, at 31 years old. If Spanish women had their first child two to three years earlier than they currently do (around 28-29 on average), as is the case in France, and had their last child, at the latest, at age 35, the birth rate in 2015, according to our estimates, would have been 0.07 to 0.1 additional children per woman (approximately 5% to 7% more births), just through the reduction in the number of spontaneous abortions suffered by women who wanted to have children.

The risk of miscarriage also increases significantly when the father is over 35 years old (about 30% more, according to a 2005 study by Dr. Rémy Slama of the French institute INSERM, published by the American Journal of Epidemiology[76]). Coincidentally the median age for male progenitors of children born in Spain in 2014 was 35 years old. In other words, in about half of all pregnancies in Spain, if not more, there was a significant increased risk of miscarriage because of the father's age, although there are no data on how many miscarriages this caused.

In addition to a woman's lower probability of becoming pregnant, and the higher likelihood of miscarrying as parents are older, there are at least two more factors having a negative effect on the birth rate when women try to become mothers at an advanced age: pregnancies and deliveries are more unpleasant and potentially dangerous experiences than at a younger age. This, logically and everything else being equal, should lead to fewer women getting pregnant again after their first or second bad experience. The older the mother, the higher the probability of giving birth by caesarean section, the higher the percentage of dystocic births (abnormally slow or difficult labor or delivery), and the higher the probability of pregnancy being ectopic (extrauterine).

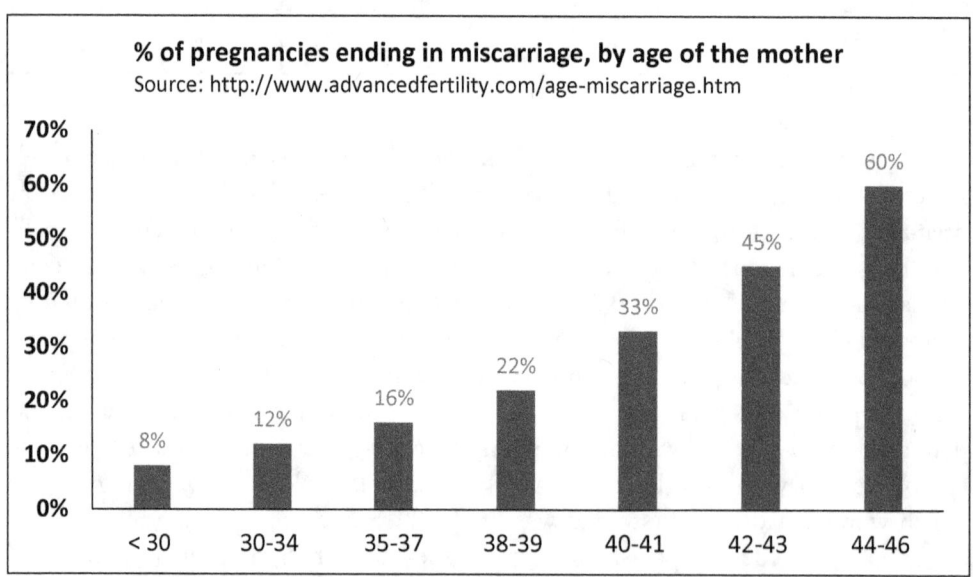

% of pregnancies ending in miscarriage, by age of the mother
Source: http://www.advancedfertility.com/age-miscarriage.htm

As for the higher percentage of cesarean sections with age, it is a clear sign that the body is no longer in such good shape to bear children. In addition, the readiness of mothers to have more children after a cesarean delivery is certainly lower than when the birth is natural, either because of the (very) unpleasant experience or because of medical advice.

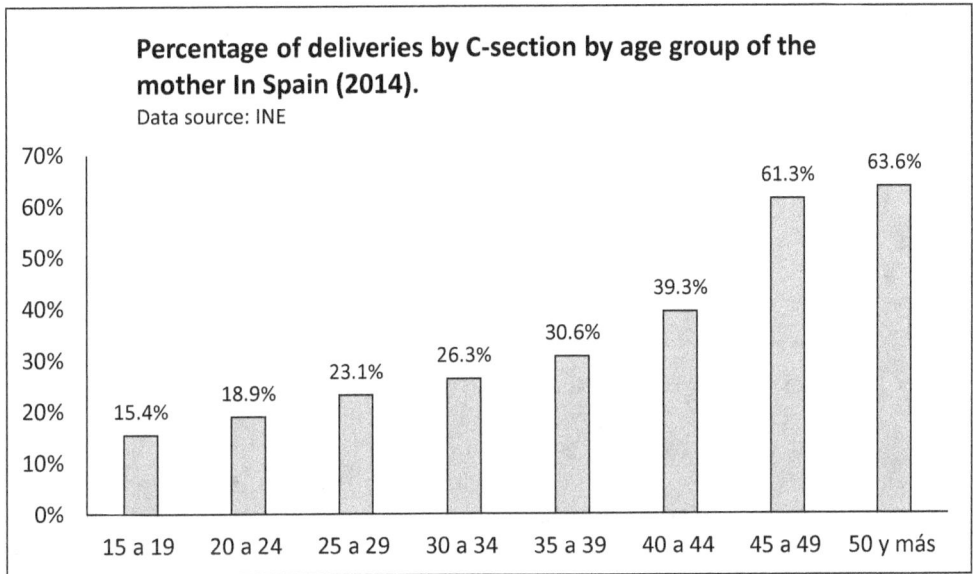

Percentage of deliveries by C-section by age group of the mother In Spain (2014).
Data source: INE

Likewise, the rates of dystocic births (deliveries that are abnormally slow or laborious, due to fetal or maternal reasons) grow with the mother's age, with a sharp increase starting at approximately 38 to 40 years old. Again, presumably, after a dystocic childbirth, all other things being equal, the woman is less inclined to have another child.

Finally, age also increases the likelihood of experiencing risky pregnancies and with more discomfort, such as ectopic or extrauterine pregnancies. These, in particular, are four times more likely in women aged 15 to 24 years (according to Roger P. Smith, Frank Netter (May 2003) Netter's Obstetrics, Gynecology and Women's Health: ISBN 978-1929007257).

Ah, one more thing: the "Kissinger Report" also proposes that, in order to reduce birth rates in the "Third World," the legal minimum marriage age for children must be raised. The idea is clear: the older people are when they get married, the fewer children they will have.

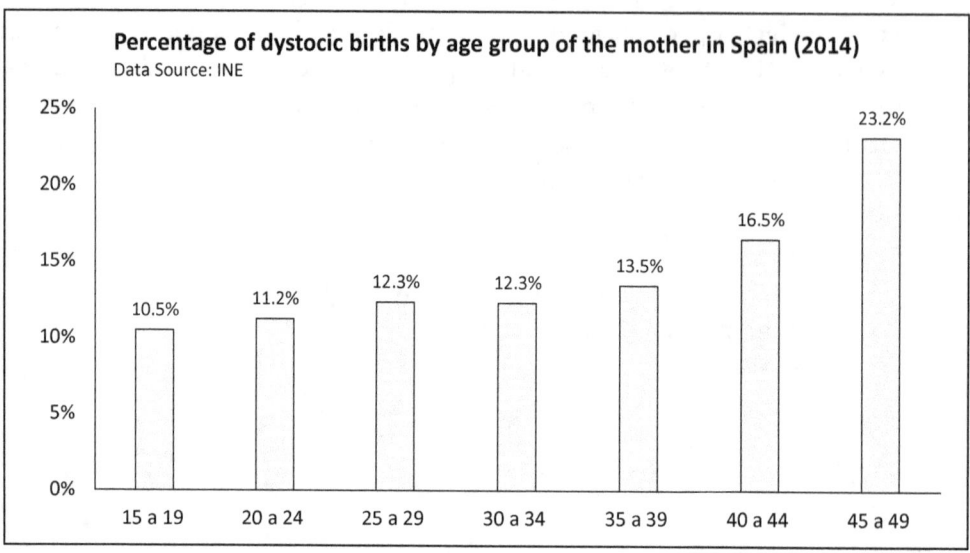

Percentage of dystocic births by age group of the mother in Spain (2014)
Data Source: INE

Delay in the age of juvenile emancipation

One of the things that most contributes to not having children at a young age is the delay in the emancipation of young adults from the parental home. In general, the earlier this emancipation takes place, the earlier we begin to live as adults, the earlier we have our first child, and the more children we have in total. Although this connection is not always so clear, as there are countries in the EU with emancipation rates above the European average for children under 30 years old and birth rates lower than the European average, there is, in general, a positive correlation between the two variables (that is, the sooner the independence from the parental home takes place, the more children people end up having). As is the case with most of what we are discussing in this chapter, this is not the only, or even the main, key for the low modern birth rate, but it seems to be one of the main ingredients, especially in a good number of developed countries.

This connection can be appreciated through visual inspection of the following graph, which shows the percentage of European women aged 25 to 29 years who no longer live in the parental home, by country, together with the fertility rate, in parentheses, after the country name. Our estimate is that in 2013 there was a 75% mathematical correlation between both indicators, which is very high (100% would indicate a linear correlation between emancipation before age 30 and birth rate;. We do not have such precise data on these two factors for the US, although the mean age at (the first) marriage is several years younger than in Europe, the vast majority of young people who attend higher education leave home to go to the university (college) around the age of 18, and the age of first-time American mothers is several years younger than the European average. The Yankee birth rate, in the period

2010-2014, was approximately 20% higher than the European average.

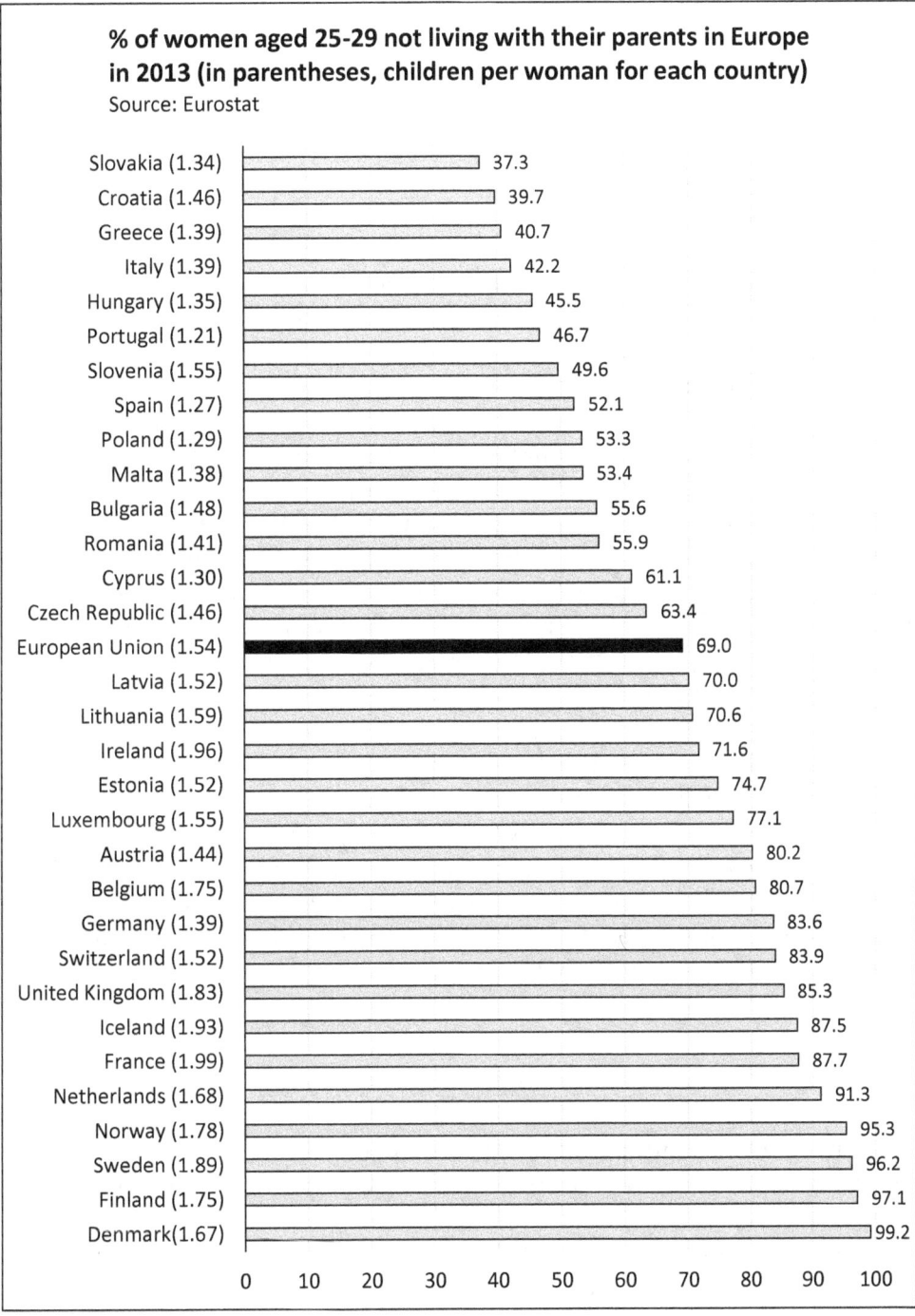

% of women aged 25-29 not living with their parents in Europe in 2013 (in parentheses, children per woman for each country)
Source: Eurostat

Slovakia (1.34)	37.3
Croatia (1.46)	39.7
Greece (1.39)	40.7
Italy (1.39)	42.2
Hungary (1.35)	45.5
Portugal (1.21)	46.7
Slovenia (1.55)	49.6
Spain (1.27)	52.1
Poland (1.29)	53.3
Malta (1.38)	53.4
Bulgaria (1.48)	55.6
Romania (1.41)	55.9
Cyprus (1.30)	61.1
Czech Republic (1.46)	63.4
European Union (1.54)	69.0
Latvia (1.52)	70.0
Lithuania (1.59)	70.6
Ireland (1.96)	71.6
Estonia (1.52)	74.7
Luxembourg (1.55)	77.1
Austria (1.44)	80.2
Belgium (1.75)	80.7
Germany (1.39)	83.6
Switzerland (1.52)	83.9
United Kingdom (1.83)	85.3
Iceland (1.93)	87.5
France (1.99)	87.7
Netherlands (1.68)	91.3
Norway (1.78)	95.3
Sweden (1.89)	96.2
Finland (1.75)	97.1
Denmark(1.67)	99.2

Abundance of cheap contraceptive instruments and systems

The abundance of contraceptive methods, instruments and mechanisms (pre and post-coital pill, condoms, abortion, IUD, vasectomy, tubal ligation, better knowledge of infertile days in the menstrual cycle, etc.) greatly facilitates that we have fewer children than before. There can be no doubt. In the "Kissinger Report" of 1974 against fertility in the least developed countries, the massive use of contraceptive methods in poor countries is one of the main pillars of the anti-birth rate plan the report contains.

However, and this is important to point out, modern contraceptive methods do not fully explain low birth rates, not by a long shot, since in many countries, such as European countries, the USA, or Japan, birth rates were already much lower than historical rates when these mechanisms started to be widely disseminated. As we saw in the first chapter of this book, the birth rate in the West was already much lower than the historical norm around 1950-1960, just before the arrival of the birth-control pill and the legalization of abortion. Even later, in 1975 in Spain at the end of the Franco regime, when both the pill and abortion were prohibited, the birth rate, at 2.8 children per woman, was already half of what it was a century to a century and a half before. In West Germany, in 1960, the birth rate was already at around only 2.4 children per woman, even without the birth-control pill (which began to be used in the US only in 1960) and when abortion was not yet legal (abortion became legal in West Germany in 1972).

Does it make sense that States should publicly fund access to contraceptive treatments or methods in countries experiencing a significant demographic winter? It does not seem logical in places where what is needed are more children, and where the current cost of contraceptive means is very small compared to what it costs to raise a child from conception to emancipation from the family home (between tens of thousands of euros / dollars and several hundreds of thousands, depending on the type of household).

Abortion and birth rates

"I will not give to a woman a pessary to cause abortion"
(one of the tenets of the "**Hippocratic Oath**," classic ethical code of physicians)

Especially important among contraceptive means is abortion. In addition to being the most controversial of them all for ethical reasons, and of the psychological harm inflicted on the woman who undergoes it—in some cases, moderate, but hardly void; in many cases, considerable; and in more than a few, simply devastating—abortion in Europe, Northern America and other areas of the world takes away a large number of human babies, who, incidentally, had they not been eliminated during their gestation per instructions of their mother, would have greatly softened the shortage of births suffered by countries affected by the demographic winter, and, in a few of them would even have reversed it by elevating the birth rate above the replacement level.

It is true that, in the vast majority of contemporary societies, there is no consensus as to whether voluntary abortion is a murder or an absolute right of the mother, as we hereby mention bluntly the two opposite manners of categorizing abortion. However, without delving into the substance of the moral debate, it is undeniable that its mass practice results in the *preventive* elimination of an enormous number of future babies, in societies where what would be needed to enjoy a good demographic health would be just the opposite: many additional babies. Thus, the facilitation of abortion by the State in countries afflicted with infertility, including almost all the most developed countries, to the point of offering it for free to women who wish to abort in many Western European countries, financing it with taxpayer money[77], is at the very least "eye-catching," since these are countries suffering from birth deficit levels between significant and very alarming, especially when the price for an abortion in private clinics (from 200 - 300 to 2,000 – 2,500 euros / dollars) is the equivalent of a very small fraction of the average annual per capita income in those countries (10 to 200 times higher), and the full cost to the parents of raising a child until emancipation would add up to between 25 and 2,000 times that amount, according to our estimates, variable by country, social class, family habits, schooling, and higher education, among other factors. It is indeed striking because pregnancy is not a disease, nor does it pose serious health risks except in extreme cases, because countries suffering from demographic winter need more live children, not aborted fetuses, and because almost all European women would have the means to pay for an abortion out of their own pocket, given its moderate economic cost, and without a doubt those who were determined to have an abortion would still have one, because in purely economic terms, the cost of raising a child is incomparably greater than that of an abortion.

---

[77] In the USA, according to the article "Are American Taxpayers Paying For Abortion?", published in Forbes magazine, taxpayers would be subsidizing 24% of the cost of abortions https://www.forbes.com/sites/theapothecary/2015/10/02/are-american-taxpayers-paying-for-abortion/. In Spain, not only does the State cover the cost of abortion, but the Public Health Ministry also includes it in its so-called "health services portfolio," which is equivalent to saying that pregnancy is a disease and a disease worthy of being "cured" with taxpayer money, if the pregnant woman so desires, since the portfolio of health services is designed to cure diseases and to prevent and solve health problems.

In the European Union, in the last decade, approximately five million children were born every year and there have been over a million legally recorded abortions. In 2007, the latest year for which almost complete statistics are available from Eurostat—not all countries report abortion data in a homogeneous and timely manner. Is it because they are an inconvenience?—there were approximately 1.2 million abortions and 5.3 million births, with a birth rate of 1.56 children per woman in 2007. This means, more or less, that 18% of pregnancies that did not end in miscarriage ended in induced abortion. This huge number of abortions corresponds to 2/3 of the babies that would have been required to reach 2.1 children per woman, the level of generational replacement.

In the case of Eastern European countries, such as Russia or Ukraine, the data are even more severe and more striking. Between 2006 and 2009, both years included, the last years for which Eurostat provides both abortion and birth statistics for Russia, in the Eurasian giant there were almost 1.77 million more deaths (8.33 million) than births (6.57 million), while a total of almost 5.39 million abortions were performed, meaning that 45 out of 100 pregnancies ended in abortion by the mother's decision (not counting miscarriages). If those pregnancies had ended with a baby born from the womb of its mother, Russia would have gained 3.62 million people between 2006 and 2009, instead of losing almost 1.77 million people, excluding any migratory balance.

Cumulative number of births, deaths, natural change of population and abortions in Russia between 2006 and 2009					
Data source: Eurostat					
Births (B)	Deaths (D)	Natural change of population (NCP) (Births minus deaths)	Abortions	(Theoretical) NCP without abortions	% pregnancies ending in abortion
6,565,393	8,333,645	-1,768,252	5,387,511	3,619,259	45%

Nevertheless, the available abortion data, not always accurate [78], do not indicate a clear negative correlation between abortion rate and birth rate, as would

---

[78] The information available from trustworthy public sources about abortions, used in this book, refers to those that are legal and are reported to official agencies. In some countries, this official figure is probably quite accurate but there are nations where abortion is very restricted, such as Poland, or Ireland (until the May 2018 referendum about this issue), where there is surely a significant number of illegal abortions as well as women who abort abroad (the so-called *abortion tourism*). The latter, in turn, would misleadingly increase the official abortion figures of the countries where foreign women go to abort, such as the United Kingdom (a country where several thousand Irish and Polish women go every year to abort), Germany (also Polish women), or Spain (from 1,500 to 2,000 abortions per year performed on non-resident women, according to the Spanish Ministry of Health). Likewise, there are voices that express doubts

be expected a priori (i.e. fewer abortions, higher birth rate), as can be seen in the following table, whose accuracy and reliability with regards to abortion rates, as was said before, is not unquestionable, as explained in the previous footnote.

The following table shows that there are developed countries with fairly high abortion rates per 100 pregnancies, such as Sweden, France, or the United States, that also boast a birth rate that is clearly higher than the rest. There are other nations with very low official abortion rates, such as Poland (where it is prohibited except in extreme cases, such as pregnancy being the result of rape or posing a serious danger to the mother's health, and where fewer than 1,000 abortions are practiced legally per year) or Croatia, and at the same time with very low birth rates. Moreover, there are other countries with strong legal restrictions on abortion, such as Ireland (not included in this table, since the author does not have official abortion data for St. Patrick's land) and with high birth rates. On the other hand, the birth rate in Germany is only marginally superior to that of Spain or Italy, but its abortion rate per 100 pregnancies is noticeably lower.

---

about whether, even in countries where abortion is fully legal and funded by public health, such as Spain, all abortions practiced in private clinics are reported to official sources, due to privacy concerns. On the other hand, the official statistics available on abortions are partial/deficient in countries of the development level of Japan, Australia, or even the US. In the United States, the CDC (Center for Disease Control) does not receive abortion data from all the states because there is no mandatory reporting from them As a result, for example, the CDC report on abortions in the US in 2012 lacks information from California, Maryland, and New Hampshire, and therefore, the total abortion numbers published by the CDC for the United States are incomplete. Official statistics in France or Sweden on abortion have not been published for years either, since the last available figures, are, respectively, for 2007 and 2010. Clearly, abortion is an inconvenient issue. For all these reasons, while I feel very comfortable, as the author, with the reliability and precision of the bulk of the figures contained in this book, even with the difficulties that may exist in their measurement, with regards to abortion data, I have more doubts about the accuracy of the numbers shown here.

Estimated abortion rate and fertility rate in European Union countries, the United States and Canada		
Data source: Eurostat, US Census Bureau, Guttmacher Institute, CIHI	% of pregnancies ending in voluntary abortion	Children per woman
Latvia	36.5%	1.65
Estonia (2013)	29.9%	1.52
Bulgaria	29.4%	1.53
Romania	28.9%	1.52
Hungary	25.9%	1.44
Sweden (2010)	24.6%	1.98
France (2007)	21.6%	1.98
United States (2011)	21.1%	1.89
Denmark	21.0%	1.69
Canada (2011)	19.7%	1.61
United Kingdom (2012)	19.2%	1.92
Latvia	19.4%	1.63
Spain	18.0%	1.32
Portugal	16.8%	1.23
Czech Republic	16.6%	1.53
Italy (2012)	16.2%	1.43
Slovakia	16.1%	1.37
Slovenia (2012)	15.8%	1.58
Finland	14.6%	1.71
Belgium	13.2%	1.81
Germany	12.2%	1.47
Croatia	7.1%	1.48
Poland	0.3%	1.32
NB-1. 2014 numbers, unless otherwise specified.		
NB-2. There are missing EU countries as they did not report those data to Eurostat		
NB-3. The rate of aborted pregnancies does not include miscarriages, for which there are no data. Total pregnancies are calculated as the sum of births and induced abortions		

We end these pages on abortion with some additional factual elements, referring to Spain, that seem of clear interest to us to better illustrate the complexity of this phenomenon and its incidence on the birth rate, which are in no way positive.

First, when legal abortion started to be performed in the country (1986), the birth rate was already very low (1.56 children per woman, 44% lower than only 11 years before, and 70% or so lower than the traditional rate until the mid-nineteenth century). On the other hand, in both 2004 and 2014, the birth rate in Spain was 1.32 children per woman, and, yet, the percentage of aborted pregnancies doubled in those 10 years, from 9% in 2004 to 18% in 2014. In other words, there were many more abortions in 2004 than in 2014, for an equal birth rate.

Second, the rates of aborted pregnancies in Spain vary tremendously according to the geographical origin of the woman who aborts, being especially high in the case of women residing in Spain and born in the Americas (virtually one pregnancy aborted for every two), more than 90% of which are Hispanic-American. In general, immigrant women in Spain have abortion rates much higher than native Spanish women, with the exception of North African women, the vast majority of whom are Moroccan. In 2013, 20% of women of childbearing age living in Spain were born outside of Spain, and abortions for that group accounted for 38% of the total number of abortions.

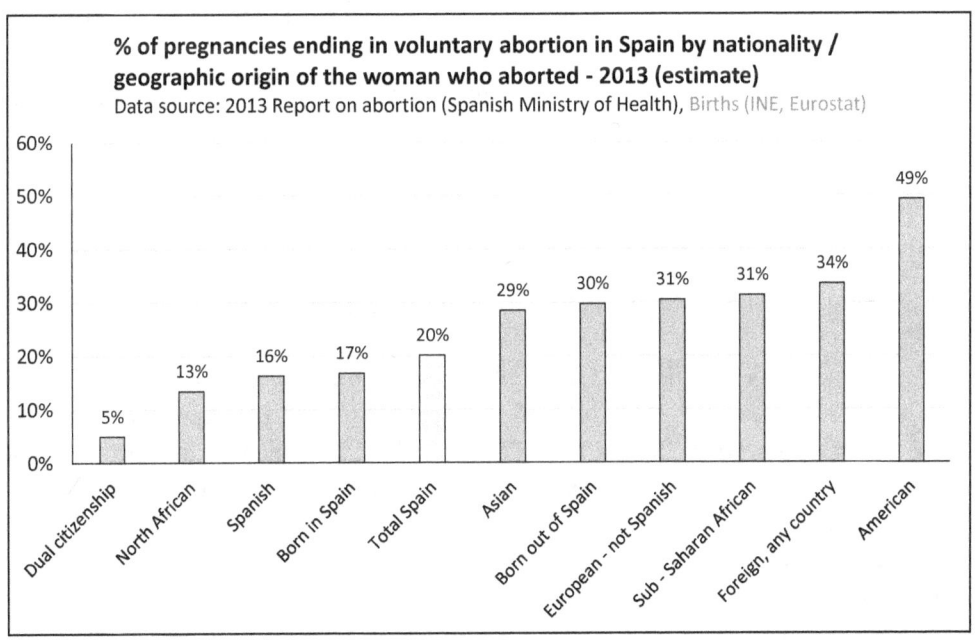

Third, the impact of the "morning after" pill is difficult to gauge as a substitute for surgical abortions. It has not been observed, since the liberalization of its acquisition in 2009 by the Ministry of Health of the government of José Luis Rodríguez Zapatero[79]—whose heads claimed, despite the potential danger to women's health of self-administrating without prescription such a powerful hormonal cocktail, that they took this measure to "reduce unwanted pregnancies and, therefore, the number of abortions"—that its use in Spain resulted in a reduction in the total number of abortions, or the percentage of aborted pregnancies, or that it substantially altered the numbers of births and fertility, especially in relation to other things that did have that effect. Data on births and abortions indicate that either the actual efficacy of the post-coital pill is not complete, that, in many cases its consumption is unnecessary, or that it is used as a substitute for other contraceptives, or that it is acquired "just in case" but is not ingested. Or a little of all the above, in proportions unknown to the author of this work.

Abortions, births, fertility rate and consumption of the "morning-after" pill in Spain							
Data source: Spanish Ministry of Health, INE, "La Razón" newspaper quoting IMS Health	2008	2009	2010	2011	2012	2013	2014
Voluntary abortions on women living in Spain	113,780	109,351	110,966	116,398	110,349	106,756	93,279
"Morning-after" pills sold in pharmacies	N/D	388,745	710,715	736,099	698,922	676,061	671,439
Births from women living in Spain	519,779	494,997	486,575	471,999	454,648	424,440	426,076
Apparent pregnancies (births + voluntary abortions)	633,559	604,348	597,541	588,397	564,997	531,196	519,355
Pregnancies ending in voluntary abortion (%)	18.0%	18.1%	18.6%	19.8%	19.5%	20.1%	18.0%
Fertility rate (children per woman)	1.44	1.38	1.37	1.34	1.32	1.27	1.32
Women aged 15-44 living in Spain by mid-year	9,937,775	9,881,452	9,758,497	9,631,339	9,477,613	9,259,243	9,056,230
Abortions per 1,000 women aged 15–44	11.4	11.1	11.4	12.1	11.6	11.5	10.3
NB. Abortion figures are the legal abortions to women living in Spain that were reported by the Ministry of Health. It does not include miscarriages							

Our final conclusions on the abortion-birth rate relation would be:

✓ The generalized practice of abortion does not help to have higher birth rates, but rather the opposite, for obvious reasons.

✓ Performing abortions using public funds sends a signal from the State to society that for the authorities, pregnancy can be considered, if the pregnant woman so wishes, a disease to be cured through surgery, a signal that is not exactly the best for encouraging fertility in countries where it should most be encouraged.

---

[79] As an anecdotal note, who knows whether with real effects, it is worth mentioning of that government that it was perhaps the most sterile in the history of Spain in the literal sense of the term, since almost 40% of its members did not have children. Of its eighteen members, four women ministers—including the one who liberalized the use of the abortion pill, and the advocates of an abortion law reform to facilitate abortion—and three men ministers lacked offspring.

✓ If we succeeded in voluntarily reducing the number of abortions, with many women who abort today when they become pregnant opting not to do so (either to keep the child for themselves or to give it for adoption after birth to one of the many couples who would welcome it, or even to its biological father), birth rates and the number of births would undoubtedly increase.

✓ Nevertheless, if people do not want to have (more) children and if it is not possible to have an abortion, since there are many other contraceptive methods available, and the possibility of getting pregnant for those who do not want to is so undesirable, many women who today have an abortion would use one or more of these contraceptive methods to prevent pregnancy. Therefore, there would still be few children born. If motherhood/fatherhood is abhorred, people will try to avoid it with the means available to women and men of childbearing age, including abortion or not. Recall that birth rates had already fallen by about half from the historical rates or even more in many developed countries before contraceptive methods became available and abortion was legalized in these countries.

Fewer weddings, higher percentage of children born to unmarried parents, and more divorces equal...fewer children in total?

If in the past in Europe and the West in general almost all children were born to married parents "for life, until death do us part," who on average had several children, now a large and increasing percentage of the children are born to unmarried mothers, be they women with a partner to whom they are not married—the vast majority of this type of birth—or women directly without a partner. If before children were raised, in their overwhelming majority, by both their biological father and mother until their emancipation from the family home[80], now in many cases they suffer during their childhood or adolescence the bitterness and misfortune of seeing their parents separating. What impact does this have on the birth rate? The logic tells us that it should impact the birth rate quite negatively—and the data support it—for several reasons:

---

[80] The most common exception to being raised by both father and mother was a consequence of the premature death of one of the parents, a frequent misfortune in the past. Nowadays, this misfortune occurs much less than in the past as mortality rates are now much lower, but it does afflict a not insignificant fraction of children as parents of young children and adolescents are several/many years older, on average, than ever.

✓ Some of the couples who break up do so before they have had all the children they would have wished for. In fact, single-parent households with children have fewer children than households with married parents.

✓ The traumatic experience of divorces, and all of them are traumatic to some extent—although there are some that are much softer than the average, there are also some that are much more dramatic than the average—is even harder if there are children involved, and especially if the little ones have not yet reached adolescence but are no longer babies. People very close to the victim of a traumatic divorce—brothers, sisters, children, close friends—knowing firsthand the pain their sibling or friend feels when going through a divorce, or having gone through it themselves as the son or daughter of a marriage that broke, may be less inclined to marry/pair up in a stable relationship and have children than those who are not as aware that marrying and having children, in our times, carries a high risk of experiencing that trauma in their own flesh as a spouse or parent. "Why should I risk such an ordeal?" think some or many of those who have seen up close and personal horror stories of this type. In fact, fewer and fewer people get married, and a higher and higher percentage of children are born out of wedlock.

✓ Cohabiting partners have fewer children than married couples. This may be due, among other things, to the fact that their rates of rupture are higher than those of married households, which is logical, since these couples have less formal mutual commitment than married couples and fewer legal impediments/procedures to overcome to get separated.

✓ Unmarried mothers have, on average, fewer children than married mothers, as common sense would indicate, because of the superior proof of mutual commitment to fidelity and stability that marriage implies in relation to other forms of coexistence and management of parenthood. There is a higher and higher percentage of children born out of wedlock. By 2014, births from unmarried parents, on average, totaled around 40% of the total births in Northern America and Europe. In 1980, this percentage was about four times lower on average, although in some of the countries that tend to set trends in many things, such as Sweden or Denmark, it was already very high (33.2% and 39.7%, respectively, according to Eurostat data).

In a country of the size and importance of the United States of America, according to the CDC, the birth rate per 1,000 American women aged 15-44 in 2014 was twice as high for married women than for non-married women. Twice as high! According to the US government's CDC[81] in 2015, the birth rate for married women aged 15-44 was slightly more than twice that for unmarried women: 89.0 births for married mothers per 1,000 married women aged 15-44, compared to 43.5 births for non-married mothers per 1,000 unmarried women aged 15-44.

Births per 1,000 women aged 15-44 in the United States, by legal marital status						
Data source: CDC (Births - Final report 2015)	1990	1995	2000	2005	2010	2015
Rate for married women (1)	93.2	82.6	87.4	87.9	84.3	89
Rate for unmarried women (2)	43.8	44.3	44.1	47.2	47.5	43.5
Birth rate (BR) married women / BR unmarried women	2.13	1.86	1.98	1.86	1.77	2.05
(1) Births from married women per 1,000 married women, aged 15-44, in the USA						
(2) Births from unmarried women per 1,000 unmarried women, aged 15-44, in the USA						

Even in countries where currently most children are born out of wedlock mothers—a growing trend in almost the whole world—such as Sweden, households where a married couple lives have more children than the rest, whether households with children with adults who are in a domestic relationship or single parent households. This is because, on one side, married couples have more children than other types of family, and, on another side, in Sweden and other countries, many people have reversed the traditional order: marriage first, children second. First they have children, or at least one of them does, and after that, the parents get married, as is the best thing to do for their little child(ren)) and their own partner. In particular, in 2014, according to our estimates based on the distribution by type of household of the "Statistics Centralbyrån" (Statistics of Sweden in English), the average number of children per Swedish household with non-adult children was as follows:

- Households headed by a married couple: 2.1.
- Households headed by a domestic partnership: 1.8.
- Single Parent household headed by a woman: 1.7.
- Single Parent household headed by a man: 1.6.

Likewise, in Spain, even though more and more children are born to unmarried mothers (44.4% of the total in 2015, four times the figure 20 years earlier, when these represented 11.1% of all births), we can easily calculate, using the birth

---

[81] Reference: Center for Disease Control report "Births: final data for 2015" (https://www.cdc.gov/nchs/data/nvsr/nvsr66/nvsr66_01.pdf).

statistics by civil status of the mother and the birth order, that married mothers have, on average, more children than unmarried mothers. Based on these data published by the INE in 2015, we estimate that the expected value for the average number of children per woman was 1.51 for unmarried mothers and 1.74 for married mothers.

Size of households with a couple, married or not, and at least one child under 25 in Western Europe, in 2011			
Source: Own analysis with 2011 Census (Eurostat)	Average number of dwellers (children) -not counting the couple- in households with a married couple	Average number of dwellers (children) -not counting the couple- in households with a cohabiting couple	Extra number of dwellers (children) in households with a married couple, relative to those with a cohabiting couple
Germany	1.78	1.46	22.2%
Austria	1.89	1.48	27.4%
Belgium	2.00	1.67	20.0%
Denmark	1.93	1.54	25.6%
Spain	1.75	1.50	16.4%
France	1.97	1.67	18.1%
Netherlands	1.99	1.59	24.9%
Ireland	1.89	1.71	10.6%
Italy	1.79	1.52	18.0%
Luxembourg	1.94	1.61	20.9%
Portugal	1.64	1.49	10.2%
United Kingdom	1.94	1.68	15.3%
Sweden	1.97	1.59	24.3%
Switzerland	1.92	1.56	23.2%
NB. On top of the couple, we assume that the overwhelming majority of the other dwellers are children			

Without a stability framework/horizon in a couple, it is difficult to venture having as many children as when that framework does exist. Having children is one of the most transcendental decisions in life, one that commits you forever, fills you with joy if things go well, and gives you quite a bit of dissatisfaction when it does not go well, besides costing a lot of money and personal freedom in any case. In a broad and figurative sense, but also literal in material terms, having children resembles a great economic investment, even though the goal is not an economic and material benefit, but rather an intangible return consisting in giving and receiving affection, a personal projection beyond one's own life, genetic continuity, and for some (nowadays) and many (in the past), the fulfillment of a spiritual duty. As far as the money that children cost and the limits they impose on the freedom to do other things through their upbringing needs, in practice, parenthood is the most important and expensive investment that the vast majority of parents undertake in their life. What do investors need to start investing, and to invest more, instead of less, money? Something very simple: good return on investment expectations, with the lowest possible risk, something that needs a stability framework and material security as well as security of any type, so that their investment can fructify. That frame/horizon of greater stability and security, when one invests a large part of their life and wealth in having children, even in times when divorce is easy, is provided more strongly by marriage than by a cohabiting partnership, which, in general, implies a lesser degree of mutual commitment and a greater ease in breaking the bond between the parents. Let's not even talk about single parenthood, one of the greatest causes of poverty, even relatively, in the modern world.

As the percentage of children born to unmarried parents has skyrocketed in all developed countries in the last decades, while marriage rates fall, family breakdowns increase, and marriage age is delayed, with respect to the factor "type of family" (married couple, cohabiting partners or a single parent), a factor with a lot of influence in the matter at stake, it is not surprising that birth rates are low in those countries. It is not surprising either that, for the same reason, birth rate does not rebound steadily and vigorously even in countries where the rates have experienced significant improvements from their lows in recent decades (Scandinavia, France, United Kingdom, United States), improvements partly induced, especially in Europe, by the economic support their States provided to motherhood and child rearing. No matter how much money and conveniences we are offered to have children, without a stable partner, or without expectations of stability with the current partner, we will always have fewer descendants on average than if we commit to another person—at least to start with, forever—and we can count on stability and expectations of stability in the home.

One of the phenomena that influences there being a lower marriage rate and fewer children is that we get married for the first time—if at all—at more and more advanced ages. The following charts give an idea of the delay in the age at which European women contracted their first marriage in 1993 and 2013 (the first and only for the great majority of them, either because they never divorced, or because if they got divorced or were widowed at whatever age, they did not remarry). It is curious to note that, although Eastern European women marry younger, since the fall of communism, they have also become closer to the women of Western Europe in this aspect. We do not have homogeneous data prior to 1993, but undoubtedly, the average age of the brides on their first marriage was overall lower. In 1980, the average age of Spanish women during their first marriage was 24 years old, versus 26.5 in 1993. We do not have the data on the average age of brides in their first marriage for the USA, but rather the median age (source: US Census Bureau), a value generally similar to the average, and following similar trends: it increased three years between 1993 and 2013, from 24 to 27 years old. It was 21 in 1973. As for the grooms, who are always several years older than brides on average, the trend is similar.

Mean age of women at first marriage in Western Europe in 1993 and 2013				
Source: Eurostat, own analysis	Mean age in 1993 (years)	Mean age in 2013 (*) (years)	Increase 1993-2013 (years)	% increase 1993-2013 of the difference between mean age and 18 years
Portugal	24.3	29.4	5.1	81%
Ireland (*)	27.5	34.3	6.8	72%
Spain	26.6	32.2	5.6	65%
Austria (*)	25.8	30.6	4.8	62%
Belgium (*)	25.1	29.4	4.3	61%
Italy	26.4	31.1	4.7	56%
Norway	27.0	31.5	4.5	50%
Luxembourg	25.8	29.7	3.9	50%
Germany	26.4	30.5	4.1	49%
Sweden	28.3	33.0	4.7	46%
France (*)	26.8	30.8	4.0	45%
Finland	26.8	30.4	3.6	41%
Netherlands	26.9	30.3	3.4	38%
Switzerland	27.3	30.1	2.8	30%
Denmark	28.8	31.9	3.1	29%
Simple average	25.1	29.2	4.1	57%
Mean age of women at first marriage in Eastern Europe in 1993 and 2013				
Czech Republic	22.1	28.5	6.4	156%
Hungary	22.5	29.0	6.5	144%
Bulgaria	22.0	26.7	4.7	118%
Lithuania	22.4	27.1	4.7	107%
Estonia	23.6	28.8	5.2	93%
Romania	22.5	26.3	3.8	84%
Poland	23.0	26.6	3.6	72%
Slovenia	24.8	29.6	4.8	71%
Simple average	22.9	27.8	5.0	102%
(*) For some countries, most recent year available: 2010 (Belgium), 2011 (Ireland and France), 2012 (Austria). Data not available for the UK and some other Eastern Europe countries.				
(**) Relative increase with respect to the adulthood age threshold (18 years)				

The total first marriage rate is used to estimate the probability that people of a certain society marry at least once in their life (the expected value for it), based on marriage statistical data for each year. In many countries it has fallen enormously, in a correlative way to the fertility rates. For instance, 40 years ago, in Spain, weddings were so frequent that this indicator predicted that everyone would marry sometime in their life (something practically impossible, because even in historical times of high marriage rates, there were always people who never married, but this gives an idea of the very high propensity to marry Spaniards had in those years). Currently, the value of this indicator, clearly below 0.5, implies that, if marriage rates do not increase with respect to the current ones, most young Spanish adults will never marry. In these same 40 years, the birth rate has followed a similarly declining trend, though not strictly parallel, to less than half of what it was towards 1976.

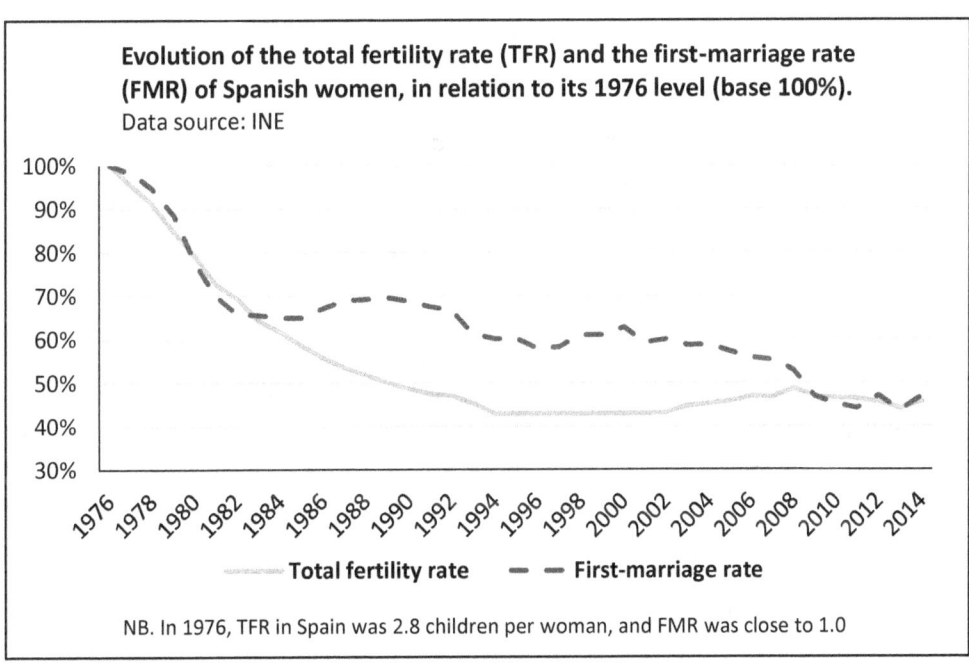

Evolution of the total fertility rate (TFR) and the first-marriage rate (FMR) of Spanish women, in relation to its 1976 level (base 100%). Data source: INE

Total fertility rate — — First-marriage rate

NB. In 1976, TFR in Spain was 2.8 children per woman, and FMR was close to 1.0

We have fewer children because there is less religiosity than before

The average intensity of religious beliefs of common people in Europe and the Americas, of mainly Judeo-Christian spiritual roots, is clearly inferior to the traditional one. Among the central biblical commands is that of "grow and multiply." Having (many) children permeated the sense of religious duty of deeply believing populations. Thus, among deeply religious English settlers in North America in the early and mid-eighteenth century, the birth rate per woman was approximately double that of the English metropolis, as Benjamin Franklin observed at that time[82]. We have already seen in the first chapter of this book that the birth rate of the US white population in 1800 was about seven children per woman.

Nowadays, as a large part of the population in the West and in Eastern European countries is atheistic, agnostic, or expresses a religiosity of medium-low intensity (as evidenced by the very low attendance at Sunday Masses in Europe, much lower than traditionally, the reduced number of vocations to priesthood and monasticism, and the decrease in the percentage of religious weddings in relation with the exclusively civil weddings), religious beliefs are no longer a motivational factor to have children as they may have been in the past for the bulk of the population in those societies. It is however still a factor for those people who maintain that intense religious feeling. In Spain, there is a particularly high percentage of very large families by today's standards—at least 4 or 5 children, if not 6 or more—among those where the parents are linked to religious movements such as Opus Dei, Regnum Christi, Legionaries of Christ, or Neocatechumenal Way. As mentioned earlier in this book, American states with the highest birth rates have, on average, a more religious (Christian) population than those with lower fertility rates. In Israel or the United States, there is a huge difference in fertility between the very orthodox Jews who have a large progeny and the rest of the Hebrew population. According to the Israel Central Bureau of Statistics, Jewish women had the following fertility rates: ultra-orthodox (Haredim), 6.5 children on average; orthodox, 4.3; traditional, 2.6 (women with religious faith, but not orthodox); secular, 2.1. Globally, the fertility of Muslims in the world is greater than that of Christians, although the birth rate of the former is also falling sharply. Moreover, the observance of the precepts of their theoretical religion is much greater, in general, in countries with a large majority of Muslims than in those of (large) Christian majority. And Muslim populations are globally more fertile.

---

[82] Although the population of the American colonies in the mid-eighteenth century was quite small, in view of the enormous birth rate of its very religious people, in addition to the arrival of immigrants, Franklin predicted that the colonies would outnumber the English metropolis, which happened not many decades later. He made another prediction, even more clairvoyant in these matters: "In the future, as people here prosper, they will tend to have fewer children, as I have observed that the better off people are, in general, the more they have to think about whether or not to have (many) children." He himself was faithful to that thesis. Franklin had sixteen siblings, made much more money than his father, and had only two children. In addition, he had an extramarital child, whom he recognized—and from whom he later severely separated as father and son took opposite sides in the US war of independence—who, given the time, certainly was not conceived on purpose.

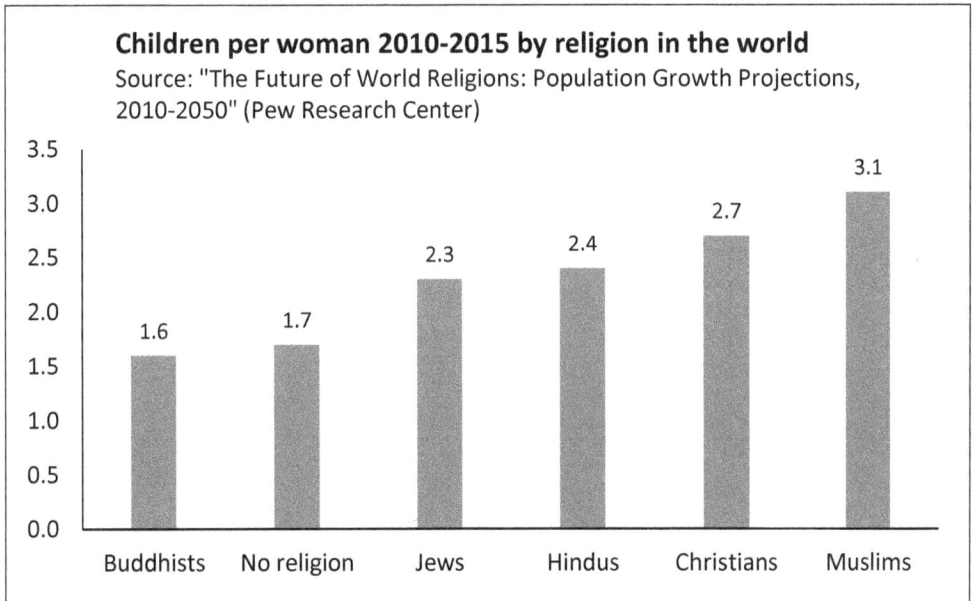

That said, as a small or partial antithesis to the thesis that "the more religiousness, the more children," it should be noted that in four particularly religious nations—at least in theory—and despite their religiousness, the birth rates have been experiencing a tremendous fall and/or are already very low.

Iran was the country that started the wave of Islamist reassertion that has had so much transcendence in the last decades in the world, with the revolution led by Ayatollah Khomeini. Following his rise to power in 1979, there was a return to more traditional Islamic values in his country with respect to women and other matters. The fertility rate, traditionally very high, even increased slightly in the following five years. After that, there was a 70% drop in just 20 years, from 6.54 children per woman, on average, in the five-year period 1980-1985 to only 1.97 in the years 2000 to 2005. Something similar can be said of Saudi Arabia, a deeply Muslim country if ever there was one—the land of the Prophet Muhammad, Mecca, and Medina—which has gone from seven children per woman towards 1980-1985 to about 2.2 in 2014, according to sources such as Index Mundi[83]. As in Iran, this is an extraordinary collapse in the fertility rate, although in the Saudi case, unlike the Iranian, it has been accompanied by a growing material prosperity in the country [84].

---

[83] See http://www.indexmundi.com/g/g.aspx?c=sa&v=31

[84] In Saudi Arabia, there is a large foreign population proportion (between 21% and 33%, according to various sources), especially of working age (and therefore also of childbearing age),

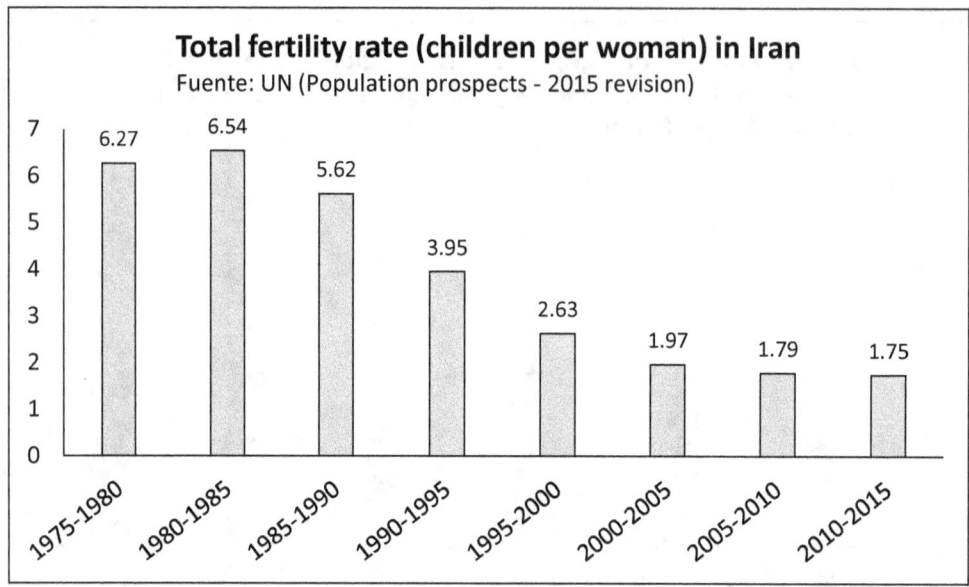

As for countries with a very Christian and specifically Catholic population, we would look at Italy—the country of the Catholic Church par excellence, where the Papacy is located—and Poland, the birthplace of Pope John Paul II. Both countries have had among the lowest birth rates in the world for some time. Italy, moreover, has one of the oldest populations. It is true that, in Italy, Catholics who regularly go to Mass already make up less than half the population, but in Poland they still represent around 60% or more of the population. The birth rates in both countries are in a category called "lowest low," between 1.2 and 1.4 children per woman.

In fact, the birth rate of Christians worldwide in the Pew Research Center's previous table of fertility rates by religious creed, if they are still moderately high (2.7 children per woman), is mostly / only thanks to those who are faithful to Christ who live in sub-Saharan Africa. If it were only for the other geographical areas of the globe, the worldwide fertility of Christians would be less than / around two children per woman, since throughout Europe—including Russia—the USA, Canada, Australia, and New Zealand, it is at levels ranging from 1.2 to 2.0 children per woman. In Latin America, it does not top 2.1 to 2.2 children per woman globally, with Brazil already clearly below 2 and Mexico around 2.1 to 2.2.

---

which has a large impact on the country's fertility rates. Therefore, to compare homogeneously the current birth rate with that of 30 years ago, when there were far fewer immigrants, we should look only at the fertility of the Saudi women, for which I lack data. Whatever that rate was in 2014, with the country as a whole at about 2.2 children per woman, versus around seven 30 years earlier, it is certain that the drop in fertility in Saudi Arabia over the last three decades has been colossal.

By way of synthesis, after the thesis and the antithesis, we believe that the thesis is substantially correct, at least among Christians, i.e., that more religious people have, on average, more children. Therefore, the loss of religiousness among the European and American populations has a lot to do with the decline of the birth rate. We believe, however, that we have to be very careful with simplistic analyses and "broad-brush" interpretations of global and per country data, as we have seen with respect to the current global fertility rate of Christians, inflated due to the high fertility of black/sub-Saharan Africa—an area of the globe that contributes to keeping the global fertility rate of Muslims higher than it would otherwise be, although to a much lesser extent than its impact on the global Christian fertility rate—the only region on Earth that still displays very high fertility rates, rates that are expected to decline as the countries of the area develop, as is already happening indeed. One would also have to see if in supposedly still very Catholic nations, like Poland or Italy, people are truly very Catholic. It is one thing for the vast majority of people in Italy or Poland (or Spain or Portugal) to declare themselves Catholic and another thing for the bulk of them to live in tune with their theoretical creed with the intensity with which they once did, including its collateral heritage of customs and rules.

We have fewer children because of the decline in patriotic sentiment (among the people and the elites)

France is one of the Western countries with the highest patriotic sentiment—which in its exaggerated version is known as chauvinism, and in a balanced and positive version is a healthy love for *sweet France* and a legitimate desire for grandeur of the homeland—more pro-birth elites and a higher birth rate. One of the main historical reasons its government has been promoting higher birth rates, possibly the only truly important reason, is the three hard wars it fought against neighboring Germany, between 1870 and 1945, which we have already discussed. The last two wars (the two World Wars) saw a clear and growing French demographic inferiority. In fact, after the costly victory of 1918, one of the keys in the Treaty of Versailles was the territorial mutilation of Germany—and with it of its population—largely motivated because the numerical superiority of the German population compared to the French population was considered a permanent source of threat to France. Repairing the territorial dismemberment of Germany was one of the popular recruiting flags of Nazism, a key element for its power consolidation and for the growth of its military potential. In the inter-war period, prominent sociologist and demographer Alfred Sauvy predicted that, because of its poor demographic health, France could badly suffer if there was a war with Germany. When the Spring of 1940 came around, France was defeated in a heartbeat by the German steamroller. Starting in 1945, after the harsh experiences of war, France undertook pro-birth policies, through economic aid of diverse types and openly pro-birth policies. Among other things, official publicity campaigns are made with slogans of such evidently patriotic style as "France a besoin d'enfants" (France needs children).

Russia has lost a lot of its population since the dissolution of the Soviet Union, as it has fewer births than deaths (as we have already mentioned, there was a shortage of 13 million accumulated births with respect to deaths between 1991 and 2011). Thanks to the fact that many ethnic Russians who were not at ease in the other former Soviet Republics, especially in those where they became second citizens after 1991, emigrated/returned to the mother country to live after the fall of the Soviet Union, the ancient nation of the Tsars was able to offset 60% of this human bloodletting, but the population reduction still figured in the millions. Very alarmed, President Putin declared that the birth rate increase be an essential priority for his government several years ago, because it is what his nation needs, in addition to facilitating the return to the "Great Mother Russia" of ethnic Russians from the former Soviet Republics. This Russian government's pro-birth stimulus seemed to be bearing some fruit, judging by the increase in births since the fertility rate in Russia hit a low in 1999, although it is still too early to know whether this rebound is sustained or temporary, after a huge drop in births in 2017 (-10%).

The government of the Former Yugoslav Republic of Macedonia, among other countries, also uses the patriotic argument in its pro-birth campaigns. In Denmark, a campaign about having more babies by a travel agency with the slogan "Do it for Denmark", followed by other resounding ads with the same goal, has had worldwide echo[85]. The governments of Hungary and Poland, as well, are undertaking big efforts to boost fertility in their respective countries.

We do not have enough children due to insufficient equality between men and women

This argument is now invoked by some of those concerned with insufficient births as one of the main causes for a low birth rate, but it does not fit the historical and current birth rate data, no matter how much equality in rights, personal dignity, and opportunities for all citizens, with the counterpart of the equality in public obligations, regardless of sex, beliefs, social origin, etc., are indisputable modern values, to which the author of this work adheres 100%.

When there was no such equality between men and women (same legal and real rights; same access to childhood and higher education; workplace with equal

---

[85] See https://www.youtube.com/watch?v=vrO3TfJc9Qw. It has surpassed 10 million viewers.

basic access to jobs for men and women; etc.), or in the income contribution to the household, or in the distribution of childcare and domestic tasks, people had many more children than now. These inequalities are disappearing legally, one after the other, and tend to also diminish in people's daily lives. For example, how many dirty diapers do current fathers change for a clean one and how many did our fathers change? This author changed no less than 50% of the total diapers his children wore. In the past, fathers did not change diapers, excluding anecdotal exceptions. Although globally nowadays, in developed countries, fathers still do not change as many diapers as mothers do, they change diapers at a much higher percentage than their own fathers did and that is certainly a significant number. Nevertheless, even with much greater equality in this day and age, both legal and real (of which the change of diapers is just an example), now is when we have very few children.

Is it necessary for almost all men and women to be practically equal in almost everything (employment rate, childcare, performing household chores, etc.) to have a greater birth rate in our societies? In defense of this argument, the model of the Nordic countries, and especially that of Sweden or Norway—one of the groups of developed nations with the highest birth rate in Europe and with a supposedly theoretical and real equality between man and woman a lot higher than in other countries— is usually presented. However commendable the pro-birth effort is in the Nordic countries, its example is dodgy in providing sufficient scientific strength to validate this hypothesis, for a number of compelling reasons and data.

First, apart from the issue of equality or inequality, Sweden, Norway, Denmark, Finland, and Iceland are among the countries with the highest per capita income in the world, and with a particularly high economic investment in the pro-birth measures. Denmark, in particular, is at the head of Europe with respect to its GDP in aid and compensation to parents. This investment is difficult to match in less wealthy countries, because the extra money to be invested in pro-births efforts must be achieved at the cost of other budget items, significantly higher taxes or a higher public deficit, all difficult and painful to manage, unless they are done very slowly, taking advantage of the greater fiscal revenues economic growth brings.

Second, the birth rates of the Nordic countries remain very low by the historical standards of 4 to 6 children per woman, are insufficient to assure the generational replacement, and have had a clear downward trend in recent years (minus 15.1% on average from 2010 to 2017). In 2017, the birth rate was 1.79 children per woman in Sweden, 1.62 in Norway, 1.77 in Denmark, 1.49 in Finland, and 1.71 in Iceland.

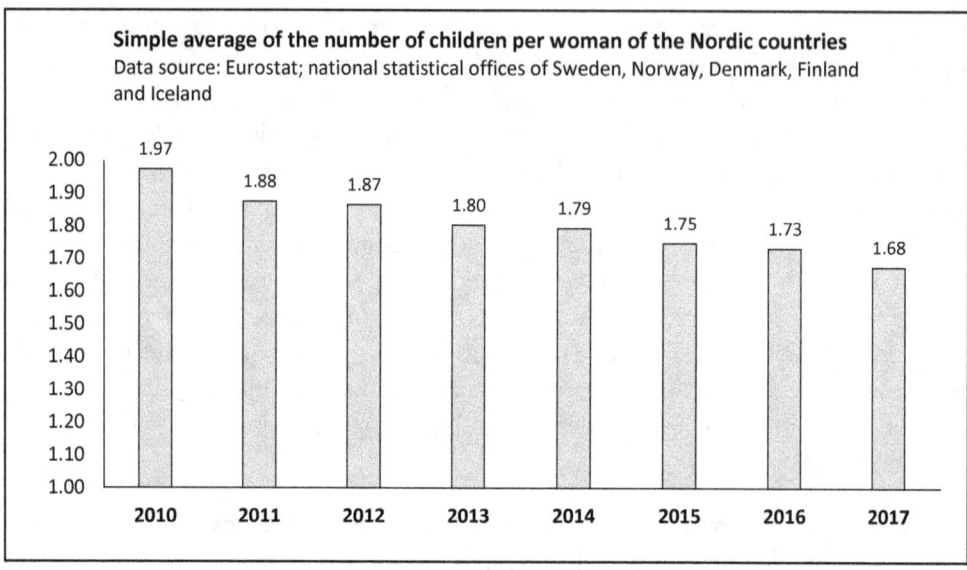

Simple average of the number of children per woman of the Nordic countries
Data source: Eurostat; national statistical offices of Sweden, Norway, Denmark, Finland and Iceland

Third, overall, the birth rate of the Scandinavian countries is not superior, but rather generally lower, to that of other Western countries with a relatively high birth rate, but without such an extreme theoretical degree of egalitarianism between men and women, such as France, Ireland, or the United States. Indeed, France alone, let alone the United States, has a population several times higher than that of all the Nordic countries put together (all together, just over half that of Spain).

Total fertility rate (children per woman) in the Nordic countries									
Data source: Eurostat; national statistical institutes of Sweden, Norway, Denmark, Finland and Iceland	2010	2011	2012	2013	2014	2015	2016	2017	Change 2010-2017
Sweden	1.98	1.90	1.91	1.89	1.88	1.85	1.85	1.79	-9.6%
Denmark	1.87	1.75	1.73	1.67	1.69	1.71	1.79	1.77	-5.4%
Norway (*)	1.95	1.88	1.85	1.78	1.76	1.73	1.71	1.62	-16.9%
Finland (*)	1.87	1.83	1.80	1.75	1.71	1.64	1.57	1.49	-20.3%
Iceland (*)	2.20	2.02	2.04	1.93	1.93	1.81	1.74	1.71	-22.2%
Simple average of fertility rates of the Nordic countries	1.97	1.88	1.87	1.80	1.79	1.75	1.73	1.68	-15.1%
(*) NB. In 2017, fertility rate was the lowest on record in this country									

Fourth, a very high percentage of births in Scandinavia, especially in Sweden and Norway, is due to immigrant women (28% to 29% of those born in both countries in 2016, a percentage that has risen steadily for years, had a mother born abroad), who significantly raise these countries' overall fertility rates. Moreover, year over year, there is a steady growth in the number of babies with foreign mothers and a decrease in the number of babies from native Scandinavian women (including among those a good number of daughters and granddaughters of non-Nordic immigrants). Certainly the homes of these immigrant women who are far more fertile than the native Swedes or Norwegians and who come from very poor countries, many of them of Muslim religion, are not as egalitarian as the native Scandinavian women households. To illustrate the decisive contribution immigration made to the—relatively better—global/theoretical demographic health of these countries, it is worth noting that more than 100% of the growth of the Swedish population over the last 20 years is due to the sum of its net immigration and Swedish babies whose parents were both born abroad, not including Swedes born to children of immigrants, or those who have only one foreign-born parent.

Births in the Nordic countries from foreign-born mothers								
Data source: Eurostat	2010	2011	2012	2013	2014	2015	2016	Change 2010-2015
Sweden	27,468	27,389	28,376	29,394	30,697	31,717	33,545	15.5%
Denmark	9,904	9,642	9,814	10,423	11,154	11,722	12,831	18.4%
Norway	12,673	13,418	14,896	15,465	16,117	16,727	16,799	32.0%
Finland	5,696	5,798	6,299	6,358	6,878	6,893	7,200	21.0%
Iceland	849	845	840	786	788	769	806	-9.4%
Total	56,590	57,092	60,225	62,426	65,634	67,828	71,181	25.8%

Births in the Nordic countries from native mothers								
Data source: Eurostat	2010	2011	2012	2013	2014	2015	2016	Change 2010-2015
Sweden	88,089	84,265	84,673	84,061	84,030	82,952	83,534	-5.2%
Denmark	53,507	49,356	48,102	45,444	45,711	46,474	48,779	-8.8%
Norway	47,647	45,688	45,152	43,257	42,728	42,088	42,091	-11.7%
Finland	55,234	54,112	53,148	51,723	50,271	48,474	45,506	-17.6%
Iceland	4,058	3,647	3,693	3,537	3,581	3,356	3,224	-20.6%
Total	248,535	237,068	234,768	228,022	226,321	223,344	223,134	-10.2%

Fifth, it is questionable whether this supposedly greater Nordic equality between men and women actually applies to all aspects of the couples, and certainly not in such essential and elemental areas as respect for the life and physical integrity of the woman. For example, the rates of women killed by their partners per 100,000 inhabitants, or the rates of rape, are significantly lower in the supposedly more sexist Spain or Italy—countries with very low birth rates—than in Scandinavia.

In conclusion, effective equality between men and women is desirable, but the data do not support that increasing equality further than all the progress already made is the key to achieving higher fertility rates. We lack substantial adjustments in the modern society model—of which an increasing equality of rights and opportunities without distinction of sex, a massive female participation in higher education (largely a majority in this field), and the labor market (still a minority, but less and less), and greater statistical parity between the sexes in economic and other contributions to households, are central elements—to make this model compatible with an adequate birth rate. So far we are not getting it. We will deal with this in the next chapter.

Less parental authority against the State in relation to children

The daughter of a good friend of mine once fell while she was playing on a swing set, when she was a little under three. There was a good blow to the forehead, one inch or so above the eyebrow, and the bruise that came out extended to the eyelid as the clot slid down due to gravity. The next day, the eyelid was as purple as a boxer's who's been hit in the eye area, and her eye was closed due to the swelling. Right after suffering this incident she was taken to the doctor, who said that, apart from her dramatic appearance, there did not seem to be anything serious, since the eye itself was unaffected and there was no fracture. The doctor advised to keep her under observation. The next day, with her purple eye closed, one of the girl's grandmothers took her to the doctor, who must have asked questions to find out if this was a case of child abuse, something that doctors, for a number of years, have been required to investigate and report in Spain. The grandmother related her dialogue with the doctor to the mother, and the mother was alarmed to discover that the doctor seemed to suspect that he might be facing a child abuse case. She told her husband, who shortly afterwards received a call on his cell phone that he could not pick up in time from a number he did not recognize. He then called that number back, asking who had called, and a kind voice answered that the call had come from the official body dedicated to the protection of the rights and the welfare of minors in their region. My friend began to shake, because this could be the first step of an unpleasant official inquiry into possible abuse that, of course, never took place. Then my friend remembered that he had a good friend who worked for that public agency, and asked to be put through to him, just in case. It turned out that the initial call had come from his friend, and had nothing to do with his daughter's accident, but rather was to propose some leisure activity between the two families the following weekend. My friend breathed a sigh of relief. Two days later, the parents returned with the child to the same doctor to see how the girl was healing from the blow and to examine the eye again. The physician, in addition to telling them that the girl was healing well and that she was not in any danger, confessed his relief in talking to her parents, hearing the actual version of the hit from the girl herself and being absolutely certain that he was not facing a case of child abuse. The moral of this story is that, with the laudable aim of pursuing child abuse cases, if cases like this are frequent, and in some of them the investigations about the alleged (but nonexistent) mistreatment go beyond the reported situation, innocent parents could suffer badly.

Something similar happens with corrective slaps to a child. How many parents dare, nowadays, to spank their child when they are on the street, however badly their child is behaving? Fewer and fewer it seems, lest they get into a mess with the authorities for possible mistreatment.

Along these lines, there is an increasing number of situations in which, for the sake of protecting children, parental authority of children is substituted by the authority of the State. The State may even completely withdraw that parental authority from the parents, or from one in particular. That, which may be justified in certain cases, because child abuse or any type of abuse is unacceptable and must be pursued, if exaggerated, can become a very discouraging element when it comes to having children. If a young individual has a close family member or friend who has suffered as a parent from being deprived of contact with his or her children, or who has seen his or her parental authority significantly diminished (for example, as a result of a divorce), by decision of the authorities, this youth is probably less likely to want to have children him or herself in the future than if he or she had not been exposed to such situations.

In short, official protection to the theoretically weak—in this case, the child—is good, beneficial, just, and necessary in the correct degree and manner. Taken to an excessive degree and at the expense of others, it can end up seriously damaging the very weak we want to protect. In Spain, for example, for decades, it had been very difficult to evict a tenant who did not pay rent. As the perception that renting was very risky became widespread among apartment owners, the number of properties offered for rent became less and less. Exaggerating a bit, but not much, it is possible to say that, for wanting to overprotect tenants, authorities almost managed to make them disappear in Spain! In the protection of children and in limitations to parental authority by the State, it is better to have as much firmness with parents with a genuinely harmful behavior as care against false imputations and overregulation that limit the authority of the parents. Otherwise, it could end up being a strong deterrent when deciding whether or not to embark on the adventure of parenthood, since human beings—as is the law of life— tend to avoid getting into trouble and painful situations when they know they can be affected.

The negative impact of feminism 2.0 and environmentalism 2.0 on birth rates

"Children yes, husbands no."
(**Dolores Ibarruri**, Historical Spanish communist leader, in the 1930s)

Nowadays, equal opportunities and legal equality between men and women and respect for the environment are two of the most important values of humanity. I fully adhere to them. I consider myself as feminist 1.0 (men and women are and should be equal in political and legal rights of any kind, opportunities, respect and dignity, as well as in legal and other duties) and as ecologist 1.0 (the environment must be protected from contaminating elements and excessive human alterations, including the visual ones. It is necessary to prevent the earth from being polluted, and those who do it must pay and be punished) as anybody else. I completely agree up to that point. However, the next historical versions of feminism and environmentalism present clear elements hostile to fertility, both direct and indirect, and both ideologies are very influential in our societies.

Important currents of opinion from modern feminism, more radical than what we have previously deemed 1.0—the original feminism from around a century ago—have a negative or very negative effect on the birth rate, in two ways:

- In many cases, these currents see children as a direct burden for what they judge to be essential for the full life of adult women: to develop a successful career. The idea of prioritizing female work outside the home above motherhood, instead of trying to reasonably combine the two, has a negative impact on fertility.

- They are androphobic (rejection of the male and the figure of the father) and against marriage, in line with the previous quote of "children yes, husbands no." As over 97%-98% of births are still the product of a male and female couple, whether through a legal or a de facto marriage (cohabiting couple), who wishes to have and raise children, to be against males simply because they are male is to be against fertility. It is also against fertility to be against marriage, since, as we saw earlier, married couples have households with more children, by a long shot, compared to households formed by de cohabiting couples or single parents.

As for the green movement, it was just and very necessary in its beginnings, because there were then plenty of reasons for this movement, with factories, power plants, motor vehicles, and residential fireplaces everywhere that significantly polluted, and a poor environmental management of garbage and waste. It continues to be necessary in general, since dirtying the environment is harmful to our health as well as the health of all living beings that share the planet with us. However, after achieving the fact that virtually the whole developed world now has a basic ecological awareness and abhors the deterioration of the environment, and that many rules have been modified to reduce or suppress human aggression against nature, a large part of the modern environmental movement, which we could call "environmentalism 2.0," seems to have crossed the sensible line. Such is the case, for example, of some of its current leaders and sympathizers who rage against those who have more than one child—as did the media mogul Ted Turner[86]—or two, due to their "ecological footprint," claiming that on Earth, "there are already too many" human beings—a debatable and in no way scientifically proven claim. This ecological "anti-baby" discourse is catching on for many people, among other things, because it makes people feel more comfortable in not having children, or in having only one, because they say and/or think that by doing so they are "helping the environment."

Even if it were true that in the world we are too many, something by no means demonstrated with scientific, objective, and irrefutable data—although it is logical to think that, if humanity continues to grow indefinitely, at some point we will be too numerous, by the magic of geometric progressions and compound interest, as in the story of wheat grains and the chessboard—this would not apply to the countries suffering from an intense demographic winter, such as Spain, Germany, Italy, or Japan. Even if there were truly too many people globally, Europeans, Americans, Canadians, or the Japanese would not be responsible, since, if humanity as a whole had grown proportionally to the European, American, or Japanese rhythm since 1950, the current world population would be appreciably lower. In 2015, the world population was 7,349 million people, according to the UN. The following tables show global and regional population variations from 1950 to 2015 and how many humans there would now be, by region and in total, if the global population and that of the various regions had grown at the same rate as that of each human-geographic group.

---

[86] Ted Turner, the founder of the CNN television network, had five children throughout his life. Despite this, a few years ago, he joined the anthropophobic ecologist current that believes that each of us should not have more than one child, since this philosophy considers human beings to be harmful to the environmental health of our planet, and therefore, it is better for the population to decrease. Imitating Hobbes, this current would include those who think along the lines of, "Man is a wolf to the Earth."

World population and by region in 1950 and 2015 (millions of people)				
Data Source: UN (World propulation prospects - 2015)	Population in 1950	Population in 2015	Compound annual growth rate 1950-2015	% change of population share of each region in global population 1950-2015
World	2,521	7,349	1.7%	N/D
Africa	221	1,186	2.6%	84.1%
Asia	1,402	4,393	1.8%	7.5%
Europe	547	738	0.5%	-53.7%
Latin America & Caribbean	167	634	2.1%	30.2%
Northern America (*)	172	358	1.1%	-28.6%
Oceania	13	39	1.7%	3.7%
(*) United States + Canada + Greenland + Bermuda + St. Pierre et Michelon				

What global and regional populations would have been in 2015 if .... (millions of people)			
Data Source: UN (World propulation prospects - 2015)	Actual world population in 2015	World population in 2015 if all regions had grown at the same rate as this one since 1950	Population by regions in 2015 if all of them had grown at the average world rate since 1950
World	7,349	7,349	7,349
Africa	1,186	13,529	644
Asia	4,393	7,899	4,087
Europe	738	3,401	1,595
Latin America & Caribbean	634	9,571	487
Northern America (*)	358	5,247	501
Oceania	39	7,621	38
(*) United States + Canada + Greenland + Bermuda + St. Pierre et Michelon			

As can be seen in these tables, Europe and Northern America (basically the US and Canada) have lost much human weight in the world since 1950, especially the former, whose current "market share" in the whole of humanity is less than half of what it was in 1950. Moreover, both regions would have lost even more demographic weight in the world, to the benefit of others, had it not been for people from outside Europe and Northern America who emigrated to those areas from poorer ones and the children they bore in their adoptive countries. If worldwide population had grown at the same rates as those in Europe, there would be only 3,401 million human beings in 2015, not 7,349 million. If it had grown like the United States and Canada, humans would be 5,247 million in total that year.

The same can be said for Japan, as its population grew by 54% between 1950 and 2015, while the world population increased by 191% over the same period. Therefore, if the ecological argument to limit birth rates for environmental reasons, as well as the economic welfare argument according to the Malthusian hypothesis—that resources grow at a slower rate than the population—were correct, or scientifically proven, they should be applied, mainly or exclusively, to regions of the planet and countries with the highest fertility and whose population has grown more in the last decades and not to those afflicted by the demographic winter, whether in its very serious (Europe) or moderate-severe (Northern America) form, given the contribution of each region of the globe to the supposed overpopulation. If all the regions had grown in population like Africa, we would now have over 13.5 billion people on Earth, or almost 9.6 billion if humanity had grown at the rhythm of Latin America and the Caribbean! Facing the future, these trends continue. The UN predicts that Europe will lose another 25% of its human weight between 2015 and 2050.

Fewer children due to the increase in homosexuality and gender ideology or theory

There are those who claim that one of the key reasons we are having fewer and fewer children is the fact that—according to those individuals—there are more and more homosexuals, and that the so-called gender "theory" or "ideology" (which basically says that what is important is not the sex with which one is born, that which is written on the chromosome that defines sex, present as the others in all cells of our body, but rather the sexual orientation which one chooses to have) is establishing itself in the official and legal environments of many countries.

This is certainly a very controversial subject, full of prejudices and ideological and religious apriorisms, while scientific rigor and irrefutable data are scarce. Except for praising diversity in terms of sexual orientation, there seems to be less and less freedom of speech in the public media regarding this subject. This climate of undermining the freedom of thought and speech is making it difficult to investigate the subject with scientific rigor (for example, the everlasting debate called "nature versus nurture," whether one is born with or acquires a homosexual orientation[87])

---

[87] Towards 1990, when I was living near New York City, I remember when the press published the news that a group of researchers had discovered that a small part of the brain in male homosexuals was much more similar to the same area in the typical female brain than in the typical male brain. I remember also reading, as a result, statements from homosexuals and others celebrating this discovery: "no one should ever attack homosexuals because they are homosexual, since it has finally been discovered that their sexual orientation is determined by nature." I also remember other groups that questioned the discovery, interpreting it just the other way round: "This is unacceptable, because there will be those who will thus say that

and to freely present the conclusions of such investigations without fear of reprisals, even if those conclusions are not to the liking of some.

If, in the future, the number of homosexuals and people whose sexual orientation is different with respect to the theoretical one written in their DNA were to increase significantly, we could expect this to carry negative consequences for birth rates. Until now, the "hard" data—from reliable sources—that exist in this regard, beyond partisan propaganda, unequivocally show that homosexuals represent a small minority of the population and that their numerical incidence is irrelevant in every way with respect to its effects on the demographic winter. Let's see:

✓ In countries where same-sex marriage has been legally recognized, once the first years of novelty have passed and their annual numbers have stabilized at their "cruising levels," gay marriages represent between 1% and 3% of the total. It is unknown—or at least, I know of no conclusive study in this regard—if homosexuals, once the legal possibility of getting married is within their reach, are more likely to marry or not than heterosexuals, as the propensity of the latter to get married is currently much lower than traditionally, not just in the more developed world, given the global drop in marriages in country after country[88]. Unless that propensity is very different, higher or lower, gay marriage statistics would imply that, as an order of magnitude, the homosexual population would represent between 1% and 3% of the total population, more or less. Indeed, the most recent data on same-sex marriages that we have been able to collect, in relation to the total number of weddings (source: national statistical offices[89]), are as follows: 1.1% in Portugal in 2015; 1.3% in Denmark, Norway, and Finland [90] in 2015; 1.9% in the Netherlands in 2013; 2.5% in Spain in 2016; 2.6% in Belgium in 2014; 4.3% in France in 2014 (the first full year of legalized gay marriage), 3.3% in 2015, 3.1% in 2016. Along these lines, in Canada, for example, according to a study by Statistics Canada, the Canadian central

---

homosexuals are physically anomalous people, and that will increase the discrimination they suffer." It is impressive how we humans react differently to the same facts, on controversial issues like this one!

[88] For example, in Mexico, according to data from the National Institute of Statistics and Geography (INEGI) of the Aztec country, the number of marriages celebrated per 1,000 inhabitants fell by 33% in just two decades between 1994 and 2004, from 7.2 to 4.8.

[89] Not all countries report these data. For example, at least in its section in English, I was not able to find them in the central statistical office of Sweden.

[90] In the case of Finland, these are registered same-sex couples.

statistics office, in 2014, 1.3% of the population aged 18-59 considered themselves homosexual and 1.7% considered themselves bisexual.

✓ In Germany, according to its national statistical office, Destatis, households with a homosexual couple with children were 0.09% in 2015 (7,000 out of 8.023 million households with children in Germany).

✓ In Spain, currently one of the countries in the world with the most favorable legal environment for homosexuals in all these matters, in 2015, same-sex couples represented 0.83% of households formed by a couple, according to the Continuous Survey of Households of the National Institute of Statistics INE. Likewise, although homosexual couples in Spain appear to be growing as a percentage of the total, at a relatively significant pace in relative terms, these are not explosive growths. Specifically, they would have gone from 0.73% in 2013 to 0.83% in 2015, although it should be noted that these are figures whose theoretical accuracy is lower than the margin of error of the survey. Nor is there any reliable data—at least, none that I have—on whether homosexuals are more likely to live as couples than the rest of the population, which again leaves the open question of how many there really are.

✓ In Spain, households made up of homosexual couples with children in 2014 were estimated at around 7,600, representing 0.12% of the total number of households with a partner and children (1 in 833), according to the INE's Continuous Household Survey. They had fewer children, on average, than households formed by a heterosexual couple and their children. There are no data on the percentage of single-parent households with children in which the adult is homosexual. As 68% of homes with heterosexual partners in Spain have children living with them, versus only 8% of those formed by a homosexual couple, composing both proportions, this would imply that it would be almost 8 times more likely that a heterosexual couple have at least one child than a homosexual couple. Of households with a homosexual couple with children, 46% have more than one, versus 53% in the case of heterosexual households.

✓ In Canada, one of the first countries in the world to legalize gay marriage, the proportions are very similar. According to Statistics Canada, in 2011, a total of 9,600 Canadians under the age of 25 were living with a same-sex couple (7,700 with women, 1,900 with men), which represents a scant 0.1% of all residents under 25 in Canada. As there were 64,575 households formed by homosexual couples according to the 2011 census, crossing both data gives us an average of 0.15 children (under 25 years old) per household with a homosexual couple. Among households made up of an adult couple, married or de facto, with or without children, same-sex couples accounted for 0.82% of all Canadian households with two adults in 2011.

✓ Finally, the transsexual population is still a smaller minority than the homosexual population, and therefore, even more irrelevant for the purpose of the birth rate of a country. There are no accurate universally accepted estimates, but it is said that rates of the incidence of this type of sexual orientation are between 0.0025% and 0.01% among the population.

If there were a strong non-heterosexual population growth in the future, we could expect a negative impact on overall birth rate figures. Until now there is no hard evidence, based on available data, that there are significant increases in the homosexual or bisexual population at the expense of the heterosexual, while birth rates have been falling for a long time in developed countries before almost anyone knew the paradigm gender vs. sex, people's "gender" was increasingly mentioned rather than referring to their "sex," or homosexual marriage was legalized. Fertility has also plummeted in the past 30-40 years in countries where the social-legal incidence of this theory or ideology is irrelevant or completely absent (Iran and Saudi Arabia are two especially striking examples in this context, both countries where, at the other end of the pendulum, homosexuality can be legally punishable by death).

For this reasons, no significant incidence among the great causes of why we hardly have children can be attributed to the ideology of gender, up until now. This is what the data tell the author of the book that you are holding in your hands, who is a friend of his ideas, beliefs, and prejudices, like every human being, but who does not cling to them when he encounters irrefutable data that disrupts them. Those of us who do not have children in sufficient numbers—a phenomenon that started over a generation ago in developed countries—are heterosexuals as a whole, who are the immense majority in any human society, an uncomfortable truth to assume for some or many of those who see the scapegoat as their best friend in the animal kingdom (something that, admittedly, is very human and happens at times to almost everyone, and very often to more than a few of our fellow human beings). Facing the future, there are no solid data that strongly support the hypothesis that the homosexual population will be much larger than usual. Although their numbers seem to grow in recent years, among other reasons due to the growing visibility in the media of well-known gays, it is not clear if there are actually more gays in total or if there are simply more of them who, in recent times, as it is popularly said, are "coming out of the closet," as the social environment tends to be much less adverse to homosexuality than in the past, and more fellow human beings tend to lose their fear of openly showing their non-heterosexual preferences. In any case, we insist, if and only if the homosexual population (for example, if it were to double or triple), and in particular the female homosexual population, were to grow, would there likely be significant negative effects on the overall birth rates in places where this would happen. As long as this does not happen—and there is no solid evidence that it will—what is fair and correct to say is that we, heterosexuals, who do not procreate enough among all of us, should not look for scapegoats: the problem of low birth rates is globally caused by "us" and essentially, is caused voluntarily and not by "others."

Parents who do not encourage their children to have (many) children

In more than a few cases, the parents of (possible future) parents are the ones who tell their children, especially if they are still fairly or relatively young, to think long and hard before having (more) offspring, including the not infrequent situation where it is these same parents who encourage their pregnant young daughters—or their sons' partners— to abort, with phrases ranging from "Think well, son/daughter, having children will complicate your life and you do not have a comfortable economic position yet," to "It's crazy for you to have (more) children," even going through arguments like "Don't make me a grandmother at such a young age." Grandparents generally enjoy grandchildren very much. Before having them though, more than a few people in this day and age are horrified at the prospect of becoming grandparents, either because of the connotation of "old" that the concept carries, or because the potential grandparents sense that they're going to have to assume part of the childcare duties, which is not a small effort ("now that I have spent a few years free of taking care of children, here comes my daughter/son and I am back at it all over again").

In many cases, children listen to the *anti-children* advice of their parents, postpone the arrival of their own offspring and end up without children of their own, or with only one, to their desolation, and in more than a few cases also to that of those parents who did not support that their children give them grandchildren when they were younger and were beginning to consider it.

Increasing cost of raising a child until he/she is emancipated

Although the real personal income level of the general population is now much higher than at any other period in history in developed countries and increasingly in emerging countries—what is earned after taxes from a job, revenue from invested capital and/or revenue received from the State, plus the value of free services and benefits received from the State and other agents such as NGOs, including government subsidies on such products as medications—many people claim that it is increasingly more expensive to raise children until they are emancipated, since they now have needs that did not exist before (for example, in developed countries, vacations and weekend trips, stays abroad, sports, and other extracurricular activities, electronic devices, expensive Masters degrees, brand-name clothes, etc.). This is a question difficult to evaluate with data and to arrive at conclusions that can be accepted by the majority of people, since what some call "new needs" that deprive couples of enough money to have and raise (more) children, others consider them "unnecessary luxuries" compared to something as important as having at least a couple of children.

It is true that, traditionally, the many children raised in rural areas, with very scarce means, did not seem to be very expensive to families in relation to their income, among other things, because of their precarious means and health. Personally, I would like to refer to a phrase that was quoted earlier in this book: "The best gift you can give your child is not to pay him a master's degree at Harvard, but to give him a little brother." I also think a lot of children, nowadays, in the developed countries, are over-pampered and over-served by an excess of toys and gifts, costly entertainments, paid extra-curricular activities, trips, and other non-essential things which contribute a great deal to depriving them of having more siblings—in many cases, of having just ONE sibling—because of the money they detract from their parents. In addition, those children are so well served materially with non-essential elements that it creates in them a feeling that things are easier to achieve than they actually are, and they are not educated to become hard-working and austere adults, the latter a value that, if it does not degenerate into stinginess, has always been considered an essential virtue.

Taxation to ordinary people far greater than in yesteryear

In line with the previous idea that we have few children because raising a child is (much) more expensive now than before, there are people who ask "why was a salary per household (the husband's/father) enough before and now we can't make ends meet well with two salaries (man and woman)?" This, in turn, makes it difficult to have children, by forcing the woman in the household to also work outside the home to bring in an income essential to living well. It is a debatable argument, since it does not include the possibility that women work outside the home to be able to have economic independence and/or because they like their work, in addition, of course, for the household to have more money, which is appreciated with or without children. It is however probably true in a fairly large number of cases.

One of the main reasons that one salary may now not suffice is that public spending and the tax burden represent a much greater percentage than before of what people earn, between direct and indirect taxes. Now, in almost all developed countries, the vast majority of citizens work between 30% and 60% of our time to pay the direct and indirect taxes collected by the State which correspondingly shrinks the personal income we have available to spend. In Spain, for example, in 2016, an employee whose total labor cost for his company is 42,000 euros receives a gross salary of about 30,000 euros, after deducting employer and employee's Social Security contributions, of which he/she pays 3,500 to 4,000 as personal income tax (IRPF). Just accounting for these two deductions, the employee does not receive 38% of what he/she costs the employer. From the money left, a substantial part is spent on other taxes such as VAT (almost all consumer products are taxed at 10% or 21%), excise taxes (on gasoline, alcohol, tobacco), IBI (property tax) and in many municipalities, garbage collection taxes (if you own your home, like most Spaniards do), motor-vehicle tax, traffic fines, and parking fees on city streets (which act de facto as taxes, as they cost tens or hundreds of euros per year to the average Spaniard). Add taxes on interest, dividends, and capital gains and even from a salary cost of just 42,000 euros a year, the State, through many avenues, can end up receiving 50% in tax revenue, if not more!

It is true that, in exchange for their taxes, citizens receive many more benefits from the State than they once did, including, when they get older, retirement pensions and expensive medical care. The people who pay taxes are not necessarily those who receive benefits from the State, or, at least, they may pay more at one stage in their lives and receive more at a different stage. For example, retirement pensions in developed countries account for between one-fifth and one-third of what States spend. A typical worker, in present-day Spain, works 15% to 25% of his time not directly for him, but for pensioners. It is true that, in doing so, he generates a theoretical right to receive, in turn, a retirement pension when he goes into retirement, although without the certainty that this commitment will be respected by the State, due to the more and more generalized evidence and belief that the demographic winter puts the traditional system of pensions at risk, or the knowledge of how much his pension will amount to. 50 or 60 years ago, as Spanish society was much less aged, the Spanish worker also generated this theoretical right to receive a pension in the future, but only had to devote a much smaller part of the income he generated to those needs. Simply with this difference, workers then had a significant amount of additional money for themselves and their family, compared to what they now have left once all taxes, contributions, and fees have been paid.

Insufficient wages to have and raise children, high unemployment rates and job insecurity, high housing prices, lack of aid from the State, etc.

These are very common complaints in my country, Spain—and I'm sure Spain is not the only one. There is no doubt that it is reasonable to think that a general improvement in some of these areas could help to have more children. Nevertheless, if this were the main, the great, the true cause for the birth rate deficit in Spain (and in other countries where many people probably allege similar problems, like Italy, Portugal or Greece), the following would not make much sense:

✓ Those who have more children per woman in Spain and the entire West belong to the segments of its population, on average, with lower income and asset levels: foreign non-Western immigrants.

✓ In very prosperous countries, with little unemployment, with great social cohesion, relatively affordable housing (at least for rent) and greater pro-birth aid, such as Germany, Switzerland, Austria, Luxembourg, or the Scandinavian countries, birth rates are not overflowing and are only higher by 0.1 to 0.6, and not 1 to 2, children per woman than the birth rates in Spain, Italy, Portugal, or Greece.

✓ In Spain, towards 2006, with full employment and a sense of economic euphoria after twelve consecutive years of uninterrupted economic growth at enviable rates—an annual average GDP increase of 3.7% in 1994-2006, starting at 2.4% in 1994, the year with the lowest growth of those thirteen years—and with an unemployment rate of 8%, the birth rate of Spanish women was practically as slim as in 2014, with a 24% annual unemployment rate and a society feeling much worse about its economic situation, after six very hard years of economic crisis: 1.31 children per Spanish woman in 2006 and 1.27 in 2014. Only 3% lower in 2014 than in 2006! If the key to a low birth rate were unemployment and ease of access to housing, fertility in 2006 for Spanish women should have been much higher than by just 3% in 2014. Delving some more, children born in 2014 in Spain were conceived almost entirely between the second quarter of 2013 and the first of 2014, both inclusive, when the average unemployment rate in these four quarters was 26%, according to INE. To split hairs, the birth rate in 2007—a year that still had economic euphoria, and more so at the time when those born that year were conceived, between a great part of 2006 and the first quarter of 2007—no longer of the "Spanish" women, including immigrants with dual nationality, but of Spanish-born women, was 1.26, versus 1.28 in 2014, according to our estimates. It was therefore slightly lower before the crisis than after six long years of it!

✓ In the Spanish province where I live, Madrid, without looking at small towns, the average birth rate is approximately the same (as low) in the municipalities with the highest per capita income and lower unemployment, a good part of which are also among the most prosperous in the country (Pozuelo de Alarcón, Las Rozas, Majadahonda, Boadilla del Monte) and in those with the lowest income per capita and highest unemployment among the largest in the province (Parla, Fuenlabrada, Móstoles and Torrejón de Ardoz, with about half the per capita income than the former group).

Regarding the effect of public aid on birth rates, in the OECD countries, there is little connection between the share of GDP devoted to supporting fertility and families, and the number of children per woman, as can be seen in the following table. The third numeric column shows how many percentage points of GDP were invested in 2011 in this type of aid per country, per point of the birth rate (one point = one child per woman). Hungary employed more than 3 percentage points of GDP, while Luxembourg, Denmark, the UK, and Germany had to spend more than 2 percentage points. There were no fewer than 17 countries that would have "spent" (assuming a cause-and-effect relationship between the percentage points spent on pro-birth programs and the birth rate itself) less than 1.5 percentage points to achieve each point of the birth rate. Among these countries, it is worth mentioning the minute 0.63 percentage points of GDP in aid per child per woman in the US, which despite this was one of the OECD countries with the highest birth rate, as well as the special case of Mexico, the country with the lowest level of economic development of this group, which devoted the lowest percentage of its GDP in pro-birth aids and yet had the highest fertility, after Israel, of all of them.

On the other hand, although pro-birth investment in the era of infertility is praiseworthy in any case, because it is fair and signals the priorities of the State, it is not clear in which direction the potential cause-effect relationship between what is spent on fertility and the number of children per woman in the country works. Since what the State invests in aids/compensation to births is more or less proportional to the number of children people have (so much money per child, so much money for pregnancy / maternity/paternity leave, etc.), if a country spends a higher percentage of GDP in support of births, and the birth rate is higher, only with these two numbers (birth rate and % of GDP invested in births) we cannot know if people have more children than in other places because that particular country gives them a larger share of the wealth the country produces, or if it spends more because people have more children for other reasons, and having them causes the State to devote a larger part of GDP to births in an "automatic" way. To

Public spending on family benefits in cash, services and tax measures -in per cent of GDP-, and number of children per woman, in OECD countries in 2011					
Data source: OECD, Eurostat	(A) Total public spending on family benefits, in percent GDP 2011	(B) Total fertility rate (children per woman) in 2011	% of GDP spent on familiy benefits per chidren per woman (A / B)	Number of times the per capita GDP is received by parents per birth	Public spending on family benefits in constant dollars PPP, divided by number of births, in 2011
Hungary	3.99	1.24	3.22	4.54	100,044
Denmark	4.05	1.75	2.31	3.82	160,961
Germany	3.05	1.39	2.20	3.68	153,938
Luxembourg	3.65	1.51	2.41	3.35	284,732
United Kingdom	4.26	1.91	2.23	3.33	121,569
Sweden	3.64	1.90	1.91	3.08	131,130
Austria	2.71	1.43	1.90	2.92	125,324
Finland	3.22	1.83	1.76	2.91	113,663
Belgium	3.32	1.81	1.84	2.87	113,677
France	3.61	2.00	1.81	2.84	103,746
Norway	3.20	1.88	1.70	2.62	153,586
Iceland	3.55	2.02	1.76	2.52	108,979
Ireland	4.00	2.04	1.96	2.47	107,003
New Zeland	3.36	2.09	1.61	2.41	76,769
Czech Republic	2.44	1.43	1.71	2.35	64,657
Estonia	2.45	1.61	1.52	2.20	50,149
Italy	2.01	1.39	1.45	2.19	75,429
Slovakia	2.43	1.45	1.67	2.15	54,241
Japan	1.74	1.39	1.25	2.09	70,392
Australia	2.79	1.92	1.45	2.06	88,909
Slovenia	2.19	1.56	1.40	2.04	56,668
Netherlands	2.13	1.76	1.21	1.97	89,187
Suiza	1.88	1.52	1.24	1.85	95,417
Switzerland	1.76	1.30	1.35	1.72	37,280
Portugal	1.44	1.35	1.07	1.57	41,573
Spain	1.51	1.34	1.13	1.49	47,679
Greece	1.37	1.40	0.98	1.40	36,833
Canada	1.43	1.61	0.89	1.30	53,297
South Korea	1.16	1.24	0.93	1.21	37,844
Israel	2.32	3.00	0.77	1.09	32,371
United States	1.19	1.89	0.63	0.94	45,571
Chile	1.31	1.88	0.70	0.91	17,324
Mexico	1.13	2.26	0.50	0.52	8,085
OECD average	2.55	1.50	1.70	2.25	86,607

illustrate this with an example, if there were two countries with equal GDP per capita, equal population structure by age, and equal assistance schemes to birth rate, but one had a birth rate 20% higher than the other, that country would mechanically dedicate 20% more of its GDP to births than the other would.

Inconvenience of having children with current lifestyles, due to the freedom, time for fun and money they take away from parents, and the responsibilities they create

In the author's opinion, this is by far the most important cause of the current low birth rates in developed countries, and increasingly, in developing countries. For many of our fellow human beings, nowadays, having children is something that is inconvenient, takes away money, leisure time and freedom, indebts us, makes us vulnerable, and loads us with heavy responsibilities. For those reasons, children are something to avoid, or of which to have one at the most, because the instinctive and/or rational desire to have children, for many, does not compensate for those potential drawbacks. Perhaps it is shocking that in a book like this, with so many words and data, so many twists, turns, straight lines, curves and meanders, one of the most important conclusions is exposed in so few lines. I have no doubt, after years of studying this subject, of processing massive amounts of data, of reading/listening to countless other views, and of reflecting on the subject by land, sea and air, that this is the main cause for the lack of births in so many countries, such as mine. I believe that everything else that plays a role in the fact that we have few children, if at all, although having its importance, is less relevant. If we really wanted to have children, we would brush aside many of the real obstacles and have them.

CHAPTER 4
HOW TO COMBAT DEMOGRAPHIC SUICIDE?

"For every complex problem, there is an answer that is clear, simple, and wrong."
(**H L Mencken**, American journalist)

We are reaching the final part of the main body of this book, dedicated to solutions to the grave demographic problem that insufficiently fertile societies suffer or will suffer (Europe, the United States, Canada, Australia, Brazil and a growing number of South American nations, Japan, China, Taiwan, South Korea, Thailand, Iran, etc.) from. We will also subsequently give some pointers on how to avoid falling into the path of demographic suicide to the numerous nations with birth rates that have declined dramatically in the last 20 to 40 years but is still above the population replacement level, or has just recently and barely fallen below it.

Because preaching and criticizing is much easier to do than actually correcting what is wrong and complex to repair, it is quite likely that what follows includes some failures, errors, naive ideas, incomplete solutions, etc. Therefore, putting the bandage beforehand on the possible site of the possible injury, I apologize in advance to the reader. But this book would be incomplete if we confined ourselves to describing how bad things are in matters of demography and what consequences they imply, without proposing solutions and strategies to tackle the problem at hand.

Main options to fight the demographic suicide

Synthetically, given the serious demographic problem that so many nations suffer from, there are three possible strategies or attitudes that can be described, by analogy, with the colors of a traffic light:

- <u>Red</u>. Do nothing, as was the case until recently in many countries, and keep looking the other way, ignoring the problem. This attitude is extremely unwise because it leads to demographic disaster and its collateral penalties, without preparing us to face it with certain possibilities of reducing or delaying its damage. Fortunately, although no country affected by a low birth rate and social aging is doing what is necessary to confront such thorny and interrelated problems, awareness of its gravity is growing exponentially everywhere, and with it, the adoption of measures to combat these problems, no matter how much these measures still fall between insufficient and very insufficient, and in more than a few cases, wrong and even counterproductive.

- <u>Yellow.</u> Adapt to the process of demographic suicide, in order to avoid and minimize its painful consequences as much as possible. It is a smarter attitude than the previous one, since at least in this scenario the problem is acknowledged and what is proposed is to weather the consequences of an unfavorable demographic environment in the best possible way. In economic terms, this adaptation, as individuals, for profit and non-profit companies, and governments and public administrations, involves:

  ✓ Saving money. Faced with difficult times and predictable economic shortages that come with demographic decrepitude, it is better to have our saddlebags as full as we can, and with little debt in our financial baggage. This is indeed just the opposite of what Japan, Europe, and North America have been doing in their public sector for decades, whose public debt tends to grow in relation to the size of their economy, with exceptions and occasional moments when their debt relative to GDP was reduced, because of the fiscal deficits of their governments, generated among other reasons by increasing expenses for the elderly (pensions, healthcare, and dependency care).

  ✓ Structural reforms, investment, and innovation in better technologies and productive processes, to increase productivity and competitiveness, and eliminate waste in public (and private) spending. Since the economy and the public sector are going to be weighed down by demography, the goal would be to alleviate or compensate this negative impact by producing more at a lower cost, and spending less on the superfluous, in order to generate and keep more wealth, and for the public sector to use it for true social utility purposes, such as a good quality of life for our seniors and elderly.

  ✓ Robotics and artificial intelligence, which, in terms of new technologies, would be especially useful in a scarce and aging workforce environment, both in business and home environments, and especially if capabilities such as those of the robots in science fiction films soon developed. Even without reaching so far, for example, the driverless car is already a mature development. Likewise, biomedical technologies that extend life expectancy with good health will be of particular interest, especially in helping to extend the working life and to save medical expenses due to illness or health deterioration (although for public finances, in relation to pensions, longer lives imply a higher overall cost per person after retirement).

✓ Extending the working life in societies with many elderly people—which is already being done or expected in many countries—for the savings on pensions that it represents for the State, and for its material and mental health benefits for people (according to the concept of "active aging"). It must be done with care so as not to harm companies, since many workers close to retirement have high salaries, but that closeness, with customary exceptions, often is a detriment to their motivation and productivity.

✓ Exporting and investing in markets not (yet) adversely affected by demographics. In fact, in the emerging countries, demography will favor economic growth over the next 15 to 30 years as there is a growing mass of young and middle-aged population with an equally increasing consumption capacity.

✓ For the most adventurous and savvy entrepreneurs, launching/exploiting businesses to provide specific infrastructures, products and services for the elderly, and taking advantage of the bargains generated by the depreciation of assets and properties negatively affected by demographic developments, such as real estate.

✓ Ultimately, emigrating to countries with a demographic-economic profile relatively better than ours (for example, for Europeans, the USA).

- Green. Try to solve the demographic problem:

✓ We must have more children: the only true solution. Our elites and the population must regain the primordial value of having children and of motherhood/paternity, understand the sad decline of collective infertility, and make the sustained rise in the birth rate one of the main socio-political priorities. This implies the rethinking of generalized social patterns and practices that impair total fertility rates (such as the empowerment of anti-birth values and poor family models, the facilitation by the State of anti-birth practices such as abortion, or the things that structurally cause people to delay the age at which they have their first child by too much), including the substantial modification or even the repeal of some laws. In addition, since children are a resource for society and their upbringing costs a lot, the parents must be compensated/incentivized economically for a substantial part of the cost of their upbringing, by means such as income tax and Social Security contribution deductions and retirement pension bonuses, depending on the number of children of each person, among others. Companies should also be relieved of the costs and disadvantages of seeing their employees, particularly women, but not only women, have children.

✓ A serious management of foreign immigration, in those countries with an economy that can attract them, facilitating the orderly arrival and good integration of immigrants that may be needed as a complement to the depleted native population and the low birth rate. This immigration should preferably be from the cultural background that best integrates in each country. Although immigration can be a good palliative and part of the solution to the demographic problem derived from a low birth rate, it is neither sufficient nor free of economic costs and social and moral risks.

Let us then develop the "green" and "yellow" options of this virtual traffic light. The "red" color is described by itself, since it leads slowly but inexorably to the precipice, collective and individual, and deserves a phrase that was made famous in 2016 in Spain by a socialist politician, Pedro Sánchez: "no means no" ("no es no").

What to do to foster the birth rate and a demographic renaissance

In countries with an insufficient birth rate, trading the cold winter demographic for a promising "demographic spring," i.e., that we have more children and recover fertility, at the very least, to the levels necessary for the replacement of the population, is something that is in the interest of all (individuals, the State, companies). We would all benefit from the arrival of the demographic spring—a sustained increase in the number of births—which we might well call a "Demographic Renaissance" due to the positive historical resonances of the term "renaissance" as well as its literal meaning[91]. Of course, it would take 20 to 25 years

---

[91] With the same idea, the author of this book, with the invaluable help of a group of friends, launched a foundation called Demographic Renaissance in 2013 in Madrid (Spain) (www.renacimientodemografico.org). It is a think tank whose purpose is to study the demographic problem derived from low birth rates and its possible solutions and to contribute to raising the awareness of this very important issue among society and elites.

to notice the effect of this possible birth rate recovery in the job market, but long before that we would have the joy of seeing more children and young people in our streets and cities. From the very moment when fertility rebounded, future expectations would begin to improve, starting with the industries that supply products and services to kids and young people, which is especially important in a world that moves based on expectations.

But how do we get there? It will not be easy. To avoid painting an all too gloomy picture, we can start with four good pieces of news.

The first is that the demographic suicide has potential consequences so horrific that it is extremely advisable, just, and necessary to avoid it.

The second is that few people are currently aware of the true scope and immediacy of the demographic problem in the making, so we can hope that, when they come to realize it and its severity, many people—ordinary people, ruling classes, including the political class—and ultimately, the great majority of society, change their attitude towards generalized reproductive absenteeism and its implications, which could end up facilitating a significant rebound in the birth rate.

The third is that what is needed in this area does not seem unattainable because of its magnitude: in order to ensure a generational change in the countries and regions affected by the demographic winter, it would suffice on average that women (and men) have between 0.2 to 0.3 and 1 additional children, i.e., that in the countries least affected by this ailment, one in every three to four women had one more child, and in places of extreme voluntary sterility, such as in my native Asturias—the beautiful Spanish region at the bottom of all of Europe in birth rate rankings—it would take one or slightly over one more children per woman. We are absolutely not talking about the 4 to 7 traditional children per woman; we are talking about having a total of 2.1 children per woman on average. That would be enough, thanks to the fact that nowadays barely any children or young people die[92].

The fourth is that several developed countries have made significant improvements in their fertility rates from their previous lows (e.g. France, Sweden, USA, or Ireland), partly as a result of economic and moral stimulus pro-birth policies, although it is true that with these rebounds they have not recovered

---

[92] In places that have had very low birth rates for many years such as Japan, Germany, Italy, Spain, or Portugal, and even more so in regions such as Liguria in Italy, or Asturias, Galicia and Castile and Leon in Spain, ideally fertility would recover to somewhat higher levels, about 2.5 to 3 children per woman, and remained at those levels for some years, in order to replace the loss of demographic force that occurred in the preceding decades. Having said that, since those countries and regions start from such low fertility rates, simply reaching 2 to 2.2 children per woman and staying there would already be very beneficial.

enough fertility levels in a sustained way, that in recent years there is another downward trend and that a significant part of this higher birth rate is due to immigrant women, not the native ones, in almost all cases.

5 + 1 strategic directions for the birth rate to rebound

In our opinion, in order to succeed in achieving a sufficient and significant rebound of the birth rate, it is necessary to take at least five (plus one) major strategic poles of activity, which are summarized in the following table, very seriously. Only the first one seems relatively easy and is a prerequisite for the others to be addressed with reasonable chances of success.

The five (plus one) great things that we would need to increase birth rates
1.- Massive awareness of the problem. Raise awareness among society and elites of the problem first and its solutions later.
2.- Knowledge. Study the problem and its solutions in depth, with rigor, data, and objectivity and without partisanship or ideological prejudices.
3.- Priority. Give this issue the very high public priority it deserves and requires.
4.- Money. Compensate parents for a large part of the cost of raising their children, as an incentive as well as for reasons of social equity.
5.- Values and laws. A cultural pro-birth change, and a change in certain laws currently against birth rate, whether directly or indirectly.
In addition and very important: **To not leave this matter in the hands of the State alone.** The whole society should be concerned with supporting those who can have children.

1.- **Raise an awareness in society that it has a grave problem** due to a lack of births, a moderate problem in some countries, serious in others, and very serious in more than a few.

2.- **Study the problem thoroughly, with rigor, objectivity, and data**, to better understand its causes, what it really implies, and what its possible solutions would be. What is the biggest difficulty in this issue? Aside from the fact that designing and implementing efficient and cost-effective solutions for such a complex issue is not an easy feat, in a world as ideologized/politicized as the one we live in, it is foreseeable that the recommended optimal outcome is not the family model/society that appeals to many and that, for starters, what needs to be done is something unpopular among broad layers of the electorate and very powerful political-ideological-intellectual lobbies. Yes, we live in an ultra-politicized world, because political power is extremely beneficial to those who desire it, because of how much those from party X, and not Party Y, make if they are in power, and the retributions that can be obtained in the form of subsidies from the political power for those who contribute to make sure the same ones keep the control. The burden of the egos and particular interests of so many intellectuals, pseudo-intellectuals, and intellectuals who make a living based on the fact that their preaching and particular theories resonate with the audiences that applaud and/or feed them must be added to this. For this reason, I am afraid that only if we are truly frightened by the demographic decline we are heading towards can we expect researchers to be truly objective and to embrace the truth rather than their political or religious (or antireligious) prejudices, in the case the accurate diagnosis and the correct solutions do not match their ideology, political interests, or particular prejudices.

During World War II, the British cabinet presided by the conservative Winston Churchill was a government of national unity, with Clement Atlee of the Labour Party as vice president. The justified terror of Hitler's victory in the war wrought this miracle of joining, for the first time—and as far as I know the last— Labour and Conservative members in the same government in London. In the decisive round of the French presidential elections in 2002, center-right candidate Jacques Chirac won 82% of the vote because the French center and left voted for him in order to not elect the much more right-wing Le Pen. Fear of Jean Marie Le Pen wrought this miracle. We might need something similar in terms of research and solutions to the demographic winter. Either it really scares us, thus allowing partisan politics and ideologies and equivalents to be left out of the investigation of causes and solutions, and of the implementation of what must be done to combat it, or we will probably stop halfway in the research and results, or when we are at the same point or worse than we are now. Do not worry, however, dear politicians—if you separate the demographic suicide from the political struggle to win and lose elections, you will still have many other things to attract the electorate, to fight over, and to manage at your convenience!

3.- Give the problem and its solutions the priority they deserve in the social and political agenda (maximum). In the public agenda, and in the budget of the States, there are dozens of issues that have to compete with each other to be the ones to receive the most attention and the largest public budget, because of the interests and/or ideals of the people who defend them. Of course, if everything had the highest priority—as I recall, in a business administration class I took, when the teacher asked us to assign priorities to three different action plans, a not very dedicated student proposed the highest for all three—by definition, nothing would really have the highest priority, because prioritization is a "zero sum game": what increases in priority does so at the expense of other things. Here it is worth repeating what was said before: either there is a large awareness, both popular and among the elites, of the danger that the demographic suicide entails, or fighting it will not receive the priority it deserves. Thus, for example, the beautiful Galicia, in the northwest of Spain, is one of the regions with the oldest population and the lowest birth rates of the country, Europe, and the world. In two of its four provinces, more than twice as many people have died as have been born for many years, and throughout the region, deaths have outnumbered births for decades. Its regional government, very meritoriously, was the first in Spain to promote a Demographic Dynamization Plan (in 2013) with the primary objective of promoting more births. The economic budget dedicated 90 million euros over three years to measures supporting maternity and the birth rate, which, in an economy with about 50 billion euros of annual gross domestic product, accounted for approximately 0.06% of the annual GDP. Why did it not have a bigger budget, despite the dramatic demographic outlook in Galicia? Logically, because the Galician rulers thought that's what this issue deserved and/or what was possible for them to dedicate to this issue, given the many other socio-political determinants of their region, the competing interests of the various lobbyist groups and voters there are in every society, and the perception of the electorate of what is and isn't most important. Fortunately, since the Galician regional government embarked on this endeavor, popular awareness of the seriousness of the problem has grown enormously, which allows and will allow more in the future, to increase the priority and the budget initially granted in Galicia to combat its icy demographic winter.

4.- **Adopt effective and socially affordable measures of economic incentives to increase birth rates**, involving parental compensation for a very significant part of the full cost of having and raising children (by means such as direct distribution of money to parents, lower taxes, prolonged maternity and paternity leave, childcare subsidies, pension bonuses based on the number of children, greater compensation to companies for the maternity of their female employees, etc.), and that help to motivate parents to have more children. In very rich countries with no net public debt, such as Norway[93], this could be relatively easy to kick-start without electoral cost, due to the excellent financial health of its government. In other countries—with high accumulated public debt and annual deficits—in order to gather sufficient resources to promote more births, through increases in public spending on this line item, no solution is void of significant potential political cost and in some cases could be economically unworkable, as it would be based on one or more of the following things: higher public deficit, more net taxes for non-parents (otherwise, if what you are given with one hand is taken away by the other, the stimulus/compensation would be a trick, whose effectiveness would tend to be null), or cuts in other budget items.

5.- **Achieve a change in both culture and social values, and modify some laws and regulations, in favor of natality**. If all of the above seemed complicated, but was theoretically in the hands of political and social leaders willing to push it to its ultimate consequences, and they could do so in a relatively short period of time[94], a pro-birth change in culture and in social values would require a time difficult to estimate and which could be prolonged. Worse still: it is not (always) in the hands of political leaders and influential people to achieve change. Reforming laws and practices that have a clear impact on birth rates is, however, in their hands, something which, on the other hand, like all the legislative action governments undertake, influences the cultural values of the society the government directs. As an example, the State has laws that regulate marriage and divorce and influences—for example, with tax laws—the decision to marry or divorce. As for the birth rate, marriage has a positive effect on the birth rate and divorce has a negative effect. Likewise, marriage has a positive impact on the development and happiness of children. States can enact regulations and favor behaviors related to marriage and divorce that favor marriage and family stability, or the opposite. Something similar can be said about abortion laws. As far as promoting cultural changes, States are continually pursuing campaigns that seek to positively influence citizens' values, such as prudence on the road, rejection of

---

[93] Norway's average per capita income 2011-2014 in international dollars was 65,615, according to the World Bank. Its total net assets, minus foreign debts (public plus private, in both cases), were more than 1.5 times its GDP. Nonetheless, its birth rate in 2016 was a modest 1.71, with the birth rate of the native Norwegians (with higher per capita income than immigrants) being less than 1.7.

[94] Imagine, for example, that the President of Germany or Italy, the King of Spain or the Emperor of Japan, publicly summon political parties with parliamentary representation, major businessmen/women, and intellectuals to finalize a great national pact to promote birth rates, as a measure to save the country in the mid and long-term. After that, a national pro-birth plan, and other specific parallel plans by regions and provinces/departments, would be designed and approved. If there were a serious will to do it, this movement could be set in motion in a matter of 3 to 12 months.

domestic violence, or respect for the environment, just to give a few examples. Of course, they can also host pro-birth advertising campaigns, as has been done in France, in the former Yugoslav Republic of Macedonia, or more recently in Italy, to provide examples the author knows about, telling the population how beautiful being a parent is; how sad it is, for the vast majority of people, to not have children; the need their country has, in the end, for more little ones to be born; and the advisability of not waiting to be much older to decide to have children, because fertility wilts with age.

Finally, in addition, and **very importantly, this concerns us all. This is too important a matter to only leave in the hands of politicians, an easy** temptation in a modern, hyper-politicized society, in which the state spends 40 to 50 percent (or more) of what is produced in developed countries and has regulations and offers apparent solutions for almost everything. If the French president Clemenceau, who concluded the costly victory for his country in World War I, said that "war is too important to be left in the hands of the military" (meaning, in the interpretation of the aphorism fair to the military, that war was something that affects everyone in a society, and therefore, that in its political aspect, its conduct must be in the hands of the political authority of the country), with as much or more reason, the fight against the demographic suicide is too important to leave exclusively to the hands of politicians, among other reasons, because they cannot have all the children for us, nor is there any way they can force us to have children, unless we fall into a much greater evil than the one that we are currently in with regards to this matter: a totalitarian State that forces us to mate to procreate[95]. We should all help as much as we can to spread knowledge of the problem, while there is not enough popular awareness about it; we can all support those who have or can still have children, one way or another, even if only through encouragement. Whoever does not contribute to this effort, even if only through verbal/moral support to the parents of kids, should not complain if their country is slowly falling down the path of the demographic suicide, if they have a very low pension when they grow old, and if they suffer from other economic and affective ailments that are characteristics of a society with a marked demographic decline. We can all do something to help increase the birth rate. Although helping a little is not much, it is always more than nothing.

---

[95] Although fortunately it seems unlikely that this will happen in the future, just over 40 years ago, the diabolical Khmer Rouge of communist Cambodia did something like this. They forced an indefinite number of Cambodians, which could amount to several hundred thousands, to marry and procreate. If they did not mate "by hook," the husbands were forced to rape their wives as a way to ensure that the couples would produce children for the country. What a horror!
http://kh.boell.org/sites/default/files/forced_marriage_study_report_tpo_october_2014.pdf

To begin with, people should be aware of the gravity and immediacy of the demographic problem

It is very difficult, if not impossible, to tackle a serious and complex social problem with success and rigor if people are barely aware it exists, and if, when they do know it exists, do not consider it important and/or necessary enough to address it urgently. They are less inclined to consider the problem if its solution involves efforts and sacrifice, and recommends to significantly favor those who contribute personally to solve it in relation to the rest, and even less if, as in this case, its solution requires a change in the model of society, in its blueprint, since not having children is not something secondary or accessory, but is at the core of the current model of society in the entire developed and much of the developing world. Therefore, it is something that will hardly improve in a significant and sustained way with a few patches, two or three isolated pro-birth measures from the government, and an advertising campaign. Desperate times call for desperate measures. You cannot cure cancer with aspirin. Moreover, you will not undertake any type of cancer treatment if you don't know you have it, and much less if, in addition, your treatment involves undeniable doses of sacrifice.

At the European level, opinion polls, called "Eurobarometers," are regularly carried out, typically with about 1,000 personal interviews per country of the European Union. In particular, in November 2015, the thirteen issues of greatest concern to Europeans were listed. The concerns were the following, in order of importance: immigration, terrorism, economic situation, unemployment, the state of public finances of the EU members, crime, inflation/cost of living, climate change, EU influence in the world, the environment, taxes, pensions, and energy sources. Of course, there was no mention of the European problem of lack of births, although in the countries of the current European Union, the aggregate birth rate has been insufficient to assure the population replacement for at least 30 years, and in 2014 it was 25% below 2.1 children per woman, despite the fact that fewer native Europeans have been born than those who have died for years, and in 14 of the 28 EU member states, there are more deaths than births, even including immigrants[96], despite the fact that in in 2015, 34% of people over 90 in the world were European, but fewer than 6% of babies.

Similarly, in Spain, my country, when the state-run Center for Sociological Research (CIS, Centro de Investigaciones Sociológicas) asks a statistically large sample of Spaniards, several times a year, about the three main problems of their homeland, a score of issues or so appears in the results the CIS publishes, listed in an order according to how many people quote them, typically headed by things like

---

[96] In 2015, for the first time, foreign immigrants included, there were more deaths than births in the European Union.

unemployment, terrorism, corruption, politicians, drugs, etc. Since 1985, when that survey was first carried out, almost fifty distinct kinds of topics have been quoted over the years. Although some of them are related to demographics and the birth rate, such as "immigration," "abortion," or "pensions," a low birth rate has NEVER appeared among the concerns of the Spaniards, the most infertile people on Earth in the quarter of a century before this book was written[97]. With social strands like this, how are we going to take serious measures to promote births in Spain? How will modern politicians, who move with/from/to/by/according to public opinion polls, do anything to give fertility the place of preeminence that should correspond to it in the Spanish public agenda? They themselves have not made any effort so far to create the necessary pro-birth opinion climate, unlike, for example, the neighboring and significantly more fertile France. If we analyze all the great public speeches of the two Spanish Kings and the five or six presidents of the government—Christmas and New Year's speeches, investiture as presidents of the government, debates on the State of the Nation, etc.—who have led Spain since it was first noted that the country was not doing well with its birth rate (towards 1980), until the writing of this book in 2016[98], the very serious birth rate problem of the Spaniards has never been publicly mentioned. This is in spite of the fact that, privately, one of them stated to me in person, when he was no longer president of the government, that indeed, Spain had a tremendous deficit in births and I believe another president thinks this way as well.

Therefore, what is first, secondly, and thirdly needed to effectively combat the demographic suicide are that people and elites be fully aware of its threatening existence, of the extent and transcendence of its consequences, and have the conviction that this is something we have to start facing now, and not, for example, when pigs fly.

---

[97] See http://www.cis.es/cis/export/sites/default/Archivos/Indicadores/documentos_html/TresProblemas.html

[98] The bulk of this book was written in 2015 and 2016, and was reviewed and finished in the first half of 2017. In January 2017 (at last!), the Spanish government began to talk about Spain's "demographic challenge," and created a High Commissioner to tackle this issue (Comisionado para el Reto Demográfico). However, it was amazing for me to verify, in the text of the government decree creating such high commissioner, that there was no explicit mention in it to the need to foster / boost the number of births / birth rate / fertility in Spain. See https://www.boe.es/boe/dias/2017/01/28/pdfs/BOE-A-2017-915.pdf. I wish the best for this endeavor! The Spanish Senate, as well, at the beginning of 2017—at last—, created a special committee about the Spanish demographic evolution.

Study the subject in depth, with reliable data, with rigor, and without bias in the diagnosis and the solutions due to ideological prejudices or particular interests

> "If I had 6 hours to chop down a tree, I would spend 4 of those hours sharpening my axe"[99]
> (Attributed to **Abraham Lincoln**)
>
> "Men willingly believe what they wish to be true."
> (**Julius Caesar**)

The demographic problem of countries and geographical areas that are in "demographic suicide" mode, as seen throughout this book, is extremely complex and multifaceted (state of development, consequences, causes and solutions), as well as important. It is not an easy problem to successfully fight, as is demonstrated by the fact that no country that entered the path of demographic suicide (less than 2 to 2.1 children per woman in developed countries) has steadily managed to exit it, and much less with regard to its own native population, since the global birth rates in almost all Western countries, let alone birth numbers, are greater thanks to the contribution of foreign immigration.

It is therefore essential to understand the problem very well and to refine the plans and measures to combat it, since, to deal with it satisfactorily, measures and actions should simultaneously combine:

✓ Effectiveness. Measures that, if applied, would yield results, i.e., a higher fertility rate.

✓ Efficiency in the use of public resources. The selected measures should cost the least possible, for the same increase in the birth rate. The worse the public finances and growth prospects of a country are, the more important

---

99 NB. Cecilia Mabilais, who translated this book into English from Spanish, did more than just translating it. She double-checked part of its content, like this statement. She found that it is uncertain whether the great Abraham Lincoln actually said it or not. Despite this feedback from Cecilia, I decided to keep it, adding the words "attributed to," since Lincoln might still have said this sentence or something very similar. And more important, because its advice is very good for facing complex issues and challenges.

this requirement becomes. In Norway, Switzerland, Singapore, or Luxembourg, for example, very wealthy countries in excellent financial shape, where it is still better to spend less than more, it is less important to do so than in countries like Spain, Italy, Portugal or Greece, where efficiency in the use of public resources is critical.

✓ Economic/political/public viability. The cost of the pro-birth measures should be affordable and there should not be significant impediments due to social unpopularity or politico-social opposition so significant they put an end to the effort.

In countries experiencing a demographic winter, we need to achieve a relatively rapid, substantial, and sustained rebound in births and fertility. We also need to adapt, in any case, to a society inevitably aged in the coming decades, since, even if birth rates shot up tomorrow, children born today will take an average of 20 to 25 years to join the productive economy. We also need to achieve the previous goals while saving the resources we need and must ensure that all the above be politically and socially viable. Easier said than done.

In this case, the solution involves that the many people who do not want to have children, or who want to have only one, because the possibility of having and raising children inconveniences them, have more children, <u>because they want to, and they want to before they are too old for it</u>. It also involves other people and social agents either helping those who can have children or, at the very least, not obstructing them from having children while accepting the fact that those individuals should be favored.

One thing that greatly complicates the demographic problem and its solutions being studied objectively and impartially is the hyper-politicization and hyper-ideologization that we suffer from in the modern world, where so many things are politicized and analyzed in a partisan/ideological way, such as, for example, the relationship between fertility and female labor, marriage, divorce, abortion, etc. In our experience, it will be difficult for a sufficiently unbiased and thorough investigation into such issues to take place (especially on solutions, causes, and consequences), accepted by the vast majority of people, as long as the demographic suicide does not frighten society so much that the bulk of the actors in the political-social-intellectual life feel it necessary to leave demographic suicide at the margin of the political brawl and ideological prejudices. One great risk countries in the process of demographic decline face in this matter is that we only massively accept the gravity of what happens to us and what needs to be done to remedy it when our degree of depopulation and aging reaches or is near catastrophic degrees. At heart, ultimately, this is the great purpose of this book: to help us realize how bad the port our ship is sailing towards is so that we can turn towards a different direction as soon as possible and head toward better waters, without ever reaching that port.

To know the causes of infertility well, and to conceive optimal ways to overcome (only) those that are worth overcoming

(Main measures proposed in the 1974 "Kissinger Report" for the reduction of birth rates in less developed countries. See Annex)

1.- Improvements in health and nutrition that contribute to lower infant mortality.

2.- Universal education and fight against illiteracy, with emphasis on women.

3.- Raise the legal age of marriage.

4.- Create more employment opportunities for women and promote equal pay for men and women.

5.- Social Security protections for old age that reduce the need to have children to take care of the elderly.

6.- Improvements in agriculture and other areas of the economy to increase the standard of living, specifically, of the poorest population, since it is the one that has more children, precisely because it is poorer. The desire to form large families diminishes when more money is earned.

7.- Providing access to contraceptive means and methods.

8.- Educate/indoctrinate children, from elementary school, that it is desirable to have small families.

In the previous section of this book we analyzed a number of potential causes as to why we now have so few children. As we have seen, some of these causes seem to easily defy the test of logic and empirical data; others are somewhat less solid; and there are those that seem more to be myths than anything else, directly contrary to reality. Although I believe that the analyses that have been detailed in this book are essentially correct, with humility, I think that all this must be studied much more in depth than I have modestly been able to do through more means, data, tools, surveys, and in-depth interviews with mothers, fathers, and those who do not have and/or do not want to have children, and to those who would like to have children. These studies should also be reevaluated periodically, because society changes continuously, sometimes little by little, sometimes abruptly, in its motivations, conditioning, and behaviors. The data loses relevance over time[100].

Main causes of infertility on which we can and should act

Let us subsequently analyze those which, in our opinion, based mainly on data, but also on reflections and intuitions—which, with humility, may or may not be correct—are the main causes of excessive infertility in developed countries, and in many developing countries, which can be acted upon in a significant extent:

1.- Children take away freedom, comfort, tranquility, security, and lots of money. There is a very common and certainly not unreasonable or irrational notion that children take away freedom, comfort, tranquility, security, and economic wealth, that it is very uncomfortable for women to be pregnant and give birth, for both parents to raise the children, and that it can hurt career opportunities for women, so that it does not make sense to have children (or to just have one, or two

---

[100] As an example of outdated data, let us see a bad example of my beautiful and (voluntarily) infertile country, Spain. Our National Institute of Statistics (INE) provides very valuable and detailed information on demographics and many other things, which this work depends upon. Generally it publishes data with an acceptable delay with respect to what is informed, although, as almost everything can be improved, in some matters it would be desirable that this delay be smaller. Where the INE has had a resounding failure in the field we are studying is in something vital to understanding who has children and not, how many, etc. We refer to the National Fertility Survey, whose last completion, at least until mid-2017, when this work was completed, occurred in 1999, with a sample of 7,749 women between the ages of 15 and 49. That no new fertility survey has been carried out in Spain since 1999 indicates the priority given by the Spanish authorities, the INE executives—and the intellectuals and influential people who interact with them—to the collection and publication of data and opinions on this issue, so that researchers can better understand the reason for the low fertility of Spanish women and in what contexts and circumstances it is not so low and why: a low or zero priority. Although this 1999 survey may continue to be a non-negligible source of data today, and in any case for historical research, it would be very risky to rely primarily on it to draw valid conclusions at the publication of this book and in subsequent years because Spanish society has changed a lot since then. When I was ending the review of this manuscript, I was informed that a new National Fertility Survey would be published in 2018 (19 years after the previous one!). I was informed as well that the survey would only include responses / opinions from women. But men matter as well a lot in this issue, indeed! I wish it finally contains, as well, responses / opinions from men. Otherwise, this survey on fertility would be incomplete, lame.

at most). Of course, if a person of childbearing age who has not yet had children, or already has one, observes/calculates/intuits the difference in the levels of effective disposable income per adult in households with children and in those who do not have children, and even more so in the case of women, because of how motherhood affects their careers, and if that person thinks only or mainly of material things, the conclusion is obvious: having children is bad economic business (unlike in the past, when they became labor in the field in relatively few years, and a little older, staff of the old age for the parents).

2.- The increasing family disintegration and instability. The traditional family, formed by a stable marriage that began its conjugal journey with a wedding in which the bride and the groom were quite young, was an environment in which there were always (quite a few) children. Even today, data available and presented earlier in this book unquestionably demonstrate that households headed by a married couple have more children than those formed by de facto couples or single parents. Nonetheless, we are getting married less and later and more children are born to unmarried women. A significant number of children are even born directly into single-parent homes[101]. Rates of divorce and family breakdowns, which were minimal in the past, are nowadays very high[102]. Of course, just as investors put much less money in unstable economies and in countries without security and legal stability, or legal frameworks that protect their investments, in our private lives, we humans have fewer children if we do not marry and spend many years in stable marriages/couples.

---

[101] Let's look at data from two specific countries of children born from single mothers, an aspect that many countries do not report specifically in their official statistics. According to the Norwegian Statistical Office (Statistics Sentralbyrå), 1/8 of Norway's births in 2014 and 2015 were the offspring of a mother who was not married or cohabiting with a partner. It is a minority of births, but not insignificant. In Spain, children without a declared father represented 2.3% of the total number of births in 2014.

[102] In the European Union there are almost 5 divorces for every 10 marriages celebrated, with countries like Denmark, Spain, Luxembourg, and Portugal having more than 6 divorces for every 10 weddings in 2013. In Belgium there was an average of 7 divorces for every 10 weddings between 2004 and 2012. This does not exactly mean that almost 50% of marriages in the EU end in divorce, since that there are many divorces contributes as much to the rate as the fact that people marry much less than before. It does give an idea, however, that the frequency of divorces is certainly not small and especially of the poor health of the institution of marriage in today's European society, among the young and middle-aged population, whether because of more break-ups or fewer weddings. On the other hand, the bride was divorced from a previous marriage in 16% of the weddings celebrated in 2013 in the European Union (not including in this statistic France, the United Kingdom, and Ireland, which did not report these data to Eurostat). This means that in one of every six weddings included in the (high) ratio of divorce to marriage, on top of all, there is implicitly at least one prior divorce involved.

3.- The delay in the age at the first child, which causes—as already mentioned—many women to end up not having any children, or only having one, to experience more difficult pregnancies, childbirth and child rearing, resulting in fewer births with more miscarriages, etc.

4- The difficulty in harmonizing motherhood and women working outside the home. This problem did not exist before, since few women of child-bearing age worked outside the home and there was no clear distinction in many rural households as in the cities between "working" and "not working" in the case of women/mothers. Today it is a real problem, in many countries poorly resolved, both for women/mothers/families and for companies, and certainly for the birth rate and society in general.

5.- Very closely linked to the above, that **modern States and the media, in general, promote women as being "workers" above being "mothers,"** instead of encouraging **both at the same time**, and in any case trying to make sure that, in general—although there will always be those who do not have children—they be the latter. A society can survive without women working outside the home, but not without mothers. The goal, ideally, is not simply to survive, but to lead a full life in all its aspects. But without surviving, in the long run, no other goal, however desirable, is possible.

6.- The legal devaluation of the figure of the father, which, in addition to being unfair and inconvenient for the children and the fathers, tends not to favor that more boys become fathers, or that many of them not be as involved in the upbringing of the children as would be desirable, which, in the end, is an element that weighs negatively on the birth rate. The mother is indispensable in the decision to have children, to bear them and to raise them properly, but, for the vast majority of women who want to be mothers, and for the children, the male/father is also of great importance, to decide whether or not to have children and how many to have, as well as to raise them.

7.- The facilitation of free access to contraceptive means to the population, and, in particular, one as arguable as **abortion**—which eliminates not a possible pregnancy but a human baby "in progress"—by the governments of countries in the process of demographic suicide.

8- The surrounding cultural magma of public values, indifferent, if not hostile, to fertility and stable marriages. This, in turn, translates into multiple aspects of laws, rules, and regulations that result in additional obstacles or risks for parents, since these try to optimize other things, although their net effect is to reduce the desire to have children in people. It also translates into a hostility with which the mothers of very large families are treated (many call them "rabbits!" in countries like Spain) and the lack of support many parents give their children to have their own children (even if, in the end, they do help and melt over the grandchildren, as grandparents), and contempt for women who do not want to work outside the home, typically to focus on motherhood and family (they are contemptuously called more or less like "house cleaners!" in Spain), as traditional moms at home.

9.- The indifference or insufficient attention of the elites to the deficient birth rate in countries where it is too low. *Sensu contrario*, in those nations whose governments have taken this issue more seriously and for a longer time, such as France, Ireland, or Sweden, birth rates are significantly higher than the European average.

Causes of a lower birth rate over which we cannot or should not act

There are also primary causes for a low birth rate that either cannot realistically be suppressed or that would not be advisable to suppress (typically both). The first of these causes is the 99% or more reduction in infant and child mortality rates, which allows us to spare more than 50% of the pregnancies, births, and first years of child-rearing that were previously necessary to achieve the same adult offspring, as parents, and the same demographic value for our country as now. It is neither possible nor would anyone in their right mind propose to recover the patterns of infant and juvenile mortality of yesteryear to try to regain the levels of fertility of that time!

Another very clear cause in this category is the modern system of retirement pensions and of medical and long-term care for the elderly provided by the State and/or private companies. This system has eliminated the peremptory need to have children to care for the elderly, although it is still very desirable to have them, for reasons of affection and quality of life in our most advanced ages, and not only at these ages. Moreover, the financing of the cost of retirement pensions takes away a good chunk of the income the young and middle-aged adults generate in their active years, part or all of which could be used, at least theoretically, to raise (more) children. As with mortality, no one would want the pensions and medical care for the elderly that are enjoyed today to disappear, in order for us to be compelled to have more children so they can care for us when we become old. Even if the public pay-as-you-go pension system—workers pay with their mandatory contributions in Social Security and tax the pensions of today's retirees—was replaced with a private pension system, the effect on birth rates would be similar to the public system, in this case, as it would similarly take the fear of poverty in old age away (in fact, if, as the logic seems to indicate and its proponents defend it, the private pension system by capitalization, such as the Chilean system, allowed us to have a higher pension as retirees, then its effect on birth rates would not be less than the current pension system).

The same can be said about life in cities, with non-agricultural occupations, very much the majority nowadays, versus the predominantly rural society of the past, in which children were conceived, among other reasons, to generate arms that worked in the family terroir as soon as they left their early childhood behind. That will not happen again, among other reasons because, with the modern farming and livestock raising techniques and technologies, and farms becoming increasingly professionalized, agriculture now requires 95% fewer people, or even less, to produce the same foods as before. For example, in the Eurozone countries, the agricultural sector currently employs only one in thirty workers.

Finally, there are other causes that would be intermediate in terms of their impact and how much can be done about them, such as the loss of religious and patriotic values in the population and the elites. It seems logical to think that a social recovery of both values would be beneficial to the birth rate, based on what was already exposed in previous pages, but it is not something that can be acted upon so easily, as it belongs to the sphere of personal conscience—especially religion—so in this book we will not emphasize it much, beyond stressing that a greater popular degree of religiosity and patriotism than the present ones, at least in Europe and the Americas, would do no harm to birth rates, but rather, would have a high probability of producing the opposite effect.

Very importantly, let's not be blinded by the myths and fallacies that are erroneously blamed for causing the declining birth rate

The main cause of low birth rates is not a problem of low income per capita and/or high unemployment, as already mentioned in the previous chapter, although both are undesirable per se, and we all want the former to grow, especially for people who have less, and for unemployment to be virtually zero, beyond the so-called "technical" (3% to 5%). If these two were the main reasons for a low birth rate, there would be no way to understand the following:

✓ That the birth rate of countries like Norway or Switzerland, without high unemployment and enormous wealth per capita, not be impressive (65,000 euros in income per capita in 2015 in Norway, for example), instead of the mediocre 1.71 children per woman in Norway in 2016 (and less than 1.7 among native Norwegians) and the paltry 1.47 average from 1994-2014 in Switzerland (1.33 among women of Swiss nationality, even richer than the rest of women, the immigrants who had 45% more children on average than the native Swiss women during that same period). Looking beyond Europe, the same is true of another of the most prosperous and developed societies, Singapore, with an equally stratospheric per capita income and an average fertility rate between 2011 and 2014 of 1.23 children per woman. The table in next page shows the fertility rates in the richest countries in the world: very mediocre; and the lower the per capita income, the higher the birth rate—not the other way around.

✓ That people do not have more children in the developed world than in the underdeveloped (it's the other way around).

✓ That people do not have many more children per woman now than they did 100 years ago, when, on average, people were much poorer.

✓ That the birth rate of Spanish women fell by only 3% between 2007 (after 12 years of economic expansion) and 2014 (after six years of hardship for the Spanish economy), and nothing if we exclude for this purpose the children of immigrants with dual nationality. Also in Spain, the birth rate of Basque women is lower than that of Andalusian women (with a much lower per capita income and much higher unemployment).

✓ That the birth rate is practically as low among German, Austrian, or Italian women as it is among Greek, Polish, or Romanian women, or among the women in the four municipalities with the highest per capita income in the province of Madrid and the four that have the lowest (among the municipalities with more than 50,000 inhabitants of that province), although the former have twice the wealth per inhabitant as the latter.

✓ That the birth rate in Taiwan, with a much higher per capita income, and without resorting to totalitarian policies of one child only, has been lower than that in China for many years.

Total fertility rate in the countries with the highest GDP per capita (excluding petro states)			
Country	GDP per capita (2011-2014), in international US dollars	Total fertility rate (children per woman) in 2014	Children per native woman in 2014 (*)
Luxembourg	98,460	1.50	Est. 1.30 native women
Singapore	82,763	1.25	N/A
Norway	65,615	1.75	Est. 1.72 native women
Switzerland	59,540	1.54	Est. 1.43 Swiss women (**)
Hong Kong	55,084	1.23	N/A
Simple average of 5 richest	**72,292**	**1.45**	**1.39**
United States of America	54,630	1.86	N/A
Ireland	49,393	1.94	Est. 1.97 native women
Netherlands	48,253	1.71	Est. 1.71 native women
Austria	47,682	1.47	Est. 1.36 native women
Germany	46,401	1.47	Est. 1.37 native women
Simple average of 10 richest	**60,782**	**1.57**	**1.52**
Australia	45,926	1.77	N/A
Denmark	45,537	1.69	Est. 1.71 native women
Sweden	45,297	1.88	Est. 1.83 native women
Canada	45,066	1.59	N/A
Belgium	43,435	1.74	Est. 1.59 native women
Simple average of 15 richest	**55,539**	**1.63**	**1.58**

Source: World Bank, Eurostat, CDC, Indexmundi, own estimates based on data from the former
(*) Only in countries from which we have data to estimate it. In the rest, it is assumed to be equal to the overall rate
(**) Average fertility of Swiss women between 1994 and 2014 was 1.33 children per woman

The same goes for other myths and false explanations about the main causes of low birth rates, which are commonly cited, such as the following:

✓ Insufficient employment rate for women. This rate is the highest in history and we have fewer children than ever before. There is no mathematical correlation in the set of developed countries between official fertility indicators and the female employment rate. In these nations, however, women who do not work outside the home usually have more children than those who do. In Spain, in particular, according to our estimates, the rate was 50% higher in 2014.

✓ Insufficient gender equality. We live in the most egalitarian societies between women and men in history, and at the same time, we have fewer children than ever before. In the supposedly exemplary countries in this area (the Scandinavian countries), as in almost all other European countries, non-European immigrant women, who generally live in less egalitarian homes than the native ones, have a much higher average fertility. Native Scandinavians also have few children, and lately, have been having even fewer.

✓ Uncertainty about the future. The degree of uncertainty—and economic precariousness—that existed in Spain in the middle of the civil war between 1936 and 1939 and during its postwar era was infinitely superior to that experienced in the last years of the economic crisis, but the birth rate then was much higher than the current one. In Nazi-occupied France—one of the most unpleasant socio-political situations imaginable—there was a rebound in the birth rate: in 1942, fertility rose, increasing in 1943 and 1944, and surpassing that of the pre-war level (!!!). Fertility in the United States also began to improve, for the first time in more than a century, when it was still in midst of the Great Depression of the 1930s. There was always, and there will always be, uncertainty about the future. People used to have many children and now have few.

✓ Difficulty of young individuals in obtaining access to housing. This is something that is argued in countries like Spain, in particular. Before the economic-financial crisis that began to be noticed in 2008, there was no such difficulty, and the birth rate was equally low. In most of Europe, where young people emancipate themselves at younger ages than in Spain or Italy (and therefore are able to establish a home of their own), fertility is equally low, or, at least, not significantly higher.

✓ Unreasonable schedules which prevent reconciling work and family, and therefore, having little ones, something that is increasingly blamed for the lack of children in Spain. Of course, work-family reconciliation is good for parents and children, and probably for some to have one more child, but the indices we have about female public servants in Spain (the number of female public servants has been multiplied in Spain in recent decades, while birth rates have drastically dropped in the country), or the insufficient fertility in countries with reasonable and among the shortest working hours in the world, as in most of Western Europe, would not substantiate that this is the main cause for the lack of births, unless we conclude that female labor and birth rate have an intrinsically difficult compatibility, and starting from this premise, seek ways to improve it. The following table shows the number of hours worked per year together with the fertility rate of the main countries. In the table, there is no correlation between the two scales (mathematically, the correlation coefficient is -4%, i.e. virtually zero)

Average hours worked per employed person and fertility in 2014 in OECD countries			
Source: OECD, Eurostat, Indexmundi, own analysis	Average hours actually worked per worker in 2014	Children per woman in 2014	Children per native women in 2014 (only countries for which we have data to estimate it)
Germany	1,371	1.47	Est. 1.37 native women
Netherlands	1,425	1.71	
Norway	1,427	1.75	Est. 1.72 native women
Denmark	1,436	1.69	
France	1,473	2.01	Est. 1.84 native women
Slovenia	1,561	1.58	
Switzerland	1,568	1.54	1.43 Swiss women
Belgium	1,576	1.74	Est. 1.6 native women
Sweden	1,609	1.88	Est. 1.83 native women
Austria	1,629	1.47	Est. 1.36 native women
Luxembourg	1,643	1.50	Est. 1.30 native women
Finland	1,645	1.71	Est. 1.69 native women
Australia	1,664	1.77	
United Kingdom	1,677	1.81	Est. 1.74 native women
Spain	1,689	1.32	Est. 1.27 native women
Canada	1,704	1.59	
Japan	1,729	1.42	
Italy	1,734	1.37	Est. 1.29 native women
New Zeland	1,762	1.92	
Slovakia	1,763	1.37	
Czech Republic	1,776	1.53	
United States	1,789	1.86	
Chile	1,990	1.85	

And if we analyze the hours worked by women in Western Europe (the previous table refers to the entire labor force, because either the OECD does not provide data broken down by sex, or I was not able to find it), the result, with fertility data from 2015, and with data reflecting the quarters when almost all children born in 2015 were conceived, we find that the correlation between typical weekly working hours and fertility by country is also very weak, if any. This is shown in the following table. A notable case is that of the Netherlands, where women work, on average, about 25 hours per week in their main job (for the vast majority the only job), far below the average. And its fertility in 2015 was 1.66 children per woman, slightly higher than the very low European average, but certainly insufficient and very low by historical standards. Other notable cases contrary to what might be expected (fewer hours of work, and therefore better balance, higher fertility rate) are the two most populous countries in Europe,

Germany (fewer hours worked, low birth rates) and France (more hours worked than the average, the highest fertility in Western Europe). And if we compare Spain and Sweden, we see that the average working day for a female is practically the same, yet the birth rate in Sweden is 0.5 children more per woman than in Spain, or almost 40% higher. In the case of Italy, the length of the working day is just above average, but fertility is much lower than average. Thus, a good balance between personal / family life and work life is a desirable goal in modern societies. Logically, it would be beneficial in order to have children, as well as a better upbringing of children, which is also very important. But the available data do not support that this is a sufficient and decisive condition for a significantly greater fertility. Otherwise, in these tables it would be clearly seen that this is so, but this is not the case. And if people do not want children, no matter how easy society makes it for them ... they will not have any.

Average number of usual weekly hours of work per woman in main job and fertility rate in Western Europe betwen April 2014 and March 2015 (*)		
Source: Eurostat	Average number of work hours per woman in an usual week in main job (*)	Total fertility rate (children per woman) in 2015
Netherlands	24.5	1.66
Switzerland	29.1	1.54
Germany	30.5	1.50
Denmark	31.0	1.71
Norway	31.1	1.72
Ireland	31.5	1.91
United Kingdom	31.7	1.80
Austria	31.9	1.49
Italy	32.7	1.35
Belgium	33.3	1.70
Luxembourg	33.8	1.47
France	34.2	1.96
Sweden	34.4	1.85
Spain	34.6	1.33
Finland	34.9	1.65
Iceland	35.1	1.80
Portugal	38.2	1.31
Simple average	**32.5**	**1.63**
(*) Average Q2-2014 to Q1-2015. All babies born in 2015 -except some premature born, and some late-born- were conceived in this time span. In the vast majority of cases, this is the only job.		

Give a high priority in the public agenda to the rebound of birth rates

In the modern world there is such an abundance of options and possibilities for almost everything that very few things triumph in each category. There are so many books that can be read, so much music that can be listened to, so many products that can be bought for the same need, so many leisure alternatives, so many ideas and ideologies, so many theories about anything, so many interesting social programs for governments, so much of everything, that what does not achieve priority status is left with nothing or almost nothing, because the time and the brain at our disposition are limited, and so are economic resources. The fight against demographic suicide, in order to be successfully addressed, requires a very high priority in the politico-social-intellectual agenda of countries afflicted with this ailment, since, as previously mentioned, the low birth rate is an essential part of the model of modern society and is something that cannot be changed just like that.

Such high prioritization could, among other initiatives, take the form of strategic national/regional/local demographic plans, as well as at the European level, in the case of the old continent (indeed, as a friend acutely pointed out to me, "old" applies to Europe now more than ever!). That would not be enough. Issues in a country or in a society are not a priority just because a law says so. The problem of birth rates, and its prioritization, must be something that permeates what the Germans call the *Zeitgeist*, the intellectual climate of the moment. As we mentioned, it is not enough that the State, the politicians, give priority to the rebound in birth rates. If non-political elites and society, as a whole, do not take up this issue as their own, not much will be achieved, or much less will be achieved than if they did take it seriously.

Incentives and financial compensation for births

If we start from the premise that children are an asset for society/the State, and that raising them costs parents a lot of money, it makes sense for society, through the State, to return/compensate families for a substantial part of that cost, for reasons of social equity. If we further believe that this high cost is one of the current brakes to having (more) children, something that seems logical but is not the only or the main cause of a low birth rate, it also makes sense to encourage more births.

As in so many things, however, the aphorism that "the devil is in the details" applies here. In order to specify and go into the details of how the economic incentive/compensation of birth rate should be carried out, we must ask ourselves at least four important questions:

1.- How much does it cost to raise children until they are emancipated?

2.- What part or percentage of the cost to raise a child should society return/contribute, through the State, to their parents?

3.- Who should receive the financial compensation/incentive for each child? The mother? The father? Both?

4.- Through what fiscal mechanisms, taxes and/or payments by the State, should that money be returned to the parents?

How much money does it cost to raise a child?

In the same country, region or locality, the cost to raise a child from birth until emancipation from the family home—even in economic terms—is not the same for all social classes. With equal income and starting wealth, not all families save or spend the same amounts. Of course, the cost to raise a child who starts working at age 18 and emancipates then is not the same as having a child who goes to college and does not start working until 23-25 or older. Nor does it cost the same, per child, to raise a single descendant as it does two, three, or any additional children, as there are obvious economies of scale for families in the unit cost per child, linked to the number of children. To further complicate the picture, there is an implicit cost, not easy to calculate, but, in some cases, perhaps the biggest of all: the opportunity cost for mothers, nowadays, to dedicate themselves (more) to their children, instead of, partially or completely, to their professional career[103]: the money they stop earning because of their loving dedication to raise the next generation of our compatriots and their own family saga.

---

[103] There may also be this opportunity cost for certain fathers, although in far fewer cases than for the typical mother. A father who essentially only goes to work, and hardly spends time with his children and family, in our opinion, is not an ideal father. He can be a great professional director, intellectual, politician, artist, academic, or whatever, but he is not a proper father. A good father, who does spend time with his family, and more if he is one of those who we colloquially call "superdads," for that same reason, has less time for his professional career, which can cause him to miss opportunities against those who are almost exclusively dedicated to their career, something not uncommon among business executives, outstanding politicians, very successful professionals in the sciences, the arts, the academy in general, etc. In all these fields there are outstanding men who, unfortunately, are not the best fathers for their children, for whom some of them have no time, nor the best husbands for their legal or de facto wives, which, for that matter, poses increased risks of divorce, a great harm for children.

On the other hand, there are important cost items related to child-rearing that are already covered by the State in developed countries, in whole or in part, for all families, such as health care—including medical expenses related to pregnancy and childbirth, or school and college education, although a considerable percentage of people in those countries incur themselves considerable expenses on private health and education, in addition to paying taxes like the others.

The economies of scale of families grow with the number of children, with significant unit savings per additional child raised

Housing, furnishing and other home items	✓The cost per square meter usually decreases with the size of the home. In a large percentage of houses, one or several additional children can be accommodated with zero incremental cost. The same is true of a large part of the household items and tools.
Clothing and footwear	✓ Among siblings, the younger ones can reuse much of the clothes and footwear of the older ones, especially when are of the same sex and/or they are very young
Fuel / energy	✓ The cost per child in fuel and energy decreases sharply with the number of children. Gasoline consumption with one more child in the same car barely increases 2%-3%.
Toys, leisure, books	✓ The cost per child in toys, vacations, books, and many similar types of consumer items decreases with the number of children.
Education and medical expenses	✓ Families with more children make it easier for the local school and health care center to achieve scale advantages. In textbooks, if they can be reused by siblings, there can be a noticeable saving for each additional child.

In total, for their parents, in a country like Spain, we estimate, on average, that raising a child, from birth to emancipation, in constant 2016 money, over 16-18 years to 25 years (or more), would cost a cumulative total of between €40,000 - €80,000 and €300,000 - €600,000 (at an average per month and child of €200-300 to €1,500 - €2,000 between birth and 16-25+), depending on the social class, the lifestyle, the age of emancipation, the studies pursued and the types of school chosen, the region and the locality, etc. In more prosperous countries with higher price levels, these quantities should probably be increased by 10% to 100%. In any case, it is a very considerable amount of money that presents enormous variability.

How much money should be repaid/compensated to parents of the costs to raise a child, both to incentivize them and for the sake of social equity

It would not be right for the State to include, when calculating the cost of raising children, for the purposes of what we are talking about, unnecessary luxuries or to reimburse the same percentage of that cost to middle-high and high-level families as it would to lower economic level families, since the latter have less economic comfort. However, *sensu contrario*, if all families were compensated/given the same amount per child, it would over-incentivize, in relative terms, the lower classes, which are largely composed of immigrants, and would not affect the well-to-do and the wealthy in their decision to have or not to have children.

It would also not be right for the State to cover the full cost of raising children by granting money—unless a substantial part of the compensation was deferred, for example, to retirement pensions—because there would then be people who would end up having children just to receive a salary, which can lead to undesirable phenomena such as the promotion of teenage single mothers of very modest economic level—which has occurred in some developed countries, in suburban slums—situations that are not exactly ideal for raising children. Nor is it ideal for the academic and professional development of these women, who in more than a few cases, like those mentioned, are still just adolescents and not mature adults. On the other hand, the State should not bear the full cost of raising children, because those who have children already receive a benefit that is not economic but includes the emotional/spiritual well-being to living a full life.

A much trickier issue would be the compensation for the job opportunity cost for mothers and their families to have and raise children—which in the long run costs them, as they earn less money, if they devote much to their children, and less or nothing at all to their company—because this could lead to enormous fraud and discrimination and because these women already have a great emotional and vital reward in the satisfaction produced through the upbringing of their little ones. Nevertheless, this cost of opportunity for "working" mothers (at least until they have children) undoubtedly exists in many cases and counts significantly for many women when deciding to have fewer children, or even none at all. Ergo, something must be done about it. At minimum, for example, compensation for social security contributions (and, in the long run, retirement pensions) is being done or announced in some places. In a non-economic order, but of social prestige, it would be very different if women who begin their maternal stage and prefer to temporarily or permanently abandon work outside the home for the care of children were to be exalted in the collective values of a society ("what a great woman, she prefers to take good care of her children rather than earn more money"), than if the generalized environment was the opposite ("how old-fashioned/stupid. Giving up her work/professional career to raise kids! What a loser!").

Finally, like so many other things in this book, we do not have THE solution to this question, among other reasons, because there is probably not a single possible answer, but we can point out avenues that seem clear to us, besides recommending further research to refine the response(s).

This compensation should increase with the income level/tax contribution to the State of the parents, because otherwise it would not promote more births, although those who make more effort with respect to their standard of living should always be relatively more compensated. It is more likely that money will be less motivating for those who have more economic comfort than for those who have meager resources, when it comes to having children. We also believe that this compensation should be somewhat tailored to the place of residence, since the cost of living is very different by localities, and even by neighborhoods.

What we believe is risky is to encourage having children with money as an incentive when neither parent has income, except in temporary and unfortunate situations of unemployment, because it can foster something so morally reprehensible, dangerous for the newborns, that their parents would want to have them for the money they would receive. What kind of parenting will children receive in a home like this, with both parents unable to earn money through work, and who had children so they can get paid? A baby should be a commodity that people have because it provides immediate economic benefits to its parents. On the other hand, for people with very little economic resources, encouraging them to have children may be something similar, *mutatis mutandis*, to the obsession that took place in the US for the lower class to own a home (a different approach is to provide them with low or very low cost housing), which gave rise to the famous phenomenon of "subprime mortgages," when these people could not pay their mortgage loans and ended ruined as a result. Following this crisis, and because of its (mis)management, the entire American economy, and by contagion, the Western economy, collapsed. Incentivizing those who, by themselves, cannot minimally take care of children to have children is to contribute, perhaps, to ruining their lives. And above all, poor children—the children of parents who had them for money!

For that very reason, and because children are wonderful for parents, we are not in favor of reimbursing the full cost of having children, or at least not immediately, while they are being raised, but rather a substantial portion, 50% and 75%, for example, and maybe some more, but deferred to old age, when the time comes to collecting the retirement pension. It is essential that having at least two children is not a deterrent for the vast majority of the population because it is expensive, while avoiding that people have them because of the money they would bring.

Who should receive the financial compensation/incentive for each child? The mother? The father? Both?

The temptation, in many modern societies, officially more or less feminist, is clear: everything directly to the mother, nothing to the father.

In some countries, such as Ireland, the State gives a monthly amount to the mothers for each child they have and gives nothing to the father. It is something that encourages more single mothers, and as such, does not favor marriage and marriage stability, which, in the long run, would be detrimental to the country's own birth rate, as well as to affected children. In Spain, the government introduced a retirement pension bonus in 2015, in line with an electoral promise from the ruling party, but only for mothers with two or more children. It also introduced fiscal aid for single-parent households with children, where in 80% of cases the mother is the head of household, although in more than half of cases there is also a father who lives elsewhere but contributes to the maintenance of the children, and in many cases, of the woman herself, and gets none of that financial help[104].

In France, however, there is a mechanism called "family quotient," which serves to offer economic benefits to families, especially those who have children, without discrimination by sex. For example, on the income tax return, in the case of marriages, all income is added together and the total is divided by the number of people in the family (counting each adult, for purpose of the divisor of the family income, as one unit, the first two children as a half unit each, and the additional children as one unit each). This leads to a substantial reduction in family taxes by reducing the effect of progressive taxation scales, something that is particularly valuable if one spouse—typically the woman—has no personal income and there are several children. There is, however, a ceiling on tax savings per person that is not particularly high.

From the point of view of the contribution to births as such, there is no doubt that the role of the woman-mother is appreciably greater than that of the man-father. The female contribution is exclusive in terms of physical wear due to pregnancy and childbirth, although it is not usually exclusive in the decision to have children or not, and when there are already children, in the decision to have one more or not. The man counts, a lot, when deciding to have or not to have children.

---

[104] In Spain, slightly more than 40% of single-parent households are the result of the misfortune that one of the spouses, typically the father/husband, passed away, and more than 50% are due to divorce / couple breakup. The rest of the cases are due to voluntary decisions of solitary motherhood, to mothers of children of unknown fathers—for example, prostitutes—or to women who got pregnant by a man who left them.

Almost all the children are born to a male and female couple. What to say about unexpected pregnancies. The situation is very different when the father of the future little baby welcomes the news with joy, and encourages and supports the woman to continue with the pregnancy, than when his attitude is the opposite, asking her to abort.

In terms of economics, in the raising of children and adolescents, the tradition was for the father to contribute, at the very least, the necessary economic resources, apart from being more or less involved, depending on the families, in the education of children and other related tasks. Nowadays, apart from its economic contribution, which is no longer exclusive in the majority of couples in developed countries, but still predominantly superior to that of the mother, the father is significantly involved in a growing number of couples in almost everything young children need (except their gestation, delivery, and natural breastfeeding): giving them the bottle, changing diapers, taking the children to school, etc.

Therefore, in terms of financial support/compensation/pro-birth incentives, focusing only on women/mothers is as unfair with respect to rewarding and offsetting the cost related to more births as it is surely counterproductive in stimulating the birth rate. In addition, as such, it is an element that does not foster the father's co-responsibility or promote that families remain united, which creates a family stability that, in addition to be good for the upbringing of offspring in all aspects—affective, educational/formative, economic, etc.—is the home environment in which people have more children, as has been sufficiently demonstrated in this work.

Having said that, as it is also true that the contribution and wear of the mother is higher than that of the father, and that in the real world in which we live, a significant percentage of couples with children end up breaking up. Hence, it makes sense that the economic compensation and incentives to promote births are greater for mothers than for fathers (and exclusive, for example, in relation to the coverage by the State of social security contributions of mothers who stop working outside the home when their children are small, so that they are not penalized in their retirement pensions in old age). Perhaps, for the purpose of mere illustration, a reasonable distribution of the compensations/economic incentives between mother and father could be 60% for the former and 40% for the latter.

Through what fiscal mechanisms, taxes and/or payments by the State, should money be provided to the parents for being parents?

The ideal mechanism, to avoid the drawback of people who have children mainly for money and to achieve a similar motivation to have children among all social classes, would be that for each child individuals have and using a basic level for those who do not have any children as reference, to grant significant personal income tax reductions, reductions in social security contributions, and increases in public retirement pensions, as well as in unemployment benefits for parents who lose their job. This scheme also has its difficulties in being a motivational factor:

✓ Young adults, who are at the ideal age to have children and represent the bulk of births in Europe and developed countries (between 20 and 35 years, especially in the case of women), generally have lower wages than those who are 10 to 25 years older and who are the ones who notice the effect of fiscal progressivity on their pocket much more. Ergo, in young adults, maternity/paternity tax cuts, when they are considering having children, are less noticeable than when they can no longer have them because they are older. In the case of people with low income, it has very little or even no impact.

✓ The reduction of Social Security contributions, in countries like Spain where the lion share of the contribution is in charge of the company, and not the worker, would be felt especially by the employer, which would have beneficial effects in the employability of mothers but would not directly stimulate mothers and fathers, since they would not obtain a great personal improvement.

✓ Bonus on retirement pensions based on the number of children. The problem with it is that young adults must believe that governments will respect this acquired right within 30 or 40 years.

As a way to overcome the above issues, we can think of some possibilities. In relation to the reduction of social contributions and taxes, apart from introducing "negative taxes," which mean a significant injection of net income depending on the number of children for those with low income levels—although money should never be given to those adults who do not have income for having children, because of the moral problems and risks already mentioned for the children, derived from only having children for money—tax credits, as are already used in certain countries, could be created to be used in the future.

With respect to retirement pensions, something that would give almost total credibility to this incentive/compensation would be for the State to deposit the bonus based on the number of children on a pension savings plan for the parents, under conditions similar to those of private savings plans: money that cannot be redeemed until retirement except in situations of prolonged unemployment and that can be invested in what the account holder wishes, with various low risk options. Thus, although such money received as compensation and incentive to have children could not be used immediately, it would "be seen" to exist and its future enjoyment would not depend on the government in power several decades later.

In summary, although we firmly believe that the proposed solution is directionally correct (it is fair and necessary to give a significant economic compensation/incentive to people for having children), the concrete details must be the product of a rational study, based on real data, without ideological biases, and taking the pros and cons of each possibility into account, since its optimal implementation is not trivial.

Changes in values and laws

People cannot be forced to have children (something that only totalitarianisms as frightening as undesirable would do, such as in Khmer Rouge communist Cambodia). Ergo, in order to increase the birth rate, it is necessary that people's desire to have children increase and that the objective and subjective obstacles that induce them not to have children, or to have very few, be reduced or eliminated. We listed multiple causes in the section of the book dealing with causes of infertility. We will now focus on the reasons we believe have the most impact and on which we can/should act, as there are some that should not be addressed, either because it is virtually impossible or because it would be very undesirable.

Create a pro-birth and pro maternity/paternity/family climate, which favors and honors parenthood

In our opinion, this is the most important of all to get out of the demographic winter. Vladimir Gjorcev, a parliamentarian from the former Yugoslav Republic of Macedonia, on the occasion of the 1st Forum #Stop Suicidio Demográfico, held in Madrid on 06/10/2016 at the headquarters of the newspaper ABC, as an example, said that everything would be very different in countries like Spain if newspaper covers featured pictures of large families with headlines such as "These are our heroes: the such and such family, with N children, whose mother and father are raising the Spain of tomorrow with love, effort and dedication" or "This mother of so many children is a wonderful woman who creates what our country needs most:

tomorrow's Spaniards," as examples, instead of so much news and praise on much less valuable subjects and personalities. This applies to all countries with a lack of births that are in the process of demographic suicide. Instead, for much of Spanish society and other countries, the woman who has many children is a "rabbit," instead of being admired. If this mother is also a traditional housewife, who does not work outside the home, in Spain she is called "maruja" (something of the kind of "house cleaner,") a qualifier that is borderline derogatory. Perhaps this hostility or contempt occurs because the mother of a very large family annoys more than one, as she proves that "yes, you can," in this day and age, have many children, generally be happy, and consider yourself a vitally accomplished woman. What a pity. The mean part of the human condition is so ugly, yet its noble and generous part, which also exists, is so beautiful, as in the case of these selfless mothers and fathers, or those who, not personally having children, applaud those who do.

A climate of prestige for births and parents in countries with few children, especially for adults who have a large progeny, fostered from public institutions and private organizations, which emphasizes that a typical full human life is a life with descendants, with children, who far compensate, through affection and vital personal projection, more than the cost and effort they require, would do much for the birth rate and would surely provide the best return in terms of cost versus efficiency, in addition to facilitating the implementation and acceptance of all the other measures needed. In France, indeed, parenthood has been promoted for many years and it is no coincidence that its fertility is appreciably superior to that of its neighbors, especially that of its traditional Germanic enemy, now its great ally and first partner, of its trans-Pyrenean and transalpine neighbors, Spain, Italy, and Switzerland, and of the richest dukedom in the world, Luxembourg.

Likewise, in the modern world, which revolves heavily around the celebrities we see/hear/read about in the media, great soccer players, renowned artists, politicians, and respected intellectuals appearing in those media with their families, saying that having and raising children is the best thing they have done in life, would very much contribute to having a pro-birth climate that is so needed in countries like mine and many others.

Warn of how sad a life without children can be

A big-hearted woman I met while researching these issues told me: "I have not had children because, when I was young, I gave priority to my professional career. When I tried to have any, I was too old. I deeply regret it." I replied to her, "I'm so sorry, but there is one thing you could do for Spain and other younger women: if you and other women who have had the same experience could tell it to the media, transmit to young girls and boys the vital sadness you have because of this emptiness, it would be a warning that could do a lot for the birth rate." It seemed like a good idea to her and she volunteered for an advertising campaign as such. Personally, I think such actions in the mass media could have a great impact.

Educate the new generations about the desirability of forming families with several children

"The great necessity [in order to reduce fertility] is to convince the masses of the population that it is to their individual and national interest to have, on the average, only three and then only two children. There is little likelihood that this result can be accomplished very widely against the background of the cultural heritage of today's adults, even the young adults, among the masses in most LDCs [Least Developed Countries]. Without diminishing in any way the effort to reach these adults, the obvious increased focus of attention should be to change the attitudes of the next generation, those who are now in elementary school or younger."

(Excerpts from the 1974 "Kissinger Report" for the reduction of birth rates in least developed countries)

In 1974, the Kissinger Report against fertility in the least developed countries, mentioned throughout this work —an analysis of which is included in an Annex— indoctrinating young children on the desirability of having small families, ideally with only two children, was pointed out as one of the key measures to achieving sustained future reductions in the birth rate. In order to achieve the opposite, i.e., to improve the birth rate in countries suffering from lack of births, the opposite would have to be told in schools: how beautiful and desirable large families, with several children, are for individuals and their country. In particular, the following would have to be told in schools—perhaps not to children as young as those proposed in the Kissinger Report, but certainly to teenagers:

✓ The future well-being of their country/state/region/province is seriously threatened if, when they are somewhat older, they do not have at least two children, on average, per person. It is an unprecedented situation in history.

✓ Although children cost money and effort, they provide unique joy and are an essential part of a typical complete human life. That is why all their direct ancestors, without exception, for millions and millions of years, had children. Having children should be one of the main wishes of the vast majority of individuals in the next 20 to 25 years.

✓ More and more people between 40 and 60 years of age are frustrated because they indeed wanted to have children, but when they were too old to do so when they tried. It is advisable to have the first child at no later than 30 years old, and if possible, somewhat earlier.

✓ We should have children mainly for the pleasure of having them. Whoever does not have any, especially if the welfare state cracks because of the demographic problem, could spend old age alone, without anyone to take care of him/her.

✓ Our future and their own well-being when reaching old age depend on their having children!

More marriages and matrimonial stability

If legal marriages, as might be expected, produce more children, on average, than other households with children (cohabiting couples and single-parent households), and their stability is very valuable for children born within them, especially until adolescence, durable marriage is something that should be promoted by the State and society in general, especially when the couple has young children. How can this be achieved?

There could, of course, be economic incentives for marriage, and for keeping it stable, especially as long as there are young children involved or if there exists a possibility of having children [105]. There could also be affective education at school,

---

[105] *Sensu contrario*, a married couple that, in the end, does not have any children—given that economic resources are scarce, and that the social model promotes women working outside the home—in our opinion, does not have to be privileged or protected as such by the State, which in economic terms is the whole of society. If a couple wants to live together, it is better for them: they enjoy the benefit of having care and mutual support. By sharing a roof and a good number of expenses, they achieve savings in spending per adult out of the reach of those who live alone and of course of those who have children not yet emancipated. If the couple is married by the church or by a religious ritual of another type, the individuals obtain, through marriage, an additional and superior significant value. Therefore, the rest of society, in our opinion, does not have to pay any type of tax improvement or pensions to the couple that has no offspring. This is especially clear in the case of widowed pensions, which were invented so that the traditional mother-woman, who was not working outside the home, would not be left indigent or in a dreadful economic state if her husband died before her, something very likely to happen in marriages that do not end in divorce before one of the spouses dies. It is much more likely to be a widow than a widower, because, on average, women marry younger and live longer than men. In particular, in 2011, according to the population census carried out that year, there

provided to adolescents by competent psychologists/educators, on how to better choose a partner who approaches the ideal "better half" and how to manage this relationship, in prosperity and in conflict, since society in general, and people in particular, have so much at stake in this decision (with whom to marry and whether to marry or not), and it is as important as it is difficult. Not in vain does the Spanish saying go: "Whoever marries correctly, in no way errs."

Furthermore, the marriage and divorce rates would not be the same in a society in which the magma of values fostered from above and by the media, including the laws, and the one that flows in the environment, was very pro-marriage and pro-children, as in another society completely indifferent to people marrying often or not, divorcing often or not, and having few children or none.

Recovering marriage and matrimonial stability, in any case, will not be easy because the collapse of the propensity to marry, the large number of divorces, and the high percentage of children born out of wedlock are three characteristics of our time, as well as being the era with low birth rates. It is not by chance that all this is happening at the same time. More and more children being born out of wedlock is occurring in all countries—except in some where those rates have already reached very high levels and do not seem to go any higher in recent years—with typical rates between 40% and 60% of the total children born to unmarried mothers in North America and Europe. Although in some of the countries with the highest percentage of out of wedlock births, such as France or Sweden (55% to 60%), the birth rate is higher than the average of developed countries, this is not the case for others, such as Ireland or the USA, with lower percentages (20% and 40%) of babies born to unmarried mothers. An extreme case is that of Israel, the western country with the highest fertility rate and one of the lowest, if not the lowest, percentage of births by unmarried mothers. Moreover, in any country, as mentioned earlier, married parents have more children than cohabiting couples and single-parent households do.

As far as marriage is concerned, half or more of the people in Europe tend to not marry, as, for example, the total first marriage rate, which roughly estimates the probability of marrying at least once in life and is based on the number of people

---

were 4.5 widows per widower in the European Union. As this situation of indigence by widowhood is no longer the case with women who receive a retirement pension for having worked and contributed to Social Security, which today tends to be a very large majority of women in developed countries, such pensions should disappear for the new generations, except for women who have children, resulting in a partial or total reduction in the retirement pension to which they would have been entitled had they not had children and had they worked the same as any typical male.

marrying for the first time in a given year, indicates. According to this indicator, for example, if marriage rates did not rebound, between 40% and 60% of adults under 60 in Europe would never marry. In the not too distant past, the vast majority of Europeans, about 90%, traditionally married at least once in their lifetime[106]. In the last 50 years, between the mid-1960s and the middle of the second decade of the 21st century, the number of weddings per 1,000 inhabitants in the countries that now make up the Eurozone fell by about 50%, while the number of divorces per 1,000 inhabitants tripled, as 2014 saw almost one divorce for every two weddings, whereas in 1964, there was only one divorce for every thirteen weddings

.

Evolution of total first marriage rate in Spain
Source: INE

---

[106] About 90% of the 80-year-olds who died in 2012 in the European Union, i.e., people born in 1931 or 1932, died married, widowed, or divorced, according to Eurostat. In other words, they had married at least once in their lives.

In general, the fall of the birth rate and the marriage rate have gone hand-in-hand, as can be seen in the following table for Europe, which also shows that for every hundred weddings in Europe, there are around fifty divorces.

Evolution of total fertility rate and crude marriage rate, and divorces as a percentage of weddings celebrated in Europe			
Source: OECD, own analysis	Change 1964-2014 in the number of children per woman	Change 1964-2014 of weddings per 1,000 inhabitants	Divorces as a % of weddings celebrated in 2014
Eurozone countries (1)	N/D	-49%	48%
Germany	-42%	-44%	43%
Austria (2)	-48%	-46%	44%
Belgium (2)	-37%	-45%	62%
Denmark	-35%	-40%	69%
Slovakia	-54%	-30%	39%
Slovenia	-32%	-64%	38%
Spain	-56%	-54%	63%
Finland	-34%	-41%	56%
France (1)	-32%	-49%	56%
Netherlands	-46%	-54%	54%
Hungary	-22%	-55%	51%
Italy	-49%	-62%	28%
Luxembourg	-37%	-55%	88%
Norway	-41%	-32%	42%
Poland	-50%	-32%	35%
Portugal (3)	-62%	-63%	70%
United Kingdom (4)	-39%	-41%	46%
Czech Republic	-35%	-48%	59%
Sweden	-24%	-28%	49%
Switzerland	-42%	-33%	40%
NB-1 Only European countries for which there are complete data (many are missing from Eastern Europe)			
NB-2 In almost all countries with the smallest drops in birth rate and marriage rate, these rates were already low in 1964			
NB-3 Without the births from immigrant women, the drop in fertility would have been higher in almost all countries			
(1) Most recent data on marriages in 2012 and divorces in 2011, not available in 2014			
(2) Most recent marriage and divorce data for 2012, not available for 2014			
(3) Most recent divorce data for 2013, unavailable for 2014			
(4) Most recent marriage and divorce data for 2011, not available in 2014			

Lower the age at which we have our first child

Men and women are becoming increasingly older when having their first child. Although male fertility lasts longer than female fertility, it also declines with age. In addition, a relatively old father at the time of conception is not desirable, as he has to subsequently raise his child properly, as well as to avoid a very old father when the child becomes an adult, and for him to not be reluctant to have more children, if he wishes. In addition, the genetic make-up transmitted by a younger father has fewer mutations and defects, as the probability of these increases with age. In the case of the mother, in addition to the above, age also causes the aforementioned disadvantages of infertility, more miscarriages, more difficult pregnancies and deliveries, etc. Now, how do we get people to have children at a younger age?

Some things that could be done—partly from the State, partly from civil society—are the following:

1- Tell adolescents, in schools, and the population in general, the problems a delayed maternity/paternity generates. The vast majority of people do want to have offspring sooner or later—as the surveys and the increase in the fertility rate of women over 40 in recent times demonstrate. In other words, people wait until very late to have children. Young people need to be told that if they push childbirth off for too long (in women, from 30+, and especially after 35), they are exposed to the previous risks (not having children or not as many as they would like, risky pregnancies, failed pregnancies, etc.)[107].

2- Shorten the long modern educational cycle. I was born in 1960, and in my time you went to college the year you turned 17, if you had never repeated a course. Nowadays, individuals start college at 18, in Spain and in other countries, and as far as we know, young people do not reach the university world better prepared than when it was time for me to do the same. A fortiori, it would be good to advance, perhaps by a year, the typical college entrance age of women, whose neuronal, physical, and affective maturation is faster than that of males, but whose fertility drops earlier.

3- Stimulate and facilitate an early enough emancipation of the youth from the parental home which, in countries like Spain and other Mediterranean

---

[107] In the former Yugoslav Republic of Macedonia, for example, the government made a masterful video with this idea and broadcasted it as an advertisement on the country's public TV during prime time hours. It tells the story of two young couples, who both want children, but one couple never makes the decision because there is always something that must be done first (studies, work, a bigger house, improvements in the couple's material life, etc.). At the end of the video, you see the two older couples: the couple who decided to embark on the adventure of parenthood is shown happy with their children already grown and even with grandchildren, while the other couple grows old in solitude (title: "Two parallel families" https://www.youtube.com/watch?v=EyFcdegD07w)

countries, occurs at very advanced ages. This is not just the responsibility of the State and of society, which can facilitate such emancipation from an economic standpoint, with programs providing cheap rent for young people or the like. Conveying to parents the idea that, after a certain age, it is not beneficial to continue in the comfortable parenting home for the ultimate development of their children as adults would also be good.

4- Sentimental education for teenagers, to help them to better choose their partner and decide before "settling down." Finding the "love of your life" late in life has clear drawbacks:
-There are fewer single people who could potentially be your "better half."
-As we are used to being independent, we have less tolerance, in general, for those frictions coexistence brings, something that leads to higher divorce rates in marriages between older partners.

The following graph gives a clear picture of the fall in first marriages in general (the proportion of people marrying at least once in life, excluding second/third weddings following a divorce or widowhood), the drop in the number of women who marry relatively young, and the rise in the number of women who marry for the first time. In the case of men, the patterns are similar, though a few years older[108].

---

108 The chart of first marriages in Europe is elaborated by adding data from European countries that reported this information to Eurostat (which, in this case, excludes the United Kingdom, Russia, Ukraine, and some other Eastern European countries that have only been independent for 25 years or less and with generally small populations, although the trend is the same in all countries), and in a few cases, using the year closest to 1990 or 2014, since data for these exact years was available from all but a few countries.

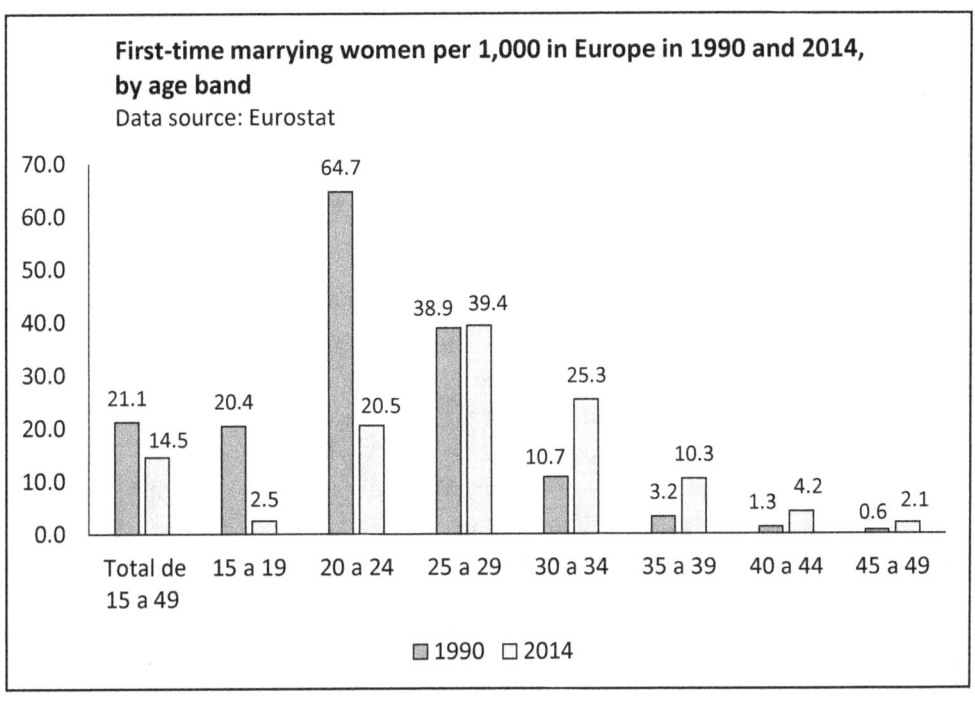

Not making companies pay the cost of maternity

"It is unbearable for any small business like mine (I have five employees) to have to pay not only the maternity leave but the seven months of absence that many pregnant women take before the delivery. And they still wonder why they are asked if they are thinking of becoming mothers, that they are discriminated against, that their privacy is invaded, but by any chance I, as an employer, have no right to choose my staff? What happens is the State should be the one to take care of this leave and the absences caused by pregnancies, at least for small businesses, which are the majority in this country, and you would see how the average (number of children per woman) would quickly rise"

(a reader's comment to the news published by the Spanish newspaper "El Periódico" on 11/07/2016 titled "Why Spain is the country where there are the fewest children," and subtitled "If I get pregnant, chances are I'll be fired")[109]

---

[109] Reference. http://www.elperiodico.com/es/noticias/sanidad/porque-espana-pais-donde-tienen-menos-hijos-5609032. Actually, in Spain, the State reimburses companies a large part of the costs of maternity leave (pregnancy and post-delivery), but not all. And of course, nothing of the loss of profit for the employer that may entail the pregnancies / parenthoods of their employees..

It is highly recommended, for reasons of social equity and of achieving a higher birth rate, that there be laws and social values that do not economically penalize women for their motherhood, that facilitate the reconciliation between personal and family life—especially when the children are young—and that facilitate the re-entry of women who decide to stop working totally or partially to become mothers until their children are old enough into the labor market.

For this to work well, however, it is necessary for laws and regulations that seek to facilitate motherhood and the reconciliation between family and work life to not be based on achieving it at the expense of companies, both for practical reasons and reasons of social equity. Both parents and society benefit from children. Some types of workers—such as women who are mothers—are potentially less profitable for companies than the rest, so companies will either try to hire them in fewer numbers or pay them less. To deny this reality is to bury your head in the sand. Maternity has a significant cost to companies and denying it only leads to the wrong port. That cost must be shared mainly between society (through the State) and parents—the beneficiaries of having children—since the bulk of companies, except those that produce goods and services for children, only benefit in the long run (if they survive). If not, we can expect women who are or may become mothers, *ceteris paribus*, to be less desired by companies, as workers, than other current or potential employees, something that would help neither the employability of these women nor the birth rate.

In Spain, for example, a woman who asks for a reduction in working hours to care for her young children, even if it is only one hour less a day—so the total time dedicated to work, including transportation, is barely lower in relative terms, and the net wage reduction is often even smaller, because a lower tax rate is applied to her salary—is entitled to a reinforced protection against dismissal, equivalent to that provided to pregnant women, until her youngest child is twelve years old. This means that any dismissal that is not due to serious misconduct of the employee or, in the context of collective dismissals, due to the company experiencing serious problems and restructuring through layoffs, is legally null, as the dismissal is assumed to be motivated because of her status as a mother, a discrimination both legally unacceptable and ethically detestable. Does this legislation facilitate or hinder women with small children or who may have them from being hired and making reasonable salaries, or do companies prefer to have and pay more people who, if they eventually produce little consistently, can be let go with the same ease or difficulty as any other? Has this enormous extra in labor protection against the rest of workers brought an apex in the birth rate to Spain? (Not at all, as far as we know). Has this enhanced protection against being fired hindered the employability of women of childbearing age and damaged their compensation? There are no authoritative data, but it seems logical and probable that this is the case, to some non-negligible extent. In contrast, in the US, where the birth rate is one of the highest in the West, working mothers barely have any legal protection against dismissal for being pregnant[110], or after giving birth. Yet, the total fertility rate is 30% to 50% higher than in countries like Spain, with very protective laws for working mothers.

Thus, it is better for us not to take side in the dilemma of "female work outside the home or maternity" but to reconcile both working outside the home and maternity in a reasonable way, since if a society opted for only the former, it would tend to disappear with time and to suffer before that a sad and impoverishing downfall, both material and affective.

Neutrality of the State and the media vis-a-vis the choice for women between occupation and maternity

For decades, the State and the media have been determined that women be mainly workers, and if that is at the cost of motherhood, so be it. What do we have now? Women have almost fully entered the workforce, but we are missing children.

Despite all these efforts, there is still a significant fraction of children born in developed countries—and many more in other countries—to women who do not work outside the home, either permanently or only during the years when their children are small. Apart from the fact that these more "traditional" women are fully entitled to freely choose this life style, without being bothered and discriminated against—as is done in Spain with certain pro-birth economic incentives exclusively designed for women who have a job—they provide a substantial number of children who are especially valuable in societies with a deficit in babies. In Germany in 2012, according to Eurostat data, more than half of the children came to the world from "inactive" mothers. In Spain, the mother of almost a quarter of the children born in 2014 was economically "inactive," according to the classification of the National Institute of Statistics (INE).

---

[110] When I wrote "El suicidio demográfico de España" ("The Demographic Suicide of Spain") in 2011, the federal legal protection of maternity said that if a woman had been working for at least one year in a company with at least 50 workers, she could not be fired in the twelve postpartum weeks. By contrast, now, in Spain, a woman who starts working for any company tomorrow, for example, in a bar with three employees on staff, and becomes pregnant the day after tomorrow, and opts for a reduction in working hours to take care of her child after childbirth, cannot be fired, except for a serious and irrefutable fault or the bankruptcy of the bar, for no less than 13 years, counting the pregnancy and the first 12 years of life of her little one (in 2011, this reinforced protection covered "only" a little less than 9 years). Nevertheless, American women, for the past decades, have had an average number of children significantly higher than Spanish women have.

Source: own analysis based on INE statistics of births activity status and age of the mother, and active women by age	Births in Spain by age and activity status of the mother - 2014							
	All ages	15-19	20-24	25-29	30-34	35-39	40-44	45-49
All births	427,595	8,477	31,030	78,244	154,190	124,572	28,902	1,923
Births from active mothers	323,109	2,189	13,832	52,914	124,274	104,489	23,706	1,571
Births from inactive mothers	104,486	6,288	17,198	25,330	29,916	20,083	5,196	352
Active women (thousands)		N/A	634.3	1,130.1	1,457.5	1,675.2	1,568.3	1,438.7
Inactive women (thousands)		N/A	514.4	209.8	209.4	273.4	326.2	385.4
Births from active mothers per 1,000 active women		N/A	21.8	46.8	85.3	62.4	15.1	1.1
Births from inactive mothers per 1,000 inactive women		N/A	33.4	120.7	142.9	73.5	15.9	0.9
Ratio de % hijos de inactivas a mujeres inactivas		N/A	153%	258%	168%	118%	105%	84%
Birth rate of inactive women divided by birth rate of active women (from 25 to 44 years)	1.51							

"Inactive" women of fertile and post-university age had, on average, 50% more children than the "active" ones, according to the birth data by activity of the mother and the survey of active population. In Germany (Eurostat data), 52% of children born in 2012 had "inactive" mothers, even though only about 25% of German women of childbearing age were "inactive." These figures give us an idea that, indeed, women have more children if they do not work outside the home and that the weight on the birth rate in Europe of women who do not work outside the home, a significant minority, is by no means negligible.

Percentage of employed women aged 25-49 in 2014 in the EU-28, the five most populated western European countries, and two European countries less populated but with relatively high fertility					
Data source: Eurostat	Childless	One child	Two children	Three children	Change in employment rate from 0 to 3 children
European Union	**76.9**	**72.1**	**70.5**	**55.2**	**-21.7**
Germany	85.6	77.8	73.4	53.1	-32.5
France	77.5	78.8	78.5	58.4	-19.1
United Kingdom	85.4	78.3	73.1	49.7	-35.7
Italy	61.9	58.6	54.2	40.7	-21.2
Spain	68.4	62.3	60.5	48.1	-20.3
Ireland	79.0	67.6	64.0	52.2	-26.8
Sweden	78.5	82.2	88.0	81.0	2.5

Percentage of full-time employed women aged 25-49 in 2014 in the EU-28, the five most populated western European countries, and two European countries less populated but with relatively high fertility					
Data source: Eurostat	Childless	One child	Two children	Three children	Change in full-time employment rate from 0 to 3 children
European Union	**61.5**	**49.5**	**42.9**	**30.3**	**-31.2**
Germany	63.9	31.6	18.6	11.8	-52.2
France	62.5	59.3	51.7	33.3	-29.2
United Kingdom	71.5	43.5	30.6	18.9	-52.6
Italy	44.7	37.7	31.4	22.3	-22.3
Spain	53.7	43.8	42.4	33.3	-20.4
Ireland	66.2	45.5	40.2	27.5	-38.7
Sweden	59.3	55.2	55.4	48.0	-11.2

Moreover, with the exception of Sweden, it is clearly visible in the first of the two tables just above, with data from the European Union as a whole, its five most populated countries, and two that are not as populated but that have a birth rate level higher than the European standard (Ireland and Sweden), that the higher the number of children per woman, the lower the percentage of women who work. On the other hand, in all countries, including Sweden, the percentage of women in part-time employment increases with the number of children they have.

Do not ignore the father figure

That the mother has a greater role, and much more physical wear and tear in pregnancy, in childbirth and parenting children than the father, is undeniable. Therefore, in birth policies, maternity/paternity incentives/aids/compensations should place greater emphasis on the mothers than on the fathers, especially in times like these when, unfortunately, divorce is so frequent. Now, that's one thing, but another is to almost completely ignore or devalue the father in the incentives and compensations for having children, as well as in the public recognition of his contribution to the birth rate and the upbringing of the next generation.

Although some countries are starting to revert from this trend, the role of the father tends to be generally more and more ignored or minimized in relation to natality/incentives/custody of children, except when he takes paternity leave and his role is thus equated with the mother's. This begins even with the fertility statistics, which, except in a few countries that also speak of males/fathers, always refer to numbers of children per woman, including those in this book[111]. The male in the human species, however, is not like that of the bears or other animal species in which all he does is fertilize the female. That is not at all the case. The male has a lot of influence and even co-decides in almost all couples as to whether to have children or not. He can encourage to have a child, or to have more, or the opposite—something that, in cases of unwanted pregnancies, is especially crucial. Although the law makes the father a bump on a log in matters of abortion, subject to material and legal obligations of all kinds to the child if the mother decides to have it—a striking legal asymmetry between rights and duties in times of equality between the sexes—in practice, when a woman who has become pregnant asks herself whether or not to have the child, there is a world of difference between when the father of the child supports the woman and is committed to being a good

---

[111] As the statistics of children per woman seem to place all the "responsibility" and "weight" on whether or not we have children on the women, and I think it is as unfair (fathers contribute a lot) as wrong (if males are not more involved, fewer children will be born, and those born will be raised poorly), some time ago I started to speak in my lectures of "children per person" instead of "children per woman." I realized, however, that, apart from having more accurate numbers on women, many people did not understand me very well, because they were accustomed to hearing "children per woman." For this reason, I stopped speaking of "children per person" but emphasize that the paternal figure, except in the small minority of cases in which the child lacks a recognized father-male (in Spain, for example, less than 2.5%), counts and should count a lot at the time of having children or not, and, later, in their upbringing.

father for the little one, and the opposite. At the economic level, of the money necessary for raising the children, the fathers contribute a lot. In fact, up until now, and as long as there is a higher rate of male than female employment in families with children and the average income per male is higher than that of women, and although there are increasing exceptions to this rule, fathers contribute and have contributed much more economically to the upbringing of children than their mothers have.

Facilitate (guarantee?) the placement for adoption of unwanted babies

Abortion deserves a special mention. This is a matter that has no social consensus and undoubtedly has potential negative psychological consequences for the woman who aborts—and not infrequently, for the father and other relatives. Without entering into the substantive debate on its prohibition or the opposite, and whether it is immoral or not, that it is legally defined as "a right," as in Spain, seems somewhat unfortunate, to mince words. As the demographer and former socialist politician, my friend Joaquín Leguina, says, killing can never be defined as a right, even if possible exculpatory circumstances can be applied, which can even be complete when dealing with self-defense when there are no other alternatives. In addition, the State, having made abortion—a so controversial and divisive issue in modern societies—a "right" sends a clear signal to society: "I do not care much if you do not have children, since I do not consider them an asset to protect."

Things could be very different in this matter if the State, for example, facilitated—or even guaranteed—that pregnant women could give the initially unwanted baby up for adoption, if finally, after the birth, they would continue to not want to care for the baby. In that case, the structural life change implied by having a child, due to the economic cost and the effort in their upbringing until their emancipation, these great elements that—in addition to the fear of pregnancy and the pain childbirth—push many women to abort, would no longer be a reason for the pregnant woman who does not want to take care of the human being in development she bears inside, to ask that a physician, transgressor of the Hippocratic oath, dispose of it. With such measures, there would be a smaller number—or much smaller—of abortions, and consequently, more —or many more—births, between women who would finally decide to keep their child, once the initial scare of unintended pregnancy has passed, and families that would welcome a baby without the complications and risks of international adoptions. Currently, private or public organizations that help pregnant women who are planning to abort, to freely decide not to abort after all, because they end up accepting the arrival of their child with joy, or because they can give it up for adoption, perform a commendable human labor and produce an undeniable good to society. For example, in a country like Spain, with an average birth rate, from 1985 and 2015, of 1.3 children per woman, and an average abortion rate of about 0.3 to 0.4 abortions per woman in recent years, if a third of the abortions did not occur, because the woman finally decided to have the child, whether to raise it herself or to give it up for adoption, the country's overall fertility would increase by 0.1 children per woman, or slightly more. Just by converting these abortions in births, about 1/8 of the birth rate deficit in Spain would be covered until reaching the replacement level, which is very valuable.

The "stick" and the "carrot" in the motivation to have or not have children

In order for people to want to have children again in sufficient numbers, as in so many other motivation problems, it is advisable to use simultaneously the two great complementary mechanisms of motivation that are known in a classic and metaphorical way as "stick and carrot." Pictorially, one of the greatest thugs of the twentieth century, the sadly famous Colombian drug lord Pablo Escobar, a criminal/diabolical individual so effective in achieving his goals, used to say that he offered "silver or lead," i.e., money or bullets, to judges in charge of the cases concerning himself or his followers, so that these judges would leave them alone and unscathed. He was using the two great complementary elements of motivation at the same time, the stick and the carrot: "If you leave us alone, I will not kill you, and on top of that you make money. I give you two great reasons, not just one, for you to do what I want."

Here, in order to convince people that it is bad that so few children are born and it is good that a sufficient number of them are born, the "stick" would mainly be the fear of the following:

1.- For society at large, the impoverishing consequences of rampant aging and a declining population. In this respect, retirement pensions have long been what worries the most a large part of the population in societies that are already quite old. When people realize that the problem of pensions, even if the problem is large, is not the only one or even the biggest one that results from the demographic suicide, their level of alarm will increase.

2.- For political elites, the loss of political/geopolitical and economic power of their respective countries or areas of influence.

3.- For the economic elites, business leaders, and owners of wealth in general, the loss of markets and the devaluation of assets in general due to the decrease in the number of consumers and members of the workforce, and because of their aging.

4.- For individuals, realizing all this, as well as their own loneliness and worse affective quality of life, in the case of having no offspring.

The pro-birth "carrot" would be a mixture of the satisfaction of freeing ourselves from those ailments, and of motivating economic elements, as well as emotional and moral factors, linked to having more children, such as the social recognition granted to parents in general, and especially to mothers of several/many children.

Do you melt over your kids? Yes, by the gallon

The first and most important of these motivating elements, in our opinion, would have to be the generalized recovery of something undeniable, which is one of the main reasons why people always had (many) children: the awareness that young children delight us and are part of a typical full human life. It does not seem mission impossible, since we are programmed by Darwinian natural selection and/or by God to make having and raising children one of our main missions in life and one of our greatest motives for joy, and to not kill or stop having them out of laziness or fear. The woman isn't the only one programmed this way. The human male, whose traditional and instinctive role in caring for the mother of his children and for protecting the family and contributing to the formation/education of the children, is one of the keys to the evolutionary success of the human species, from our ape ancestors to homo sapiens[112]. Yes, we love to see faces like the smiling baby in the photo. When my brother Ricardo had just had his first child, when I still didn't have any myself, I asked him: "So what, do you melt over your kid?" "Yes, by the gallon," he replied. Something as basic as this is, and should be, the greatest motivator for having children.

---

[112] Human being is the living being with the most powerful brain, by far, but is born especially defenseless and immature, and needs between fifteen and twenty years of development so that his body and brain reach their full adult stage. For this reason, according to scholars of human evolution, natural selection has rewarded those whose parents—not only the mother but also the father—paid more attention to the care of their family and the education/training of their children, who survived to a greater extent and developed a more capable intelligence than the descendants of parents who did not. In other words, natural selection would have favored the survival and prevalence not only of the most "maternal" and prolific women, but also—and this is something unusual among the males of most animal species—of those males to whom, when they have children, we call colloquially "superdads," for the attention and the care that they dedicate to their offspring. A similar argument could be made about why we melt over babies and toddlers so much, who are the most helpless, and for the longest time, of any animal species. Their best weapon for survival—and practically the only one, if their parents lack religious/moral beliefs that include the duty to engender and raise their descendants—is that to adults, and especially to their mothers—but also to fathers—babies and toddlers are charming, they seduce us, they inspire us with great tenderness. In colloquial language, we "melt" because of them.

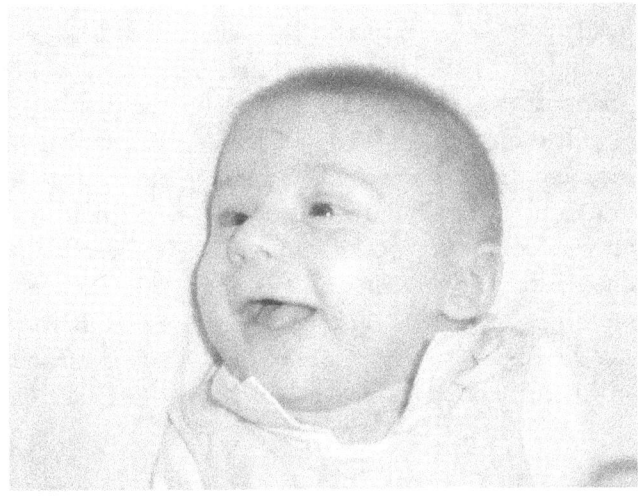

Without entering into religious or patriotic motivations that not everyone shares, having offspring is a command that we humans carry in our DNA, like all animals, from the simplest fly to the most gigantic blue whale: our genes must be mixed with those of a fellow male or female, as appropriate, to give rise to "little fellows" that carry a mixture of the DNA of both. All human beings that are present on Earth owe our existence to the fact that ABSOLUTELY ALL our direct ancestors—in an uninterrupted chain of life, which scientists believe to be several hundred million years old—fulfilled that basic biological mandate. Not a single one of them skipped it. Had they not, neither you, reader, nor I, would be here. Of course, it is not problematic that in a society there be a certain number of people without descendants or with very few, as long as the rest of the people, with more children, compensate. That a fraction of the people has no children, or only one, has always happened and will always happen. When the global average number of children per adult is well below the population replacement levels as is currently the case in almost the whole developed world and much of the developing world, there is something very deep that does not work well in the current society, which is bound to suffer painful problems because of its low collective fertility, if it were to persist in time and not just be a passing phenomenon.

Do not forget those who do not want to have or who do not have children, or can no longer have any: they matter a lot

As important as motivating those who still can or will be able to, in the future, have children—adolescents, young adults, and adults still in fertile ages—is, it is almost as important that the rest of the population—those who have not had children and can no longer have any, or those who have had children but their offspring are already adults—support and encourage, or at least, not hinder, those who wish to have and who have children. Because their opinion and support count significantly in many cases, when the time comes for the possible parents to have children or not (with reactions like "congratulations, my daughter, give me (more) grandchildren" or the opposite "how are you thinking of having a child now, in this complicated world, and especially now, when you are starting to do well at your company?", both very common types of comments). It is very desirable that those who do not want children or who can no longer have them understand and accept that it is necessary to favor, at least differentially, those who have children and are raising them, since we all benefit from more births. Otherwise, it will be much more difficult to afford the economic and other benefits that are just and necessary for parents[113].

Let us imagine, for example, that large direct taxes and social benefits (in countries such as Spain and many others, personal income tax, social security contributions, and retirement pensions) establish a basic or reference level for each type for those who do not have children. For every additional child there would be a bonus of, say, 25% (and therefore, in the case of having five children or more, one would receive net money from the State as "negative taxes "). Thus, with this framework of a 25% improvement for each not emancipated child, with four children, one would not pay personal income tax each year, nor contributions to Social Security, and would receive twice the retirement pension in old age than someone who did not have children. With two children, their improvement would be half in personal income taxes, social security contributions, and retirement pensions. I am not sure that the appropriate percentages of fiscal and pension

---

[113] Years ago, in a colloquium following a talk I gave about the demographic suicide in Spain, one of the attendees said in public: "I believe that those who have not had children should not receive retirement pensions, since they have been able to save more than the others and have not contributed with children so that pensions can be paid in the future." Then another person from the audience, looking about 60 years old, jumped like a spring: "Not at all. I have not had children, but I have religiously paid my taxes and social contributions for the pension and I have full right to it when I retire". Well, in our opinion, fairness is something intermediate between both positions. Of course, anyone who has contributed during their working years should be entitled to a retirement pension. It is also not fair, nor motivating to have children, that the same pension is received, at equal social contributions during the working life, if someone has had several children (and even more if they have had many) than if someone has only had one, let alone none. Those who have been parents have contributed through their spending and effort in raising their descendants so that the next generation can pay the pensions of the retirees of the moment, and to the functioning of the economy, and the more children they have had, the more they have contributed. The better those who do not have children, or who have few, understand this, the less they will oppose this better tax and pension treatment that should be given to the (more) fertile, with the understanding that it is fair and that it has also benefited them that others have had more children.

incentives to have children and the differential disincentives when not having them should be exactly those. Directionally, however, things would have to be more or less that way. These tax and pension benefits should be clear, substantial, explicit and well known, in order to be more motivating. Such a plan would probably be even more stimulating for the birth rate if the tax and pension tables were explained in terms of a bonus/malus above or below a reference or base level set for those with two children. In other words, people without children or with only one would perceive that they have a fiscal surcharge that would result in a significant reduction in their pension, and those who have three or more children would receive a substantial fiscal relief and a higher pension. Every additional child, if not considered a blessing, as we used to say, at least would bring immediate fiscal improvements. Moreover, if these advantages were applicable from the moment a woman becomes pregnant, they could play a significant role in reducing the number of abortions and increasing the number of births.

Of course, it is logical that this type of measure will seem good to all parents. It is also desirable that those who have one child or none, which is the case for many of the adults in countries with a low birth rate, or at least in a large number of them, also accept it, so that fiscal programs such as these be politically viable, because in democratic systems it is very difficult to establish rules like this if they are opposed by many—let alone the majority of—layers of the electorate. Hence the vital importance of raising the awareness of the ENTIRE population that the problem of low birth rate affects all of us and that we all have to do our part to solve it, including those who can no longer have or who do not want children.

What ordinary citizens, and civil society, can (should?) do to combat the demographic suicide

The demographic suicide in the countries that suffer from it affects and will affect, first and foremost, everyday people, ordinary folks. Politicians and the ruling classes, as we know, live very well with the way things are, while they last. Moreover, many of them have prospered thanks to ideologies that go precisely against motherhood and fatherhood. That is why ordinary people—you, me, your cousin, my friend, your brother-in-law—should not leave the solution of this problem exclusively in the hands of politicians, as French president Clemenceau suggested about war and the military[114]. The demographic suicide is also too serious

---

[114] "War is too important a matter to be left in the hands of the military," said Clemenceau. This is something reasonable with respect to the political conduct of war, but not to military strategy and tactics per se.

to leave exclusively in the hands of politicians. Among other reasons, because, since there has been a problem of low birth rate in the vast majority of countries afflicted with that ailment, the bulk of politicians have been indifferent to it, if not elements that have contributed to its deepening and entrenchment.

The first thing the common citizen must do, in this matter, is to get informed, and understand its extreme gravity. After that, they should contribute as much as possible to a general revaluation of motherhood and childrearing, whose devaluation since the last third or fourth of the twentieth century in so many countries has brought us here and is leading us to very dark times. Of course, ideally, the vast majority of those who are of childbearing age and do not have children or have only one, if possible, should try to engender some more before they no longer can—for biological reasons, for their personal good, and for the good of their country/society (and in the long run, their own good, and that of their children, in addition to the great joy they will give their beloved parents, as grandchildren are one of the few benefits of old age and allow the rigors of old age to soften). There is something we can all do, whether we have children or not, and whether or not we are past our fertile age: once we understand the colossal gravity of the demographic problem, we can share this knowledge with our fellow citizens, who do not yet know that we are facing a tremendous problem, many of whom still believe that the fact that people in their country are having too few children is not serious. Modestly, this is what we have tried to do with this book the reader has in his hands: to do our bit in this endeavor. Along these lines, citizens and organizations that create opinions and disseminate ideas in mass media, forums and public platforms of all kinds, and organizations whose main purpose is the search or improvement of the common good have a special opportunity and a greater responsibility.

The right amount of immigration, controlled, which can integrate well economically and culturally

Controlled and well managed immigration can be a palliative or a partial remedy to the demographic winter, as has been commented on throughout this work. To rely exclusively on the solution to a society's demographic suicide on the arrival of new immigrants, however, is not a good strategy at all, because of the obvious risks this entails, which were exposed earlier in this book, and is rather an easy and incomplete way.

Reality proves that "good management" of foreign immigration is extremely complicated, since:

✓ It is very difficult to adjust the inflows and outflows of foreigners in quantity and in professional qualifications, to what is more suitable for each country, something that would only be achieved if the immigrants were chosen in their countries of origin according to the needs of the recipient country by the latter's officials and employers. In practice, much of the immigration that has come in recent decades to Western Europe or the US has been illegal. As for the exit from the country of foreigners who are in a situation of long-term or indefinite unemployment, theoretically a situation that should be a reason to leave the country, by symmetry with the condition that they had to have a job to be able to reside in the host country legally, for political and humanitarian reasons, it is equally complicated.

✓ In countries with generous welfare states, and with anti-discrimination public values, it is very difficult to prevent that a non-negligible part of the foreigners who emigrate and remain in those countries do it mainly or exclusively for the subsidies and free social benefits they expect to receive or already receive there. It is not their "fault" that this basic concept of immigration ("I go to country X, richer than mine, to work to make a living") is deformed, since it is not the immigrants who establish and grant such generous benefits at the expense of the taxpayer of the host country. Traditional immigrants, prior to the existence of modern welfare States, only had a "plan A": work, work and work. Now, immigrants who go to Western Europe, besides the traditional "plan A", has also a "plan B": live on welfare, subsidies and free services provided by the State[115]. Of course, the net balance of immigration for host countries is quite different if foreigners just fill labor market gaps or launch their own businesses / enterprises (like the people who colonized the American West between from the seventeenth to the nineteenth centuries), or if they know that they can rely on a welfare State "plan B." As an example, according to the Spanish Municipal Register (INE), in 2016, no less than 80,000 net working age immigrants came to Spain from non-European countries. Without such "plan B," does this inflow make any sense in a country with a mean unemployment rate that year around 20%, and 4.5 million unemployed people?

✓ The socio-cultural integration of certain immigrant communities in Western countries is not easy, as evidenced by the numerous terrorist attacks by Islamic

---

[115] Let us insist: it is neither fair not correct to blame immigrants of such subsidies and free public services to foreign newcomers that have never contributed any taxes to the country, or to immigrants structurally unemployed, and that this acts as a magnet to attract new crowds of immigrants that are not needed for the productive economy of the host country, and to retain them in it. It is not foreign immigrants who approve legislation and public budgets that make possible such bounty for them at the expense of the local taxpayer, but local politicians (and ultimately, to some extent, the people who vote for them).

fanatics who were either immigrants or sons of immigrants, or the frequent incidents and debates that have taken place in recent years on issues such as whether the burka is admissible as a dress outside the home, or whether girls and young women can go to school with veils, or about the *burkini* on the beaches. Thus, on December 20, 2010, news was published in Spain that the parents of a Muslim student had sued a local teacher for praising the delicious ham of Trevélez during class, accusing him of a "crime of workplace abuse with xenophobic motivations "(c'mon, "this is unbelievable": now you can't even speak publicly of ham in Spain, the country of "jamón" par excellence!). The lawsuit was later dismissed in court, but the effective right to free speech of Spanish teachers with Muslim pupils was damaged by such incident, since nobody wants to risk being sued, if this can be avoided. Japan, fearing the same kind of things and increased crime would happen in its country, prefers not to roll the dice with immigration, despite its worrisome demographic decline.

As is often the case with patch strategies to address serious underlying issues, instead of going to the root of the problem and curing it in a holistic way with medicines that may have a bitter taste and uncomfortable therapy, resorting exclusively to immigration to cure the demographic illness of countries with low birth rates and much aging is a rather "pseudo-solution" or "semi-solution," better than the evil itself, but with significant shortcomings, drawbacks, and risks. Reasonably well managed, although immigration cannot solve the whole demographic problem of the host country, it can help make it smaller. But developed and very aged countries should be very careful with its downside and potential risks, which can ultimately happen to be even more harmful than the problem to address.

How to avoid the demographic suicide of countries close to falling into it

In many emerging countries, fertility has fallen dramatically in recent decades, as recorded in this book, and they currently have a birth rate slightly above or slightly below the replacement level. Lest they fall squarely into demographic suicide processes like the bulk of the developed countries, it would suit them to not imitate these countries in these matters and to adopt pro-birth policies before the low birth rate also permanently sets foot in them. Perhaps their elites and ruling classes should read this book and/or others of the kind, to gain a better understanding of the kind of country that their children and grandchildren will receive from them, if birth rates in their respective countries keep falling. Hopefully, in this matter, they will not see the countries that historically first developed modern economies as an inspiration model to be replicated.

Emerging countries with a fertility rate slightly lower or higher than 2.1 children per woman				
Below 2.1 children per woman			Above 2.1 children per woman	
Country	Children per woman 2015-2020 (P)		Country	Children per woman 2015-2020 (P)
Colombia	1.83		Myanmar	2.13
El Salvador	1.87		Mexico	2.14
Malaysia	1.90		Nicaragua	2.16
North Korea	1.94		Turkmenistan	2.22
Qatar	1.95		Azerbaijan	2.22
Vietnam	1.95		Honduras	2.25
Bahrain	1.98		Argentina	2.27
Uruguay	1.98		Suriname	2.28
Jamaica	1.99		Venezuela	2.28
Turkey	2.01		South Africa	2.28
Sri Lanka	2.03		Libya	2.32
Kuwait	2.04		Uzbekistan	2.33
Tunisia	2.07		India	2.34
Bangladesh	2.08		Peru	2.35
Nepal	2.09		Indonesia	2.36
			Panama	2.36
			Dominican Republic	2.38
			Morocco	2.38
Source: UN (World Population Prospects 2015 - Medium variant scenario)				

How to adapt to the demographic suicide and to protect ourselves from it

Even if the number of births in countries in the midst of a demographic winter recovered drastically tomorrow—something technically complicated, at least in those countries that have experienced a low birth rate for thirty years or more, since the number of women of childbearing age is lower every year in these countries as a consequence of the declines in the number of births of the previous decades, and therefore, except if there are continuous improvements in the fertility rate, a year-to-year reduction in births is expected—the negative consequences of a persistent low fertility and the significant degree of social aging are already unavoidable. The reason is that these additional hypothetical children, if any, would still take 20 to 25 years to enter the workforce, although the investment in raising them made by their parents and society would result in a significant revitalization of the sectors of activity which provide the products and services that babies/children/young people consume (such as diapers, food, clothing, schools and educational materials, tourism, and leisure, etc.), as well as an improvement in the country/society's future expectations, something of great importance for the economic agents. Therefore, apart from developing pro-birth plans and possibly well-managed immigration plans (as already discussed, something not trivial at all), the three main economic elements or agents of society (individuals/households, private for profit or non-profit companies, the State and the public sector in general) will have to adapt to an unavoidable demographic decline, trying to minimize its harm.

In all cases, since the demographic winter results in a collective impoverishment and higher costs in caring for the elderly, to alleviate this poverty effect caused by demography, the following lines of action would be advisable.

✓ Save money. If the future holds less economic comfort, there is no alternative.

✓ Invest resources taking the demographic prospects very much into account. This applies to all economic agents: individuals, companies, governments…

✓ Structural reforms, to improve the productivity of the economy, as the economy will be burdened by demography. At an individual level, better personal training, to increase one's productivity.

✓ Eliminate superfluous public expenditure and rationalize the welfare state, in order to be able to address properly the most important social needs, and in particular, those related to the growing elderly population.

✓ Complement public traditional pay-as-you-go retirement systems with private pension systems. Although the system of retirement in which each one saves while in activity for its own pension, the so-called capitalization system, has clear theoretical advantages (among others, increased savings, greater transparency and legal security, the ability to bequeath the savings not spent to children and the spouse, a higher return for the retiree when the funds saved are properly invested), in many countries it could only be implemented without trauma over a transition of several decades, since otherwise the current retirees would stop receiving a pension for which they contributed for many years in their time. However, public-private plans for pension savings, such as those existing in Sweden, can be implemented at any time, or individuals can simply save on their own what their level of income and expenses allows them to. In any case, through instruments with or without tax benefits, individuals should save for their retirement age as much as they reasonably can.

✓ Invest in preventive medicine—medical checks, vaccines, increased practical healthcare education for common people, etc.—and promote healthy lifestyles

—food, physical exercise, techniques to control stress, etc.[116] —to prolong the working life in its later stages, to save on disease treatments, and to benefit individuals.

✓ Encourage active aging, to harness more work/professional productivity in the years prior to old age, from the age of fifty-something—people who lose their job and have problems finding another because of their age—through the 60s, and even, if desired, 70 years and over.

✓ Create infrastructures and services for a larger mature and elderly population and adapt the current ones.

✓ Export and invest abroad.

✓ Launch/exploit businesses that serve/care for seniors.

✓ (Possibly) emigrate to places with a better demographic-economic profile and move business abroad.

Something that would be extremely desirable, from the standpoint of the State and civil society, would be to educate the growing retired population so that the coverage of their needs (pensions, health care, long-term care) is not done so generously that it asphyxiates the productive economy and taxpayers. If a moderation of the increase in the funds allocated to the retired population is not achieved, which would be very difficult to achieve without the acquiescence of a significant part of it, with retirees understanding that it would be very harmful to "kill the goose that laid the golden eggs" (the productive economy in general and the taxpayers) in order to satisfy their aspirations as a top priority, societies in demographic decline are headed towards a gerontocracy detrimental to the economy, to an intergenerational conflict between the "old" and the "young," and/or the massive emigration of young and middle-aged people to places more favorable to them.

---

[116] Cortisol is an essential hormone for human metabolism. It is generated in larger amounts when we are under stressing circumstances / perceived dangers, to be able to overcome them in a better way. But if we persistently have high levels of cortisol in our blood —for instance, if we constantly live stressing situations—this produces harmful secondary effects on our health, ultimately leading to earlier aging. It is believed that, in ancient / primitive times, cortisol long-term secondary effects were much less important than the benefit of having an increased chance of surviving dangers such as a lion or a bear near us, and hence, these side effects were not punished by evolution mechanisms. But in modern, developed societies, where we very seldom face such life threatening dangers, reducing our levels of stress is very important to stay healthy through the years, as well as for the benefit of serenity.

EPILOGUE-RECAPITULATION: EITHER DEMOGRAPHIC RENAISSANCE OR DEMOGRAPHIC SUICIDE

"In our own time the whole of Greece has been subject to a low birth-rate and a general decrease of the population, owing to which cities have become deserted and the land has ceased to yield fruit, although there have neither been continuous wars nor epidemics. [...]For as men had fallen into such a state of pretentiousness, avarice, and indolence that they did not wish to marry, or if they married to rear the children born to them, or at most as a rule but one or two of them, so as to leave these in affluence and bring them up to waste their substance the evil rapidly and insensibly grew. For in cases where of one or two children the one was carried off by war and the other by sickness, it is evident that the houses must have been left unoccupied, and as in the case of swarms of bees, so by small degrees cities became resourceless and feeble. About this it was of no use at all to ask the gods to suggest a means of deliverance from such an evil. For any ordinary man will tell you that the most effectual cure had to be men's own action, in either striving after other objects, or if not, in passing laws making it compulsory to rear children." (Polybius, Greco-Roman historian, during the middle of the second century BC, in the midst of the decline of classical Greece, in the Histories, book XXXVI, V, 17.1)

"The problem of Europe, which it seems no longer wants to have children, penetrated my soul. To foreigners this Europe seems to be tired, indeed, it seems to be wishing to take its leave of history. Why are things like this?" (Pope Benedict XVI ["Pensées sur la famille," page 71 – 12/22/2006)

Since ancient times, any living species with an abundance of nutrients and livelihoods has had equally abundant offspring. The opposite is happening broadly to the modern human being. The more economic development and material well-being, the more security and social peace, the fewer children he has. It already happened in decadent classical Rome and Greece, and both ended as badly as they did. Since the second half of the 19th century in Western Europe, and since the first half in North America, and more recently in the whole world, economic development and the fall of birth rates have gone hand-in-hand. In the early stages of this process, as mortality, especially infant and juvenile mortality, generally dropped at a rate faster than the drop in fertility, there was no demographic damage, but a rather accelerated population growth. In the developed world, however, and very soon in large parts of the world that is emerging from underdevelopment, the fall in the birth rate is no longer demographically innocuous, but potentially catastrophic, because fertility has settled below the threshold needed for generational replacement. If we continue along this route, we slowly but inexorably tend towards extinction, first going through an impoverishing and sad social decline. With this phenomenon, the human being is unique in the animal kingdom, not just because of his superior intelligence, and for the believers, but because of his soul. Additionally, the present human being is unique with respect to all our ancestors, since we branched out from the other apes and/or were created in the image and likeness of God, because of his minuscule birth rate. With abundant nutrients and livelihoods, as exist now, a security in almost all areas of material life incomparably greater than the historical norm[117], our offspring are no longer large in number, as they once were, and are now insufficient to create the next generations that will take over from the previous generations[118]. Without a doubt, this is a singularity with profound implications and philosophical by-products, whose mystery is increased by noting that, nowadays, having children no longer represents the enormous death risk it once traditionally implied for the mother. When it was dangerous to bear children, we had many. When it is no longer dangerous, we have far fewer. Will we not be able to survive our own

---

[117] Homicide rates in Western Europe, around the year 1300, were around 40 per 100,000 inhabitants, and since then have been progressively declining to around 1 per 100,000 today, according to data presented by the experimental psychologist from Harvard University in his work " The Better Angels of Our Nature: The Decline of Violence in History and Its Causes" published in Spain by Paidós (Barcelona) in 2012. In Spain, according to historical INE mortality tables reviewed by the author, the number of homicides per 100,000 inhabitants in the second half of the 19th century was about 10 times higher than the current rate.

[118] In general, living beings of any species produce fewer offspring or embryos (living descendants, eggs, seeds, spores, successors through bipartition, etc.) the higher the chance of survival of their descendants is. This is why fish caviar is made of so many eggs. And this is why females of many wild animals heat up if a predator eats her offspring, or, as in the case of bears, a male kills the cubs, trying to have the mother heat up again to copulate with her. Therefore, to some extent it is normal that human birth rates tend to decrease with the reduction in infant and juvenile mortality. But in case of abundance of food and scarcity / absence if lethal enemies, even with lower baseline fertility, all animal species tend to grow exponentially in number. Even if they have fewer descendants when their mortality is lower, in a favorable environment, they still produce many more offspring than needed just for population replacement. This is not the case of humans in many countries, where the number of children is much less than the fall in mortality would have entailed in any other living beings.

success as a superior species of evolutionary development on Earth and/or from Creation, because by reaching very high levels of material well-being, civility, and political development, we become voluntarily sterile? With this breeding anomaly, we are squandering the inheritance of human capital—material, social, and spiritual—that all our direct ancestors, without exception, helped to cement and increase with their generosity in procreation and upbringing. We no longer feel, in Europe and other parts of the world, the sense of duty to conserve and increase that centuries-old human legacy, a heritage that paleontologists say began with the ancestral mother of mankind, *Australopithecus afarensis* Lucy, the first hominid, about 3.2 to 3.5 million years ago, in lands that are now part of the current Ethiopia.

What direct and indirect consequences does this anomalous phenomenon have, among all animal or plant species, and in the long history of human beings? Why does it occur? How do we get out of this spiral of demographic death in Europe, the West, and the Far East, and how do emerging countries avoid falling into it? These are the three major questions this book has tried to respond to, using, for this purpose, the best data and arguments its author has been able to obtain, conceive, analyze, and expose. The reader will decide if, in his or her opinion, the effort has been successful. Subsequent investigations by third parties and the author himself, in greater depth, and with more and better data, will corroborate, qualify, or refute what is being told in this book, to which, possibly, readers will find some other error—hopefully minor. As for the value judgments and projections it contains, if they include mistakes, hopefully these err on the side of too much pessimism rather than the opposite.

Beyond arguable nuances, the (small?) errors these pages may contain, and admitting the theoretical possibility of being wrong, as I conclude this book, I will "go out on a limb," as an author, and recapitulate the fundamental aspects of what I think is happening and can happen in the matter at hand. After over seven years of in-depth research on the subject, during which I have faced tons of data and a multitude of tables, graphs, analyses, simulations, conjectures, readings, and conversations with experts and lay people, I hold no substantial doubt about the following:

✓ With fertility below the replacement level, as in much of today's world, the medium and long-term future of a nation, region, or locality tends to be very gray: a tendency to lose population; social aging; economic and affective impoverishment; political gerontocracy; increased risk of loneliness, mistreatment, and undesired "euthanasia" in old age; weakness as a country against its neighbors and geopolitical weakness. In the end, extinction.

✓ These negative expected consequences can be amplified/accelerated or attenuated/delayed, depending on how far or close the fertility is from the replacement level and according to the emigration and immigration of the place in question with the rest of the world.

✓ Migration flows can result in different social consequences for countries with a low birth rate (very positive, positive, neutral, motley, negative, or catastrophic, or ...), depending on their breadth, their net balance (more immigration than emigration, or vice versa), and how they are managed. Immigration net effect, specifically, depends on whether or not it is successfully integrated into the host society. Well-managed immigration can be part of the solution to the demographic problem, but has not been a sufficient solution in any country with a demographic winter, even in those that have done a better job at integrating it, among other reasons, because immigrants also age and end up receiving pensions, and their fertility tends to fall, as they get accustomed to the habits of the host country. Let's not even talk about places where good / effective integration has not been achieved.

✓ By far, the demographic problem is the biggest root/long-term problem of nations that have had very low fertility for decades (Germany, Italy, Spain, Portugal, Austria, Switzerland, Eastern Europe and Russia, Canada, Japan, South Korea, Taiwan, etc.) and one of the main baseline problems of those countries that have a somewhat higher, but still insufficient birth rate (the rest of Western Europe, USA, Chile, Australia, New Zealand, etc.). For their part, the developed or emerging countries that have been immersed in their own demographic winter for not too long, or that are on the verge of falling into it, and that therefore still have a significantly young population, such as China, Thailand, Iran, part of the Arab world, Brazil, Mexico, Colombia, Cuba, Puerto Rico, etc., will begin to clearly notice, within the next 5 to 20 years, that they also suffer from this problem. These latter countries run the risk of becoming very old before completing their process of socio-economic development ("risk of being old before being rich").

✓ The decline of the long-standing family, whose essential characteristics were having a large number of children and marital stability, which has gone from being largely a majority to a minority in the homes of the developed world, is one of the main features of the demographic suicide and is its cause and effect. It has been favored by laws and customs promoted by the political power and the mainstream media in the public opinion and has been accepted de facto and followed by the majority of the population aged less than 50-60 in developed countries, and increasingly in emerging countries as well.

✓ If someone really wants to have children, whatever obstacles exist can be overcome, in the vast majority of cases. If people, in this day and age, believed in the stable family and its importance as they once did, there would be many weddings and far fewer divorces. Nobody prevents anyone from getting married and nobody compels any couple to divorce. No one prevents anyone from having children, except for the not-so-infrequent cases, but a very small minority, of adolescent girls who become pregnant and receive irresistible pressure from their relatives and/or their partner to abort[119].

✓ The fundamental cause of having so few children, in addition to the low infant and juvenile mortality, is the model of society and socially prevalent values in which forming/maintaining a family and having children are secondary and dispensable for lots of people, compared to goals such as material prosperity, professional success, and a life free of family commitments that limit access to the many options available for leisure and entertainment. By contrast, in yesteryears, forming one's own family and keeping it together and having children were priorities for almost everyone.

✓ In today's model of society, having and raising several children, for a large part of the population, is too uncomfortable and uneasy, appears to be too much effort to embark upon, and does not compensate because it takes away money and personal freedom and requires a significant effort to perform. Going a step further, this anti-children sentiment has much to do with how comfortable the economic development and security we enjoy has made us, with the new social role of women and the objective and subjective difficulties of reconciling maternity and women working outside the home, with the delay in the age when having the first child, with the majority living in cities and not in the countryside, and with a decline in infant and juvenile mortality, among other reasons. It also has to do with the trivialization—and in some ways, facilitation—of divorce and abortion by States and a large part of opinion makers. It also has to do, at least, but not only, within the West, with the social decline of religiosity and patriotism and their collection of practical collateral

---

[119] The immense majority of abortions are undergone by adult women and the vast majority of these are undergone by pregnant women over 25 years of age. Between 2012 and 2014, based on Eurostat figures, we estimate that 94%-95% of the abortions practiced in the European Union (plus Norway, Switzerland, and Iceland) were undergone by adult women, 18 or older; 88%-90% for women 20 or older; 64%-67%, for women 25 or older. In other words, the vast majority of voluntary abortions are undergone by grown and mature ladies, adult women, who, if they abort, do so freely and assume full responsibility for their own actions. If they want to have the child they harbor in their womb, even if the pregnancy was not sought or initially desired, they end up having that child.

values.

✓ The world has changed—perhaps forever—on very important issues having a negative impacting on fertility, such as a large part of the factors contrary to having more births mentioned above. In relation to many of these changes, either because they are hardly reversible—such as living mainly in cities and not in the countryside—or because some would be absurd and/or undesirable to reverse—the lower child and juvenile mortality, or the fact that it is normal for women to wish to develop a career—we cannot count on their reversibility to recover the lost birth rate. At the same time, there are other positive changes that should lead us to have more, and not fewer, children than before, such as the virtual disappearance of maternal mortality. Yet we have the meager fertility from which we suffer.

✓ If we do not recover part of the attributes of the traditional society model, and above all, the importance it gave to the family and to having children, even with the adaptations pertinent for the twenty-first century and subsequent centuries, we will not get out of this process of demographic suicide.

✓ The politicians, intellectuals, and great social leaders who do not include the low birth rate among the main social problems of countries and regions affected by a demographic winter in their public actions and speeches/writings/programs—either because they do not know the gravity of the problem or because they do not dare to or want to talk about it—deserve to be mistrusted. Those who, while giving apparent importance to the subject, focus on proposing very inadequate or erroneous solutions, either because they do not give it the relevance it deserves or because of ideological/partisan prejudices contrary to factual evidence and common sense, also deserve that same mistrust.

✓ There is a need for politicians to take pro-birth measures, such as those presented in this book, with an economic component, to incentivize/compensate parents—and businesses, if the goal is that there be many working mothers, and that these women have several children—for a large part of the cost of raising children, with an emphasis on the mother without forgetting the father, and with another component of pro-birth laws and values, and of recovering a family that has more children as a model, in the immense majority of cases: stable marriages.

✓ This issue is, however, too important to leave exclusively in the hands of politicians and "important" people in our societies. It affects all citizens, and we all must contribute, to the extent that we can, to increasing the birth rate, for those who can, to having children, and for all in general, in supporting, to the best of our personal ability, those who have children and those who promote reasonable pro-birth policies. The demographic suicide is also too serious to leave exclusively in the hands of politicians. Among other things because, since there has been a problem of low birth rates in the West and other parts of the world, the vast majority of our politicians have been indifferent to this issue, if not elements that contribute to its deepening and entrenchment.

Eventually, we will have what we deserve. If in Europe, the West, the Far East, and half the world we really understand that we have a serious/very serious birth rate problem, and that having several children per adult is very good for society and an essential part of a typical full life, we will do what we must to address the problem and its causes, and the "demographic spring" or, "demographic renaissance," will arrive. If we continue to ignore this essential problem or consider it secondary, let alone promote laws and customs that tend to amplify it, as in a significant number of countries, there will be no escape from the demographic suicide, a human decline that will be faster, more intense, and more painful in countries with a particularly low birth rate, such as that of the author of this work, Spain. There is no alternative.

APPENDIX 1

THE 1974 KISSINGER REPORT. "Implications of Worldwide Population Growth for U.S. Security and Overseas Interests" (National Security Study Memorandum NSSM 200).

The so-called "Kissinger Report" was a secret memorandum of the United States government of December 1974[120,] later declassified (1980) and made publicly available (1989), on the implications for the national security of the US and its interests abroad of the explosive growth of the population that then was occurring in the world, and what had to be done to try to slow it down. The report, after arguing why this is a major problem for US security, contains a plan of action to achieve a drastic reduction of the birth rate in less developed countries, where the population at that time doubled, on average, every 25 to 30 years, a rate that would have seen that population multiplied by 10 to 16 in a century[121], by 100 to 250 in two centuries, by 1,000 to 4,000 in three centuries, by 100,000 to a million in five centuries...This memorandum was produced when the trauma of the first major oil crisis (oil embargo from October 1973 to March 1974, which quadrupled oil prices) was still very much vivid, a sequel to the Arab defeat by Israel in the Yom Kippur war of 1973. It was also very close in time to what happened in 1972, a year of adverse weather in much of the globe, which resulted in a sharp decline in food production, and thus in the almost complete exhaustion of world food, and mainly North American, reserves that could not be replenished in 1973, despite that being a year of high food production. The report said of this event: "A repetition under these conditions of 1972 weather patterns would result in large-scale famine of a kind not experienced for several decades – a kind the world thought had been permanently banished.."

---

[120] It can be accessed in http://pdf.usaid.gov/pdf_docs/Pcaab500.pdf

[121] For example, the population of Pakistan, whose growth has moderated in the last decades, increased by five times from 1950 to 2015, according to data from the UN. If it continued with the same average growth rate of the last 65 years, in 2050, it would be twelve times the population of 1950 (!!)

In summary, the document expressed the tremendous concern of the US government, in the midst of the cold war, that the high birth rate of the less developed countries, and the strong population growth it led to, as mortality rates were also declining in less developed nations—especially among children and youth—had the following consequences:

1) Make it difficult for poor countries to get out of misery/ underdevelopment, as a very large part of their GDP growth was absorbed by the increase in population, and therefore their per capita income increased very slowly. This, together with higher unemployment and underemployment rates, due to an excess in the workforce, led to increased risks of revolutions, coups, and political instability, especially in the years of poor harvests and famines.

2) As a consequence of these risks, scenarios were generated, which highlighted risks of shortage (price increase and scarcity) of strategic mineral raw materials (metals and oil), because this politico-social instability and the consequent coming to power of governments hostile to the West would hinder/prevent the investment in exploration and operation of new deposits, and/or would result in the governments in charge expropriating the (Western) companies dedicated to the exploration/exploitation of these mineral substances from their respective countries, and/or that their hostility would lead to a strong increase in the prices of these resources, either by decision of the third world governments through cartels such as OPEC or because of the shortage of these raw materials caused by the bad policies of those governments[122].

It seems, therefore, reasonable that the United States be alarmed in these circumstances and based on such judgments on the effect of world population growth and especially in poor countries. Unfortunately, with its policies against

---

[122] The authors of the report do not fear that, in the foreseeable future, and before there are any substitute elements, the strategic mineral raw materials in the world will be depleted. They do fear, however, that they could be in short supply and become expensive if anti-Western governments and political instability in some countries impede the discovery of new reserves and their proper exploitation. They are anti-natality, not because of a direct "Malthusianism" (the theory in which people increase in numbers more quickly than the resources they need), because, in essence, their authors do believe that, technically, resources could be generated that a larger population would require, but for fear that a runaway demographic growth in the poor countries would lead to a political instability that would prevent generating these resources.

natality in the world, the US government contributed, probably significantly and perhaps a lot, to the fact that the current population risks of much of the world are quite the opposite: a potentially devastating demographic winter.

The proposed anti-natality measures

As a consequence of the fear of a runaway population growth, the Kissinger Report recommends policies and actions for the US government, through various agencies (especially the Agency for International Development or AID) to take for the control and reduction of the birth rate in the least developed countries, whose governments and influential elites are expected to be convinced and encouraged so that it be one of its essential collateral means in their efforts to reduce the poverty of their population. The goal is for global fertility rate to decline by the year 2000 to just the replacement level, a very ambitious goal, since it meant cutting the average birth rate by half in just a quarter of a century.

Among the measures proposed by the birth rate report, in addition to committing national governments and key leaders of the various underdeveloped countries to this goal, are the following:

1.- Improvements in health and nutrition that contribute to a lower infant mortality.

2.- Universal schooling and adult literacy, with emphasis on women.

3.- Increase the legal age of marriage.

4.- Create more female employment opportunities.

5.- Social Security plans for old age that reduce the need to have children to take care of you.

6.- Improvements in agriculture and other areas of the economy to raise living standards, specifically of the poorest population (since this is the one that has the most children, precisely because it is poorer). The report says that "The desire for large families diminishes as income rises."

7.- Facilitation of contraceptive methods and means (pills, preservatives, sterilization, techniques to avoid pregnancy). On abortion, following an initial—and erroneous—apology as a means of moderating population growth[123], the report

---

[123] The report says that "No country has reduced its population growth without resorting to abortion." This is not true, starting with the US itself. When abortion was legalized in Western countries, their birth rate and population growth were already much lower than traditionally.

says the US government is prohibited from promoting abortion abroad ("None of the funds made available to carry out this part of the Foreign Assistance Act shall be used to pay for the performance of abortions as a method of family planning or to motivate or coerce any person to practice abortions"). They do, however, say that they can devote funds to activities that would facilitate abortions, such as training gynecologists in obstetric practices such as abortion, or medical research on the subject. Abortion in the Third World is also indirectly supported by helping abortion organizations such as Planned Parenthood. Therefore, the plan that drives this report is abortionist, albeit in a sneaky, indirect way.

8.- Educate (the report speaks of "indoctrinating") children, starting in elementary school, that it is desirable to have smaller families (the report literally says: "concentrating on the education and indoctrination of the rising generation of children regarding the desirability of smaller family size"), with two children.

Certainly, these measures are in line with the bulk of what, in this work, are considered fundamental elements that favor lower birth rates, even though some of them are undeniably positive and essentially irreversible: lower infant mortality; less poverty (ergo, we do not now have few children for lack of income, but, basically, because of the contrary); higher education and female employment (which implicitly underscores the difficulty of reconciling female employment and maternity); public retirement pensions (which make it less necessary to have children); that people marry later in life (to start having children at an older age, and thus have fewer); profusion of contraceptive means and techniques; instill in people, from a young age, values contrary to having many children (that it is desirable to have smaller families); anti-natality governments.

Effects of the Kissinger Report

What effects have had these American policies had on the evolution of fertility and population growth in the world and, in particular, in the least developed countries? It is difficult to accurately evaluate/measure them, since:

1.- Birth rates had already fallen dramatically in developed countries when this report was produced. Therefore, simply by helping poor countries develop, it seems normal that birth rates fell in those countries as well.

2.- Moreover, when the Kissinger Report was written, birth rates were already falling in a large part of the Third World countries. It is true that there were already policies and programs the Yankee government had put in place that were aimed at reducing these countries' fertility rates.

3.- Since 1974, birth rates have plummeted in Latin America and Asia, but not in Africa, although they have been falling there too in recent decades.

4.- Birth rate has also dwindled a lot since 1974 in countries outside the direct sphere of influence of the United States, some of them hostile to the Yankee colossus in the last 40 years or during much of that period—among them, Russia, China, Cuba, Iran, Vietnam, and North Korea. Anyway, it is true that, even as enemies, these countries also imitated the United States in many ways, or were at least influenced by the Americans. It is one thing they were not friends of the United States and another that they did not adopt many ideas and techniques that first arose in the land of Uncle Sam.

5.- An overflowing birth rate and population growth in poor countries were also not desired by their own national governments, with or without US aid, in order to combat their own misery, and because of the associated risk of political instability (due to high youth unemployment and possible famines) that could potentially turn against these governments.

6.- The central quantitative objective of the US government's anti-birth plan, that underdeveloped countries reach the replacement fertility level towards the year 2000, was not achieved, primarily because of the poorest countries of all. In the "intermediates" countries, the birth rate reached levels of about 2.6 children per woman, half what it was when the Kissinger Report was developed.

Change in fertility (children per woman) in the countries identified as top priorities for the US in the National Security Study Memorandum NSSM 200 ("Kissinger Report")				
Data Source: "Implications of Worldwide Population Growth For U.S. Security and Overseas Interests" (1974), UN (World Population Prospects 2015)	Children per woman 1970-1975	Children per woman 2010-2015	Change in fertility 1970-2015	Relative change in fertility 1970-2015
India	5.41	2.48	-2.93	-54.2%
Bangladesh	6.91	2.23	-4.68	-67.7%
Pakistan	6.60	3.72	-2.88	-43.6%
Thailand	5.05	1.53	-3.52	-69.7%
Philippines	5.98	3.04	-2.94	-49.2%
Indonesia	6.16	2.70	-3.46	-56.2%
Turkey	5.34	2.10	-3.24	-60.7%
Egypt	5.70	3.38	-2.32	-40.7%
Nigeria	6.61	5.54	-1.07	-16.2%
Ethiopia	7.10	4.59	-2.51	-35.4%
Mexico	6.71	2.29	-4.42	-65.9%
Brasil	4.72	1.82	-2.90	-61.4%
Colombia	4.90	1.93	-2.97	-60.6%
Simple Average	**5.94**	**2.87**	**-3.06**	**-51.6%**

Total fertility rate (children per woman) in various countries hostile to or not controlled by the US, in the days of the "Kissinger Report" and in 2010-2015				
Data Source: "Implications of Worldwide Population Growth For U.S. Security and Overseas Interests" (1974), UN (World Population Prospects 2015)	Children per woman 1970-1975	Children per woman 2010-2015	Change in fertility 1970-2015	Relative change in fertility 1970-2015
China	4.85	1.55	-3.30	-68.0%
Iran	6.24	1.75	-4.49	-72.0%
Vietnam	6.33	1.96	-4.37	-69.0%
North Korea	4.00	2.00	-2.01	-50.1%
Russia	2.03	1.66	-0.37	-18.2%
Cuba	3.60	1.63	-1.97	-54.7%
Simple Average	**4.51**	**1.76**	**-2.75**	**-61.0%**

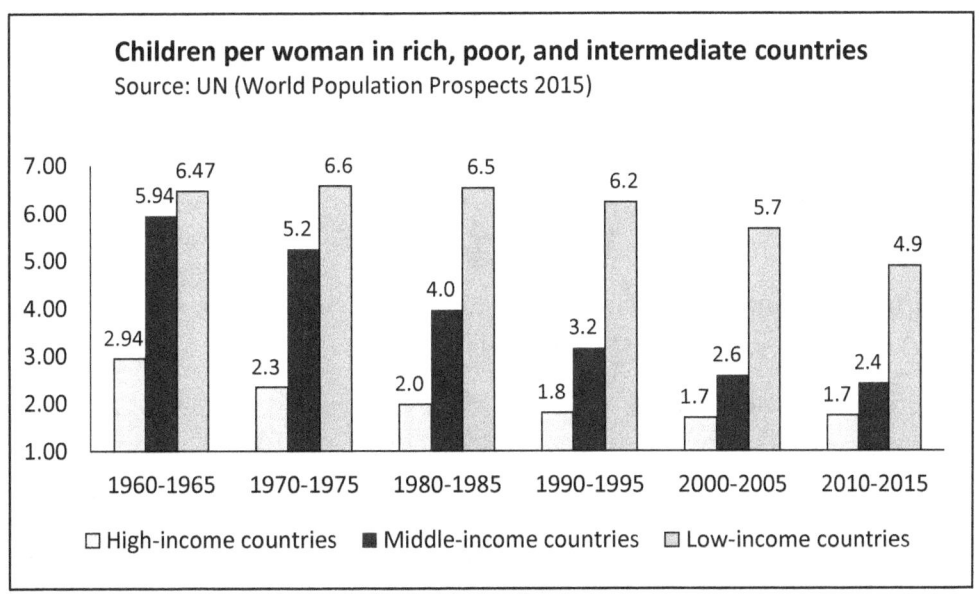

Apart from these caveats, given the enormous global influence of the United States and the large amounts of money employed by the Yankee government in its anti-natalist efforts—the report speaks of considerable sums for its fertility control purposes—and despite the impossibility to accurately measure their impact, we believe that this report and its subsequent actions have contributed somewhat, and possibly significantly, to the fall of the birth rate in poor countries that occurred at levels of development and prosperity lower than those existing in rich countries when birth rates fell there, as well as the triumph of the set of values and collateral recommendations contained in the report.

In our opinion, while the US government's fear of overpopulation in the Third World seemed reasonable in the 1970s, based on the reasons given in this memorandum, the dynamics of this report led to the opposite problem in the long-term: the spiral of demographic death. It also leads to countries being concerned that the dependency rate (population that must be maintained by every one hundred people working in the productive economy) is no longer high due to there being many children, but because there are many retirees. Let's not forget that the cost of raising a child, besides being much lower, on average, than the cost in pensions, health, and dependency care for retirees, is an investment in future human capital. Spending on retirees, certainly, is not.

From a moral standpoint and from the social model standpoint, there are key elements of the Kissinger Report that are clearly debatable, such as its pro-abortionism, or its intrusion into creating personal consciences that favor a "minimalist" future family nucleus.

A curiosity: Earth was experiencing 34 years cooling in temperatures when the Kissinger Report was elaborated

On page 36 of the report you can read the following paragraph, a true gem in our times when one of the great world concerns is the fear of the warming of Earth's surface: "There is great uncertainty whether the conditions for achieving food balance in the LDCs can in fact be realized. Climatic changes are poorly understood, but a persistent atmospheric cooling trend since 1940 has been established. One respectable body of scientific opinion believes that this indicates that there will be a period of much wider annual frosts and possibly a long-term lowering of rainfall in the monsoon areas of Asia and Africa." In other words, at the time of its writing, it was thought that the atmosphere had been cooling down for 34 years.

Apostille: Political paradoxes of the Kissinger Report

At the time of the writing of this memorandum of the US government, there was much talk in the world of "American imperialism," whose values were supposedly "right-wing" and conservative, particularly under Republican presidencies in the United States, as was the case in 1974. Henry Kissinger, a politician, possibly no less famous in the world than presidents Nixon and Ford, whom he served, embodied in particular that imperialist and right-wing image. Yet, this very important report—initially secret, and therefore presumably sincere in relation to what its authors knew and thought—reveals paradoxical recommendations with regards to this stereotype, since:

1.- The report is feminist, as it emphasizes the incorporation of women into paid labor, the education and social advancement of women, equal pay as men, few children, and is pro-abortion.

2.- The report is in favor of introducing and promoting one of the pillars of the social-democratic welfare state in poor countries: Social Security for Retirement.

3.- The report especially recommends efforts to improve the economic and health status of the poorest of the poor countries, in line with the typical demands of the political left and anti-poverty NGOs.

4.- The report recommends instilling in children, from an early age, the idea that it is best if they do not have many children, and that they do not, themselves, form families with a large progeny, unlike the traditional way.

Seeing the world through our lens, it is very interesting to read, in the Kissinger Report, that the atmosphere had been cooling for 34 years (from 1940 to 1974) when it was developed, and that this would lead to bad harvests and severe droughts. Only 23 years later, in 1997, the Kyoto protocol was signed, when the opposite concern, that the planet was warming, had already taken root, a concern which equally threatened to cause droughts and famines. Moreover, the fear of global warming has generated yet another argument to have few children, and that the family be further reduced, up to one or two children at most: the "ecological footprint" generated by the human being is harmful to the health of the planet and is therefore responsible for the potentially catastrophic warming of the atmosphere. That is to say, when we believed that the surface of the Earth was cooling down, we were told: please, have few children. If we think it is warming up, as it currently is, we are told something similar: please, have few children. How about that!

APPENDIX 2

COMMENTS ON THE ACCURACY OF NUMBERS AND GRAPHS CONTAINED IN THIS BOOK

The numbers in this book are based on data from public sources of the highest theoretical solvency. In some cases, we have transcribed them literally. In many others, we have made estimates and elaborations from them (in such cases, instead of saying "source" for the data, the expression used is "Data source." Or it is written "own analysis"). These are very interesting numbers, because they illustrate, clarify, and explain what is happening, but the reader should not take them literally and should not pay too much attention to their exact precision, because demographic phenomena are often not easy to measure with total accuracy, and in certain cases are subject to further revisions. In addition, of course, as time elapses between the moment of writing these words and when the reader reads or re-reads these pages, these numbers will be less current. Of course, the older these numbers are, such as certain demographic data contained in this book dating back to the nineteenth century and earlier, the more likely they are to be less accurate, though in any case they represent the best estimate available, and a good estimation is generally much better than nothing.

Having said that, beyond the exactitude of the decimal portion in the numbers in this book, and that the figures that appear in it are gradually becoming outdated, the large series and trends contained therein, except for possible errors in our calculations or in the data source used, provide a fairly reliable picture of what is happening and has happened to demographics in the various places for which we offer data. Beyond the concrete decimal in the many numbers in this book, and without recourse to more indicators than the estimated number of children per woman, it is evident that a society with a very insufficient number of children and in which life expectancy continues to increase, such as the German, Spanish, Italian, Russian, Chinese, or Japanese societies, just to mention some of the many countries that suffer this problem intensely, cannot but grow old in a rampant way, and ultimately, experience its native population, as well as the total population, shrinking in numbers, if there is not sufficient foreign immigration to compensate that native blood loss.

APPENDIX 3

DATA SOURCES AND BIBLIOGRAPHY

For better or worse, this work is essentially an original work, not intensive in third-party bibliography. It is a mixture of research work, essay, and manifesto, essentially built through the analysis of demographic, economic, and sociological data from public sources, accessible through the internet.

Main sources of data used

-Eurostat (statistical office of the European Union). http://ec.europa.eu/eurostat/data/database

-US Census Bureau International Database https://www.census.gov/population/international/data/idb/informationGateway.php

-UN – Population Statistics and Prospects https://esa.un.org/unpd/wpp/

-OECD https://data.oecd.org/

-CDC (Center for Disease Control) US Government, regarding birth data (https://www.cdc.gov/nchs/nvss/births.htm)

-CIA Factbook.(https://www.cia.gov/library/publications/the-world-factbook/rankorder/2119rank.html)

-National Statistics Bureaus from several countries: INE – Spain (www.ine.es), INSEE – France (https://www.insee.fr/fr/accueil), DESTATIS – Germany (https://www.destatis.de/EN/Homepage.html), ISTAT – Italy (http://www.istat.it/it), Office for National Statistics – UK (https://www.ons.gov.uk/), Statistika Centralbyrån – Sweden (http://www.scb.se/en /), Denmark Statistics – Denmark

(http://www.dst.dk/en/Statistik#), Statistik sentralbyrå – Norway
(https://www.ssb.no/en/), Office fédéral de la Statistique – Switzerland
(https://www.bfs.admin.ch/bfs/fr/home.html), CBS – Netherlands
(https://www.cbs.nl/en-gb), Instituto Nacional de Estadística y Geografía de
México – Mexico (http://www.inegi.org.mx/), Statistics Canada
(http://www.statcan.gc.ca/eng/start), etc

-Wikipedia. Searching for "Demographics of _____" (any country), results in an
excellent Wikipedia Web page with con demographic data generally very precise,
coming in large measure from the official statistics institutes of the respective
countries (NB. On numerous occasions, I have verified demographic data from
Wikipedia in the sources cited there, and they always matched the originals)

Reference Books

"An Essay on the Principle of Population." Thomas Malthus, 1798.

"Brave new world revisited." Aldous Huxley, 1958.

"The population bomb." Paul R. Ehrlich, 1968.

"La Peste Blanche" (the White Plague). How to avoid the suicide of the West?"
Pierre Chaunu and Georges Suffert. Gallimard, 1976.

"La France ridée" (France wrinkled). Alfred Sauvy, Pierre Chaunu, J Legrand and
Gérard-François Dumont. Hachette Iittératures, 1979. (NB: GF Dumont was the
one who coined the term "demographic winter").

"History and Decadence." Pierre Chaunu. Perrin, 1981.

"The economics of population". Julian L. Simon. Transaction Publishers, 1998.

"Prosperous Paupers & Other Population Problems." Nicholas Eberstadt, 2000).
Brunswick, New Jersey: Transaction Publisher, 2000.

"The death of the West." Patrick Buchanan. Thomas Dunne books, 2002.

"Introduction to demography." Livi Bacci, Massimo., Ariel. 2007

"Reflections on the Revolution in Europe: Immigration, Islam and the West".
Christopher Caldwell. Ed. Debate, 2010.

"El suicidio demográfico de España" (The Demographic Suicide of Spain).
Alejandro Macarrón Larumbe. Ed homo Legens, 2011.

"The rise of post-familialism: humanity's future?". Joel Kotkin 2012 (https://www.chapman.edu/wilkinson/_files/The%20Rise%20of%20Post-Familialism.pdf)

"Dizionario dell'estinzione" (Diccionary of Extinction). Giuliano Cannata. NdA Press, 2012.

"What to Expect When No One's Expecting: America's Coming Demographic Disaster." Jonathan V. Last. Encounter Books, 2014.

ABOUT THE AUTHOR

Alejandro Macarrón Larumbe was born in 1960 in Avilés (Asturias – Spain). He is a telecommunications engineer and a graduate of the Universidad Politécnica de Madrid and holds an Executive MBA from the Madrid Business School – University of Houston.

He was a co-founder and partner of several strategic consulting firms, including Otto & Company, of which he is the managing partner for Spain. He has worked as a research and development engineer at Telefónica R&D, and AT&T Bell Labs; As a business consultant at McKinsey & Co and with AT Kearney (freelance at the latter); And as a manager at the satellite telecommunications operator Hispasat and IT solution providers Heyde AG and Infoglobal. He has professional experience in a number of economic sectors and countries—in addition to Spain—including a two-year stay in New Jersey (USA).

With respect to the low birth rate and the aging of the population, he is the author of the book "El suicidio demográfico de España" (The Demographic Suicide of Spain (2011), the founder and CEO of the Fundación Renacimiento Demográfico - Demographic Renaissance (www.renacimientodemografico.org), has published dozens of articles, given numerous lectures, and has been interviewed in multiple Spanish and other media outlets. In other arenas, he is also the author of the essay book "Coopetencia. Cooperación y competencia en cada paso de nuestras vidas" (Coopetition – Cooperation and Competition at every step of our lives) (2006).

www.ingramcontent.com/pod-product-compliance
Lightning Source LLC
Chambersburg PA
CBHW081205280526
45787CB00006B/2328